Wartguon
DEUTCH

Writers in
Hollywood
1915-1951

ALSO BY IAN HAMILTON

Robert Lowell: A Biography
In Search of J. D. Salinger

IAN HAMILTON

Writers in Hollywood

1915-1951

1817

An Edward Burlingame Book

HARPER & ROW, PUBLISHERS, NEW YORK

GRAND RAPIDS, PHILADELPHIA, ST. LOUIS, SAN FRANCISCO
LONDON, SINGAPORE, SYDNEY, TOKYO, TORONTO

Photographs in the insert that follows page 166 are credited to:

1: Culver Pictures; 2: Museum of Modern Art/Film Stills Archive; 3: Courtesy of Fay Wray; 4: Museum of Modern Art/Film Stills Archive; 5: Museum of Modern Art/Film Stills Archive; 6: Museum of Modern Art/Film Stills Archive; 7: UPI/Bettman Newsphotos; 8: Culver Pictures; 9: Museum of Modern Art/Film Stills Archive; 10: Culver Pictures; 11: Culver Pictures; 12: Museum of Modern Art/Film Stills Archive; 13: Museum of Modern Art/Film Stills Archive; 14: Museum of Modern Art/Film Stills Archive; 15: Museum of Modern Art/Film Stills Archive; 16: Culver Pictures; 17: Courtesy of Writers Guild of America; 18: Museum of Modern Art/Film Stills Archive; 19: Culver Pictures; 20: Museum of Modern Art/Film Stills Archive; 21: Martha Holmes/*Life* Magazine © 1947 Time Inc.; 22: UPI/Bettman Newsphotos; 23: Museum of Modern Art/Film Stills Archive.

FIRST EDITION

Designed by Barbara DuPree Knowles

LIBRARY OF CONGRESS CATALOGING-IN-PUBLICATION DATA
Hamilton, Ian, 1938–
   Writers in Hollywood, 1915–1951/Ian Hamilton.
      p. cm.
   "An Edward Burlingame book."
   ISBN 0-06-016231-7
   Includes index.
   1. Motion picture industry—California—Los Angeles—History.
2. Screenwriters—California—Los Angeles. 3. Motion picture
authorship. 4. Hollywood (Los Angeles, Calif.)—History.
I. Title.
PN1993.5.U65H35   1990
384'.8'0979494—dc20   89-45665

90   91   92   93   94   CC/RRD   10   9   8   7   6   5   4   3   2   1

FADE IN on a general view of Skull Island, at dawn, with the bridge of the ship in the foreground. Captain Englehorn is leaning over the rail looking out at the grandeur of the spectacle. Sea and jungle are still in purple shadow. But high above, the east has drenched the mountains in the glory of its burning. One by one the columnar peaks of snow are kindling downward, chasm by chasm, each in itself a new morning; white glaciers blaze their winding paths like fiery serpents; long avalanches cast down keen streams, brighter than lightning, each sending its tribute of driven snow, like altar smoke, to the heavens. The rose light of the silent domes flushes that heaven about them until the whole sky, one scarlet canopy, is interwoven with a roof of waving flame and tossing, vault beyond vault, as with the drifted wings of many companies of angels.

—Scene description from script of *King Kong*—a black-and-white film

PREFACE

Fifteen years ago, a book about Hollywood screenwriters would almost certainly have been taken as a riposte to those theories of screen authorship that pay exclusive homage to the "vision" or "personal signature" of the director. I have a three hundred-page compilation on the subject, put together by John Caughie for the British Film Institute. Called *Theories of Authorship*, it was published in 1981 but draws heavily on material from the late sixties and early seventies. According to the index, *screenplay* receives two passing mentions, *scriptwriter* only one, and we will search the book in vain for serious consideration of any individual writer's contribution to the "language of the cinema." And this fairly reflects a prodirector prejudice we now take pretty much for granted—in spite of nobly conceived counterattacks like Richard Corliss's *Talking Pictures*, in which the methods of archauteurist Andrew Sarris are lovingly devoted to the construction of a pantheon reserved for Writers Only, or—as Corliss dubs them—"Author-Auteurs."

The escalating prestige of the director was of course viewed with much indignation by the old school of Hollywood screenwriters, with their history of neglect by other means. They had weathered the contract system, they had survived the blacklist, and then—in the early 1960s—they found themselves more or less eliminated from the critical-historical map. *Un film de John Ford* was the designation: Dudley Nichols, Ford's faithful wordsmith, might, if he was lucky, get a footnote. The "Capra touch" owed little or nothing, it turned out, to the speechwriting facility of Robert Riskin. The "writer in Hollywood" for most people evoked images of Scott Fitz-gerald, HUAC, and perhaps a scene or two from *What Makes Sammy Run?*

I remember conversations in Oxford circa 1960, when I used to go to the cinema five times a week, if I could manage it. Outside the darkened theaters, in junior common rooms across the land the "auteur theory" was beginning to take hold. On one occasion I was particularly struck by the dialogue in a film called *Sweet Smell of Success* (the "Match me, Sidney," "You're dead, go get yourself buried," sort of thing), and I was eager to acquire a copy of the script—actually not possible in those days, and not so easy now. To disdainful *cinéastes* of my acquaintance this seemed a pretty low response to what I'd viewed on screen. I should have been concentrating instead on the "voice" of the director, the recurrences and antinomies by which he had marked the narrative as "his."

It so happened that the director of this wonderfully hard-boiled, urban-American toughie was a Scotsman called Alexander Macken-drick. Briefed now, I was on the lookout for other films "by him." The best known of these, it transpired, and the first I came across, was a soft-focus tearjerker about a deaf-and-dumb juvenile. This time I didn't want to read the script and, apart from a possible link between the charms of the delectable little child star Mandy Miller and the repulsive sister-fixation of Burt Lancaster in *Sweet Smell,* I could see nothing at all that the two films had in common. Evidently, Mackendrick was a pro for hire, and very good at whatever he was paid to do. "But that's the point!" the *cinéastes* would cry. "Look harder. Seek out the clandestine." Since this would have meant reliving the near-intolerable trials of Mandy Miller, I gave up. Evidently my attachment to the cinema was essentially a slob attachment, that of an addict or at best a fan. "Movies," I now understood, would have to be filed away along with Broadway musicals, Guy Mitchell, and the Glasgow Rangers football club: low-cultural distractions from the wrath of F. R. Leavis.

But I still wanted to read the script of *Sweet Smell of Success* and over the years I have kept a vague eye on the fluctuating fortunes of the Hollywood screenwriter (an eye not vague enough, alas, to avoid noticing that Ernest Lehman, author of *Sweet Smell,* went on from there to pen *The Sound of Music*). Nowadays the Hollywood writers we know about are usually powerful, deal-fixing "hyphe-nates" (writer-producers, writer-directors). Figures like William Goldman, Paul Schrader, and Robert Towne are known to have real clout; they are bankable, like stars. And yet in no sense are these men fugitives from some more elevated literary zone. They are genuine "film people" in a way that very few of the old contract writers would have wished to be. In a recent interview, Schrader sums up the attitude of the new men very plausibly, and also by implication reveals much about the predicament of his forerunners:

> If I wanted to be *just* a writer, I could be just a writer very easily. I am not a writer. I am a *screen* writer, which is half a filmmaker. . . . If I wanted to be a writer, I would not be writing screenplays, that's for sure.
>
> I want to be a filmmaker; therefore, I *can* write screenplays. If you want to make a good *living*, you *can* be that bastardized thing called the screenwriter. But it is *not* an art form, because screenplays are not works of art. They are invitations to others to collaborate on a work of art, but they are not in themselves works of art.

To the literary film fan, this kind of talk is likely to sound intelligent, correct but inherently unglamorous. For someone who is, or would prefer to be "just a writer" there is more to be learned—about compromise, self-delusion, money distractions, and the like—from contemplating the writer-in-chains saga that emerges from any study of Hollywood during its so-called golden years—the period I have marked as running from 1915 to 1951. Nineteen fifteen was the year of D. W. Griffith's *The Birth of a Nation.* In 1951, the studio system at last knew itself to be defeated by antitrust legislation, the threat from television was accelerating, and the blacklist had, from the writers' point of view, added a final insult to the various injuries they believed themselves to have suffered since the first day they decided to "go Hollywood."

It is not a saga to be bathed in tears. Too much has been made of what Hollywood *did* to X or Y. Those writers, as we will discover, were in the movies by choice: they earned far more money than their colleagues who did not write for films, and in several cases they applied themselves conscientiously to the not-unimportant task at hand. And they had a lot of laughs.

Even so, there are moments when the sometimes pure in heart might read their story as an admonitory parable: a not untimely reminder that to be "just a writer" is not, and will never be, as easy as Paul Schrader makes it sound.

I am grateful to the following for their advice and practical assistance during the preparation and writing of this book: Gillon Aitken; Philip Dunne; Sam Gill and Howard Prouty of the Production Code Administration Library; the staff of the Margaret Herrick Library at the Academy of Motion Picture Arts and Sciences; Brigitte J. Kuepers of the Theater Arts Library at UCLA; Jackie Morris of the National Film Archive at the British Film Institute; Abraham Polonsky; Mrs. Preston Sturges; Patricia Wheatley of the British Broadcasting Corporation; David Zeidberg, head of Special Collections at the University Research Library, UCLA; the staff of the UCLA Film and TV Archive; and the staff of Video Plus, Sepulveda Boulevard, Los Angeles.

1

We do not fear censorship for we have no wish to offend with impxroprieties or obscenities, but we do demand, as a right, the liberty to show the dark side of wrong, that we may illuminate the bright side of virtue—the same liberty that is conceded to the art of the written word, that art to which we owe the Bible and the works of Shakespeare.

These are the words of a prologue to D. W. Griffith's *The Birth of a Nation,* released in 1915 and now widely agreed to be the first American movie that can be talked of without condescension as a work of art. Griffith's text is titled "A Plea for the Art of the Motion Picture," and much of its rhetorical demeanor we can now recognize as "vintage Hollywood": on the one hand, a grandiose wish to be (or possibly outdo) both Shakespeare and the Bible; on the other, a just as sizable nervousness about mass-audience reaction. With Griffith, Hollywood began to thrill to the idea of its own potency. It also began to worry about how long this magic gift could last and to devise methods of protecting it.

Griffith himself had started out as a writer, and like most others of that trade, he had always been vaguely contemptuous of the movies. From his teens he remembered the penny arcades, the nickel-in-a-slot Kinetoscopes and Mutoscopes with their two-minute vaudeville routines, their circus turns and boxing bouts, their Samoan dancers and Lady Fencers Without Foils. By the turn of the century (Griffith was twenty-five in 1900), these slot machines had been replaced by small picture houses that offered visitors a thirty-minute package of projected spectacle: comic setups, chases, scenes from hit plays, simulated news events, big moments from world history. The writer's contribution, if he made one, was in note form; rarely was there scope for "fiction." A fortunate scenarist could get twenty dollars for sketching out the movies in, say, *The Pretty Stenographer; or, Caught in the Act:*

> New York studio—26 feet—An elderly but gay broker is seated at his desk dictating to his pretty typewriter. He stops in the progress of his letter and bestows a kiss on the not unwilling girl. As he does his wife enters. She is enraged. Taking her husband by the ear she compels him to get on his knees. The pretty typewriter bursts into tears.

More often than not, the moves would need no script assistance: everybody knew them by heart. In the same catalog in which the "gay broker" does his stuff, we read of *How Bridget Served the Salad Undressed:*

> New York studio— 22 feet— This is an old and always popular story told by motion photograph. Bridget of course mistakes the order and brings in the salad in a state of deshabille hardly allowable in polite society.

"In their utter simplicity," the films of that day "had no more use for words than a caveman had for a Christian name."[1]

And this remained true for a few years, even after the first so-called story films made their appearance, starting with Edwin S. Porter's *The Great Train Robbery* in 1903. The script for this ten-minute film could have been comfortably jotted down on the back of an envelope: "a train holdup, a dance-hall episode, and an escape." After all, Porter's great discovery was that movies were not just "motion photographs": they could indeed tell stories, defy the unities, move compellingly from A to B. As Hollywood's first narrative-film editor, he would have taken some pride in keeping his language links down to the bare essentials.

By 1908, when D. W. Griffith reluctantly took a job with this same Porter ("I haven't reached the point where I have to work in films," said Griffith, a day or two before he signed on at the Biograph studio[2]), the writer in Hollywood was still a mere provider of ideas and synopses. Screen titling had just begun, and it was a primitive business: many filmmaking establishments kept big rolls of titles on their shelves—"The Next Day," "Ten Years Elapse," "Forgiven," "Wedding Bells," etc. A cost-conscious director made sure that his story avoided language that could not be found in stock.[3]

Although directors and even actors often concocted their own stories as they went along, there were professional screenwriters, studio employees whose sole job it was to provide plot material and dialogue. Indeed, there had been such since 1898, when Roy L. McCardell, a caption writer for the *New York Standard,* approached Biograph with the claim that he could write ten Mutoscope quickies in a day: "the first man on either side of the water to be hired for no other purpose than to write pictures."[4] By the time Griffith went to work for Biograph, the screenwriter was an established presence on the lot. He was usually, like McCardell, an ex-newspaperman, and if he was reasonably diligent he could make around two hundred dollars a week (more than four times what he would earn at his reporter's desk).

As the story films developed, so the screenwriter's tasks became a shade more taxing (characterization, subplots, and the like began to seep into the pictures around 1910), and the price of photoplays went up. Studios began to buy in material from the outside. Biograph, for instance, advertised for "problem stories in which effective contrast is made between rich and poor." Some motion picture companies mounted "scenario contests." Story departments were set up, both to sift the unsolicited manuscripts that were beginning to pour in (only about one in a hundred of these "amateur" submissions was accepted) and to monitor Broadway, the bestseller lists, and the big New York magazines for filmable ideas. A tightening of the copyright law in 1911 had made it harder for the studios to plagiarize any plots they liked the look of—their cheerful custom, it seems, until a lawsuit involving the authorship of *Ben-Hur* precipitated an expensive legal clampdown.

It was as if, in 1912 or thereabouts, the film industry came to an agreement that "the screen story of today cannot all be told by the camera."[5] Certainly, it was in response to some such acknowledgment, and to the rich rewards it seemed to promise, that "serious" writers began to think of Hollywood as seductive and corrupting:

When I left New York for Hollywood in 1914, my friends unanimously agreed that I was committing professional hare-kiri, that I was selling my pure, white body for money, and that if my name

were ever mentioned in the future, it could only be . . . by people
lost to all sense of shame and artistic decency. This attitude on the
part of my friends merely reflected the way in which motion
pictures were regarded at the time by all legitimate writers, actors
and producers.[6]

Thus spoke William de Mille, elder brother of Cecil and a man of the
theater (as a writer-producer) for some thirteen years before a friend
not of the sort described above revealed to him: "They'll pay you
$25 a reel, Bill. You can do several in a day, and they'll keep your
name out of it."

With *The Birth of a Nation,* a certain softening took place in
literary circles; the contempt could no longer be quite so automatic.
This was partly because Griffith's new filmic devices were interesting enough to be *envied* by the literary fiction writer: the scale of
his 140-minute movie was unprecedentedly ambitious, his deploy-
ment of vast hordes of lifelike extras almost godlike in its manipula-
tive verve. The film offered not one family saga but two, and—
excitingly—it showed that merely by slick cutting from one family
to the other a film narrator could sustain a sense of pace and tension
that a novelist would surely have to labor for and even then perhaps
not capture quite so fluently. And to agitate even the most delicate
of literary spirits, there was of course the pioneering Griffith close-
up (at the first sight of which an early mogul is said to have declared:
"When I buy a whole actor, I want to see *all* of what I've bought").

The slight relaxation of critical hauteur was assisted also by the
way in which *The Birth of a Nation* was received. A Hollywood
director had "taken on" a large subject—the reconstruction of the
South—and had treated it not with the bland documentary zeal with
which the movies usually approached Our History but with polemi-
cal intent. The film reeks of authorial prejudice. Griffith was a Southerner, and he dared here to portray the Ku Klux Klan as "the organization that saved the South from the anarchy of black rule" and to
suggest as a proper outcome of the conflict that "the former enemies
of North and South [be] united again in common defense of their
Aryan birthright."

The idea of the cinema as an agent of ideas was relatively new;
the idea of the cinema as a spur to serious social controversy was
pretty well unheard of. *The Birth of a Nation* was the object of costly
boycotts organized by the NAACP; liberal opinion denounced it as

"a flagrant incitement to racial antagonism," "a deliberate attempt to humiliate ten million American citizens and portray them as nothing but beasts." Commercially, it was a triumph. The film's female star, Lillian Gish, recalls the fuss:

> Part of the early success of *The Birth* may have arisen from the immediate raging controversy it incited. Everyone wanted to see the film that the NAACP and the Booker T. Washington clubs were trying to have outlawed. Fist fights and picket lines occurred at many premieres of the film. The opening at Clune's had nearly been halted by rumors of a race riot. Extra police stood guard around the theater just in case. The same thing happened in New York. Two weeks before the film's showing in Boston, birthplace of the abolitionist movement, it was assailed from rostrum, pulpit and classroom. . . . When it opened at the Tremont Theater, 5,000 Negroes marched on the state capitol building demanding that the film be banned. Outside the Forrest Theater in Philadelphia fights and rioting broke out between 500 policemen and 3,000 Negroes. War news in the papers gave way to stories of this violence. Cities all over the country clamored to see the film.[7]

As for Mr. Griffith, Miss Gish claims that he "reacted to the violence and censorship with astonishment, shock and sorrow. Not even he had realized the full power of the film he had created, a film that raised the threat of legislation for national censorship. Then slowly his reaction turned to anger."

Anger does sound a more plausible response. It is hard to believe that Griffith did not know that his film was hugely offensive to abolitionists, indeed to anyone who was not zealous "to prevent the lowering of the standard of our citizenship by its mixture with Negro blood" (the words of Thomas Dixon, who wrote *The Clansman,* the book on which Griffith's film was based). What might have astonished and shocked Griffith was the scale of the response, the impact. But even this should have brought with it a certain exhilaration, a pride in the immense power of his medium—after all, in 1915, only Griffith knew how films like his were made.

Although Griffith is famous for not having used a shooting script (and thus, some would say, for being better at big visual moments than he was at narrative construction), the titles that run through *The Birth of a Nation* reveal a considerable literary pretentiousness.

Presented on the screen in framed boxes, with the initials "DG" at every corner, like the most vulgar of calling cards, the texts regularly strain toward a state of vivid metaphor:

> For her who had learned the stern lesson of honor we should not grieve that she found sweeter the *opal gates of death* [DG's italics].

This of a young girl who falls to her death as she flees a Negro pursuer—an innocent pursuer, as it happens, but how was she to know?

When the Ku Klux Klan assembles for one of its ceremonies, the language soars to incoherence:

> Here I raise the ancient symbol of an unconquered race of men, the fiery cross of old Scotland's hills. . . . I quench its flames in the sweetest blood that ever stained the sands of Time!

And when a Klan-contrived settlement of the hostilities is promulgated, the words begin to drip:

> Dare we dream of a golden day when the bestial War shall rule no more?

> But instead—the gentle Prince in the Hall of Brotherly Love in the City of Peace.

Sometimes the titles are straightforwardly informative—explanatory footnotes to the historical paintings that Griffith was fond of animating on the screen, or simple underscorings and asides: "The first negro regiments of the war were raised in South Carolina," or "A mother's gift to the cause— Three sons off to the war." But many of these shorter tags contrived to carry a literary flourish: "In the red lane of death others take their place"; "War claims its bitter, useless sacrifice." One can well imagine that a hard-up New York writer, however serious, might have perceived an opening here for his off-duty muse.

2

Stop a minute and think. Literature is old, centuries old. It started way back; possibly before the flood. It ought to be good by this time if, like wine and cheese, it gets savor from age. Photoplay writing is no bearded veteran. Photoplay writing was born some time or other in 1909. Can you ask the six-year-old to have the erudition of the ages?[8]

This almost touching plea from Epes Winthrop Sargent was typical of the period: a combination of new-dawn optimism and give-us-time defensiveness. Sargent knew his stuff; an ex-vaudeville reviewer for the *Daily Mercury,* he had done "several hundred stories for Lubin, two for Imp, two for Vitagraph and seven for Edison. Also about half a mile of photoplay advice and several miles of short stories and novelettes." In his column "The Literary Side of Pictures" in *Motion Picture World,* he would burble on about the screenplay trade, bringing news of old-timers, giving the nod to new recruits, checking out the current rates of pay, reporting on the whims and personalities of story editors: "The Universal staff is headed by Captain Leslie T. Peacocke. Captain Peacocke is also a dramatist and novelist. Walter MacNamara was once a member of the staff, as was Pop Hoadley, to say nothing of Hal Reid, who bought more stories for $10 cash than any man alive or dead." Sargent's consistent message was: We are on to a good thing, and it can only get better:

It has been a big jump from the $10 to $20 of 1909 to the $50 to $100 of today, but the changes to come will be still more marked and it is reasonable to suppose that the story of a few years hence will make these prices seem absurd. Already $1,000 and even more has been paid for book rights without the advantage of simultaneous publication in the newspapers, and it is only reasonable to suppose that in the time to come, when the best of the book rights shall have been exhausted, the author who writes photoplays for photoplay production will command a better price than the man who writes books that may be adapted.[9]

A fond hope, and for a time it looked as if Sargent could be right. If we look at the earnings of Anita Loos for her first photoplays, we discover a substantial leap around 1915–16, a year or so after Sargent made his prophecy. But then Anita Loos was in many respects untypical of the trade: her appearance in Hollywood more or less coincided with the studios' abandonment of their established policy of anonymity, and, with other factors also working in her favor, she became one of the first "name" writers, the first to have any sort of presence in the public consciousness.

Loos had no real background in newspapers or magazines; she simply mailed scripts, unsolicited, from her home in San Diego to the Biograph story department, was lucky enough to have Griffith direct a one-reeler called *The New York Hat,* and luckier still perhaps to have her text performed by Mary Pickford, Lionel Barrymore, and Lillian and Dorothy Gish. This was in 1912, and—as with writers—the notion of star acting talent was just beginning to take shape. Loos got on well with actors, and as they prospered, so did she. In 1913, she sold nearly forty scenarios, at an average payment of twenty-five dollars each. Three years later, in line with Sargent's prediction, her price had shot up to five hundred dollars, and in this same year, 1916, she was given her first movie credit, for *Macbeth*—by William Shakespeare and Anita Loos. ("If I had asked, [they] would have given me top billing.")

Loos is often spoken of as the first literate screenwriter, and although little of the early evidence survives, she herself preserved a few of her manuscripts. In 1913, Biograph paid her twenty-five dollars for *A Girl Like Mother:*

> Maude is in love with Sidney, a youth who has sworn he will never wed until he finds "a girl like Mother." In an attempt to learn what sort of girl his mother is, Maude frequents Sidney's neighborhood to study her from a distance. But through an unfortunate error, she mistakes the town trollop for Sidney's mother. Although it goes against the grain of a modest girl like Maude, she proceeds to whoop it up in a manner that ruins forever any chance to win the man she loves.

Even here, one can detect a note slightly more acerbic than Hollywood was used to at the time (although it was provided with a happy ending, *A Girl Like Mother* never reached the screen), but only when the use of dialogue titles became fully fashionable was Loos able to be seen as possessing a distinctive gift. Dialogue had had a

hard time muscling into films. At first, there was much resistance to
the idea that a writer could *overtly* contribute to the on-screen
entertainment or that words could augment the star appeal of a
Douglas Fairbanks and a Norma Talmadge by making them seem
witty and shrewd as well as wonderful to look at. Griffith himself,
although he was responsible for getting Anita Loos her first contract,
remained suspicious of what his author liked to call the "refreshing
impudence" of her screen repartee. Loos tells the story of the director John Emerson (later to be Mr. Loos) chancing upon a bundle of
synopses in the studio's script department and taking it to Griffith:

> "There's some fellow named Loos who's turned out just what I
> want for a Fairbanks picture. When can I meet him?" With a glint
> in his eye, D. W. said, "Right now," and ordered A. Loos to be
> fetched from the script department.
>
> But then he proceeded to warn Emerson that the script he had
> picked out was deceptive. "If you study it," Griffith said, "you'll
> notice that most of the laughs are in the dialogue, which can't be
> photographed." When Emerson asked why he bought the stories,
> D. W. said because they made *him* laugh. Emerson ventured they
> might do the same for audiences if the laugh-lines were printed
> on the film. "But people don't go to the movies to read," Griffith
> argued.[10]

Griffith was partly converted when, in a film called *His Picture in
the Papers* (1916), Loos's dialogue transformed Douglas Fairbanks
from a buffoonish athlete (a Keystone Cop, was Griffith's first verdict
on the actor) into a thoroughly credible screen smoothie. But even
then Griffith's instinct was to kill the picture. Loos's biographer
records:

> Griffith sat through the first screening without a smile. His disap-
> proval kept the picture on the shelf until a booking crisis forced
> Triangle to put it in circulation. A huge critical and popular hit,
> it guaranteed the future of Fairbanks and the printed caption as
> a legitimate form of screen humor.[11]

Triangle was a new company set up in 1915 by Griffith in partnership with Thomas Ince and Mack Sennett; the idea was that Triangle
would buy up theaters in key cities and that the three directors

would supply these theaters with four films every week: two hundred films per year. Triumvirate might have been a better title for the company: Griffith, Ince, and Sennett were Hollywood's top directing talents of the day, and among them they covered the main money-spinning genres. If Griffith was in charge of history and ideas, there was no disputing that Sennett was in charge of laughs and Ince in charge of action, Western-style.

The head of Triangle's story department was C. Gardner Sullivan, probably the most celebrated and certainly the highest-paid screenwriter of the silent days. Another ex-newsman, Sullivan had arrived in Hollywood in 1914 and had worked with great success on Ince's two-reeler Westerns starring William S. Hart. With the founding of Triangle, Ince was ready to move on to five-reel features, and Sullivan was more than ready to move with him: Sullivan may not have been the first talented screenwriter, but he probably was the first to take a near-solemn view of what his talent had to offer. As a result, he is now credited with introducing to the screen the soon-to-be-hallowed concept of the good bad man, the seeming blackheart whose essential virtue is unlocked by the love of a good woman. Did a cowboy ever tell a gal: "I reckon God ain't wanting me much, Ma'am, but when I look at you I feel I've been ridin' the wrong trail," or mumble to his buddy: "When women like her say there's a God, there *is* one, and he sure must be worth trailin' with"? If we are pretty sure he did, some of the credit should be given to C. Gardner Sullivan.

Like Griffith, Ince and Sullivan had no qualms about getting to the point when it came to treating racial themes. Just as good and bad could get all muddled up sometimes, so, too, could black and white. Here is an Ince-Sullivan synopsis for *The Aryan,* subtitled "The Story of a White Human Heart Turned Black":

> The hard cruel face of a man who has learned to hate, looks into the trusting countenance of a girl whose whole life has known nothing but love and trust. The man has sworn vengeance on the whole white race, and especially its women, because of a vile deed that one woman had done—a deed that has left its black impress on his very soul. The trust of the child, her confidence that he will help her and the other white people who have besought him for food and shelter, at first makes no appeal to the man who hates.

She shall be one more victim of his vengeance, her companions shall suffer with her. He glowers at her, and sneers at her pleas.

Still the great dark eyes follow him about, with no indication of fear or doubt. He has told her that he will show no mercy to her or to the white women of her party. Very well—she will not believe him. He is a white man, she can see that, although he lives among half-breeds and Indians, and she knows he will run true to the creed of his race—to protect its women.

He does. He bursts the shackles of hatred and revenge which have held his spirit in bondage and justifies the girl's absolute confidence in him.

Sullivan certainly enjoyed troweling on the prose, and his subtitles are not often merely functional. In *Hell's Hinges,* for example, the characterization is both deft and definite. When Silk Miller appears on the screen, Sullivan hangs this label around his neck:

SILK MILLER: MINGLING THE OILY CRAFTINESS OF A MEXICAN WITH THE DEADLY TREACHERY OF A RATTLER, NO MAN'S OPEN ENEMY, AND NO MAN'S FRIEND.

Silk Miller is *all* bad, as some folks are. Blaze Tracey, on the other hand, can at once be recognized as savable (if only because he is played by William S. Hart):

BLAZE TRACEY, THE EMBODIMENT OF THE BEST AND WORST OF THE EARLY WEST, A MAN KILLER WHOSE PHILOSOPHY OF LIFE IS SUMMED UP IN THE CREED Shoot first and do your disputin' afterwards.

Sullivan is now most often praised, when he is praised at all, for his confident psychologizing, but his real value to Ince might well have had more to do with the zeal with which he approached the task of visual composition. Although Hart did much of his own on-set directing, Ince and Sullivan seem to have left very little to chance when they devised their scripts:

SCENE L: CLOSE-UP ON BAR IN WESTERN SALOON

A group of good Western types of the early period are drinking at the bar and talking idly—much good fellowship prevails and every man feels at ease with his neighbor—one of them glances off the

picture and the smile fades from his face to be replaced by the
strained look of worry—the others notice the change and follow
his gaze—their faces reflect his own emotions—be sure to get over
a good contrast between the easy good nature that had prevailed
and the unnatural, strained silence that follows—as they look, cut.

And sure enough, alas, the next thing we, and the cowboys, see is
Satan MacAllister.

More than once, Sullivan's imagery would transcend the camera's
resources. In *Hell's Hinges,* for instance, a church has been burned
down by the local baddies. The audience sees a close-up of a spire
in flames, with Sullivan's prose superimposed:

STANDING LIKE A MARTYR OF OLD, WITH THE SYMBOL OF ITS FAITH
PROUDLY UPLIFTED TO THE CRIMSONING SKY.

Later on, a born-again Tracey decides enough's enough; in revenge
he takes a torch to the local saloon. The fire spreads, and pretty soon
the whole of Hell's Hinges is ablaze. Sullivan makes sure that we
don't miss any final, purifying intimations:

AND THEN FROM THE MOTHERING SKY CAME THE BABY DAWN, SING-
ING AS IT WREATHED THE GRAY HORNS OF THE MOUNTAINS WITH
RIBBONS OF ROSE AND GOLD.[12]

Small wonder, we might now think, that by 1917 Sullivan was
earning over fifty thousand dollars per year; seven years later, this
salary was trebled, making him by some distance the best-paid
writer of the era, the "dean of silent screenwriting," as *Variety* once
called him. A listing of his credits can now and then read like an
extract from a soft-porn catalog—*The Marriage Cheat, Wandering Husbands, Cheap Kisses, Other Men's Wives*—but even though
relatively few of his 375 scenarios seem to have survived, we feel
confident that, whatever the film's title, Silk Miller rarely got away
with it.

Anita Loos and C. Gardner Sullivan are names that are now mentioned in the histories: Loos because she went on to do other, celebrated works; Sullivan because he is closely identified with the shaping of a genre. In the world of silent comedy, though, the "author"
rarely got a credit: the performer *was* the script, or so it seemed. In

any case, the "Gag Room" at Mack Sennett's studio was no place for nourishing the ego. Frank Capra worked there for a time, and he has recalled the atmosphere with a fond and fascinated horror:

At the top of the stairs was the Gag Room—square and all windows. The "furniture" was a dozen kitchen chairs, two battered tables, two old typewriters, yellow scratch paper everywhere, and two long, high-backed depot benches—with built-in armrests to fiendishly discourage stretching out for a nap. Felix introduced me to the writers.

"Frank Capra, meet the prisoners of Edendale: Tay Garnett, Brynie Foy, Vernon Smith, Arthur Ripley. . . . It's eight hours a day up here, Frank, and nights, when the Old Man can't sleep. Here's the way we slave: Two men work up a story line, then all the others pitch in on gags. Sennett holds story conferences up here or down in his office. Sometimes he takes us to the projection room to see the rushes. You can scribble out your own ideas, but no scripts for directors. You tell them the story and they shoot from memory. Got it?"

Arthur Ripley, a tall, lugubrious character with the lean and hungry look of Cassius, put in his two-cents worth. "And Frank. You're good for six weeks here if, when Sennett's around, you make like Rodin's 'Thinker' and don't open your mouth."[13]

It was not in Capra's nature to keep his mouth shut for long. He managed it for two weeks, and then, at a projection room story conference, he made his first bid to ingratiate himself with Sennett, that "Napoleon of the cap and bells":

A scene came on the screen in which Eddie Gribbon, the villain, tried to break through a door. He pulled and rattled the doorknob until it came off in his hand. Then he kicked, pushed, and hurled his shoulder at the door. It wouldn't open. So the villain tore his hair and walked off.

"That's not funny," said Sennett. "We need a topper for the scene. Who's got the topper?"

"I got one, Mr. Sennett," spoke up a writer. "After Gribbon has knocked himself out trying to open the door, let him turn to the audience and say a one-word title: "Locked!" Sennett roared, "That's it. We'll use it."

"I got a topper for *that*, Mr. Sennett," I heard myself saying.

There was a hush in the room. Felix Adler and the other writers made all sorts of silent gestures for me to keep quiet. Sennett took a shot at his spittoon, then slowly turned his leather rocking chair in my direction.

"You have?" he asked, jingling gold pieces in his pocket. "Let's hear it."

My fellow scriveners raised their eyes to heaven and uttered a few muffled groans.

"Well, Mr. Sennett," my voice had a break in it, "after the heavy says 'Locked!' he looks down and sees a little cat come up to the locked door and push it open with his paw."

Sennett roared—and my co-gag men roared louder, for my benefit. "Great, Frank. That's a helluva laugh. Then what, Frank?"

"Oh-h-h. Well—uh—then the door closes quietly behind the cat. Gribbon gets an idea. He squats down on hands and knees, crawls up to the door like the cat, and pushes lightly on the door with *his* paw. No soap. Door won't open. Then the heavy throws himself at the door all over again."

"Great!" says Sennett. "We got a routine going. Come on, you guys, keep it rolling. What's next?"

And that's how comedy routines were created by gag men, one idea sparking another, sometimes slowly, sometimes like a string of firecrackers.[14]

After six months, Capra was offered a better contract ("I think it's time you lost your apprentice bug and rode the stake horses because you've won your wings. Know what I mean?"), and when he responded that what he really wanted was to be a director, Sennett hit the roof: "A director? And lose a good gag man? You're nuts."[15]

3

By the beginning of the 1920s, most American film production had moved to the West Coast, and most of the "major studios," as we now know them, were thoroughly in business. By 1920, Fox and Universal were already names to conjure with, the Warner brothers had just opened their first small lot on Sunset Boulevard, Harry and Jack Cohn had founded Columbia, and Loew's, Inc., the theater chain, had just taken over Metro Pictures, inaugurating a series of mergers that would eventually give birth to MGM. A year earlier, in response to this influx of corporate muscle, four of Hollywood's most revered "creative" figures had set up their own production company; when Mary Pickford and Douglas Fairbanks joined with D. W. Griffith and Charles Chaplin to form United Artists, a famous jest was coined: "The lunatics have taken over the asylum!" Of the other big-name studios, RKO would come later, with the beginnings of sound, and Paramount was already formidably there, but under another name: Adolph Zukor's Famous Players–Lasky.

In later years—indeed, quite soon—it would become impossible to weigh up a screenwriter's individual predicament without knowing which of these companies he worked for: each of the studios swiftly evolved a recognizable house style, and this style was largely determined and sustained by the ruling mogul, together with one or two of his henchmen. And these men were in turn answerable to their backers in New York.

In the early 1920s, Wall Street began to take a serious interest in Hollywood: financiers liked the idea of an industry that could reap big profits even as it lulled the masses into a cheerful, not to say grateful, acceptance of the status quo. The postwar Red Scare was well into its stride, and the cinema was beginning to attract a new middle-class, "thinking" audience. Bolshevism would be outgunned by money, and the bankers could get richer by seeming to be worthy. They could be in touch with show biz glamour; they could cash in on the burgeoning real estate possibilities; they could open up the European markets. Via Hollywood—this "foremost entertainer and educator of the world's millions"—they could plausibly present themselves as Christian patriots, both shaping and investing in a good America.

With Hollywood itself reeling from the effects of the 1920 money panic (not to mention the cinema-emptying flu plague of two years earlier), an alliance between East Coast cash and West Coast "creativity" was unavoidable. Without such an alliance, Hollywood might have crumbled there and then. Having accepted the alliance, though, Hollywood turned itself from a place into a definition. When H. L. Mencken was asked (by himself) in the late 1920s: "When do you think the Shakespeare of the movies will appear?" his answer was:

> The movies today are too rich to have any room for genuine artists. They produce a few passable craftsmen, but no artists. Can you imagine a Beethoven making $100,000 a year? If so, then you have

a better imagination than Beethoven himself. No, the present movie folk, I fear, will never quite solve the problem, save by some act of God. They are too much under the heel of the East Side gorillas who own them.[16]

Hollywood's self-definition was, of course, taking shape well before its pact with Wall Street was complete. By 1920, most film-makers in California saw themselves as "bound by rules that set stringent limits on individual innovations" and had already agreed that "telling a story is the basic formal concern," that "realism"—both Aristotelian and historical—was always to be aimed for, and that the teller of the tale should be invisible. It was also established that the tales themselves should be "comprehensible and unambiguous" and possess "a fundamental emotional appeal that transcends class and nation."[17] These so-called classical Hollywood criteria would dominate the industry for the next thirty years and show themselves able to accommodate the very best and the very worst in a (numerically) breathtaking output of film fiction.

Where the Wall Street alliance made a difference was in the moneymen's assumption that since the filmmakers were already of such an agreeably populist bent, it ought to be easy to manipulate and bully them into a total subservience to market values. As David Robinson has gloomily described it:

Big business left permanent marks on the creative aspects of production. The bureaucrats and accountants, eager to overcome the unpredictable and intractable elements in the creation of films, began to codify certain principles of commercial production that still prevail in the industry: the attempt to exploit proven success with formula pictures and cycles of any particular genre which temporarily sells, at the expense of other and perhaps unorthodox product; the quest for predictable sales values—star names, best-selling success titles, costly and showy production values—which in fact have little to do with art.[18]

Robinson goes on to find himself "astonished" that in spite of all this, "so much of real worth came out of this cinema and this era." Another definition of Hollywood might call it a realm in which everything happened in spite of something else.

2

The screen needs a Shakespeare. And history has proved that every time there is a real need someone rises to the occasion.

The screen will eventually have its Shakespeare—that I believe. A man will come who will tower head and shoulders above past writers and contemporaries in the construction of original screen stories. He will bring to the screen something new, some great thought, some finely wrought form of construction and story telling. He will open our eyes to new possibilities, to new dreams of the screen as a medium of art, and when he passes will leave a creative monument behind him that will be something for many generations to gaze upon with awe.

I do not predict the arrival of a screen Shakespeare this year, or next, or possibly during the lifetime of any of us. But there is a crying need and I, for one, am sure that the super-author of pictures will in the not too distant future rise like a colossus in our midst.[1]

The cadences are assuredly not those of H. L. Mencken. The speaker here is Jesse L. Lasky, partner of Adolph Zukor in Famous Players–Lasky, and we can tell from his prose what sort of Shakespeare he would settle for. It is strange how often the name Shakespeare crops up in the early days of movies and how rarely it gets mentioned in the days that follow. The search for a "Bard of Hollywood," as Lasky calls him, began in earnest in July 1919, when Sam Goldwyn—who had recently been ousted from Famous Players–

Lasky and had set up on his own—issued a thirty-two-page brochure as an insert in two leading Hollywood trade papers. It was, boasted Goldwyn, "the largest and most elaborate insert ever used in the industry," and yet it advertised not forthcoming Goldwyn features, nor current Goldwyn stars, nor even—except by the way—Goldwyn himself. Remarkably, it heralded the formation of a new body called Eminent Authors.

With the help of novelist Rex Beach, Goldwyn was attempting a riposte to Zukor's Famous Players concept (the contracting of eminent stage stars): he had assembled a stable of what he called "classy writers" to inject a bit of verbal eminence into his films. He signed up the novelists Gertrude Atherton, Gouverneur Morris, Rupert Hughes (uncle to Howard), Mary Roberts Rinehart—writers forgotten now but at the time big names, not just classy but also extremely popular. To help these prose writers with any dialogue problems, Goldwyn had also acquired a handful of playwrights, including Elmer Rice. Under the terms of their contracts, these authors granted Goldwyn a ninety-day option on the film rights of their forthcoming works. If the work was accepted for filming, the author would receive "a $10,000 advance against one third of the film's earnings." This was real money, betokening a surprising confidence in the usefulness of literary talent. After all, this was still deep in the days of silent films.

The experiment failed. The eminent authors complained about the cavalier way in which Goldwyn's story department handled their material; the Goldwyn actors and directors were suspicious of their boss's new valuation of the writer's status. Feuds and bickering ensued. Elmer Rice's disillusionment was typical:

> I had accepted Goldwyn's offer largely on the strength of his promise of free creative scope. But he had reckoned without the scenario department's entrenched bureaucracy. The practitioners of the established patterns of picturemaking saw in the invasion from the East a threat to their security. Beneath the surface affability there was a sort of struggle for power.[2]

The bureaucrats, needless to say, prevailed, and Goldwyn's own attitude to writers soon settled into the cautious skepticism that was to stay with him for the rest of his career (although the craving for literary class stayed with him too):

The great trouble with the usual author is that he approaches the camera with some fixed literary ideal and he cannot compromise with the motion picture viewpoint. . . . This attitude brought many writers whom I had assembled into almost immediate conflict with our scenario department, and I was constantly being called upon to hear the tale of woe regarding some title which had either been left out entirely or else altered in such a way as to ruin the literary conception.[3]

From what little we know about the Eminent Authors fiasco, the authors were probably at fault, being too grand, too disdainful of the "mere technicians" who had the impudence to tamper with their sense of how a story should be told. But then Goldwyn himself had been no more conscientious than they in his planning of the scheme. All in all, the episode is best remembered for various anecdotes involving the Belgian playwright Maurice Maeterlinck. Maeterlinck happened to be on a lecture tour of the United States and, on the strength of his known eminence (he'd won the Nobel Prize), found himself signed up by Goldwyn to write films.

Goldwyn, although disconcerted that Maeterlinck had never heard of Gertrude Atherton et al. ("What is he? A dumbbell?"), was at first immensely proud of his new acquisition, announcing to the world: "I feel proud to have allied to the production forces of my organization, the brain and inspired pen of Maurice Maeterlinck and to establish as a policy of Goldwyn the desire to secure the greatest creative brains from the world's literati." The trouble started when the Belgian set to work. He spoke no English, so, to get in the mood, he produced an adaptation of one of his own novels, *La Vie des abeilles.* The scenario was translated and turned over to the boss. "My God!" yelled Goldwyn when he read it. "The hero is a *bee!*"[4]

Even this Goldwyn turned to his advantage. He took to introducing his author as "the greatest writer on earth. He's the guy who wrote *The Birds and the Bees.*" Maeterlinck's next contribution was called "The Power of Light." After this, Goldwyn persuaded him that perhaps he ought to watch some films. This he did, for hours on end, eventually coming up with his next, much more professional scenario. According to Goldwyn, it began with "the lid slowly rising from a sewer in a street of Paris; up from the sewer came the face of a gory and bedraggled female Apache with a dagger gripped between her teeth." Maeterlinck was paid off and sent back to Belgium, or wherever. Legend has it that Goldwyn took him to the station, patted him on the shoulder, and said, "Don't worry, Maurice. You'll make good yet."[5]

Goldwyn had had rebuffs from authors more eminent than the ones he ended up with—H. G. Wells regretted that he "never could write on order" and would certainly "fail abjectly when it came to doing it for the screen," and George Bernard Shaw declined on the grounds that "There is only one difference between Mr. Goldwyn and me. Whereas he is after art I am after money." In response to Goldwyn's busy recruiting, though, Zukor and Lasky began to wonder if there might not be something they were missing. They, too, began canvassing for eminents and managed to import Somerset Maugham and Elinor Glyn. Maugham's flirtation was brief. He sold Jesse Lasky a script and left town as quickly as he could, later to "look back on my connection with the cinema world with horror mitigated only by the fifteen thousand dollars." In 1921, he wrote an article in the *North American Review;* the gist of it, by this time, most of his co-eminents would have applauded:

> There are directors who desire to be artistic. It is pathetic to compare the seriousness of their aim with the absurdity of their attainment. . . . I believe that in the long run it will be found futile to adapt stories for the screen from novels or from plays, and that any advance in this form of entertainment which may lead to something artistic, lies in the story written directly for projection on the white screen.[6]

Even so, as Maugham's biographer has written, "There was probably no writer who sold as many stories, plays and books to the movies as Maugham."[7]

The popular novelist Elinor Glyn set off for Hollywood in June 1920, in response to an offer from Lasky that she might like to "study the technical and other problems of film-making" and, having done that, "write a scenario specially for filming and herself supervise its production as a moving picture." At age fifty-six, Glyn still cut an exotic figure, and according to report, she made an immediate impact on the social scene: "her great beauty, her real presence, and her personality made her, effortlessly, one of the outstanding figures." She was a queenly, organizing type, and she soon carved out a role for herself as Hollywood's resident expert on "refinement." It was not Hollywood's treatment of her work that bothered her. Not only did she deliver a filmable scenario called *The Great Moment,* she was also astute enough to turn the script into a novel—possibly the first "book of the film." Her real quarrel with American movies was that they seemed to her rather vulgar and ill-bred:

> In vain she protested that English Duchesses did not wear their hair like frizzy golliwogs, that the drawing rooms of English country houses did not contain bamboo tables, aspidistras or the various knick-knacks usually associated with seaside lodging houses; that ducal castles did not have a line of spittoons, even gold ones, down the middle of the drawing room.[8]

Few of Hollywood's design people had ever been abroad, and for them Glyn was "the sole representative of European high society in Hollywood." She proved her seriousness in almost shocking style by ordering scenes from the film of her novel *Three Weeks* to be reshot, at her own expense. Real class. Glyn spent two years in Hollywood, and apart from whatever impact she made in the matter of removing gold spittoons, she is best remembered now for two major contributions: she invented the term "It" to denote sex appeal (Clara Bow became famous as the "It" girl), and she taught Rudolph Valentino how to kiss a lady's hand—palm upward was the Glyn decree.

The promise to Elinor Glyn that she would be allowed to supervise the production of her scripts was not as generous or foolhardy as it sounds today. In spite of schemes like Eminent Authors, there was not always a clear demarcation between the various filmmaking roles. For example, June Mathis was one of a group of powerful young women scenarists who, during the silent era, seem to have had more than a mere writing hand in the pictures they were set to work on. There was Anita Loos, of course, and her long association with D. W. Griffith; after her came tough, reliable professionals like Bess Meredyth, Frances Marion, and Jeannie Macpherson. Each of these began as a performer—Meredyth, for example, started out as a Griffith extra and Macpherson, Cecil de Mille's favorite, had been something of a star. The producers liked these women writers, it seems, because they could inject a money-spinning "female touch" into their scripts. It was a Hollywood doctrine that "wives and shop girls can always get their men to the movies they want to see, but a man can't get a woman to one that doesn't interest her." Another advantage, though, was that each of these women had been created by the industry; they all knew about films and they believed in them—unlike the ex-newspapermen and failed short story writers who had drifted to Hollywood in search of a fast buck.

June Mathis is remembered now for having discovered Valentino and for shifting him to Famous Players–Lasky after Metro refused to double his salary. A near-contemporary account of that discovery gives some idea of the sort of influence a staff scenarist could be permitted in the 1920s. Terry Ramsaye, in his splendid *A Million and One Nights,* recalls how Metro boss Richard Rowland followed "with a fatal fascination" weekly advertisements in the *New York Times* for a book called *The Four Horsemen of the Apocalypse,* by Vicente Blasco Ibañez:

> It was a novel of war, and through these months when all the world was trying to forget the war its circulation was mounting, mounting, mounting.
>
> Here was a success which seemed to flaunt itself in the face of every index of the times. It was something to engage the attention of the busy-minded Rowland, alert in that game of chance and wits that is the motion picture. But, curiously typical of the world of the motion picture, Rowland's curiosity did not lead him to investigate the book, to read that rapid, cloying tale of horrendous glamours for himself. The book was nothing, but those weekly figures in the Literary Section of the *New York Times*—"fortieth printing— forty-first printing—forty-second printing"—were enamoring and compelling. A dozen times he decided to order negotiations for the motion picture rights, and then one word, "War," intervened, and he did not make the step. It would be a folly against all experience. War pictures were dead.[9]

But those ads continued to torment Rowland, and in the end, despite opposition from his colleagues, he bought the book. His next step was to call in June Mathis: "Take this book and make a continuity. When you get one you like bring it to me. You've got to make good on this one for me. Everybody in the world thinks I'm crazy." Mathis delivered a script. "Rowland thumbed it over rapidly. It looked like a script and he had faith in Miss Mathis." Rowland then asked Mathis who should direct the picture. She told him. And what about the cast? She knew an Argentinian dancer called Valentino. Rowland concluded the interview by telling her: "Say, you take this script and go out there and make this picture—hire anybody you like. It's your job."

It need hardly be added that the picture was a smash hit and Valentino became a star. The film wasn't a war film, after all. "It was a triumph of a new Don Juan of the screen, a victory for Latin love and suppressed desire among the movie millions":

> Not so long ago, Richard Rowland, now at the helm of First National, picked up the novel of *The Four Horsemen* to read it for the first time. He turned a few pages and then threw it under the radiator. He had had all the excitement there was in that story.[10]

Mathis's success with *Four Horsemen* led to her appointment as supervisor, or on-site studio representative, on a new version of *Ben-Hur*. This time her luck ran out. She decided to film in Italy, where it was believed labor would be cheap: labor was cheap, but it was also (or perhaps therefore) anxious to prolong the filming for as long as possible. Costs soared, the rushes didn't look as wondrous as they should, the studio took fright and recalled the company from Rome. Mathis was blamed for "lack of supervision."

In accounts of the making of *Ben-Hur*, June Mathis is usually cast as the artist-victim. Her next big supervisory assignment, the cutting of von Stroheim's *Greed*, has no such kudos attached to it. Just as *The Birth of a Nation* announces the beginning of "serious cinema," so *Greed* is often taken to mark the point at which Hollywood once and for all defined the limitations it would impose on any maverick creative hirelings, however brilliantly gifted those mavericks might seem to be. Erich von Stroheim was not one of Hollywood's postwar European imports, schooled in Berlin experimentalism; indeed, he liked to describe himself as a "graduate of the D. W. Griffith school of film making," having worked for Griffith, as actor, assistant director, and "military adviser," throughout the war years. He began writing and directing his own films in 1918. His first three efforts were successful at the box office, and by 1922 he was the leading director at Carl Laemmle's Universal Studios. In spite of clashes with the studio head, Irving Thalberg, von Stroheim was valued for his "Continental" subtlety and sophistication: so far, these qualities had flourished within accepted boundaries.

No shrinking violet, von Stroheim had set his heart on a major triumph, a Griffith-style masterpiece that would extend the medium's sense of its own possibilities. He had bought the rights of a novel called *McTeague*, by Frank Norris, and he wanted his treatment of it on the screen "to go the Master one better as regards film realism":

> I was not going to compromise. I felt that after the last war, the motion picture–going public had tired of the cinematographic "chocolate eclairs" which had been stuffed down their throats, and which had in a large degree figuratively ruined their stomachs with this overdose of saccharose in pictures. Now, I felt, they were ready for a large bowl of plebeian but honest "corned beef and cabbage." I felt that they had become weary of insipid Pollyanna stories with their peroxide-blonde, doll-like heroines, steeped in eternal virginity, and their hairless flatchested sterile heroes, who were as lily-white as the heroines. I thought they could no longer bear to see the stock villains, dyed-in-the-wool, 100 per cent black, armed with moustache, mortgage and riding crop.
>
> I believed audiences were ready to witness real drama and real tragedy, as it happens every day in every land; real love and real hatred of real men and women who were proud of their passions. I felt that the time was ripe to present screen stories about men and women who defied . . . written and unwritten codes, and who took the consequence of their defiance gallantly, like many people do in real life. People who defied prejudice and jealousies, conventions and the social mores of a hypocritical society, who fought for their passions, conquered them or were conquered by them.
>
> I knew that everything could be done with film, the only medium with which one could reproduce life as it actually was. I knew also that entertainment that mirrored life would be more entertainment than one which distorted it. The sky was the limit! Whatever men could dream of, I could and would reproduce it in my films. I was going to metamorphose the "movies" into an art—a composite of all arts. Fight for it! and die for it, if need be! . . . . Well, fight I did. . . . And die . . . I almost did, too![11]

This is an extract from an unpublished article, and one has to allow for some roughness and melodrama in the prose. Von Stroheim's credo is worth pondering, though. As a literary manifesto, it is not in the least startling; indeed, it borders on the lurid, the overobvious. Viewed in a Hollywood context, as the outline for a film, it seems touched with a sort of insane courage: how does he think he'll get away with *that?*

He didn't, of course, and yet he almost did. In 1923, the Goldwyn Company (from which Goldwyn himself had been ousted) miraculously decided to back von Stroheim's *McTeague* project. How this was managed no one seems to know: it seems unlikely that von Stroheim could have told his backers that *McTeague* was a novel about five people destroyed by greed. Perhaps he presented it as a murder yarn, since the book was in part based on an actual San Francisco killing. Anyway, he got the money and set off in pursuit of superrealism, insisting on doing most of his shooting in the house in which the real-life murder had occurred. He had decided that he would have no studio shooting at all and even went so far as to subject his cast and crew to two months in Death Valley, where the temperature was 132 degrees under an umbrella. Fourteen members of his team fell ill, and his star, Jean Hersholt, ended up in the hospital with a hemorrhage brought on by the heat. Von Stroheim's lust for authenticity often seemed merely fanatical, as if he believed that it was worth wasting time and money in order to promote an abstract faith. One of his cameramen later on recalled: "Realism got us into trouble in the gold-mining scenes at the start. Von Stroheim insisted that we went into the mine to a depth of 3,000 feet . . . instead of 100 feet, which would have got us exactly the same effect."[12] The script said 3,000; that was that. Fidelity to the book *McTeague* demanded that rooms had to be furnished in exactly the way Frank Norris furnished them, that effects of light described in the novel had to be precisely reproduced on film. And if a character was said in the book to be hate-filled, von Stroheim made sure that his performer didn't have to act. Shortly before being rushed to the hospital, Jean Hersholt played this final scene:

> The day that we staged our death fight I barely recollect at all. Stroheim had made our hot tired brains grasp that this scene was to be the finish. The blisters on my body, instead of breaking outwards, had burst inwards. The pain was intense. Gowland and I crawled over the crusted earth. I reached him, dragged him to his feet. With real bloodlust in our hearts we fought and rolled and slugged each other. Stroheim yelled at us: "Fight, fight. Try to hate each other as you both hate me!"[13]

Von Stroheim's shooting script runs to some three hundred printed pages and is an impressive document, the detail of its visual directives managing to accumulate a sort of literary power as we track them on the page. Von Stroheim hadn't simply read *McTeague;* he'd *seen* it:

> Medium shot of McTeague. He hears the squeaking of a little bird and looks around until he discovers the bird on the rail. (The camera moves back on the narrow gauge track ahead of him to include the bird in the foreground on the rail as well as McTeague.) Cut to close-up of the little bird sitting on the rail. It is apparently lame as it cannot fly away in spite of its attempts to do so.
>
> Back to medium shot of McTeague. The camera pans slightly as he leaves the car, walks cumbersomely but carefully towards the bird, bends down and picks it up.
>
> Close-up of McTeague holding the bird up to his face.
>
> Extreme close-up of him kissing the bird.
>
> Medium close-up of McTeague with the bird in his hand, examining it closely, but very tenderly.
>
> Medium long shot. Not finding anything wrong, he retraces his steps to the car, which he then pushes with his right arm while holding the bird with his left (showing enormous strength through his feat of pushing four car-loads of ore with one arm). As he starts moving, camera again moves ahead of him on the narrow gauge track for a few feet only.
>
> Cut to long shot, reverse angle, from behind McTeague, pushing towards the entrance of the mill: his car approaches another one being pushed by a miner in the opposite direction. Medium shot, inside the mill. McTeague pushes the first car in from right to left; he takes the body of the car and lifts it with one arm into such a position that the ore rolls through a chute into the stamps. Close-up of a miner's face, very ugly and mean. He looks in the direction of the bird in McTeague's hand.
>
> Shot from the miner's angle of McTeague's hand holding the bird. Medium shot of McTeague and the other miner as they meet. The miner maliciously slaps McTeague's hand with such force that McTeague drops the bird. (With his right hand he is

holding up the second car-load at an angle of forty-five
degrees.)
Close-up of McTeague. The look on his face slowly changes
from a dumbfounded, questioning, expression to a terrible
grimace of anger.

With similarly loving care, we are told how McTeague grabs the
miner and hurls him over a precipice. And then:

Medium close-up of the miner at the bottom of the ravine
feeling his bones, wiping the blood off his face and starting to
climb up again cumbersomely.
Close-up of McTeague again.
Title: "SUCH WAS MCTEAGUE."[14]

Von Stroheim's *McTeague* was always going to be a lengthy film,
but at the end of the shooting even he was surprised to find that he
had forty-two reels of it—about ten hours' worth of viewing. "Even
if I wanted the film to be shown in two parts, it was necessary to cut
half of it." Eventually, and with a heavy heart, he brought it in at
eighteen reels. By this time, though, the Goldwyn Company had
become part of MGM, and von Stroheim's old adversary, Irving
Thalberg, was now chief of production—at the age of twenty-three.
Von Stroheim was told that the film would go out at ten reels, and
June Mathis (who dreamed up the title *Greed*) supervised the cutting. Neither Thalberg nor Mathis can fairly be thought of as philistines or thugs; their job was to produce a marketable movie. When
von Stroheim saw the finished product, though, he was disgusted.
On that day, as he remembered it later:

I abandoned all my ideals to create real art pictures and made
pictures to order from now on. My film *The Merry Widow* (1925)
proved that this kind of picture is liked by the public, but I am far
from being proud of it and I do not want to be identified at all with
the so-called box-office attractions. So I have to quit realism entirely.[15]

2

Since the failure of Eminent Authors, there had been a tendency in Hollywood to steer clear of outside talent and to nurture the in-house technicians: staff scenarists at the June Mathis level were involved fairly closely in the overall production and postproduction of a movie, and the quarrel between words and pictures seems for a brief period to have enjoyed a kind of truce. By the mid-twenties, the movie business was booming, and competition between the studios (for stars, distribution outlets, and—a Thalberg motto—"superior production values") was of a new and passionate intensity. Films were longer, more elaborately plotted, and subtitles were now integral: for the first time, the quality of the titling had an important bearing on the film's box office impact. There was new talk of the need for titles that could "hit the back wall," that could induce laughs and tears all by themselves, or that could dignify some of the more pretentious items that were now being hoisted onto the assembly line: biblical epics, translations from the classics. Film audiences were getting sophisticated; they had a troubling tendency to laugh out loud when the old corny material came up on the screen:

Scene 122—EXT. Bottom of cliff
Both roll to bottom of cliff—struggle—Bob overcomes
Dick—raises gun to strike—

Scene 123—EXT. Same location. C.U. of the two—Bob has Dick
on the ground—arm raised with gun to strike—recognizes
Dick—starts in horror—his arm drops slowly to his side as he
stares at Dick—Dick tries to bluff it out—says:

SUBTITLE: FOR GOD'S SAKE, BOB, GIVE ME ONE MORE CHANCE, REMEMBER WHAT YOU PROMISED MOTHER!

Scene 124—EXT. Same location.
Bob buries his head in his hands—Dick is thoroughly repentant—and puts his hand on Bob's shoulder—says:

SUBTITLE: BOB, I'VE LEARNED MY LESSON AND—I'M GOING STRAIGHT FROM NOW ON.
Bob looks slowly at Dick—Dick looks at him with earnest sincerity. *Fade Out*

SUBTITLE: TIME HEALS ALL WOUNDS.[16]

This, a Columbia production called *The Call of the Blood,* is quoted in a 1922 manual, *Photoplay Writing,* as an example of the "way to do it"; perhaps this *was* the way to do it, but by 1925 it was seriously out of date.

Titling was, of necessity, a minimalist art. If merely functional, it had to link and explain without drawing attention to itself. If aiming for the laughs and tears, it had to work succinctly. The requirement by the mid-twenties was for the gilded, quotable one-liner. Where better to seek that sort of material than at the Algonquin Round Table in New York? Through a clever and unashamed manipulation of the gossip columns, this weekly seminar of journalists and playwrights had become famous for its mastery of the epigrammatic mode, for—in effect—subtitling its table talk. At a quick glance, it must have seemed that the Table's cryptic style was perfectly suited to the movies.

And in a sense, it was. Unhappily, though, the movies were high on the list of the Round Table's favorite satiric targets. This was not enough to prevent most of the members from taking an interest when the money offers began rolling in, but it did rather determine their approach to Hollywood when they got out there. And even today, most popular notions of "the writer in Hollywood" are shaped by versions of his plight concocted in the 1920s by characters like Ben Hecht and Herman Mankiewicz.

In 1925, Mankiewicz, a second-string drama critic and frequently failed playwright, was thought by many to be the most gifted and the most vulnerable of the Algonquin group. He had made one trip to Hollywood already, collecting five hundred dollars for a scenario about the marines, which he claimed to have thought up while sitting on the toilet. Five hundred dollars was no joke; in those days, two dollars bought you lunch at the Algonquin. In 1926, Mankiewicz was lured back to Hollywood at a salary of four hundred dollars per week, as a Paramount staff writer—a staff writer with a difference, though. As a known Algonquin wit, he was given his own office suite in the administration building and was treated more as a visiting dignitary than as a hired literary hand.

Mankiewicz, having spent some years observing the posturings of successful Broadway playwrights, had no quarrel with this sort of treatment: he got himself a big house, bought a convertible from Ernst Lubitsch, and settled down to the serious business of squandering his salary in big-stake poker games. Los Angeles was still a country town surrounded by orange groves ("A great place to live

if you're an orange" was a well-known quip), and Herman was en-
tranced by the climate and the vegetation: palms, vines, and euca-
lyptus trees could be gazed on from your office window, and on a
good day you could have lunch with Charlie Chaplin. As to the work,
the quick-tongued Mankiewicz had little trouble staying ahead of
the game. Titles like "SHE WAS COOL IN AN EMERGENCY AND WARM
IN A TAXI" or "PARIS, WHERE HALF THE WOMEN ARE WORKING
WOMEN . . . AND HALF THE WOMEN ARE WORKING MEN" seemed,
to the Paramount chieftains, to be crackling with East Coast savoir
faire. For Mankiewicz this was easier work than having lunch at the
Algonquin: here no one answered back.

Mankiewicz missed his New York friends, though, and did his best
to persuade Paramount to hire others like himself. Paramount's
production chief, B. P. Schulberg, had served long years as a writer
and story editor and was sympathetic: all the more so, perhaps,
when he found that he could regularly recoup much of Mank's
wages at the poker table. An early Mankiewicz recruit was Ben
Hecht, a Chicago newspaperman and former Dadaist poet. In late
1926, Hecht received a wire from Mankiewicz: WILL YOU ACCEPT
THREE HUNDRED PER WEEK TO WORK FOR PARAMOUNT PICTURES?
ALL EXPENSES PAID. THE THREE HUNDRED IS PEANUTS. MILLIONS
ARE TO BE GRABBED OUT HERE AND YOUR ONLY COMPETITION IS
IDIOTS. DON'T LET THIS GET AROUND. In fact, Mankiewicz himself
made sure it did get around. Nunnally Johnson, a *Saturday Evening
Post* story writer, was another 1926 recruit; he stayed for six weeks
and many years later was still trying to remember what he did: "A
fellow took me in his office and said 'Look, here are our stars':
Richard Dix, Adolphe Menjou, Richard Arlen. 'Now we want you to
do this: pick out one of the stars and do a story for him.' " Johnson
was a reserved, ironic Southerner, modest but conscientious, and
later he would become a substantial figure in Hollywood. In 1926,
though, it was Mankiewicz who set the tone. "Mank was a man who
liked to manipulate people and the job," Johnson recalled, "and
when he came out here, I think Mank figured, 'These are my kind
of people and I can handle them.' He was so damned smart he
charmed everybody from stuffed shirts like Walter Wanger all the
way down to almost idiots and hustlers. Bringing Mank to Hollywood then was like throwing the rabbit into the briar patch."17

In Ben Hecht, Mankiewicz had a kindred spirit, arrogant and
mischievous. When Hecht arrived in Hollywood, Mank thought he

could benefit from a crash course in movie writing, and he advised him as follows:

> I want to point out to you that in a novel a hero can lay ten girls and marry a virgin for a finish. In a movie this is not allowed. The hero, as well as the heroine, has to be a virgin. The villain can lay anybody he wants, have as much fun as he wants cheating and stealing, getting rich and whipping the servants. But you have to shoot him in the end. When he falls with a bullet in his forehead, it is advisable that he clutch at the Gobelin tapestry on the library wall and bring it down over his head like a symbolic shroud. Also, covered by such a tapestry, the actor does not have to hold his breath while he is being photographed as a dead man.[18]

Hecht's response to this little lecture was to concoct a story that eliminated heroes and heroines, a story "containing only villains and bawds." By this means, "I would not have to tell any lies." The script that resulted was called *Underworld,* and it was assigned to Josef von Sternberg—his first film as a Paramount director. Von Sternberg was the same age as Hecht—thirty-two—and Hecht, who had spent two years in Berlin going Dada with the George Grosz set, was in no mood to be impressed by von Sternberg's efforts to apply expressionistic touches to this modest yarn about small-time Chicago hoods. Hecht knew about Chicago hoods, and he knew about *Das Kabinett des Dr. Caligari;* to him, the Austrian von Sternberg was a poseur with a monocle: "There are thousands like that guy playing chess on Avenue A."[19]

Later on, Hecht would boast that *Underworld* (1927) was "the first gangster movie to bedazzle the movie fans, and there were no lies in it." No lies, that is, except "half a dozen sentimental touches" put in there by von Sternberg: "I still shudder remembering one of them. My head villain, Bull Weed, after robbing a bank, emerged with a suitcase full of money and paused in the crowded street to notice a blind beggar and give him a coin—before making his getaway." At the time, Hecht was indeed furious, but von Sternberg has his own tart recollection of the film:

> The discerning Academy of Motion Picture Arts and Sciences bestowed one of their gilt statuettes on Mr. Ben Hecht for the best film of the year, and he must have been so overcome with this that

he forgot to mention that he had requested that his name be expunged. He failed to show embarrassment of any sort, though he had previously stated in the presence of the press that when he saw the film he felt about to vomit, his exact words being as quoted in print: "I must rush home at once. I think it's *mal de mer.*"[20]

Although neither would have cared to admit it, *Underworld* was for each of them a crucial film. It rescued von Sternberg's career, after a number of commercial flops, gaining him useful kudos as the initiator of Hollywood's first gangster-movie cycle. Hecht shared these kudos, but more important, he got from *Underworld* his first taste of directorial authority, of having to accommodate and compromise. It made him think. Since Hecht was nobody's subordinate, he devised a set of skillful counterploys, which eventually turned him into the highest-paid screenwriter in town. The Hecht line, as it evolved, ran roughly as follows: Since Hollywood was essentially, inherently lunatic, it didn't matter what one did there so long as the rewards were correspondingly insane. By not having any qualms or pretensions, by not caring about screen credits or critical acclaim, Hecht was able to turn himself into an indispensable script-fixer, the man you called on in an emergency, the man who delivered, took the cash, and walked away. As we will see, Hecht cared more for the movies, and put more of himself into them, than he pretended. The fact remains, though, that he is now most famous in the film histories for *(a)* the huge amounts of money he earned and *(b)* the terrible things he said about the people he earned it from: "Hollywood held the lure . . . tremendous sums of money for work that required no more effort than a game of pinochle"; "Movies are one of the bad habits that have corrupted our century. They have slipped into the American mind more misinformation in one evening than the Dark Ages could muster in a decade"; "A movie is never any better than the stupidest man connected with it"; "The movies are an eruption of trash that has lamed the American mind and retarded Americans from becoming cultured people."[21] The list could be continued. But here perhaps we should remember Hecht's Dadaist beginnings and the occasion when he and the poet Maxwell Bodenheim got paid one hundred dollars to address a pretentious Chicago literary club:

When the evening arrived, Hecht walked to the foot of the stage and announced that the topic of debate would be—"Resolved:

That people who attend literary debates are imbeciles." He scanned the audience in silence. At last he said, "I shall take the affirmative. The affirmative rests." He motioned to Bodenheim, who after an equally dramatic pause, intoned, "I guess you win." The pair beat their way out the back a hundred dollars richer.[22]

3

In the year of *Underworld,* F. Scott Fitzgerald made his first trip to Hollywood. He came not in the spirit of Mankiewicz and Hecht, although like them he thought the work would be child's play. "At that time I had been generally acknowledged for several years as the top American writer both seriously and, as far as prices went, popularly. I . . . was confident to the point of conceit. . . . I honestly believed that *with no effort on my part* I was a sort of magician with words—an odd delusion on my part when I had worked so desperately hard to develop a hard, colorful prose style." He was doing Hollywood a favor, to be sure, but he also had serious ambitions: after the commercial failure of *The Great Gatsby,* he had spoken more than once about using Hollywood to subsidize his novels. When he received the call from United Artists to write "a fine modern college story," he didn't even bother to check with his agent before accepting.

Fitzgerald had had earlier dealings with Hollywood, but he had never been there. Two stories from *This Side of Paradise* had been filmed, and in 1922 there had been a screen version of *The Beautiful and Damned.* In 1926, a stage adaptation of *Gatsby* (directed by George Cukor) had been successful in New York, and it had been followed in the same year by a film treatment, of which Zelda wrote: "It's ROTTEN and awful and terrible and we left." Terrible it may have been, but was not *Gatsby* something that Fitzgerald had *given* to the screen? And had not Ring Lardner said of the stage version: "Every now and then one of Scott's lines would pop out and hit you in the face and make you wish that he had done the adaptation himself." Fitzgerald is hardly to be blamed for believing that his magic gift might bring a mysterious new luster to the business of screenwriting.

Hollywood, at any rate, gave him a big-star's welcome. He was installed in a suite at the Ambassador Hotel, and the columnists lined up to interview this new contestant in "the Hollywood game of authors." The film he was to write was to be called *Lipstick;* it would star Constance Talmadge, and for her Fitzgerald would create "one of his blonde, reckless, wilful and irresponsible girls." Of Talmadge in real life, Fitzgerald was said to have said: "Constance Talmadge is the epitome of young sophistication. She is the deft princess of lingerie—and love—plus humor. She is Fifth Avenue and diamonds and Cattleya orchids and Europe every year. . . . She is the flapper *de luxe.* "[23]

A similar weakness for hyperbole marked the Fitzgeralds' conduct as they settled in to the Hollywood social round, and several celebrated "Scott and Zelda" horror stories issue from this 1927 adventure. There is the Sam Goldwyn party story (S and Z, not invited, turned up on their hands and knees and barked until they were let in), the "ladies' purses" story (S and Z, out to tea, collected all the ladies' purses, boiled them in a pot, and served them as tomato soup), and the visit to John Monk Saunders story. It seems that Zelda had decided that Saunders, a well-known screenwriter, was too successful with women and that "measures" should be taken. At four o'clock in the morning, S and Z, accompanied by the illustrator James Montgomery Flagg, roused Saunders. According to Flagg:

> Saunders was in his pajamas and a Sulka dressing robe and sandals; smiling imperturbably and getting drinks as if nothing surprised him. He turned on his phonograph and we set about chatting, with the exception of Mrs. F., who in prowling around found a pair of editor's shears and then sat down next to Saunders on a lounge, pulled open his robe and took a deep inhalation, then called: "Scott, come here. John smells lovely!"
>
> Scott went over and sat on the other side of Saunders and they buried their noses in his manly chest. They sighed luxuriously. Then Mrs. F. remembered the shears and began gently urging her host to let her perform a quick operation on him, explaining with quiet eloquence that his earthly troubles would be over if he would submit.[24]

John Monk Saunders now has his joke niche in biographies of Scott Fitzgerald. In 1927, though, he was many things that Fitzgerald would have wished to be. Like Fitzgerald, Saunders was from Minnesota. Unlike Fitzgerald, he had been to Oxford as a Rhodes

Scholar and had served as a pilot in the U.S. Flying Corps during World War I. At the University of Washington he had been "a brilliant student and a champion swimmer"; he was the same age as Fitzgerald (thirty-one), tall, good-looking, privately well-off, and he had made a success in Hollywood without seeming to have written anything he didn't want to write. In 1926, Paramount had paid Saunders an unprecedented $39,000 for an unfinished novel called *Wings*, based on his war experience: the film version was to win the first-ever Academy Award. Both book and film were dedicated to "Those young warriors of the sky whose wings are folded about them forever."

By the time the Fitzgeralds arrived in Hollywood, Saunders was at the peak of his glamour and celebrity but was modest with it. Had he not, two years earlier, written—in a style possibly borrowed from Fitzgerald—"Shall I, at fifty, be a major figure or a minor figure? Shall I go up like a rocket, blacken against the sky, and come down like a dead stick? Or shall I go up at all?" Even without the evidence of Flagg's anecdote, we might guess that Fitzgerald would have studied the Saunders phenomenon with some unease. In a Fitzgerald novel, such a character would have been doomed.

And so it was with Saunders. He went on to write two more successful air force pictures—*The Dawn Patrol* (1930) and *The Last Flight* (1931). He stayed on in Hollywood (he married the *King Kong* actress, Fay Wray), but during the 1930s his career declined. He was securely typecast as a "flying" writer, and his screenwriting formula ("Action is the thing. Action! Action! Action!") had been shaped by silent movies. Titles like *The Eagle and the Hawk, West Point of the Air,* and *Devil Dogs of the Air* give an idea of the kind of work he was offered, and none of these scored a success. By 1938, his marriage destroyed, according to Fay Wray, by his fondness for "drinking and narcotics," Saunders crossed paths with Fitzgerald once again. Fitzgerald, on his third trip to Hollywood, was put to work on Saunders's story for *A Yank at Oxford.* Two years later, both men died, aged forty-four. Fitzgerald's drink-induced heart attack is now thought of as one of Hollywood's most famous, or infamous, deaths. Saunders, six months earlier, had hanged himself in a Florida beach cottage, using the cord from his robe.

The Fitzgeralds' 1927 Hollywood adventure lasted eight weeks and was not counted a success. Fitzgerald's script for *Lipstick* was turned down as "weak," and Zelda got inflamed with jealousy over

her husband's infatuation with the young film actress Lois Moran
(later used as the model for Rosemary Hoyt in *Tender Is the Night*).
Moran, incidentally, arranged for Fitzgerald to have a screen test—
which he also failed. Accounts of *Lipstick* make it sound a rather
silly affair, to do with flappers and Princeton undergraduates, with
unfilmable lines such as the one in which the heroine is described
as "so lonesome that she [tries] to look as if she hopes no-one will
speak to her." Its refusal by United Artists cost Fitzgerald a big
payday: the deal had been that he would get $3,500 for writing the
script and a further $12,000 if it was accepted. Scott and Zelda were
well out of pocket—they had spent far more in Hollywood than he
had earned.

But there were gains. It was during his 1927 visit that Fitzgerald
met the Last—or, some would say, the first—Tycoon. Irving Thalberg, already viewed as "Hollywood's supreme wunderkind," was
two years younger than Fitzgerald and also marked for early death
(he had a congenital heart complaint). Thalberg conformed to none
of the tycoon stereotypes, except in his dedication to huge profits.
He was slender, frail, and solemn, and spoke magisterially but with
sensitivity about matters of taste and prestige; he read books, he
philosophized, and he had a formidably complete faith in his own
moviemaking instincts: "I, more than any single person in Hollywood, have my finger on the pulse of America. I know what people
will do and what they won't do."[25]

But Thalberg wielded his considerable power unsentimentally. It
was Thalberg who recalled *Ben-Hur* from Rome; it was Thalberg
who tamed von Stroheim; it was Thalberg who, when told that you
couldn't have a moonlit seaside scene in a film that was meant to be
set in Paris, repelled all argument with the edict: "We can't cater
to a handful of people who know Paris." Tales about Thalberg are
usually recounted in a tone of what might be called qualified awe.
Fitzgerald in 1927 seems to have been straightforwardly mesmer-
ized. Meeting Thalberg by chance one day in the MGM commissary,
he not only sat through the following speech but remembered it
well enough, ten years later, to incorporate it in *The Last Tycoon:*

> Scottie, supposing there's got to be a road through a mountain—a
> railroad, and two or three surveyors and people come to you and
> you believe some of them and some of them you don't believe, but
> all in all, there seem to be half a dozen possible roads through

those mountains, each one of which, so far as you can determine, is as good as the other. Now suppose you happen to be the top man, there's a point where you don't exercise the faculty of judgment in the ordinary way, but simply the faculty of arbitrary decision. You say, "Well, I think we will put the road there," and you trace it with your finger and you know in your secret heart, and no one else knows that you have no reason for putting the road there rather than in several other different courses, but you're the only person that knows that you don't know why you're doing it and you've got to stick to that and you've got to pretend that you know and that you did it for specific reasons, even though you're utterly assailed by doubts at the time as to the wisdom of your decision, because all these other possible decisions keep echoing in your ear. But when you're planning a new enterprise on a grand scale, the people under you mustn't ever know or guess that you're in any doubt, because they've all got to have something to look up to and they mustn't ever dream that you're in doubt about any decision.

A year later, this same decisionmaker would pronounce that "talking pictures are just a passing fad." Presumably, on this occasion also, no one dreamed that Thalberg was in any doubt.

Fitzgerald would return to Hollywood four years later, this time with Thalberg as his boss. In the meantime, he was happy enough to quit this place of "almost hysterical egotism and excitability." According to legend, he and Zelda, on their last day, piled all the furniture in the middle of their hotel room and then crowned this edifice with a sheaf of unpaid bills. Back East again, they were welcomed in salty New York style by H. L. Mencken: "Thank God you have escaped alive! I was full of fears for you. If Los Angeles is not the one authentic rectum of civilization, then I am no anatomist. Any time you want to go out again and burn it down, count me in."[26]

3

"You ain't heard nothing yet!" Can this really have been the first-ever line to be spoken in a movie? And is it true that Al Jolson, who spoke it, was ad-libbing? *The Jazz Singer* opened at the Warners Theatre in New York on October 6, 1927, and whatever might be said about the film, Hollywood surely deserves praise once again for scripting its own history. We had indeed "heard nothing yet."

Jolson's threat that night was in some ways easy to dismiss. *The Jazz Singer* did have a synchronized sound accompaniment, but this was mainly used for songs; the "dialogue" added up to no more than a few lines, and when Samson Raphaelson, author of the play on which the film was based, attended the first night, he came away in two minds about the future possibilities of talking pictures. On the one hand, he felt that his play had been brutally travestied:

> Jolson didn't have any comedy dialogue. The man's a terrific co-median—and a lousy actor. He's a non-actor. They gave him "dra-matic" scenes—that is, "straight" scenes—terribly written synop-sis dialogue—and he didn't try to play them; he just read them. It was embarrassing. A dreadful picture. I've seen very few worse.[1]

On the other hand, any fool could see that if Warner Brothers' new Vitaphone technique did manage to catch on, motion pictures would never be the same again:

> I could see tremendous possibilities, once I heard sound on film. You heard background noises; as you went through the East Side,

you heard the street sounds, and so on. I could see a whole new
era had come into the theater. But from this particular picture,
you wouldn't have much hope for the possibilities of that era.[2]

Raphaelson's response was fairly typical of Hollywood in 1927.
After all, "sound films" had been under discussion there for several
years. The moguls knew how to make them, but they also knew that
it would cost millions to convert the picture palaces, reequip the
studios, and so on. As long as the fans seemed happy with the silents,
there was no need to be precipitate.

It was Warner Brothers, facing a financial crisis, that decided to
stake everything on Vitaphone—they did a deal with Western Electric, reequipped a couple of cinemas, and, after exhibiting a few
experimental "shorts," put on *The Jazz Singer,* to test audience
response. Audiences loved it, and Warners quickly followed up with
the first all-talk "talkie," a gangster movie called *The Lights of New
York,* the film that gave new meaning to the phrase "I'll take you
for a ride." This, too, scored a definitive success.

Paramount, Universal, and particularly MGM paused for a moment, as if in disbelief, and then—with astonishing efficiency—they
took the plunge. By the end of 1928, there were twenty thousand
movie houses in the United States, and of these, thirteen hundred
had been wired for sound. A year later, nine thousand had been
reequipped, and by the end of 1930 the silent picture was stone
dead. To finance this transformation, the studios needed to raise
huge amounts of capital; by 1930, the boards of all the big film
companies were heavily staffed by New York bankers and financiers.
The alliance with Wall Street was now complete and irrevocable,
with Wall Street in control. The years 1928–30 were not, after all, the
best of times in which to borrow money.

While the moguls did their sums, the filmmakers puzzled over the
new technical requirements. Cameras had to be installed in huge,
unwieldy soundproof booths—called "ice-boxes" because that's
what they looked like, and because, inside, they were suffocatingly
hot—and were thus more or less immobilized. Soon the booths
would be equipped with wheels and rails, but at first it seemed as
if the days of panning and tilting had been lost forever.

Microphones were nondirectional, "suspended from above or hidden behind flower vases, underneath tables or in back of curtains.
The actor was unable to speak while in motion from one pick-up
point to the other. Looking at some of the early talking pictures you

get the impression that it's 1-2-3-4-speak!, 1-2-3-4-speak!"[3]

Editing sound was also a problem, because the sound track was on disc, and the disc factor necessarily affected the editing of film: "In the first sound-on-disc films, scenes were required to run from 8 to 10 minutes in order to be recorded on a 16-inch disc." And of course the atmosphere in the studio changed. In a silent-film studio there was always lots of noise: spectators were allowed sometimes, and now and then the actors liked to be entertained by string quartets as they performed. Directors could yell out instructions during filming, arc lights could crackle, motors could rev up outside. With the arrival of sound, a cathedral-like *gravitas* descended: now everything seemed petrified, on tiptoe. One studio, during filming, hoisted a "Silence Please" balloon from its roof in the hope of diverting any passing aircraft. The new king on the set was not the producer or director but the sound man. As William Wyler has recalled: "He was up under the rafters of Universal's only sound stage. After a scene, everybody looked up to hear His verdict. If He had heard the words properly, it was okay. If not, you had to repeat." And Hal Mohr, cinematographer on *The Jazz Singer,* has unpretentiously reminisced:

> In the early days of making sound pictures, the experts on sound came from the telephone laboratories, and we were terrifically awed by the eggheads who came onto our stages to tell us how we were going to put sound on our silent films. They'd walk authoritatively onto the stage and say, "We have to put our baffles here," or "You can't have lights there, because that's sound-reflecting," and so on and so forth. Unsurprisingly, after we made the first sound pictures (including *The Jazz Singer*) it looked as if sound pictures were going to be very short-lived, because, by the prevailing standards of making motion pictures, they were so bad! We did suffer tremendously from the inadequacies of being unable to meet the problems that sound put to us.
>
> Those of us who had any voice at all in the making of motion pictures finally convinced our mentors—the producers with the purse strings—that they were short-changing themselves by making such an inferior amusement-product, and that we'd better start making movies again. The sound man at that time had been the supreme god on the set. If he said "You can't have that light there," then that light disappeared; or if he said "I want that

microphone down here," that's where the microphone was placed, despite the fact that an actor had to deliver the lines and we had to photograph him. So finally we reached the point where we said "Now fellows, we're going to start making movies again. You just get the best sound that you can get, and if it ain't good enough, that's too bad." We then found a happy compromise: they worked with us and we worked with them, and the result is that we're still making bad movies.[4]

Even if the first talkies had been more expertly produced, they would still have met with opposition from cineastes, those who believed, with Charlie Chaplin, that talkies were "ruining the great beauty of silence." Chaplin feared, correctly, that "the oldest art in the world, the art of pantomime," was under threat, and he was not just speaking from self-interest (for many years he refused to make a talkie). He felt, as many others did, that by 1928, the silent film was close to perfecting its own language and that it was about to emerge as the dominant twentieth-century art form.

The Art of the Film was already under heavy discussion in both America and Europe, and much of the talking against talkies came from literary intellectuals of the modernist persuasion. The first serious film magazine, *Close-Up,* printed poems by Gertrude Stein alongside essays on Eisenstein and was owned and run by literary types. Advanced works of literature were freely spoken of as "cinematic": in America there was Vachel Lindsay; in France, Apollinaire. New films from Germany and Russia had given rise to a spate of almost messianic theorizing—theorizing based always on the proposition that film language offered an *alternative* to word language: "In this mutely vivid art, comprehensible in every language and to nearly every culture, even very primitive ones, the cinema enthusiasts believed they had found a form which could not only meet the highest aesthetic standards, but also, in its intimate appeal to all people, could become a universal language."[5] But in Russia, even as sound movies were taking hold in Hollywood, V. I. Pudovkin was devising an aesthetic for scenarists that would have offered little long-term scope for Hecht and Mankiewicz:

Relationships between human beings are, for the most part, illuminated by conversations, by words; no one carries on conversation with objects, and that is why work with them, being expressed by visual action, is of special interest to the film technician. Try to imagine to yourself anger, joy, confusion, sorrow, and so forth expressed, not in words and the gestures accompanying them, but in action connected with objects, and you will see how images saturated with plastic expression come into your mind. Work in plastic material is of the highest importance for the scenarist. In the process of it he learns to imagine to himself what he has written as it will appear upon the screen, and the knowledge thus acquired is essential for correct and fruitful work.[6]

Rather as one might expect, filmmakers like Pudovkin and Eisenstein, and serious theorists like Rudolf Arnheim, were quicker to perceive the possibilities of sound, and adjust to the new order, than were most of their disciples (although it was sound effects rather than dialogue that the Russians welcomed, and Arnheim believed that "little" could "be expected of dramatists and novelists for sound films"[7]). For a year or two, even after it was evident that sound had come to stay, it was widely reviled as a typical Hollywood perversion, a bid for quick profits, for faddishness, at the expense of any serious interest in the development of cinema: how could words do other than relegate the film to a derivative dependence on literary modes of narrative? Aldous Huxley, himself later to earn large sums as a screenwriter, wrote an angry essay called "Silence Is Golden," in which he reports on a visit to *The Jazz Singer.* The talkies are described as "the latest and most frightful creation-saving device for the production of standardized amusement," and as for Jolson and the "dark and polished young Hebrews" who accompanied him: "My flesh crept as the loudspeaker spouted out those sodden words, that greasy, sagging melody. I felt ashamed of myself for listening to such things, for even being a member of the species to which such things were addressed."[8] George Jean Nathan shared Huxley's distaste but was a shade more stylish in his approach. He felt he could afford to be, because in his view moviegoers would soon tire of this new challenge: "To wish the movies to be articulate is about as sensible as wishing the drama to be silent . . . if the Vitaphone were to stick to words of one syllable, the movies might use it to advantage. That is possible. But the moment it went in for words of two or, on gala occasions, three, Mr. Adolph Zukor would have to sell his twelve Rolls Royces and 82-carat diamond suspender buckles, learn English and go back to work."[9]

2

In fact, it was the "advent of sound" that made it possible for Mr. Zukor to hang on to his possessions, unlike several other business-men of this epoch. By 1930, cinema audiences in America had almost doubled (from 60 million per week in 1927 to 110 million), and the new sound movies, far from limiting themselves to monosyllables, or sticking to music and traffic noises, had become suddenly word-hungry. Not only were there new talkies to be made; there was also a considerable backlog of silent stock to which dialogue had to be added (or, if the stars in these old films were not ready for "the ordeal of speech," dream sequences or voice-overs had to be de-vised). "An S.O.S. was beamed to the East, a hurry-up call for what was then described as real writers, to distinguish them from the continuity boys, the gag-men, the ideas men and the rest of the colorful if illiterate silent contingent."[10]

This was Budd Schulberg, being unfair to some of the Hollywood writers already in position—writers like Jules Furthman, for exam-ple. Furthman had been selling scripts to Hollywood since 1915, and by 1926 he had become established as a top writer at Paramount, home of Mankiewicz and Hecht. He worked on the scripts of *Under-world* and other von Sternberg silents, and with the arrival of the talkies (plus the arrival of Marlene Dietrich), he and Sternberg formed an effective partnership on films like *Morocco, Shanghai Express,* and *Blonde Venus.* Furthman left Paramount for Thal-berg's MGM in 1932, and his name will crop up in association with several "classic" movies of the thirties and forties. The point here is that he was neither colorful nor illiterate (although it should be said that some of his collaborators would later accuse him of various near-jaunty acts of plagiarism: "Practically word for word out of famous pieces. Things by Mark Twain and Somerset Maugham. . . . Granted, nothing's new, but Jesus, you don't just take whole lines of dialogue"[11]).

But in 1928, there *was* an S.O.S., and it was answered with enthu-siasm. By the end of 1931, there were 354 full-time writers in Holly-wood and another 435 working part-time, costing the industry $7 million (which was actually a mere 1.5 percent of the studios' total payout). Some of the new migrants from the East had backgrounds in vaudeville, but most of them were either struggling playwrights or ill-paid newspapermen and magazine writers. Even the most thrifty and disdainful found it difficult to resist the call. Samson Raphaelson, for instance, had turned down earlier Hollywood offers as "degrading"; he lost his savings in the 1929 stock market crash, and by 1930 he was more than ready to sign up with RKO at $750 per week. Robert Riskin, a former newspaperman and publicist, had worked on a few short films in New York; he, too, was burned in the crash and eagerly accepted the patronage of Frank Capra at Columbia. S. N. Behrman was a playwright in his mid-thirties, with one hit to his name *(The Second Man).* He was connected to the Algonquin–*New Yorker* circle and was thus scornful of Hollywood. In 1929, his latest play flopped, the coming Depression was much on his mind, and Fox offered him $1,250 per week to go out West. In Behrman's next play, *Biography,* one of his characters would dream of the day when "men won't have to prostitute themselves in Hollywood." This, of course, did not mean that Behrman—and others like him—were not both grateful and valuable to their Hollywood paymasters. Without Hollywood, Behrman wrote, "I would have died of malnutrition long ago." Like Raphaelson and Riskin, he turned himself into a professional screenwriter of some quality, although he was rather more Hecht-like than they in his approach: he was always glad to collaborate, had nothing against doing adaptations, and was able to remain active in New York.

Many of the new arrivals didn't need the Depression to drive them to the West Coast: whatever the state of the economy, Hollywood offered better prospects than would ever be in view back home. Jo Swerling was a Chicago journalist with a sideline in comic strips. He was also Chicago correspondent of *Variety* and had once given the Marx Brothers a rave review; it was through them that he received the invitation to "go Hollywood." Morrie Ryskind was another Marx recruit, and so, too, was S. J. Perelman. Perelman had been a magazine humorist and was originally hired by the Marxes to do radio scripts. With the coming of sound, he was a natural for Hollywood. He hated it—"a dreary industrial town controlled by hoodlums of enormous wealth"—and would sourly describe the working conditions that awaited the first wave of "real writers" from the East. The writers' building at Paramount, he recorded, was a "ramshackle warren of tan stucco," in which could be discovered

thirty or forty other scribes. They were all in various stages of parturition, some gestating gangster epics and horse operas, others musical comedies, dramas and farces. Few of them were writers in the traditional sense, but persuasive, voluble specialists adept at contriving trick plot situations. Many had worked before the advent of dialogue, in silent pictures; they viewed the playwrights, novelists and newspapermen who were beginning to arrive from New York as usurpers, slick wordmongers threatening their livelihood, and rarely fraternized.[12]

The 1929–30 intake of Eastern writers was actually Hollywood's third attempt to assimilate the World of Literature: there had been the Eminent Authors fiasco, and then the Herman Mankiewicz recruitment (which turned out to be quite durable), and now there was the Great Talkies Panic. Of this third wave of immigrants, it has been calculated that over 75 percent returned home after three months. Theirs was the predicament that is dramatized in Kaufman and Hart's 1930 stage play, *Once in a Lifetime,* a "savage"—in fact, overpitched and ludicrous—satire on the film world's mindless extravagances: highly paid writers lolling unemployed in padded cubicles while illiterates spend millions before realizing that they are working on the wrong script—that kind of thing. Of the 25 percent who didn't immediately pack their bags, many were not writers at all but composers or librettists.

The first talkies naturally tended to be musicals or melodramas: in each of these modes, the techniques of the silent film could be preserved—the dance number, the car chase. When Wells Root, a former *Time* magazine film critic, arrived in Hollywood in 1928 (summoned there by Mankiewicz), David Selznick is reputed to have said to him: "Write whatever you like as long as there's a love scene and the girl jumps in the volcano at the end."[13] A cryptic brief, not requiring much in the way of thoughtful dialogue. For "scintillating conversation," as Lewis Milestone dreamed of it, the movies had little choice but to make a raid on Broadway. The American theater just happened to be enjoying a would-be scintillating phase of genial, lighthearted satire: domestic and topical but without much weight or difficulty. And there was no problem about quantity; in 1927–28, the total number of plays produced on Broadway had reached an all-time high—264 of them flitting in and out of the city's eighty theaters during the course of the year: "There was no one shaking his head and crying Where are the playwrights, where are the directors, where are the great actors, the playgoers? There was a shortage of nothing whatsoever."[14]

And so Hollywood began to buy dialogue by the ton before anyone had really had the chance to think about how it might come across on film. Movies had to be churned out, even as the most basic rules were being changed. While directors like Milestone, Lubitsch, and Mamoulian (originally a theater talent himself) puzzled over ways of reliberating the cinematic eye, the assembly line of necessity kept moving. Between 1928 and 1931, Hollywood seemed to be "photoplaying" everything—from *Anna Christie* to *Charlie Chan*, from *Arrowsmith* to *Dracula*. Novels and stories were gutted and the hired dialogue writers were set to work on Conrad, Galsworthy, Jack London, even Dickens: his *Dombey and Son* (1848) becoming Paramount's *Rich Man's Folly* (1931). This was the beginning of the great age of Hollywoodization, an age that was shortly to bring us *Main Street* under the title *I Married a Doctor*. It is not hard to fathom the psychology behind such packaging. For instance, in 1930 we have *Experiment in Sincerity* filmed as *A Lady Surrenders;* along the same lines, *Lost Ecstasy* becomes *I Take This Woman* and poor Elmer Rice finds his *See Naples and Die* transformed into *Oh! Sailor! Beware!* Even Hollywood's own Joseph M. Schenck was moved to remark: "The trouble with the whole industry is that it talked before it thought."[15]

3

Lewis Milestone might bravely pledge that he could "hold a screen audience for two hours" with "scintillating conversation" (after all, he went on, "take the plays of Shakespeare . . . They have come down through the years because of their scintillating conversation"[16]), but Milestone was relatively lucky. His 1930 screen version of Erich Maria Remarque's novel *All Quiet on the Western Front* allowed for long sequences of silent-style battle action (plus audible gunfire and screams and the use of Universal's new crane), and the dialogue by Maxwell Anderson et al., though hardly scintillating, was genuinely novel when served up as cinema. That is to say, it was an earnest and plausible attempt to make cinema audiences think in something like the way that serious playgoers and book readers were supposed to think: consecutively, point by point, in pros and cons.

"The French certainly deserve to be punished for starting this war."

"Everybody says it's somebody else."

"Well, how *do* they start a war?"

"Well, one country offends another."

"How can one country offend another? You mean, there's a mountain over in Germany gets mad at a field over in France?"

"Well, one people offends another."

"Well, that's it. I shouldn't be here at all. I don't feel offended."

"Somebody must have wanted it. Maybe it was the English. No, I don't want to shoot any Englishman. I never saw one till I came up here, and I suppose most of them never saw a German till they came up here. No, I'm sure they weren't asked about it."

"I think it's more a kind of fever. Nobody wants it in particular, and then all at once there it is. We didn't want it. The English didn't want it. But here we are, fighting."

"Whenever there's a big war coming on you should rope off a big field and sell tickets. On the big day, you should take all the kings and their cabinets and their generals and put them in the center in their underpants and let them fight it out with clubs—and the best country wins."

Six years earlier, Maxwell Anderson had written—with Laurence Stallings—an antiwar play called *What Price Glory?* At the time, it was hailed as a landmark in the American theater, and doubtless Anderson would have found it hard to predict that his 1930 film script might turn out to have a more enduring life. Even in 1930, though, he got a taste of the cinema's inflammatory power: stink bombs were hurled at the screen during showings in America, and in Germany, Nazi demonstrators succeeded in getting the film banned. It seems improbable that a silent film would have had quite the same effect.

In *All Quiet on the Western Front*, the speeches came as a near-welcome interlude between bouts of noisy and horrific action. Mostly, though, the early talkies talked too much, and what action there was took place within stage-directed limits (vide Milestone's next effort, the movie version of Hecht and Charles MacArthur's *The Front Page*). Now and then, as Arthur Knight has well described it, writers and directors tried to break up long dialogue passages by having a conversation begin in a taxi, continue in a living room, and end up in a bedroom.[17] A promising enough sequence of events, but somehow bedrooms turned out to present a special problem for the talkies: after all, what do you *say* in a bedroom? Without fail, it seems, audiences rocked with laughter whenever a formerly adored romantic star like John Gilbert delivered an "I love you" in a not quite husky enough voice to a frozen, eyes-front costar whose own accents were then revealed to be querulous mid-European or muscular mid-Bronx, or both. For some reason, hearing these screen deities speak the "I love you" was funny in itself. As *Variety* remarked: "Seems the only type of love stuff received as intended since the advent of talkies is the comedy love scene. The screen comics are becoming the heavy lovers and the heavy lovers, comedians."[18]

Seeking replacements for several of these soft-edged silent stars again involved turning to Broadway, which, in the late twenties–early thirties, was entering a hard-edged phase: there was a small vogue for gangster plays. Edward G. Robinson in *The Racket,* Paul Muni in *Four Walls,* Spencer Tracy in *The Last Mile:* these actors, signed by Hollywood, seemed to bring their own subject matter with them. Certainly they helped to revive a screen genre that, although popular in the silent days from time to time, had always rather yearned for speech. Much gangster lore and rhetoric has to do with language: threats, blackmail, confessions, tip-offs. Similarly, there is the business of "squealing," "singing," and, indeed, "silencing." Even the rhythms of gangster-speak—quick-fire, staccato—were admirably suited to the fast film stock that had to be used for talking pictures. Add to these factors the sound of screeching tires, police sirens, and volleys of machine gun fire, and it will be understood why *Little Caesar* was the big hit of 1930.

Based on a novel by W. R. Burnett, *Little Caesar* was a lightly disguised biography of Al Capone (Al himself planted a spy on the set while the film was being made). Edward G. Robinson said later of his starring role that it "probably expressed a feeling that millions of people had about their lives."[19] The Depression had indeed made Capone a sort of underdog hero, a challenger of the establishment, a poor boy who made it big, an individualist who lived by his own rules. The actor Robinson, small, mean, and ugly, was a bracing alternative to the Ruritanian good lookers of the silent days. Nobody pushes me around: for an hour and a half, Depression audiences could believe that this was true. With *Little Caesar*—which was swiftly followed by James Cagney in *Public Enemy*—the gangster movie was reborn, as social comment. "Mother of Mercy, is this the end for Rico?" Robinson cries as he sustains obligatory retribution. The Warner Brothers answer to this was: Absolutely not. Warners, the pioneers of sound, had made a discovery. Dialogue didn't have to sound like dialogue; it didn't have to be Broadway posh or particularly intelligent. "Yeah, yeah, awright, you guys, yeah, yeah" was verse drama to the ears of a 1930s groundling. "I had a literary theory about dialogue," said W. R. Burnett:

> This was in the twenties. Novels were all written in a certain way, with literary language and so much description. Well, I dumped all that out; I just threw it away. It was a revolt, a literary revolt. That was my object. I wanted to develop a style of writing based on the way American people spoke—not literary English. Of course, the fact that the Chicago slang was all around me made it easy to pick up.
>
> Ultimately what made *Little Caesar* the enormous success it was, the smack in the face it was, was the fact that it was the world seen completely through the eyes of a gangster. It's a commonplace now, but it had never been done before then. You had crime stories but always seen through the eyes of society. The criminal was just some son-of-a-bitch who'd killed somebody and then you go get 'em. I treated 'em as human beings. Well, what else are they?[20]

Burnett had an unkind notion (many of Burnett's notions were unkind) that the Warners bought *Little Caesar* because the hero comes from Youngstown, Ohio: the Warner boys were sons of a Youngstown butcher. It seems more likely that they bought it because Burnett had a priceless knack: he knew how tough guys talked. Later Burnett stories like *High Sierra* and *The Asphalt Jungle* are now ranked as film classics rather than as works of printed fiction, but Burnett never minded much about literary critics, or so he claimed. The son of a family of Irish Ohio political bosses, he moved to Chicago in 1927, to "soak up the atmosphere," and took pride in being "among the first at the scene of the St. Valentine's Day Massacre." After the success of *Little Caesar,* he moved to Hollywood, but he signed no long-term contracts there: he worked on several screenplays—notably *Scarface* for Howard Hawks—but his favored method was to write filmable novels and then let other people sweat over the scripts. Apparently, his first contact with Hollywood taught him that authors also needed to talk tough:

> When they opened *Little Caesar* at the Strand Theatre in New York, they opened it cold, yet they had to get out the mounted police and run it twenty four hours a day. Then, I'll never forget the premiere out here [Los Angeles]. They had every goddamned person on stage—the actors, the director, the cameraman—and when they were finished introducing all of them, Ben Lyon, the emcee, finally says, "Oh yes, the *writer.* There always had to be a writer." Can you imagine that? He introduced me and I said "Screw you." I wouldn't stand up for him. That's one of the things that made it very tough for me when I came to Hollywood. I realized what the status of the writer was.[21]

4

In 1930, the status of the writer was uncertain. A tough-guy novelist feels scorned; a grandee playwright feels ridiculously pampered. A hard-up genius is grateful for the extra funds; a Great American Novelist believes the movies should be kneeling at his feet.

When P. G. Wodehouse was brought to Hollywood by MGM in 1930, he was given two thousand dollars per week and Norma Shearer's house to live in (Shearer no longer needed it because she had married Irving Thalberg), so—in MGM terms—Wodehouse had no worries about status. The playwright was also given permission to do his work at home. "When I get a summons from the studio, I motor over there, stay for a couple of hours and come back. Add incessant sunshine and it's really rather jolly." The studio, it seems, summoned him but rarely:

> The actual work is negligible. I altered all the characters to earls and butlers with such success that they called a conference and changed the entire plot, starring the earl and the butler. So I'm

still working on it. So far I've had eight collaborators. The system is that A gets the original idea, B comes into work with him on it, C makes the scenario, D does preliminary dialogue, and then they send for me to insert class and whatnot, then E and F, scenario writers, alter the plot and off we go again. I could have done all my part of it in a morning but they took it for granted that I should need six weeks.[22]

Wodehouse served a year in Hollywood, and at the end of his contract he gave an interview to the *Los Angeles Times*, which caused something of a stir:

> It dazes me. They paid me $2,000 a week—and I cannot see what they engaged me for. They were extremely nice to me, but I feel as if I have cheated them. You see, I understood that I was engaged to write stories for the screen. After all, I have twenty novels, a score of successful plays, and countless magazine stories to my credit. Yet apparently they had the greatest difficulty in finding anything for me to do. Twice during the year they brought me completed scenarios of other people's stories and asked me to do some dialogue. Fifteen or sixteen people had tinkered with those stories. The dialogue was really quite adequate. All I did was tough it up here and there.
>
> Then they set me to work on a story called "Rosalie," which was to have some musical numbers. It was a pleasant little thing, and I put in three months on it. When it was finished, they thanked me politely and remarked that as musicals didn't seem to be going so well they guessed they would not use it.
>
> That about sums up what I was called upon to do for my $104,000. Isn't it amazing?[23]

The nation's press agreed that, yes, it was amazing. The interview was extensively reprinted, and the *New York Herald Tribune* printed an editorial under the title "All So Unbelievable," praising Wodehouse for being the first to tell all, to name names, and "thus assure us of the truth in the astounding legends. He confirms the picture that has been steadily growing—the picture of Hollywood the golden, where 'names' are bought to be scrapped, talents are retained to be left unused, hiring [of distinguished authors] is without rhyme and firing without reason. It is indeed amazing."[24] Ac-

cording to his biographers, Wodehouse's interview "galvanized the
bankers who supported the film industry into action to secure reform," but it is not easy to find evidence of this. Indeed, in 1935,
"Plum" was invited back to Hollywood, again by MGM. His task? To
work on the script of a musical comedy called *Rosalie.* As for reform,
if there was any, it did not prevent Dorothy Parker and her husband,
Alan Campbell, from being hired in 1933 at a joint salary of five
thousand dollars per month.

It was in this same year that Nathanael West arrived in Hollywood. His second novel, *Miss Lonelyhearts,* had had a disastrous
publication in New York (the publisher went bankrupt), and he was
feeling anything but "classy" or "distinguished." When Columbia
offered him a job as a "junior writer" at a salary of $350 per week,
he was delighted to accept, even though his contract was renewable
on a week-to-week basis. In his seven-week stint, West completed
two screenplays: a "work-place" potboiler called *Beauty Parlor* and
a rather more portentous item entitled *Return to the Soil,* both of
them envisaged as B pictures. Nathanael West scholars now study
these texts for indications that their hero tried to smuggle some
seriousness into his scenarios. For instance, does West not mean it
when he has one of his film characters declare: "Everything comes
from the soil. Without the farms, the cities could not be built. . . .
Men lived from the soil from the beginning and will continue to live
from it until the end. When Mother Earth stops giving forth, the
world will end"?

For West, filmwriting was a job: he neither despised it nor took
pride in it. And when Columbia stopped giving forth, he, too, had
very little to fall back on—indeed, he lived for a time on money
borrowed from his brother-in-law, S. J. Perelman. In seven weeks,
West earned just a bit more than Wodehouse took in seven days, and
he gave no interviews complaining about being underused:

> This stuff about easy work is all wrong. My hours are from ten in
> the morning to six at night with a full day on Saturday. They gave
> me a job to do five minutes after I sat down in my office—a sce-
> nario about a beauty parlor—and I'm expected to turn out pages
> and pages a day. There's no fooling here. All the writers sit in cells
> and the minute a typewriter stops someone pokes his head in the
> door to see if you are thinking.[25]

There is a story that Harry Cohn, the greatly dreaded boss of Columbia Pictures, once approached his writers' building and, finding it in silence, shouted: "You people in there are supposed to be working." All at once, the typewriters within began to clatter. Cohn, enraged by this obedience, yelled: "Liars!"

5

In the year that Nathanael West was hired by Columbia, Darryl Zanuck bought the screen rights to *Miss Lonelyhearts.* The price was low, four thousand dollars, but West again was thrilled—he had been working as a hotel manager in New York, and it now seemed as if he had a chance of surviving as a full-time writer. He had no great hopes that Zanuck would do justice to his novel, but, as Perelman advised him, "the book [might] be aided in sales by the picture, even if the latter has nothing to do with the book."[26] As it turned out, what the studio mostly wanted from West's book was its title, and even this they did not use. *Advice to the Lovelorn* was released in December 1933 and made no difference to anything. By this time, though, West knew enough about Hollywood not to be surprised.

Not all novelists were as unillusioned as Nathanael West when it came to adaptations of their works. Many followed, or tried to follow, the example of Theodore Dreiser, who, three years earlier, had done battle with Paramount over the filming of *An American Tragedy.* Dreiser versus Paramount is a complicated tale of greed and amour propre, with Dreiser none too lovably attempting to get the best of several worlds, but at the time, it seemed to some writers that the novelist was defending an important principle. He had sold the film rights to Paramount in 1926, for eighty thousand dollars, but it was not until 1930 that serious moves were made to begin filming. At first, the idea was that *An American Tragedy* would be Eisenstein's first film for Hollywood—a silent twelve-reeler, with a million-dollar budget. Eisenstein prepared a script with Ivor Montagu, and Dreiser pronounced himself satisfied with their efforts; in particular, he was pleased that the Russian viewed his novel as "an indictment of American society." The Paramount moguls, however, found the script not so much an indictment as a "monstrous challenge" and decided to drop the project—or, at any rate, to drop Eisenstein.

A few months later, with Eisenstein on his way to Mexico, it was revived but in shortened form, as a talkie, with Josef von Sternberg as director. Dreiser collected a further $55,000 for the sound rights and succeeded in getting a clause in the contract that obliged Paramount to "use its best endeavors to accept such advice, suggestions and criticisms that the Seller may make in so far as it may, in the judgment of the Purchaser, consistently do so." Dreiser seems not to have noticed that the wording of the clause gave him no real protection at all. A new script was written (by Samuel Hoffenstein, author of a 1928 volume of verse called *Poems in Praise of Practically Nothing* and sometimes spoken of as one of the bright young twenties talents "ruined" by Hollywood), and Dreiser agreed to meet the writer for a script conference, in New Orleans. When Hoffenstein arrived, there was a note from Dreiser:

> On my arrival here I found the proposed scenario for *An American Tragedy . . .* and have just read it. To me, it is nothing less than an insult to the book—its scope, actions, emotions and psychology. Under the circumstances, and to avoid saying personally how deeply I feel this, I am leaving New Orleans now without seeing you. You will understand, I am sure.
>
> If, at any time, the studio should permit the construction of a script representative of the book and will seriously agree to work along the lines I know to be the most valuable for this purpose, I will be glad to co-operate, and at once, but not before.[27]

Dreiser then wrote to Paramount, asserting that "Sternberg and Hoffenstein have botched my novel." He wanted von Sternberg sacked and "radical and advantageous changes" made to the script. Paramount replied that shooting had already begun but that they would be prepared to incorporate extra material "embodying some of Dreiser's suggestions." Dreiser traveled out to Hollywood ("swooping down from the air like a corpulent eagle," said von Sternberg), made some script alterations, and left, having also given a few press interviews in which he denounced "Hooeyland" and complained that "I don't recall contacting any producing brains that assayed more than one-half of one per cent."

The film was made, and needless to say, Dreiser loathed it. Not only loathed it but tried to stop its distribution. He arranged for the picture to be seen by an eighteen-man committee appointed by himself (and including figures such as George Jean Nathan, Carl Van Doren, the playwright Patrick Kearney, and the psychoanalyst A. A. Brill). Paramount arranged a private showing for Dreiser's "jury"—whose verdict, unsurprisingly, went in Dreiser's favor. On the basis of this victory, the novelist got an injunction "directing Paramount to show cause why it should not be restrained from distributing the picture."

The case was heard at White Plains, New York, before Justice Graham Witchief, and a stormy trial ensued, with Dreiser yelling and leaping to his feet so often that Witchief had to threaten his removal from the courtroom. Paramount's attorney succeeded in defining Dreiser as a temperamental publicity-seeker, and the judge ruled in favor of the studio. On Dreiser's chief complaint, that by not creating "the inevitability of circumstances influencing Clyde, a not evil hearted boy, they had reduced the psychology of the book so as to make it a cheap murder story," the judge opined:

> In the preparation of the picture the producer must give consideration to the fact that the great majority of people composing the audience before which the picture will be presented, will be more interested that justice prevail over wrong-doing than that the inevitability of Clyde's end clearly appear.[28]

"Such being the case," commented Dreiser, "that spells the end of art, doesn't it?"[29] Von Sternberg thought that Dreiser had made a big mistake in not calling *him* to the stand: "I would have agreed with him. Literature cannot be transferred to the screen without a loss to its values; the visual elements completely revalue the written word."[30]

Unhappily, White Plains never got to hear this point of view. Many months earlier, relations between Dreiser and von Sternberg had touched a puerile low. Dreiser had come across an interview with von Sternberg in which the director spoke of him as a "so-called literary giant" who was now manifestly past his peak. In retaliation, Dreiser had his secretary mail "Joseph Sternberg" a *Times* notice of the film *Dishonored,* which von Sternberg had both written and directed. The *Times* had described the screenplay as "clumsy" and "emphatically amateurish." Von Sternberg didn't like people to forget about his "von" (even though it was awarded to him in Hollywood), so he got his secretary to write back, asking for an explanation of the "mystic significance" of the *Times* cutting. The secretary misspelled Dreiser's name in two different ways and asked leave to address him as "just plain Teddy." Of all this, Dreiser's biographer remarked: "Childishness could hardly have gone farther on either side. It was in this spirit that von Sternberg began the picturization of one of America's great novels."[31]

4

In a novel you can still say what you like, and the stage is free almost to the point of obscenity, but the motion picture made in Hollywood, if it is to create art at all, must do so within such strangling limitations of subject and treatment that it is a blind wonder it ever achieves any distinction beyond the purely mechanical slickness of a glass and chromium bathroom.[1]

This was Raymond Chandler, writing in 1950, with the end of screen censorship as he knew it more or less in sight. Chandler went on to spell out a few of the ways in which the cinema could get around the censor without seeming to, ways not available to the novelist or playwright: eloquent dissolves, suggestive transitions, luxurious movements of the camera, and so on. Clandestine resources of this kind could to some extent compensate for the extrarigorous controls that movies were obliged to live with. But if there were such compensations, they were more likely to be relished by the director than by the writer. Once the censor had made sure that everyone on screen was fully dressed, he would be inclined to turn his attention to matters of dialogue and plot, to film narrative as literature. For the writers who already felt anguished about writing for the films, strict censorship was just another insult to be added to the list. For those who were happy enough to be doing what they did, it was simply a way of defining the available terrain: there were things you could say and things you couldn't say. The most effective practitioners, one need hardly stress, were the ones who operated somewhere in between these two rhetorical extremes.

In 1915, the year of Griffith's *The Birth of a Nation,* the United States Supreme Court declared that the motion picture industry was "a business pure and simple" and was therefore not protected by the Constitution's First Amendment—the one that covers freedom of expression. In other words, right from the start, the movies knew that they were going to be monitored more repressively than any other type of entertainment or creative art. This being so, the question was: Who does the monitoring? Between 1915 and 1922, the job was entrusted to a so-called National Board of Censorship, a body set up by the movie exhibitors in 1909 when the mayor of New York, flooded with complaints about "indecency," closed down the theaters. The board was made up of representatives of civil, social, and religious agencies. In addition to this national setup, there were some state censorship authorities; indeed, by 1921, most states exercised their own controls.

This rather casually assembled system seems to have functioned smoothly until the early twenties, although all along religious bodies were lobbying for tighter controls or, best of all, for a federal intervention that would "rescue the motion pictures from the hands of the devil and 500 un-Christian Jews." In the early twenties, in a period of national recession, the picture business was booming and the producers began to feel untouchable. They started to take risks:

> The cries for censorship became louder and more furious as pictures were released with such titles as *A Shocking Night, Lying Lips, Luring Lips, Red Hot Romance, Flame of Youth, Virgin Paradise, Scrambled Wives, The Truant Husband, The Fourteenth Lover, Her Purchase Price, Plaything of Broadway.* Skirts were shorter in the pictures. Make-up was heavier. Kisses were longer. Embraces were more clinging. Cinematic sin was well on the way to becoming a billion-dollar business.[2]

By this time, the film fan was susceptible not only to what was witnessed on the screen, but could be aroused also by events in Hollywood itself, by the sexy off-screen dramas that were now being stoked by the press and, in some measure, by the industry itself. Moralists tut-tutting over Jazz Age frolics found it easy to pretend that the movies were to blame, the movies and their movie colony, their Sodom by the Sea, "where debauchery, riotous living, drunkenness, ribaldry, dissipation, free love seem to be conspicuous." These words were spoken in the U.S. Senate in 1921. In that same year, as if on cue, Hollywood plunged into a series of headline-grabbing scandals. There was the Fatty Arbuckle case (Arbuckle was put on trial for manslaughter after a girl died at one of his twenty-four-hour drinking parties); there was the Mabel Normand–Mary Minter case, in which the two stars were linked to the murder of an English film director (Normand, a year later, was tied in with another lurid murder mystery); and there was the Wallace Reid case (a prototype clean-liver on the screen, Reid died at thirty-two from drink and drugs). It didn't matter to the world at large that Arbuckle was acquitted, that Normand and Minter were proved "innocent beyond all doubt," or that Reid had become addicted to morphine after suffering bad head injuries in a train crash. Each of these scandals was used as ammunition in the campaign against Hollywood's allegedly corrupting influence. And the scandals kept on cropping up: the Charlie Chaplin case, the Clara Bow case, the Jean Harlow–Paul Bern case, and so on.

The producers, fearing that federal controls would indeed soon be forced on them, announced the formation of the Motion Picture Producers and Distributors Association of America, "to foster the common interests of those engaged in the motion picture industry in the United States, by establishing and maintaining the highest possible moral and aesthetic standards in motion picture production." The head of this new body would be brought in from outside the industry: indeed, from President Harding's own government. Will H. Hays was chairman of the Republican National Committee and was Harding's postmaster general; his appointment made it look as if the producers were almost inviting federal guidance and constraints. In fact, Hays's job—as seen by his employers—was to neutralize the opposition. For his first few years in office, Hays busied himself pulling strings and placating pressure groups. To assist him in this work, the industry had a mild cosmetic cleanup and made a show of seeking advice from the Hays Office on any possibly controversial scripts. In 1927, Hays issued a list of Don'ts and Be Carefuls, which he hoped the filmmakers would consult whenever they felt themselves in need of guidance. It was all very polite, and on the whole it seemed to work. Attacks on the industry continued, but now the producers could pass them on to Mr. Hays, who more often than not knew how to make them disappear.

With the arrival of sound, things started hotting up again. The bought-in writers were not accustomed to being given lists of Don'ts and Be Carefuls. The religious pressure groups now had the matter of "bad language" to contend with. And the producers, stimulated by dire events on Wall Street, were in any case disposed to loosen their own show of vigilance: quick profits were essential during this uneasy period of transition. To offset the new wave of protests, the producers in 1930 attempted another 1921-style ploy. This time they invited Martin Quigley, the Catholic publisher of the *Motion Picture Herald,* to redraft and extend the original Don'ts and Be Carefuls list. Quigley, aided by Daniel J. Lord, S.J. (a Saint Louis drama professor), came up with a full-scale Motion Picture Production Code—to be enforced, or so its authors hoped, by the Hays Office, with the willing cooperation of the industry. Will Hays's official historian has lovingly described the purpose of the Code:

> It is important to note that the basic moral principles upon which Quigley and Father Lord worked in creating a systematic code did not involve matters of theology, concerning which there are differences among the religions of the Western world. The basic moral prohibitions in all these religions go back to the Ten Commandments. For that reason, the Code, while originally drafted by members of the Catholic religion, was universally acceptable by the members of all Western religions. There was no other common ground upon which all who were concerned could stand. So the Code suggests the basic moral unity of Western civilization.[3]

On March 31, 1930, the Code—to be known for the next few years as the Hays Code—was officially accepted by the producers. Like their Catholic advisers, they now believed that "correct entertainment raises the whole standard of a nation" and that "wrong entertainment lowers the whole living condition and moral ideals of a race."

The Code's first, all-governing assumption is that films are different from other art forms because of their mass appeal. A film can reach "places unpenetrated by other forms of art":

(a) A book describes; a film vividly presents.

(b) A book reaches the mind thru words merely; a film reaches the eyes and ears thru the reproduction of actual events.

(c) The reaction of a reader to a book depends largely on the keenness of the reader; the reaction to a film depends on the vividness of presentation.

And it is no good retorting that a stage play also "vividly presents" its "reproduction of actual events." Films have a capacity for enlargement and emphasis, which ensures that "the screen story is brought closer to the audience than the play." This intimacy of audience involvement has also engendered a relationship with the acting personnel that is "beyond anything of the sort in history." In spite of all its icy prohibitions, the phrasing of the Code repeatedly reminds us that Quigley was himself something of a fan; he knew that of which he spake:

> The attention of the producers is called . . . to the magnificent possibilities of the screen for character development, the building of right ideals, the inculcation in story form of right principles. If motion pictures consistently held up high types of character, presented stories that would affect lives for the better, they could become the greatest natural force for the improvement of mankind.

The Code was divided into three sections, and the above insights are enshrined in Section One, under the title "General Principles." Section Two gives us "Working Principles," and the most important of these is that "Evil must not be presented alluringly":

> Even if, later, the evil is condemned and punished, it must not be allowed to appear so attractive that the emotions are drawn to desire or approve so strongly that later they forget the condemnation and remember only the apparent joy of the sin.

In short, evil and good must never be confused: a fairly major prohibition so far as any serious writer was concerned. Was this the end, not just for Rico but for the good-bad cowboy, the fallen woman, the mischievous farceur? Deciding between good and evil was not merely a spiritual affair: "The courts of the land must not be presented as unjust."

Section Three of the Code gets down to practicalities, listing—under "Plot Material"—a number of specific prohibitions, here summarized in note form:

1. The triangle: O.K. to deal with, but it must never finally imperil "marriage, the sanctity of the home and sex morality."

2. Adultery: Should be avoided. Never a fit subject for comedy. Illicit sex should never be presented as "either delightful or daring."

3. Seduction and rape: Must be essential to plot. *Never* comic. No seduction *methods* to be portrayed.

4. Scenes of passion: These must *"not* be *explicit* in action nor vivid in method, e.g. by handling of the body, by lustful and prolonged kissing, by evidently lustful embraces, by positions which strongly arouse passions." (Informally, the Hollywood rule on this became: "Lips together for 3 seconds. Come out of kiss with lips sealed.")

5. Pure and impure love: Pure love is permitted by the law of God and man and is therefore the "rightful subject of plots." *But* "The passion arising from this love is not the subject for plots." Impure love should be avoided, but if it has to be there, its presentation must not "excite sexual reactions, mental or physical, in an ordinary audience."

6. Murder: Should be infrequent, not brutal. Revenge no justification; dueling "should not be presented as right or just." Self-defense O.K.

7. Crime in general: Criminals should not be glamorized, and the audience should not be told in detail how crimes are committed; that is, "the film should not serve as a possible school in crime methods." (Interestingly, this paragraph adds that "Crime need *not always be punished,* as long as the audience is made to know that it is wrong." Subsequently, most producers seem to have reasoned that the simplest, if not the only, way to let audiences know that it was wrong *was* to have it punished.)

8. Vulgarity: Oaths "should never be used as a comedy element." The name of Jesus Christ should never be used except in reverence.

9. Costume: "The fact that the nude or semi-nude body may be *beautiful* does not make its use in films moral. For in addition to its beauty, the effects of the nude or semi-nude body on the normal individual must be taken into consideration." The troublesome areas of the body are pinpointed as: "male and female organs and the breasts of women." These "should *never be uncovered,*" nor would it help matters to have them draped with *"transparent* or *translucent* material" or to present them "clearly and unmistakably *outlined"* by a garment.

10. Dancing: Must not be suggestive. "Dances of the type known as 'Kooch' or 'Can-Can' . . . are wrong." So, too, "the so-called *bellydances*—these are immoral, obscene and hence altogether wrong."

11. Locations: No brothels or bedrooms. Bedrooms could be portrayed, if absolutely necessary, but not in comedy or farce. "In themselves [bedrooms] are perfectly innocent. Their suggestion must be kept innocent."

12. Religion: There must be no ridicule of "any religious faith honestly maintained." And there must be no irreverent presentation of clerics: they must not be used "in comedy, as villains, or as unpleasant persons."

A hasty note is appended to this Twelfth Commandment, to the effect that the Code authors do know of some villainous, unpleasant priests. Portraying such in a movie, though, would surely encourage a bad attitude toward "religion in general." The Code also incorporates what sounds suspiciously like a job application: "Ceremonies of any definite religion should be supervised by someone thoroughly conversant with that religion." After its breakdown of plot categories, the Code concludes with a list of straightforwardly "banned" subjects: "sex perversion—or any inference to it"; "miscegenation (sex relationship between the white and black races)"; "sex hygiene or venereal diseases"; "scenes of actual childbirth, in fact or in silhouette."

2

With these principles formulated, and with a toothless body appointed to "enforce" them, the producers returned to the serious business of rescuing their industry from the Depression. The Code was more or less ignored. Indeed, for the next four years—between 1930 and 1934—Hollywood movies became tougher and sexier than they had ever been before. Sin was punished, to be sure, but not before it had been given a fair hearing. Murderers came to a bad end, but the filmmakers insisted on making sure that their punishments were thoroughly deserved. *Little Caesar* was followed by a deluge of gangster pix, in which there was no attempt to deglamorize the villains. There was also a cycle of exposé films, dealing with rackets, prison brutality, bank failures, newspaper scandal sheets, and the like. As we shall see later on, many of Hollywood's most effective "social problem" movies were made during this strange, hectic period.

There was also a Fallen Woman cycle, in which the faintest of lip service was paid to the Code, even though this would seem to be a particularly vulnerable area. Witness von Sternberg's *Blonde Venus,* starring Marlene Dietrich. Dietrich has an adulterous affair with wealthy playboy Cary Grant, and she eventually drifts into prostitution. We are meant to remind ourselves throughout that she is doing all this only in order to save up for medical treatment that will save her husband's life. In other words, Marlene and Cary are *not* having a good time, even though they sometimes seem to be.

In the Hays Office files on this picture there is a memo from Lamar Trotti, assistant to the chief Hays officer in Hollywood, a man called Jason Joy. Trotti, a former Atlanta journalist brought in by Joy to cast a literary eye over possibly offensive scripts, would later become a successful screenwriter himself and, indeed, with his *The Ox-Bow Incident* (1943), would experience his own problems with the censor. In 1932, though, Trotti had no doubt about whose side he was on:

> There seems to be a very real and distressing tendency at Paramount to go for the sex stuff on a heavy scale. One gets the feeling not only in the scripts but in the conversations with the studio where talk about pictures having to have "guts" . . . is too frequently heard.[4]

As to *Blonde Venus,* the key question for Trotti was: Did Marlene *like* going off to live with Cary Grant? There had already been rows over this question between von Sternberg and the studio, and the version seen by Trotti had been toned down by Paramount. Trotti, though, was "secretly reciting [his] prayers that the fight will result in a general agreement to forget the whole story altogether."[5] In the end, the cuts made by the Hays Office included a scene in which "a white woman is shown singing in a negro cafe operated by negroes . . . this would be questionable, especially in the Southern States, where such equality is frowned upon." Also cut was the second chorus of "I'm Getting What I Want," in which Marlene was supposed to sing:

> He don't like a tennis court,
> But he sure is great at indoor sport,
> And when he's on my davenport,
> How he can entertain me!
> I could stay awake till six
> Just to let him do his parlor tricks—
> Oh, I'm getting what I want the way I like.

By September 1932, the Hays Office was ready to back *Blonde Venus*, and a letter from Jason Joy to the heads of Paramount gives some idea of how relaxed things had become. It would not be difficult to read the document as a letter *from* Paramount to Joy, such are its amenable rationalizations:

In view of the controversy over "Blonde Venus" which got into the papers, and of the infidelity and prostitution which are the fundamentals of the story, it's probable that the censors will be looking more critically than usual at this production. If so, you will want to be prepared to advance all the arguments that seem proper under the circumstances.

In forming our own conclusion that the picture is acceptable under the Code, we were actuated by the following basic facts:

1. While the woman is admittedly unfaithful to her husband, she is motivated only by a desire to save his life and not by any thought of self-gratification or personal gain.

2. While the woman enters upon a life of apparent prostitution, she does so only in response to the urge of mother-love, because she wants to keep her child at her side, and not for any benefits to herself. In fact she very definitely feels that were she not being hunted down she would find work and honestly support herself and her child.

3. When she realizes that the sort of life she is forced to live is

detrimental to her child's welfare, she gives up the child, thereby sacrificing her own happiness for his good.

4. While the woman flees to luxury in Paris, she is never depicted as happy in that situation. Rather she is unhappy in that she has had to give up her child and her home. Clothes, jewels, flowers, adulation are so many baubles—as she proves when at the very height of her success she gives them all up without a moment's hesitation to return to New York where she can see her boy. This is not the act of an abandoned woman who is finding pleasure and happiness in an unconventional life. It is the action of a mother and a good woman.

5. The woman gladly, and also without a moment's hesitation, gives up everything to return to her husband and her child—on the same economic level which she had left, thus proving that she was never after the luxuries the other life afforded.

Never is she glorified as an unfaithful wife or as a prostitute; and never are infidelity and prostitution in themselves made attractive.

These, then, are the fundamental reasons why, in our opinion, the story is not only in conformance with the Code but really a moral story.[6]

Encouraged, no doubt, by such leniency, a new sort of screen heroine made her appearance around this time: the sort that answers back—tough-talking, seen-it-all. "Brazen" was the word they used to use. Dames of this caliber were needed to spark off the Cagneys and the Gables and to keep pace with the accelerated aggression of their gangster speak. Jean Harlow, in the tropical romance *Red Dust* (scripted by John Lee Mahin), plays a laconic prostitute, and she barely delivers a line that does not crackle with "offensive" innuendo. Is she "happy"? Who can tell? Checking the parrot's cage, she asks the bird: "What have you been eating— cement?" Reading a bedtime story to the convalescent Clark Gable, she muses: "A chipmunk and a rabbit—say, I wonder how this comes out?" Another memorable moment has her taking a bath in a rain barrel, clad in soapsuds and a sponge, with the rough-hewn, all-male Gable looking on. On *his* mind is the prospect of an adulterous affair with Mary Astor. There seem to be few respects in which *Red Dust* (1930) does not breach Hays Office regulations, but far from raising any outcry, it helped to inaugurate a new style of sex-war repartee.

This style we now tend to think of as belonging to Mae West. West, a former playwright (her first play was called *Sex*) and the author of at least some of her own dialogue, was the most flagrant Code-breaker of her day, and it is believed that the success of her first two films—*She Done Him Wrong* and *I'm No Angel* (both 1933)—was responsible for Paramount's surviving the Depression. In other words, it would have taken an unusual sort of studio self-censorship to close her down.

West was, to be fair, a resplendent sight (like "the Statue of Libido," said George Jean Nathan), but it was probably her dialogue as much as her physique that rescued Paramount: "Is that a gun in your pocket or are you just pleased to see me?"; "Anytime you got nothing to do—and lots of time to do it—come on up"; "I was once so poor I didn't know where my next husband was coming from"; "I've been things and seen places," and so on. Within the space of four years, the movies had become quotable. As with W. C. Fields, West's screen witticisms were backed up by reports of her off-duty repartee, and the legends of her private life, although they portrayed her as a man-eater, invariably got their zip less from what she did than from what she was reckoned to have said when doing it. And she—like Edward G. Robinson—felt that she was speaking for the people in their hour of need:

> The Depression had gotten people out of the habit of going to the movies. I got people back in the mood 'cause I gave them something they wanted to see, and the word got round—you know, by mouth-to-mouth advertising. . . . It was overwhelming. More people had seen me than saw Napoleon, Lincoln and Cleopatra. I was better known than Einstein, Shaw or Picasso.[7]

Or Theodore Dreiser, who, apparently recovered from his lawsuit, spent some part of 1934 attempting to sell to Hollywood "a picture idea starring Mae West."

Mae West was not merely challenging the censors; she was taunting them, or so they came to believe. Of *I'm No Angel,* the Code coauthor Martin Quigley wrote: "There is no more pretense here of romance than on a stud farm . . . it is vulgar and degrading [and] its sportive wise-cracking tends to create tolerance if not acceptance of things essentially evil."[8] In April 1934, a group of Catholic bishops announced the formation of a Legion of Decency. This body, supported by a number of non-Catholic church groups, organized a nationwide boycott pledge. Signatories undertook to stay away from movies that were deemed indecent. At the height of its campaign, the Legion had collected eleven million such pledges: a serious slice of the market at a time when most of the studios were struggling to make ends meet. The producers got nervous all over again and eventually agreed to a new system of "prior restraint," a system that might work. The Hays Office appointed Joseph Breen, a Catholic journalist, to head the Production Code Administration; from now on, every film would need to have a Breen Office seal of approval before it could be distributed. Suddenly, it was in the interests of producers to show scripts to the censors before they began spending money.

Within six months, trade commentators were noting that "the obscenity that was found in four out of five pictures before last June has disappeared," and by July 1936, the cleanup was so effective that, from Rome, the ultimate "seal of approval" was bestowed. Pope Pius XI issued an encyclical in praise of the Legion of Decency campaign:

> It is an exceedingly great comfort to us to note the outstanding success of the crusade. Because of your vigilance and because of the pressure which has been brought to bear by public opinion, the motion picture has shown improvement from the moral standpoint; crime or vice are portrayed less frequently; sin no longer is so openly approved or acclaimed; false ideals of life no longer are presented in so flagrant a manner to the impressionable minds of youth.
>
>   . . . In particular, you, venerable brethren of the United States, will be able to insist with justice that the industry in your country has recognized and accepted its responsibility before society.[9]

Just in case the producers reasoned that, with the Pope happy, they could begin drifting back to their old ways, a number of church groups kept up their campaigns for federal intervention, and the Legion of Decency made it clear that boycotts would be reintroduced if there was any backsliding. The Code was now a force to be reckoned with, and it would remain so for the next thirty years.

Mae West viewed these developments with some disdain, and at the start of the cleanup she liked to tell stories about Breen Office representatives roaring with laughter throughout screenings of her films and then scissoring out the bits they had most enjoyed. She boasted that, post-1934, she learned to plant "real rough stuff" in her scripts so that the censors would be distracted from "the important funny dialogue." As she said, "it got to be an interesting battle of wits"—although not everyone agrees that West came out on top.

Not altogether mischievously, Mae West continued to antagonize the opposition by taking on subjects that, even with sanitized dialogue, were bound to be seen as inappropriate; in particular, she seemed to go out of her way to dabble in religion, as if deep down she wanted the enraged believers to believe in her. In *Klondike Annie* (1936), she even presents herself as a Quaker convert. If, as some thought at the time, this was "all calculated to raise loud hosannahs from the Production Code vigilantes," it was a serious miscalculation—especially as West wanted to hang on to jokes like "Give a man a free hand and he puts it all over you" and "When she is caught between two evils, she likes to take the one she's never tried before." The church groups and women's clubs were immediately up in arms. What right had Mae West, of all people, to climb up in a pulpit and declare:

> Any time you take religion for a joke, the laugh is on you. You know, folks, I once made the mistake of thinkin' religion was only for certain kinds of people, but I found out different. I came to realize that you don't have to wear a long face and walk around bein' sad to be good. An' that's what I want you people to understand, here and now. I want to show you that you can think right and do right and still have a good time in this world.[10]

Similar miscalculations followed—most notoriously a Christmas 1937 radio broadcast in which West played Eve to Don Ameche's Adam: "Would yuh, honey, like to try this apple sometime?" The Hearst press mounted a virulent campaign, and as the protests against West snowballed, her old fans began to look the other way: she was now in her mid-forties, with a weight problem and an increasingly unfunny sense of grievance. Her films began to get bad notices and not-so-good box office returns. In 1940, she retired from moviemaking, her last project an unproduced screenplay about the life of Catherine the Great. In 1974, a few years after her "comeback" in *Myra Breckenridge*, West was asked about film censorship. "Right now," she said, "I think censorship is necessary; the things they're doing and saying in films right now just shouldn't be allowed. There's no dignity anymore and I think that's very important."[11]

In 1934, the cleanup involved the dropping of gangster films (or the replacing of them by G-men sagas) and a buildup of musicals, costume dramas, and prestige biographies. It also required the speedy evolution of a new, cutely encoded film vocabulary, by which "audiences understood that if two young lovers clasped hands and you moved the camera into a close-up of those hands, or if a tactful camera panned away from an embrace to a view of a fire or the moonlit sea, this was an outright implication that an affair had followed." The Hays Office foreign relations division had not yet begun to make its presence felt, so the push for inoffensiveness was at this stage limited to matters of violence and sex—although Heathcliff in *Wuthering Heights* was told *not* to wrestle with that dog in case the cruelty-to-animals activists made trouble. In these early days, the business of outsmarting the censor could be seen as just another aspect of the compromised screenwriter's craft:

> One day Ben Hecht got a call from Bernie Hyman, MGM production head, asking for help on a movie about to be shot. "I won't tell you the plot," Hyman said. "I'll just give you what we're up against. The hero and heroine fall madly in love with each other— as soon as they meet. What we need is some gimmick that keeps them from going to bed right away. Not a physical gimmick like arrest or getting run over or having to go to the hospital. But a purely psychological one. Now what reasons do you know that would keep a healthy pair of lovers from hitting the hay in Reel Two?" Hecht told him that frequently a girl had values that kept her virtuous until she got married and that there were also men who preferred to wait for coitus until they had married the girl they adored. Hyman could hardly believe his ears. "Wonderful!" he cried, struck by the novelty of the idea. "We'll try it."[13]

5

By the mid-1930s, there were over a thousand writers in Hollywood, and most of them believed they had something to complain about. The highest paid, like Ben Hecht, were always ready to deride Hollywood's absurdities and to say that they were reserving their true seriousness for whatever project they had going in New York. The lowliest wanted to be treated like Ben Hecht. Hecht himself, of course, was scornful of those who could not work the system as successfully as he did: "for the most part a run of greedy hacks and incompetent thickheads. Out of the thousand writers huffing and puffing through Hollywood there are scarcely fifty men and women of wit or talent. The rest of the fraternity is deadwood."[1]

The secret of Ben Hecht's success in Hollywood was that he learned, early on, that screenwriting is an endlessly collaborative business; indeed, for him this was part of the fun—he could sit around bantering with Charles MacArthur or Gene Fowler and end up with an expensive "outline." Even without his collaborators, though,

> the loneliness of literary creation was seldom part of movie work. You wrote with the phone ringing like a firehouse bell, with the boss charging in and out of your atelier, with the director grimacing and grunting in an adjoining armchair. Conferences interrupted you, agents with dream jobs flirted with you and friends with unsolved plots came in hourly. Disasters circled your pencil. The star for whom you were writing fell ill or refused to play in

the movie for reasons that stood your hair on end. The studio for which you were working suddenly changed hands and was being reorganized. This meant usually no more than the firing of ten or twenty stenographers, but the excitement was unnerving. Or the studio head decided it would be better to change the locale of your movie from Brooklyn to Peking. You listened to these alarms, debated them like a juggler spinning hoops on his ankles, and kept on writing.[2]

For Hecht, it was all a bit reminiscent of the pressroom of the Cook County Criminal Courts Building, from which he and Charles MacArthur had covered more than twenty hangings—and on which they based their thrice-filmed drama, *The Front Page.* This was in the twenties, when Hecht was a journalist and poet: even then he had been able to keep collaborative bustle separate from lone creativity.

In Hollywood you could become famous for not caring about attribution, and so it was with Hecht. Hecht's *Underworld,* for instance, is not really his—it is also von Sternberg's, or Paramount's, or Jules Furthman's. And yet somehow it is Hecht who tends to get the credit for inventing gangster films. As we have seen, he picked up an Oscar for this film, but he did so scornfully—and this became his regular technique; his theory was that the louder you sneered, the more money you'd get paid: "My own discontent with what I was asked to do in Hollywood was so loud that I finally received $125,000 for four weeks of script writing."

Hecht's speed of delivery was also famous. He wrote *Scarface* in seven days, *Viva Villa* in fifteen—this last for ten thousand dollars plus five thousand if he finished it on time. As David Selznick wrote to L. B. Mayer:

> I do not think we should take into consideration the fact that we are paying him a seemingly large sum of money for two weeks' work, because this would merely be penalizing him for doing in two weeks what it would take a lesser man to do, with certainly infinitely poorer results, in six or eight weeks.[3]

As well as being fast, Hecht was known as the supreme fixer, the "angel over Goldwyn," the man to be called on in a crisis, to redirect a plot, to retouch a scene, or (and this was one of his specialties) to write those rolling introductory titles that tell audiences where they are:

> On an evening in 1914—when an Era was ending—when the world still wore the smile of yesterday—on an evening before the First World War began, two pleasant old fuddy-duddies stepped out of the only atrocity known in that day—a Paris taxi-cab.[4]

This sort of work was anonymous, and Hecht was glad for it to stay that way. Sometimes, though, not having a screen credit enabled Hecht to feed the "fixer" myth by letting it be known that if it hadn't been for him, such and such a film would certainly have flopped. And of course, if it had flopped, Hecht could stay silent. We might never have known, for example, that—in seven days—he "fixed" *Gone With the Wind:*

> Selznick and Vic Fleming appeared at my bedside one Sunday morning at dawn. I was employed by Metro at the time, but David had arranged to borrow me for a week.
>
> After three weeks shooting of *Gone With the Wind,* David had decided his script was no good and that he needed a new story and a new director. The shooting had been stopped and the million dollar cast was now sitting by collecting its wages in idleness.
>
> The three of us arrived at the Selznick studio a little after sunrise. We had settled on my wages on the way over. I was to receive fifteen thousand dollars for the week's work, and no matter what happened I was not to work longer than a week. I knew in advance that two weeks of such toil as lay ahead might be fatal.
>
> . . . We worked for seven days, putting in eighteen to twenty hours a day. Selznick refused to let us eat lunch, arguing that food would slow us down. He provided bananas and salted peanuts. On the fourth day a blood vessel broke in Fleming's right eye, giving him more an Indian look than ever. On the fifth day Selznick toppled into a torpor while chewing on a banana. The wear and tear on me was less, for I had been able to lie on a couch and half-doze while the two darted about acting out the story. Thus on the seventh day I had completed, unscathed, the first nine reels of the Civil War epic.[5]

This is the (probably mendacious) voice of the screenwriter-as-hero, and Hecht enjoys using it from time to time. He knew very well that so far as *Gone With the Wind* was concerned, he would be remembered for his "epic week"; he also knew that nobody was likely to blame him for the finished film.

After all, with any film, the question of authorship is always hard to settle. Between 1930 and 1950, Hecht is believed to have worked on fourteen films without a screen credit, and in these cases the size of his contribution can never be determined. The example of *Scarface* is instructive. The film was directed by Howard Hawks, who liked to be seen as a director who rewrote as he went along, at the last moment, on the set. He had helped Hecht with his original *Underworld* story, and the two of them got on well together:

> When Hecht . . . and I used to work on a script, we'd sit in a room and we'd work for two hours and then we'd play backgammon for an hour. Then we'd start again and one of us would be one character and one would be another character. We'd read our lines of dialogue and the whole idea was to try and stump the other people, to see if they could think of something crazier than you could. And that is the kind of dialogue we used, and the kind that was fun.[6]

We note that Hawks said this in 1977, long after Hecht's death, and that his description of their cowriting is markedly similar to reports we have on how Hecht and MacArthur used to spark each other off. Directors in their memoirs frequently downgrade their writers' contributions in order to enhance their own—most notoriously, von Sternberg, who makes no mention in his autobiography of Jules Furthman. Hawks may well be guilty of exaggeration; if so, he was merely doing to Hecht what Hecht would happily have done to him, if asked. Once an argument about attribution begins, there is almost no point in pursuing it.

On the matter of *Scarface,* for example, people can get quite heated about who was responsible for that film's most celebrated gimmick: the endless tossing of a coin by the character Guino, played by George Raft. In addition to Hecht, no fewer than three writers worked on the picture. Two of them, W. R. Burnett and John Lee Mahin, have had their say on the subject of the coin. Burnett recalls:

You know that coin thing in *Scarface?* It's one of the things that made the damn picture. That was Raft's idea. He realized he wasn't a good actor, which he wasn't. But he knew if he *reacted* to what other people said, he was effective.[7]

And John Lee Mahin:

Howard was such a liar. . . . Like he said he invented the nickel thing. He didn't at all. It was all in the script. Ben put it in the script. Raft flips a nickel constantly, nervously. I can remember the way Ben said: "He flips a nickel nervously."
   Interviewer: Even George Raft claims that Hawks thought that up.
   JLM: I don't think he'd read the script.[8]

But then Hecht wrote the script *with* Hawks, so who can tell? And in any case, what does it matter? In the actual film, it's the way Hawks employs the coin device that captures our attention. And if we take it further and consult the visual exegetes, we are likely to view Mahin's quibbles as bordering on the impertinent:

As Cesca sits in her bedroom, on her bed . . . she hears the music of an organ-grinder on the street below. Looking down from her window, she catches her first glimpse of Guino, who returns her gaze as he casually, pointedly, tosses his coin in rhythm with the music. The coin tossing was to be the first of many pieces of coin business in a Hawks film as well as becoming an archetypal gesture for George Raft that he himself would live to parody twenty-seven years later [in *Some Like It Hot*]. Cesca completes the sexual circle when she tosses a coin out her window to the organ grinder below. Originally the script called for her to toss one of Tony's bills, but the simple word Hawks wrote in the margin of his script— "Coin?"—shows him improvising a much subtler . . . and surer . . . link to Guino below, who has been defined by his coin tossing. Guino catches Cesca's coin, flips the musician his own, and holds onto hers, which he then begins to toss exactly as he did his own, staring and smiling up at the coin's sender. The juxtaposition of the circularly turning handle of the street musician's organ [Hawks may well have known the lurid 1920s jazz tune "Organ Grinder," made popular by Ethel Waters], the repetitive, hypnotic tossing of that metal object, and the lingering close-up of Cesca's face firmly lock Guino and Cesca in a circle of mutual desire. Hawks has used a piece of inanimate physical matter to make the internal, emotional point—Cesca and Guino share a sexual energy that is more than the mere exchange of metal. His grasping her coin in his hand is the closest he can come to grasping her hand.[9]

John Lee Mahin, it might be remarked, was originally a Ben Hecht protégé and was rumored to have served as one of Hecht's ghostwriters, employed to support the legend of the Master's productivity—Mahin's nickname in those days was "the wraith."

2

Another of Ben Hecht's high-priced attributes (and again one much envied by his colleagues) was his versatility. He could do gangster material because of his Chicago background, and he could do "scintillating conversation" because of his connections with Broadway and the Algonquin set. According to Darryl Zanuck, he was even "great on pirate stories and knows more about piracy than anyone else on earth." And of course he was an expert also in a language that he had himself helped to invent—the sonorous, tough-tender, fake-momentous cadences of Hollywood itself.

Some writers were under contract to a studio, others teamed up with particular directors, but Hecht mostly managed to stay freelance. This meant that he had to know his way around the major studios. He worked for all of them at one time or another and was able to adjust his copy accordingly: each studio had its favored style or generic tendency, and this had considerable bearing on what was expected of its writers. Paramount was known to be a director's studio; its "maximum mogul," Adolph Zukor, did not involve himself closely in the making of films, and subordinates like B. P. Schulberg and William LeBaron were not the overbearing sort. Thus a director like Ernst Lubitsch could impose his "touch"—sexy, sophisticated, "Continental." Paramount, like every other studio, churned out its quota of Westerns, dramas, musicals, and so on, but it was generally reckoned to have a certain wicked savoir faire. And this was different from the sort of "class" that MGM aspired to. MGM did everything lavishly and expensively, but it was a producers' studio, more interested in stars than in writers and directors. An MGM actor would usually feel grand enough to tamper with a script, and since Thalberg would have made sure that the script in question had been the work of at least half a dozen writers, no one greatly cared. At 20th Century–Fox, on the other hand, the script was sacrosanct. Darryl Zanuck had started out as a screenwriter, under pseudonyms like Gregory Rogers and Mark Canfield; he had written four films for the German Shepherd Rin Tin Tin, and at least twenty other silents, including *Oh! What a Nurse* and *State Street Sadie.* He had even published a book of joined-together stories called *Habit—A Thrilling Yarn That Starts Where Fiction Ends and Life Begins,* of which the *New York Times Book Review* had said: "If he were as skilled in the writing of fiction as he is ingenious in the imagining of it, and as versed in the use of the English language as he is resourceful in fancy, the author could probably look forward to a successful career as a novelist." Almost perfect credentials for a filmmaker, and enough certainly to give Zanuck confidence in his nose for a story. As a producer, he was rigorous about getting his narrative line straight before shooting began. Zanuck was loyal to the writers he hired, and they in turn knew that in dealing with 20th Century–Fox, they would be dealing with Zanuck, every step of the way. As Philip Dunne has testified, to Zanuck

> final script was as sacred as if engraved on tablets of stone. There was one boss, one arbiter of all disputes, and that was Darryl Zanuck. A director usually was assigned only after the script had been complete to Zanuck's satisfaction, and while directors could *suggest* changes, they *made* them at their peril. The writers made them—if Zanuck approved. This was forcibly brought home to me after I had taken up directing and, on the set, changed a line in my own script. Zanuck's reaction was awesome but logical: "Goddammit," he said, "for years I've been protecting you from other directors, and now you force me to protect you from yourself."[10]

Before joining Fox, Zanuck had been production chief at Warner Brothers, where he had supervised both *The Jazz Singer* and *The Lights of New York.* His efforts in the early thirties more or less defined the Warner Brothers style—tough social realism, earnest bio pix, and modest budgets ("I don't want it good, I want it Tuesday," Jack Warner used to say). Zanuck was succeeded at Warners by Hal Wallis, who tried to inject a bit of star quality and MGM-style gloss.

Wallis eventually went independent within Paramount, and the Warners reputation for social concern persisted, although some believe the studio lost its abrasiveness after Roosevelt's election in 1933. Thereafter it became, for many, the President's studio. It was also, because of its politics, thought of as a writers' studio: if a writer wanted to be "effective" in the movies, he had more chance of being so at Warners than at any of the other, richer studios. He also had more chance of being made to earn his keep:

> A writer was expected to appear at the studio at nine o'clock in the morning and leave at five o'clock. He was expected to restrict his outside calls to the minimum; they were monitored. Let's face it; you didn't say anything you didn't want heard. A writer was not permitted on the set without written permission from Jack Warner. This was a regulation. A writer was never invited to see his rushes. He was never invited to a preview. If he wanted to see his own pictures on the screen, he paid his money and went in and saw them. This was the regulation.[11]

At RKO, the newest studio, a more benign regime prevailed, under the command of Pandro Berman, usually described as "eclectic," "unobtrusive," "a shrewd enthusiast who let the younger directors and writers have their head." Orson Welles would shortly be putting these qualities to the test, but in the early thirties, RKO was clearly a pleasant, adventurous-seeming place to be. There the writers' building was called the New Writers' Building and had "large panelled woodwork offices with a room for one's secretary":

> We were treated generously. There was none of the committee writing so prevalent at other studios. Pandro permitted us to do what no other studio permitted at the time—for example, I was on the set constantly during shooting, something new for writers in those days. At other studios, those writers who were low on the totem pole were treated as a necessary evil.[12]

The Columbia headman, Harry Cohn, might have dropped the word "necessary." Of all the moguls, he was generally agreed to be the most vulgarly tyrannical: bullying, tightfisted, devious. The mystery was that his studio was kept alive by films that celebrated the little man's capacity for outwitting types like Cohn by force of simplehearted decency. But then Frank Capra, who made those films, regarded Cohn as essentially a little-man-made-good:

> His face whitened and contorted. Foam flecks appeared in the corners of his mouth as he suddenly turned on me with unexpected fury. "You think this is easy for me, you goddam dago? Yes! I'm crying! I started Columbia with spit and wire and these fists, made one-reel comedies with no money to pay bills. I stole, I cheated, beat people's brains out to build Columbia; got known as a crude, loudmouth son-of-a-bitch. But I built Columbia. Into a major studio. Yes, you helped. But I picked you out of the gutter and backed you. Now you wanna leave Columbia. It's dreck to you. Poverty Row. But to me, goddam you, Columbia is—is—not just my love. It's my baby, my *life*. I'd die without Columbia.[13]

Before this speech, Capra had been determined to resign from Columbia for the very good reason that Cohn had been cheating him: films not made by Capra were being put out in Europe under Capra's name, collecting bad reviews but making a bit more money than they would have made if they had been correctly attributed. Capra launched a lawsuit against Cohn, and now Cohn was being leaned on by his bankers. Capra to Cohn: "You'll *rot* before I walk into your studio again." This was before Cohn's speech. After it, Capra records:

> Disgust and admiration swirled through my head. I had Cohn right up to the gaff, then let him off the hook. He disarmed me with my own speciality—Capra-corn. . . . In some ways he topped them all.[14]

Did Cohn really speak those foam-flecked words, or did Capra make them up, as if for a big showdown in one of his own movies? We shall never know.

In addition to the major studios, which handled their own distribution, there were two independent moguls: David Selznick and Sam Goldwyn, who released their films through RKO or United Artists. Goldwyn we have already met—a man of more taste and distinction than his Goldwynisms give him credit for. Selznick seems to have been less earnest but more fanatical than Goldwyn: most observers speak of his excessive zeal, and his near-maniacal lust for the Big Picture. Starting out at Paramount, it was Selznick who read Eisenstein's script for *An American Tragedy* and wrote to B. P. Schulberg:

> I have just finished reading the Eisenstein adaptation of *An American Tragedy*. It was for me a memorable experience; the most moving script I have ever read. It was so effective, that it was positively torturing. When I had finished it, I was so depressed that I wanted to reach for the bourbon bottle. As entertainment, I don't think it has one chance in a hundred.
>
> . . . Is it too late to try to persuade the enthusiasts of the picture from making it? . . . I think it an inexcusable gamble on the part of this department to put into a subject as depressing as this one, anything like the cost that an Eisenstein production must necessarily entail.[15]

There is a Thalbergian note to be heard here, and indeed, after Paramount, Selznick did fill in for the sick Thalberg at MGM (Selznick happened to be Louis B. Mayer's son-in-law, a fact that weighed on him perhaps a bit too heavily). Apart from *Gone With the Wind*, Selznick is remembered for three things: his passion for filming literary classics (Ben Hecht once wired him: THE TROUBLE WITH YOU DAVID IS THAT YOU DID ALL YOUR READING BEFORE THE AGE OF TWELVE); his vast output of memos (these have been published in a six-hundred-page book and thoroughly endorse his title "the great dictator"); and his ferocious, literally sleepless commitment to the task at hand. Nunnally Johnson once turned down a writing job with Selznick, saying: "My understanding is that an assignment from you consists of three months' work and six months' recuperation."

Thalberg, Selznick, Zanuck, Wallis, Goldwyn, Cohn: not much got made in Hollywood during the thirties without the vigorous involvement of one or another of these men. And slightly below them there were other power figures to be reckoned with: tough-guy fixers like MGM's Eddie Mannix and Hunt Stromberg or independents like the Dartmouth-educated Walter Wanger, perhaps the only "regular intellectual" of high rank on the production side. A writer like Ben Hecht could deal comfortably, if not contemptuously, with these tycoons, but for most Hollywood scribes they were distant figures, monstrous and ludicrous, to be feared and to be laughed at. Writers sometimes become writers because they don't like the idea of being bossed around. In Hollywood, to be kept waiting for hours in the outer office of an Irving Thalberg, to be dragged out of bed by a Darryl Zanuck so as to attend a midnight story session, to be harassed round the clock by an overstimulated David Selznick, such indignities were impossible to reconcile with any notions about the proudly separate creative artist.

And this was particularly painful for those writers hired by Hollywood in the early thirties, writers familiar with the pleasures of solitary composition. Screenwriters' memoirs from this period are full of funny and sad tales of humiliation at the hands of the ill-read producers. But it was all very well to chuckle over Jack Warner's "I would rather take a fifty-mile hike than crawl through a book" or Sam Goldwyn's "I read part of it all the way through." At the end of the day, or at the end of a current contract, the writer had to take what he was given—or not take it, and go home.

It did not help that in several cases the producers were younger than or the same age as the writers they employed. Zanuck, for instance, was head of production at Warners at the age of twenty-six; at thirty, he was running 20th Century–Fox. Hal Wallis was thirty-two when he replaced Zanuck at Warners. Selznick was twenty-four when he joined MGM. Thalberg, when he died in 1936, was only thirty-seven, the same age as Selznick when he made *Gone With the Wind*. Ben Hecht was eight years older than Selznick, five years older than Thalberg. In the early thirties, when most celebrated moguls were beginning to consolidate their empires, few of them were over forty. Even the notoriously fatherly Louis B. Mayer was only forty-five in 1930, and in that same year Carl Laemmle, ancient head of Universal and one of Hollywood's creators, was but sixty-three. The publicity machines, of course, made much of all this youth power, but not everybody found it thrilling. Leo Rosten, indispensable historian of the period, has pointed out that "probably never in history has so immature a group been accorded such luster, such sanctions and such income."[16]

3

Orson Welles once said that in his opinion the writer "should have the first and last word in film-making, the only better alternative being the writer-director—but with the stress on the first word."[17]

Since there is no record of Orson Welles the director being over-
ruled by any writer other than himself, this edict is not as magnani-
mous as it sounds. A director with literary aspirations could indeed
exercise those aspirations in his films. A writer who wanted to direct
(as several of them did from time to time) had to be unusually
determined or well placed.

Ben Hecht, one might have thought, was too detached from the
whole circus to care greatly about what finally went on the screen,
and perhaps in the end he was. Even he, though, admitted to moments of authorial frustration:

> My chief memory of movieland is one of asking in the producers'
> office why I must change the script, eviscerate it, cripple and
> hamstring it? Why must I strip the hero of his few semi-intelligent
> remarks and why must I tack on a corny ending that makes the
> stomach shudder? Half of the movie writers argue in this fashion.
> The other half writhe in silence, and the psychoanalyst's couch or
> the liquor bottle claim them both.[18]

Hecht believed that "ninety per cent of the success of a movie (or
of its failure) lay in the writing of its script" and that film directors
were even less important than stage directors when it came to
getting across the writer's story. Mostly, directors ruined perfectly
good stories by intruding their own filmic flourishes: "It has been the
habit of great Hollywood directors to distort a script so that it would
seem a director and not a playwright was telling the tale." Like
many another writer of that era, Hecht believed that—given the
chance—he could teach the directors a thing or two about screen
narrative. In 1935, freakishly, he got that chance.

When, in the 1920s, the big studios began closing down their East
Coast operations, Paramount held back: their Astoria studio in Long
Island City continued to make pictures. Run by Walter Wanger,
Astoria kept Paramount in touch with Broadway (the Marx Brothers
could film *The Cocoanuts* during the day while performing *Animal
Crackers* on stage in the evening), and it was useful for New York
location shooting. Also, as actress Louise Brooks describes it, Astoria
was a holiday from Hollywood:

> There were writers and directors from Princeton and Yale. Motion
> pictures did not consume us. When work was finished, we dressed

in evening clothes, dined at the Colony or "21," and went to the theater. The difference in Hollywood was that the studio was run by B. P. Schulberg, a coarse exploiter who propositioned every actress and policed every set. To love books was a big laugh. There was no theater, no opera, no concerts—just those god-damned movies.[19]

In 1935, Ben Hecht and Charles MacArthur somehow clinched a deal with Paramount that allowed them to take over the Astoria studio for a period of eighteen months. During that time, they undertook to produce, direct, and write four films. Quite what Paramount was thinking of it is hard to know; according to Hecht's biographer, "it was a small expenditure well worthwhile in retaining the writers' good will and getting them off its back."[20] The offer also had something to do with Paramount's pursuit of metropolitan sophistication. For Hecht and MacArthur, it was of course a triumph to be much chortled over in New York literary circles. Instead of writers being lured to Hollywood, here Hollywood was being summoned to within a cab ride of Manhattan—and the writers were in charge:

> Neither Charlie nor I had ever spent an hour on a movie set. We knew nothing of casts, budgets, schedules, booms, gobos, unions, scenery, cutting, lighting. Worse, we had barely seen a dozen movies in our lives. Finding ourselves with all this unknowingness in sole and lofty charge of bringing movies into existence, we were, however, not for a moment abashed.[21]

The Astoria Experiment, as it was called, is now remembered chiefly for its prankishness: "a two year party that kept going seven days a week." Hecht and MacArthur were "like boys released from a reformatory."[22] Hecht hung up thirty-foot signs proclaiming that "Better than Metro Isn't Good Enough" and pasted "life-size photos of female nudes" on all the office doors. He and MacArthur hired local prostitutes as secretaries (or so it has been told) and had waiters chauffeur out lunch for twenty-five from swank Manhattan restaurants.[23]

> There were constant games, musicales, yarn-swapping marathons and athletic contests at this time. I recall one summer afternoon

in autumn. Charlie and I had organized a baseball team called "The Writers." We challenged a team who called themselves "College Athletes." . . . Our team had on it Ed Sullivan, Bugs Baer, Robert Sherwood, Billy Rose, Denny Miller, Harold Ross, Harpo Marx. Charlie played first base. I pitched. We all wore sailor suits.[24]

As to the films they made, these were of course defiantly in breach of Hollywood conventions. Too defiantly, perhaps: for *Crime Without Passion,* the montage expert Glavko Vorkapich was hired to devise a spectacular opening sequence in which three blood-dripping "sisters of evil" are made to fly around the tops of skyscrapers, popping in and out of office windows—the Furies, we are told, that haunt all mortal dreams. Avant-garde figures from the twenties like George Antheil and George Grosz were brought in to provide music and artwork, and for *Once in a Blue Moon,* the rascally producers got hold of a "Continental" vaudeville celebrity and a champion wrestler. It was all aimed at a mildly advanced New York clientele, a theater audience tuned in to European cinema and snobbish about Hollywood's lack of "adventure." But the recipe was too casually contrived: ultra-smart stage dialogue embellished with film trickery—split screens, dream sequences, dead men revisiting their former lives. Cinematographer Lee Garmes was on the payroll as associate director, and he did the best he could to visualize the whims of his oft-absent bosses, but the overall impression is of an opportunity frivolously wasted. In a Hechtian manner, these films *were* made for Hollywood.

The one movie from the Astoria Experiment that still has some admirers is *The Scoundrel,* which actually won Hecht and MacArthur an Academy Award. In this, Noel Coward plays a Hecht-like egotist—a publisher named Anthony Mallare, adored by all women, envied by all men, cynical about his trade and yet outrageously successful. "Are we on the side of radicals or capitalists?" he is asked. "Neither. We are interested in the spoils of life, not its battles." And this *is* the way he talks. "Marcel Proust, don't you admire him?" "I'm very polite to him," sighs Anthony. In the Mallare outer office there is a permanent gathering of literary hacks and hopefuls (including Alexander Woollcott, played by himself), and needless to say, the "satiric" possibilities of such a setup are ridiculously overplayed.

Mallare treats everyone appallingly, but he oversteps the mark when he trifles with an innocent young poetess, "shy, odd, with the eyes of a runaway child . . . I adore your poems . . . you are so young, so eager, so generous with your foolish heart." A month later, he drops her callously, and as he leaves for his next assignation, she cries after him: "I hope your plane falls . . . and that you're killed . . . there's not one human being on the earth who will cry for you." The next time we see Mallare, he is picking seaweed out of his hair—a ghost doomed to walk the earth until he can find one human being who will cry for him. In other words, the film seems to be saying, go easy on the epigrams.

The Astoria Experiment was not pursued after the agreement with Paramount expired, although Hecht did continue to direct films now and then (of one of these, called *Specter of the Rose,* Saul Bellow testified that he would rather eat ground glass than sit through it for a second time). Hecht also continued to make big money as a screenwriter and script handyman—although there was a falling off in the late forties, when his vehement pro-Zionism resulted in his films being banned in Britain. The British Film Institute print of *The Scoundrel* is prefaced with an explanatory message:

> We are fully aware that the name and works of Ben Hecht are at the present time looked upon with extreme disfavour in this country.
>
> It is felt, however, in view of the fact that Film Societies show films of every race and creed, also films made in Nazi Germany, not to mention films from the USSR, that in this instance the BFI remains as always impartial. *The Scoundrel* therefore is offered as an example of universal film fare which when made was a resounding commercial failure due to it being many years in advance of its time.

Surely Hecht has the last laugh here. Only movie people, he would have said, could write sentences like these.

4

After its rejection of Eisenstein's script for *An American Tragedy,* Paramount canceled the Russian's contract and would have been greatly relieved to see him catch the next boat home to Russia. Since his arrival in 1930, he had been trouble, with anti-Communists and anti-Semites campaigning for his deportation; and the reactionary mood in Hollywood was hardening. Eisenstein, however, had his own ideas about what he wanted to do next. With the help of Charlie Chaplin, he approached the novelist Upton Sinclair (who had a wealthy wife) for funds to help him make a film in Mexico.

Sinclair agreed to raise the financing, but the project turned out to be more grandiose than he'd envisaged, and eventually the backing was withdrawn. Eisenstein was furious—as he saw it, he was "transforming a shabby travelogue into a really major film" and needed no more than a further eight thousand dollars to complete the project when the Sinclairs decided to pull out. Sinclair assembled two films out of the Mexican footage, but Eisenstein—who by then had returned to Russia—refused to acknowledge these "mutilated stumps." Back in Hollywood, Eisenstein's reported excesses and general lack of "professionalism" were viewed with satisfaction. Sinclair the Bolshevik had been made a fool of by his Russian chum—dreamers both.

Sinclair was a bestselling novelist, but he was viewed with suspicion by the studios. He had sold books to Hollywood and he had written screenplays, but Irving Thalberg's line "Buy it but keep that Bolshevik out of the studio" had been pretty much the order of the day. In September 1933, after the *Que Viva Mexico* fiasco, Sinclair announced that he would be running for the governorship of California in the 1934 elections. His slogan would be "End Poverty in California"—EPIC. Nobody in Hollywood took much notice at first; Sinclair had run before, as a Socialist, and done badly at the polls. This time, though, he was putting himself forward as a Democrat, and he was aiming his message at the Depression unemployed. Seven hundred thousand workers were out of work in California, half of them in Los Angeles County, and there had already been violent clashes between migrant laborers and teams of strikebreaking vigilantes hired by the employers. It soon became evident that the Bolshevik might have a constituency after all.

And so far as the film industry was concerned, he was the worst sort of Bolshevik: he had his eye on *them*. Sinclair had just published a book about Hollywood urging all sorts of terrifying federal regulations, and sure enough, when he set forth his manifesto for the governorship, it included proposals for a special tax on the movie studios. Sinclair also suggested that empty studios in Hollywood could be rented by the state, so that "unemployed actors [could] make a few pictures of their own." In other words, state moviemaking—with a Communist screenwriter in control.

In August 1934, Sinclair won the Democratic nomination with alarming ease, and the studios began to worry. Threats were issued that if Sinclair won, the filmmakers would quit Hollywood—they would reopen in New York or start again in Florida. Sinclair stayed calm, retorting that few screen goddesses would be able to withstand the Florida mosquitoes, and he continued to gather popular support. The studios' next move was to set up a fund in support of Sinclair's opponent, Frank Merriam. MGM employees were invited to donate a day's pay to the Republican, and the clear hint was that anyone who didn't would be looked on with disfavor. The employees were actually given checks made out to Louis Mayer: "You were expected to sign it and send it in, and you were worried that if you didn't send the check in, when option time came they might not pick up your option."[25]

At Columbia, Harry Cohn set up a huge thermometer in the executive dining room to mark the progress of the "Stop Sinclair" fund and threatened staff with blacklisting (or being "marked lousy") if they failed to make a contribution. The Marxist playwright John Howard Lawson, a contract writer at Columbia, refused to pay—even though he viewed Sinclair as "diversionary and counterrevolutionary." Cohn told him to give a symbolic dollar "just to show your heart is in the right place." Lawson said no; Cohn fired him.

The fund generated over half a million dollars. With this, and with the vigorous assistance of the Hearst-owned press, Hollywood launched an aggressive smear campaign against Sinclair, with leaflets, radio broadcasts, and billboards proclaiming the Democrat's intention—and that of his "maggot-like horde"—to Sovietize California. The Bolshevik Beast, they said, would dynamite churches and nationalize children. Intimidation at the studios continued, and in such a bludgeoning manner that a group of writers, including John Bright, Philip Dunne, and Allen Rivkin, set up an "authors committee" to raise funds for Sinclair. The infant Screen Writers Guild adopted a resolution condemning the studios' fund-raising methods, their "implied coercion and intimidation." For the first time, the screenwriters were united behind a single cause. The left-wing Dorothy Parker, the liberal Nunnally Johnson, the conservative Morrie Ryskind shared a general indignation. After all, had not Louis B. Mayer said to his staff: "What does Sinclair know? He's only a writer." Allen Rivkin, a political moderate, recalls:

> We rebelled, because we felt the man had the right to a fair campaign and that we had the right to speak for ourselves. It was democracy in action and a rebellion against the control of the studios over our non-studio lives.[26]

For most Hollywood writers, this was their first taste of political activism, and some of them enjoyed it. But there was not much that the writers, or anybody else, could do to combat the studios' next move. An MGM screen-test director called Felix Feist was given a crew and told to film a series of short newsreels under the title "The Inquiring Reporter," to go out as appendixes to the studio's Metrotone newsreels. Feist's footage included interviews with voters, and these were edited (under Thalberg's supervision) so as to discredit Sinclair. All the sensible, well-dressed interviewees, and all the sweet old ladies, were for Merriam.

> Those who backed Sinclair scratched themselves, stammered or rubbed their bleary eyes. A shaggy man with whiskers and fanticism in his eyes favored Sinclair because "his system vorked vell in Russia, vy can't it work here?"[27]

Some commentators claim that these "voters" were bit-part actors reciting from a script; Sam Marx, story editor at MGM, says it was simply that "respectable people who favored Sinclair" were "left on the cutting room floor." It has also been contended that some of Feist's "documentary" scenes were in fact outtakes from old movies: footage of "anarchist and other riff-raff crossing the border to assume control of Hollywood if Sinclair was elected" came out of William Wyler's *The Wild Boys of the Road*. It was the start of "image politics" in the United States, and it worked. Sinclair was defeated soundly—at a cost to the film industry of something like ten million dollars. The *Hollywood Reporter* declared exultantly that "Never before in the history of the picture business has the screen been used in direct support of a candidate . . . it will undoubtedly give the bigwigs in Washington and politicians all over the country an idea of the real POWER that is in the hands of the picture industry." Also undoubtedly, it gave Hollywood's writing community an idea of the ruthlessness and mendacity of their employers. "But it was a dirty trick! It was the damnedest unfair thing I've ever heard of," said actor Fredric March to Thalberg after the results came through. "Nothing," replied Thalberg, "is unfair in politics."[28]

6

The seeking of contributions for the anti-Sinclair fund was not the first time that the studio chieftains had sought assistance from their troops. The year 1933 was one of financial crisis for the studios, as it was for almost everybody else. Fox and Paramount had gone into receivership, and even MGM was struggling to meet its giant payroll. In March came President Roosevelt's bank "holiday." The studio heads called emergency staff meetings and proposed that to keep the industry alive, everyone should accept a 50 percent reduction in wages for the next two months. There had been compulsory (10 percent) wage cuts before, during the crises of 1927 and 1931, but this time it was different. This time the producers were asking, nay, begging for a voluntary pull-together in the interests of elementary survival: We owe *this* much to the industry that's been so good to us, was the substance of their plea.

On March 8, 1933, Louis B. Mayer, "red-eyed and unshaven," summoned his tribe and said unto them: "My friends . . ." He then "broke down, stricken; he held out his hands, supplicating, bereft of words." The impossible had happened: Metro had run out of cash. Mayer haltingly proposed the 50 percent cut, and his audience, much moved by his distress, agreed to go along with it, in order that MGM might live. As Mayer left the meeting, he was heard to whisper to an aide: "How did I do?"[1] His audience might later have mused that production heads like Mayer got much of their own salaries in the form of massive bonuses and that these bonuses were based not on the next two months but on the overall company performance:

The really staggering production costs at the major studios were not the salaries of the artists, but the Croesus-like bonuses handed out to executives at the end of each year. In the thirties an unbelievable 20–25 per cent of the net earnings of the majors went to remunerate a tiny handful of production chiefs, studio owners and New York executives.[2]

In August 1933, the screenwriter Dalton Trumbo published, in the *North American Review*, an article called "The Fall of Hollywood": "Bankers, nepotists, contracts and talkies," he said. "On four fingers one may count the leeches which have sucked a young and vigorous industry into paresis." There was not much to be done about the bankers and the talkies. Nepotism and contracts, though, were matters that Trumbo believed could be addressed with more vigor than the writers, grumble though they did, had so far felt inclined to muster. Nepotism, of course, connected with the all-important question of screen credits: who actually wrote what? Writers tended to be paid according to the credits they had managed to amass, but these credits were often awarded either arbitrarily or corruptly, or were so "shared out" as to be almost meaningless. Commentators have pointed to the example of a film like MGM's *Stamboul Quest,* written by Herman Mankiewicz, based on an original story by Lee Pirinski, with a treatment by Donald Ogden Stewart. As if this weren't enough, the credits also tell us that "construction" was the work of Pirinski and Stewart plus three other writers, that "dialogue" was by four more writers in addition to Wells Root, who already has a credit for "construction," and that "special sequences" had been composed by a further five writers, including none other than C. Gardner Sullivan. This makes a total of fifteen writers, but not even Mankiewicz or Stewart would bother to list the film in their "filmographies."

Stewart, in fact, had a sound method for handling the credits problem:

In those days the first thing you had to learn as a writer, if you wanted to get screen credit, was to hold off until you knew when they were going to start shooting. Then, your agent would suggest you might be able to help . . , it was the third or fourth writer that always got the screen credit. It wasn't beyond you to try to possibly screw up another writer's script so that your script would come through in the end. It became a game to be the last one before they started shooting so you would not be edged out of the screen credit. They thought that if you did a script too quickly it couldn't be very good. The plot was not to be too quick. They were paying you a marvelous salary; if you took three or four months over it, that would impress them. There was a general feeling that the more money spent, the better the script must be.[3]

Sometimes, though, mysterious names would appear in a picture's writing credits: a producer's son-in-law, an agent's wife. Curt Siodmak remembers working on a film called *Aloma of the South Seas* and finding that his cowriter was "an old actress who they kept on the payroll out of kindness":

She had been a big star in the twenties. All doped up now. But maybe the old producers had had affairs with these old ladies when they were all young, you know, so they gave them jobs as writers so they could get some money. They put a young guy with them to write the story, and they got the credit.[4]

And Ogden Nash summed up the credits system in a well-known couplet: "Carl Laemmle/Has a very large faemmle."

The matter of a screenwriter's ownership of his "material" had actually been raised as long ago as 1905, when a New Jersey court ruled that "a photograph which is not only a light-written picture of some object, but also an expression of an idea, a thought, a conception of the one who takes it, is a 'writing' within the constitutional sense, and a proper subject of copyright." Several questions are begged here: so many, indeed, that the topic was left unexplored for a further thirty years. In 1933, however, these were just the sorts of questions that the younger Hollywood writers wanted to be raised. They believed that their only protection against exploitation was to begin insisting that movie writing should be treated like any other form of writing—it should be thought of as essentially belonging to the author. Many of them remembered or had heard of the Dramatists League strike of 1919, the so-called Battle of Broadway, which had ended with the playwrights winning a standard contract. Why not some similar arrangement for the photoplaywright?

As things stood, there were no agreements in Hollywood to cover minimum wages or minimum periods of employment. Writers could be fired without notice or laid off for short periods without pay—

although still "under contract." Their material could be scrapped, rewritten, retained for future action, and even attributed to someone else. If it got made into a profitable film, the writer took no share of the profits. The credits system worked according to the whim of the employer.

In theory, the Hollywood writers did have the means of voicing complaints. Since 1912, there had been clubs and associations that could, if so inclined, make statements or representations on behalf of the writing community. Epes Winthrop Sargent founded the first such club, and in 1914, Anita Loos, D. W. Griffith, Thomas Ince, and others set up a Photoplay Authors League. This League in 1920 gave way to the original Screen Writers Guild, which specifically claimed to offer "protection of its members against unfair treatment." In practice, these leagues and guilds were more social clubs than labor unions, and in 1927 it was an easy matter for Louis B. Mayer to propose that the new Academy of Motion Picture Arts and Sciences should have a "writers division," which would handle any grievances, wrangles over credits, disputes about money, and so on. To Mayer's way of seeing things, it was like a headmaster establishing a prefect system; to the young writers of the early thirties, the Academy was simply a company union—its first business was to protect the interests of the studios. Said Dorothy Parker: "Looking to the Academy for representation was like trying to get laid in your mother's house. Somebody was always in the parlor, watching."

It was the Academy's approval of the 50 percent wage cut that finally destroyed its plausibility. A month earlier, in February 1933, ten screenwriters—one might call them the original Hollywood Ten—had called a meeting at the Knickerbocker Hotel. The upshot was a relaunching of the old Screen Writers Guild, with the aim of making it "sufficiently powerful to back up its demands by shutting off the source of supply for screenplays." Power of this order could be gained only by affiliation with other writers' organizations, so that the buying of plays and novels could be blocked. Having shown itself to be capable of making trouble, the Guild would press for various reforms: a fair allotment of credits, two weeks notice of dismissal for free-lancers employed on a week-to-week basis, notification of script changes, expenses on location, and so on. Most fearsome and ludicrous of all, from the studios' point of view, was Article 4, which dealt with royalty contracts. An early member of the Guild summarized the article's demands as follows:

It provided that the author of original screen material, whether in the form of ideas, synopsis, original story, treatment, or script, must require the return of his material to him, unrestricted in any way not later than six months from the date of sale, if within that six months' period, the producer had failed to produce the material as a motion picture. A producer could extend his option on the material for another six months by paying the sum specified in the royalty contract. This Article also included the right of the author to approve or disapprove, in writing, any changes in a script which was his original work; his right to require examination, by a Certified Public Accountant of his choosing, of the producing company's books; his right to require the producer to consult him in the selection of a director and the casting of a picture. The author's royalties were to be a percentage of the producer's gross receipts.[5]

By April 1933, some two hundred writers left the Academy and joined the SWG. At the end of the year, the SWG membership was up to the five hundred mark and growing fast. The producers' first reaction to all this was part scornful, part indignant. Those who prided themselves on good relations with their writers felt betrayed. Darryl Zanuck said to Milton Sperling: "Look at all I've done for you. You gave me stories and I turned them into pictures." In a more belligerent mood, Zanuck also declared: "If those guys set up a picket line and try to shut down my studio, I'll mount a machine gun on the roof and mow them down."[6] Zanuck believed the whole thing was being engineered by leftists in the New York Dramatists League, people who "hate moving pictures and hate Hollywood, and make fun of it and ridicule it and who write plays lambasting it, and who look upon anybody associated with moving pictures as a disappointed stage playwright, who hate the salaries that are made by screen writers because screen writers receive ten times as much money for a picture as they receive for a hit play."[7] The producers' house organ, the *Hollywood Reporter,* also managed to sound genuinely plaintive: "Do they want to kill the goose that has been hatching all those beautiful golden eggs right in the pockets of the men and women who would now like to risk a new control?"

The "new control" most feared by the producers would, they believed, stem from the Guild's proposed amalgamation with the two big New York writers' guilds, the Authors League of America and the Dramatists League, and their fears seemed to be confirmed when in 1935 the Guild vowed that after amalgamation the new setup would "impose a blanket embargo on all contracts and the sale of all material to motion pictures until May 1938." Thus, not only could the resident Hollywood writers withdraw their labor; they could also see to it that the studios' story departments were prevented from buying material for adaptation.

No doubt Hollywood could have survived for a long time on remakes of properties they already owned, and there was always a sizable backlog of old screenplays. The studios were certainly troubled by the Guild's threats, but what really angered them was the idea of being told what to do by a gang of book writers and playwrights in New York. It was this specter of outside interference that had to be resisted at all costs. The Guild was told that it would not be given studio recognition unless it agreed to forgo the amalgamation. In the meantime, attempts were made to head off the threat by reviving the Academy, by setting up negotiating committees, and by nurturing opposition to the Guild by processes of inducement and intimidation.

Among the producers, Irving Thalberg was the most vehement and active opponent of the Guild, furious and puzzled that "his" writers didn't come to him when they had problems. To go running to New York for help in what was, to him, essentially a family quarrel: this was treachery indeed and clearly the work of a few Bolsheviks and malcontents. There was a story in *Variety* that Thalberg was attempting to sign writers on personal contracts that would prohibit them from joining any guild. Refusal to sign would guarantee an early exit from MGM. Frances Marion voiced a general disappointment among the writers that Thalberg should be taking this hard line:

> For the first time in this confrontation with his underlings, Irving was not the benign teacher but the little czar. . . . We would not have blinked had L.B. [Mayer] roared out a threat to close the studio unless we gave up the guild idea, but when Irving Thalberg made this threat in chilling tones we were shocked into a dread silence which revealed his enormous power over us.[8]

In November 1933, MGM introduced a new system for hiring writers: from now on, they would be signed to work on a specific film and then be laid off when it was finished. A week later, ten writers were dropped from the staff, and two weeks later, with other studios following Thalberg's lead, there were predictions in the press that staff writers would soon be phased out altogether.

Although tactics of this sort were troubling, Thalberg did have his supporters in the writing community. There was the old guard, men like Rupert Hughes and Herman Mankiewicz, who couldn't see why those young hotheads wanted to cause trouble and who saw the proposed amalgamation as "menacing the ancient freedom of the writer with regimentation, coercion and segregation."[9] Mankiewicz in particular was scathing; he even took an advertisement in *Variety,* proclaiming: "Writers of the world unite! You have nothing to lose but your brains!" and when a Guild member told him: "Herman, we're *not* doing this for the $2,500 a week writer. We're doing it for the $250 a week writer," Mankiewicz replied: "All the $250 a week writers I know are getting $2,500." And when strike talk was in the air, he would scoff:

> I think it's a great idea. Chasen's can dispense the vichyssoise on the picket line. I want to see the accounting of the first guy who applies to the union good and welfare fund—two hundred dollars a week for school tuition, a hundred twenty dollars for the psychiatrist, three hundred dollars for the cook, two hundred dollars for . . . You'll all go out on the streets carrying big signs saying "Help! Help! We're only being paid seven and a half a week." And everybody will say, "How about those poor guys? Seven dollars and fifty cents a week." And then somebody else says, "No, seven *hundred* and fifty *dollars* a week." And then duck because you'll all be stoned to death.[10]

Less jocular in its approach was a group of younger conservatives, led by John Lee Mahin and James Kevin McGuinness. They could see no profit in antagonizing the producers, and with Thalberg's backing, they began actively plotting against the Guild. Lawyers were hired to challenge the legality of the amalgamation plan, advertisements were placed, letters were sent:

> We went cloak-and-dagger, and we found out that all the heavy, hard-working guys in the Guild were members of the Party. We sent guys to meetings. Frankly, we spied on them. A couple of them admitted it. But then we couldn't convince a lot of the people that they were, and some said: "Yeah, we agree with you,

but you ought to stay within the Guild." We said, "To hell with it; we don't want to have to watch them all the time. Let's form a guild where we will welcome them in, but we don't want to be run by them." We simply felt we could deal better with Uncle Louis than with Uncle Joe.[11]

The showdown came in 1936, the year in which Dudley Nichols refused an Academy Award for his script of *The Informer* because to have accepted it "would be to turn my back on nearly a thousand or so members of the Guild." The amalgamation issue would be voted on at a meeting scheduled for May 2, and in the weeks leading up to it, there was frantic canvassing by both sides (well chronicled by Budd Schulberg in his novel *What Makes Sammy Run?*). Thalberg made a final plea to the writers at MGM, saying: "You've all gotten a great deal out of this industry. It's been good to you and what you're proposing to do is to give it away and turn it over to outside interests, and we are not going to tolerate it."[12] In another account of Thalberg's speech, it is reported that "Thalberg said he'd never allow a merger of the Screen Writers Guild and the Authors League because he had to protect the stockholders, some of whom were widows and orphans. It sounded as if he was beginning to believe his own scripts."[13]

Over at Warner Brothers on the same day, Jack Warner presented his point of view.

> He said he remembered when he was a butcher boy and how now, when he got up in the morning, he had to think which car to take to work. He said that was how well the business had treated *him*. Therefore, he wondered, why were we kicking it around? . . . He said our leaders were communists, radical bastards and soap-box sons-of-bitches. . . . He said that he, personally, didn't care because he had five million dollars in cold cash and that the studio could close up tomorrow, as far as he was concerned. He said repeatedly, "There are a lot of writers in the business who are active in the SWG now who will find themselves out of the business for good and it wouldn't be a blacklist because it would all be done over the telephone."[14]

The writers, it should be said, had their own rhetoricians. In the cutthroat atmosphere of the day, even Dorothy Parker was moved to declare that screenwriting, far from being a "soft racket" (which is how some producers were now beginning to describe it), could indeed sometimes be felt to possess a quasi-vocational appeal:

> When I dwelt in the East . . . I had my opinion of writing for the screen. I regarded it—all right, sue me—with a sort of benevolent contempt, as one looks at the raggedy printing of a backward six-year-old. I thought it had just that much relationship to litera- ture. (I still do—all right, take it to the Supreme Court.) I thought, "Why, I could do that with one hand tied behind me and the other on Irving Thalberg's pulse." . . . Well, I found out, and I found out hard, and I found out forever. Through the sweat and the tears I shed over my first script, I saw a great truth—one of those eternal, universal truths that serve to make you feel much worse than you did when you started. And that is that no writer, whether he writes from love or from money, can condescend to what he writes. What makes it harder in screenwriting . . . is the money he gets.
>
> You see, it brings out that uncomfortable little thing called conscience. You aren't writing for the love of it or the art of it or whatever; you are doing a chore assigned to you by your employer and whether or not he might fire you if you did it slackly makes no matter. You've got yourself to face, and you have to live with yourself. You don't—or at least, only in highly exceptional circum- stances—have to live with your producer.[15]

2

As the May 2 meeting got closer, the producers got extra busy "over the telephone," offering long-term contracts to several of the needier, less-well-paid writers—contracts that automatically put those writers in breach of the 1938 embargo. By the time it came to vote, many of the centrists and the "undecideds" in the Guild were secretly praying for a compromise. The radicals, suspecting this, began to worry that their own support might be more seriously undermined than they'd thought possible. The right was thus well placed to execute its master plan.

Just before the vote, McGuinness, Mahin, and Co. announced, to everyone's amazement, that they were ready to vote for amalgama- tion—but in principle only. They would also wish to see various minor amendments, and they would insist that a way be found for the Writers Guild to preserve its "autonomy." The left was taken by surprise, but the wavering moderates were able to welcome this show of flexibility by the supposed "producers' pets." The vote, when it was taken, was for "amalgamation—in principle." Although this verdict was dressed up as a healthy truce and was greeted with great celebrations on the right, with Dorothy Parker hugging the archenemy McGuinness, it rapidly became clear that the right had cunningly contrived to win the day. The SWG had indeed voted for amalgamation and could thus view itself as combatively sticking to its guns, but actually nothing irrevocable had been decided on— indeed, nothing had been decided on at all. The right had somehow transformed a protest vote into a wistful plea.

The producers now stepped up their campaign, with more overt aggression. They immediately announced their absolute refusal to recognize the SWG and vowed, in an official proclamation, that they would not buy in any books or plays that had "strings tied to them as to how and who should write the screen treatment." ("How and who"? Maybe they did need those writers after all.) They also kept up their pressure on individuals, distributing mimeographed letters of resignation from the SWG, with follow-up phone calls offering members "a simple choice: resign from the Guild or get off the lot."

All this was in the week following the fudged vote. During that same week, the conservatives—some of whom, in the euphoria of coalition, had managed to get themselves elected to the SWG board, dislodging stalwarts like Dorothy Parker and Dudley Nichols— delivered the knockout blow that they had maybe all along been holding in reserve. They resigned from the Guild. Having proved themselves reasonable men by sponsoring a coalition and by lending their names—"in principle"—to a proposal that the producers were known to detest, they could now plausibly be viewed as leaders who knew how to protect the writers without antagonizing their employ- ers. On May 9, these "oppositionists" announced that they were setting up their own union, to be called the Screen Playwrights. The SP, with John Lee Mahin as its president, condemned the "radical- ism" of the SWG and declared itself ready to undertake "sane negotiations" with the producers. Within a couple of days of this announcement, 125 rightists and centrists resigned from the Guild— 75 of them saying they would join the Screen Playwrights. Within a month, the Guild's membership plummeted from one thousand to below the fifty mark. By autumn of 1936, it was operating more or less underground.

The Screen Playwrights was officially launched on May 21, promising "an association of writers . . . with whom the producers can meet in a spirit of amicable and effective co-operation." Filmwriting was different from other sorts of writing: uniquely, it depended on a complicated network of collaboration—there was no room in Hollywood for conflicts stirred up by "a group of writers with a lust for power." The producers smilingly agreed to recognize the Screen Playwrights as the official writers' representatives, and to be fair, they agreed also to a number of proposals that, if the Guild had been across the table, would certainly have been turned down. Under a five-year contract signed with the SP, the producers granted a minimum wage (of $125 a week), notice of termination, openness on whether other writers were working on the same material, and fairer allocation of credits. Even hostile commentators have had to admit that "The SP did live up to its code of *noblesse oblige:* these contract provisions were intended to alleviate the plight of the middle- and low-rank screenwriters."[16]

On the other hand, the Screen Playwrights was more exclusive than the Guild had wished to be—more like a club than a union. It charged high fees and limited its membership to writers who had at least three screen credits in the bag. Its membership was never more than 125. As John Lee Mahin explained, this was "a deliberate attempt to protect ourselves from the elements we had left behind in the SWG." Those "elements," meanwhile, struggled on, keeping the Guild idea alive even though the actual organization was moribund. According to John Howard Lawson, the Guild's first president, "a panic hit the studios, and a blacklist blossomed in Hollywood. It was dangerous to talk about the SWG in the studios, and it was worth your life to be seen on a studio lot wearing an SWG button." Most other Guild members would probably have called this an exaggeration, but undoubtedly "There was a blacklist. More of a graylist, really, a hesitation about hiring. It was emotional rather than institutional." And John Bright, author of *Public Enemy,* has said:

There was a great deal of intimidation. It was a kind of graylist. Those of us who were active in the SWG were second choices for jobs. If you were a member of the SP, you were first choice for a job. All of the SP members were on the second floor of the Thalberg building at Metro, a new building at that time. And those of us who continued to belong to the SWG were on the third floor. There was no physical traffic between the two factions because there was bad blood, really bad blood. . . . We had no luncheon traffic and met the SP members from the floor below only in elevators. The commissaries all over town were like armed camps.[17]

George Seaton *(Miracle on 34th Street)* remembers McGuinness and Herman Mankiewicz harassing SWG members during the lunch hour, telling them: "You still in the SWG? You better get out of that commie organization or you won't be here long." Word of this reached Irving Thalberg, and he called Seaton into his office, along with another writer who had been getting the same treatment:

We went to see him and Thalberg said, "I understand you two are staying with the SWG. Why?" And we said, "Because we don't believe in company unions and we do believe in the aims of the Guild." And Thalberg said, "Well, I disagree with you about that. I understand you're being harassed in the commissary. If anybody tries to threaten you, to tell you your job is in danger, you come and tell me. You're entitled to your opinions." And he stood up and shook our hands, saying "God bless you both."[18]

Irving Thalberg died in September 1936, and Hollywood held a silence: "the whole kingdom stopped for a moment." President Roosevelt sent a message praising Thalberg's "high ideals, insight and imagination," and on the day of his burial, film star Wallace Beery piloted his own plane over Forest Lawn Cemetery, off-loading flowers onto the heads of the assembled congregation. Some of the mourners were skeptical, still unable to work out how this ruthless businessman had had the power to stir so many literary imaginations. S. J. Perelman, for instance, "seriously began to question whether Thalberg ever existed, or whether he might not be a solar myth or a deity concocted by the front office to garner prestige."[19]

Scott Fitzgerald's portrait in *The Last Tycoon* goes some way to fathoming the problem: "Success came to him young, at twenty-three, and left certain idealisms of his youth unscarred." (The rabbi who officiated at Thalberg's funeral said of him: "He was simple as a child, despite his greatness.") For the Hollywood writers, there was a fascination in the spectacle of this highly gifted man giving his whole creative self to the manufacture of mass entertainment. How could such seeming sophistication choose to operate within such limits? "I believe," Thalberg had said, "that although the motion picture may not live forever as a work of art, except in a few instances, it will be the most efficient way of showing posterity how we live now." Writers might have jeered when Thalberg spoke like this, but there was also a way in which his fervor had helped to dignify their situation.

Thalberg's perfectionism, although its aims might have seemed finally vulgar and ridiculous, was also awe-inspiring. "He didn't know," said Charles MacArthur, "how to rest, or play, or even breathe without a script in his hands." And there was never any arguing with his sense of what an audience would go for. However snooty and aloof a writer might feel himself to be, he usually harbors fantasies of crowd manipulation. Thalberg not only had power over the writers' lives, their salaries, their prospects, their prestige; he also had power over the public imagination such as could barely be dreamed of. And he was young and ill and—up to a point—sensitive in his manipulations. Fitzgerald wanted "to show that Stahr [Thalberg] left certain harm behind him just as he left good behind him. That some of his reactionary creations, such as the Screen Playwrights, existed long after his death just as so much of his valuable creative work survived him." But *The Last Tycoon* is essentially a work of homage—homage to a type of creative sensibility that had nothing in it of self-doubt or self-destruction.

3

Thalberg's Screen Playwrights did not, in fact, exist "long after his death," nor was the Screen Writers Guild utterly destroyed, as it had seemed to be in 1936. Two years later, after much tedious petitioning of the National Labor Relations Board, it was decreed by government that writers in Hollywood should be able to choose their own union, by secret ballot, and that whichever union they chose would henceforth be the "sole bargaining representative of motion picture writers." The vote took place and was crushingly in favor of the Guild. The producers, though, still withheld recognition and for a time continued to deal with the Screen Playwrights. The Labor Relations Board was eventually obliged to issue "an unfair labor practice citation" against the studios and to enforce it by voiding their contract with the SP. By the end of 1939, the Screen Playwrights gave up the struggle: they now had no vestige of legality and less than thirty members on their books.

Even the demise of the SP did not persuade the producers to grant recognition to the Guild. Indeed, it was 1941 before they gave in—some eight years after the Guild had presented its original demands. The 1941 contract granted the Guild a closed shop (but with a no-strike clause) and agreed to let the writers themselves arbitrate on disputes about credit allocation. The Guild was never very happy with the contract, since it gave them relatively little power and was potentially divisive, but for some members the eight-year struggle had been formative: "the Guild battles produced a highly politicized left wing which was to have a significant impact on the Hollywood community and the rest of the nation in the late thirties and forties."[20]

The Upton Sinclair campaign of 1934 had introduced a number of Hollywood writers to the political life, a life of funds, rallies, and committees, and the Guild saga had certainly kept this excitement on the boil. When the Guild seemed to be crumbling in 1936, there was the Spanish Civil War to attend to: the nightly meetings could now plot against General Franco as they had once plotted against John Lee Mahin. Only one screenwriter—Alvah Bessie—actually volunteered to fight in Spain, but the Republican cause provided a focus around which various styles of Hollywood progressivism could, for a time, unite.

And the styles were indeed various. There were the Communists, the party members (their numbers unknown but guessed to be around a hundred). These men were full of intrigue, discipline, and secrecy. John Howard Lawson, the Guild's first president, had been active in advanced theater projects in New York before coming out to Hollywood, and party colleagues like Samuel Ornitz, Lester Cole, and John Bright were others who had arrived on the West Coast with their political alignment already well established: "Hell, we'd all come out of the Depression. We were all New Deal progressives."[21] A combination of Adolf Hitler abroad and Louis B. Mayer at home swiftly inclined them toward party membership; also, as one memoirist recalls it, the CP had the liveliest social life and the prettiest women.

John Howard Lawson became known as the hardest of the Communist hard-liners, but his political education seems to have been haphazard. During the 1920s, his plays had had a good deal of highbrow attention, and he was one of the original members of the New Playwrights Theatre (along with John Dos Passos, who had served with Lawson as an ambulance driver during World War I). Lawson at this point was a "vaudevillesque expressionist," cynical about political solutions to the postwar malaise, although capable at times of mawkishly anarchistic "visions" for the future. His 1928 musical, *The Internationale,* gives an idea of what he and other "futilitarian" off-Broadway playwrights were up to at the time:

> The influences of vaudeville and *Le Sacre du Printemps* are obvious. The play incorporates "well-known tunes" ("The Birth of the Blues" and, of course, "The Internationale"), map and graph projections, in the style of the German director Erwin Piscator, choreography reminiscent of the "biomechanics" of the Russian director Meyerhold, topical references to Sacco and Vanzetti [the play opened five months after their execution and Lawson's first arrest for civil disobedience]—all worked into the theme of sexual and political revolution.[22]

A collaborative enterprise, no doubt, and yet it hardly makes Lawson seem an obvious target for the MGM story chiefs. But this was 1928 and the beginning of the Talkies Panic: a playwright was a playwright, more or less. Irving Thalberg "knew my plays, although he had not seen or read them. At the same time he made it clear that he was giving me a chance I did not deserve. I was a cipher at the studio, employed for a short option period at a very low salary. This was my status because my plays had not made money."[23]

For Thalberg, Lawson helped with the dialogue on *Flesh and the Devil* and *The Pagan,* and then he was hired by Cecil B. DeMille, who needed some close-to-the-earth lines for his first talking picture, *Dynamite,* the story of a love affair between a society woman and a coal miner. ("No, we wouldn't have your kind of woman where I come from. We have real women there.") He also wrote the love scenes for *Our Blushing Brides.* ("You seem like some gorgeous creature of the French court—who stepped out of a dream.") In 1930, Lawson resigned from MGM, rather haughtily, in order to have another crack at Broadway, but after some investment calamities, he was back a few months later—this time at RKO, where he wrote *Bachelor Apartment,* on which "every day's work . . . reminded me of my 'almost blunted purpose'; instead of bringing new life to the theater, I was perpetrating a stale cinematic joke." Lawson was fired by RKO in January 1932 and went to New York for a production of his play *Success Story,* but "the cash nexus was inescapable," and before the end of the year he was back in Hollywood again, at MGM. It was in this same year that he penned an attack on writers who work in Hollywood for a month or two and then "hasten back to New York with a lot of amusing stories and vow never to return to the fleshpots—a vow which is broken as soon as a new contract is offered."[24]

Lawson's new contract with MGM was for six months, and just as it was about to expire he was elected president of the revived Screen Writers Guild. He was not yet a Communist (he joined the party in 1934), but he loved the togetherness engendered by the early Guild activities: "we were all stronger together, and there was a qualitative difference, a personal emotion that flowed outward, instead of being confined and crushed, in our association." During his first busy year as president, Lawson was out of work and rather welcomed his expenses-paid trips to New York to confer with the Dramatists League and to Washington to attend National Recovery Administration hearings. But having no contract himself was embarrassing: his pleas for *better* contracts sounded more plaintive than belligerent. Thus, when RKO made an offer to film *Success Story,* Lawson was delighted—not merely because of the ten-thousand-dollar fee but because the Guild would gain the "advantage of having its president employed."

To make the triumph less than sweet, though, RKO insisted on removing the play's Jewish theme. Lawson the playwright was appalled by this:

> I had always known that my play would be cheapened in a film version, but the rejection of the Jewish theme meant the rejection of everything that gave it passion and life. Even from a box office standpoint, I believed it to be disastrous; the serious projection of Jewish character was a sensational departure for Hollywood, but

without it there would be nothing to distinguish it from other melodramas of sex and money.[25]

Not only did Lawson agree to RKO's demands—finding the whole transaction "a bizarre illustration of the writer's helplessness"—he also took on the job of adaptation. While the RKO money ensured that he could now campaign more authoritatively on behalf of the Guild, his work on *Success Story* meant that even as he argued for writers having more control over their material, he would be systematically destroying his own play. Lawson, from now on, would see himself as having a mission in Hollywood; he had grown up politically.

The John Howard Lawson sort of party member—old New Deal progressives—provided the backbone of the Screen Writers Guild and of Hollywood's left wing, but not all of their recruits in the early 1930s had come up the hard way. Budd Schulberg, for example, was the twenty-one-year-old son of B. P. Schulberg, the Paramount tycoon. In 1934, during his summer vacation from Dartmouth, Budd visited Russia, saw Maxim Gorky chair the Writers Congress, and came back "inspired." Much the same thing happened to Maurice Rapf (son of MGM producer Harry Rapf) and Ring Lardner, Jr. Lardner returned from a visit to Germany and Russia and declared that "the best hope for mankind lay with the Soviets."[26] All three joined the party.

So, too, for a time did Dorothy Parker and Donald Ogden Stewart. These two were from another distinct grouping, thought of in Hollywood, and elsewhere, as the dandy converts, the pixie revolutionists: New York wisecrackers lured to Hollywood by the big money and now self-politicized in order to assuage their guilt: guilt about writing for films and earning mammoth salaries at the height of the Depression, guilt about having had such a good time in the twenties. Stewart, for instance, had started out as a *Vanity Fair* humor writer and busy New York socialite. He drifted into films very briefly in the mid-twenties after stopping over in Hollywood during a lecture tour (his subject: "Life, Liberty and the Pursuit of Happiness"). MGM bought a book he had written, called *The Crazy Fool,* about a young man who had inherited a mental institution, and Stewart—a Yale man—was invited to stay on and write the script for *Brown of Harvard.* This he did, but soon he fled to New York, where he dabbled in the theater, as a writer and an actor. But he kept up his movie contacts, and in 1932 he was back in Hollywood, this time for good. He hit it off with Thalberg, learned how to play the credits game, and by 1934 was one of MGM's top-earning writers. His epitaph at this stage of his career, he hoped, would read: "He gave them a laugh at the End."

Stewart's conversion was an overnight affair. One story had it that he was knocked over by a truck, suffered concussion, and when he woke up discovered that he had turned into a Communist. Stewart himself claimed that it happened because he was writing a play called *Intolerance* and needed to work up some left-wing jargon for one of his characters, a young rebel who had turned against his wealthy family. A bookseller recommended John Strachey's *The Coming Struggle for Power:*

> It suddenly came over me that I was on the wrong side. If there was this "class war" as they claimed, I had somehow got into the enemy's army. . . . I felt a tremendous sense of relief and exultation. . . . I felt I had the answer I had been so long searching for. I now had a Cause to which I could devote all my gifts for the rest of my life. I was once more beside grandfather Ogden who had helped to free the slaves. I felt clean and happy and exalted. I had won all the money and status that America had to offer—and it just hadn't been good enough. The next step was Socialism.[27]

Dorothy Parker, an old New York buddy of Stewart and of his first wife, Beatrice Ames, had come out to Hollywood in 1933 as part of a double act with her new husband, who was a failed actor. Parker was already in her late thirties, a bestselling poet and, with the Roberts Sherwood and Benchley, a founder member of the Algonquin clique. She had been tempted to Hollywood once before, had sat for three months "in a cell-like office and did nothing," before fleeing to New York, where she resumed her customary stance toward the business of screenwriting: "the raggedy printing of a backward six-year-old." Parker's husband, Alan Campbell, twelve years younger than she, took an altogether different view. His ambition, when he gave up acting, was to be a writer—but he had no interest in composing plays or novels; what he wanted, above all, was to make a success of writing films.

The combination of Campbell's conscientiousness and Parker's name commanded a high price. Between 1933 and 1938, the pair of them had credits on fifteen successful movies, and they earned an estimated $500,000. Campbell, it seems, did the "body" of the script and Parker brightened it with song lyrics and snappy dialogue. At script conferences, she would sit knitting, like Anita Loos, while Campbell "buzzed" with plot shifts and trick endings—"adding," she would say, "to the compost heap we were piling up":

> Hollywood did not matter. She thought the town was as asinine as the motion picture scripts she and Alan Campbell were assigned to write. The Hollywood money was convenient, however, and the money came flooding in. It enabled her to live within marble halls, with servants at her side. She ordered huge pink jersey hats and enormous black lace hats from John Frederics at $35 apiece, and, in the same week, another hat for $86.36 from Bullocks Wilshire. She ordered $628.45 worth of hand-made lingerie from Emma Maloof in New York and $80.03 worth of perfume from Cyclax of London and she ran up a bill of $176.39 at Lilly Daché, and she gave her purchases no more thought than would a woman buying a roll of flypaper.[28]

So says Parker's biographer John Keats, writing in 1970 with full access to her check stubs. He tells us that we should multiply all amounts by three to get "the modern equivalent of the prices she paid." Keats also reports that around the same time, the Campbells spent less than a week's salary on the purchase of a Pennsylvania dwelling to which they could retreat from Hollywood: "a beautifully proportioned Colonial house . . . standing halfway down a gentle slope at the center of one hundred and twelve acres of softly folded pasture and woodland."[29] Apparently, the locals thought they had been overcharged.

These expenditures are noted because they happened in 1933–34, at the height of the Depression, and because this was the year in which Parker announced, "I am a Communist," and set up as one of Hollywood's most energetic left-wing activists. After the Guild struggle had subsided, or been squashed, she and Stewart formed the Hollywood Anti-Nazi League, and they were both prominent in the numerous other committees that were formed during the next couple of years: the Joint Anti-Fascist Refugee Committee, the Motion Picture Artists Committee to Aid Republican Spain, the Motion Picture Democratic Committee, and so on. These organizations put on readings, screenings, cabarets, and revues, and held countless rallies and meetings to raise funds for the Republican cause. A single screening of a documentary film called *The Spanish Earth* (scripted by Ernest Hemingway, Lillian Hellman, and Archibald MacLeish) netted $35,000. Another screening, of the film *Blockade* (written by John Howard Lawson), provided a dozen ambulances for Spain. "Hollywood became the place where any anti-fascist movement went for dollars." In 1951, when the House Un-American Activities Committee was making out its case against the Hollywood left, it was estimated by the HUAC counsel that "eight Hollywood Popular Front organizations collected close to $1m" during the 1930s.[30]

Some will say that wasn't much, in Hollywood terms, when we consider how much fun the fund-raisers seem to have had while they were doing their good works. As Ella Winter, Stewart's second wife, wrote at the time:

> There is hardly a tea party today, or a cocktail gathering, a studio lunch table or dinner even at a producer's house at which you do not hear agitated discussion, talk of "freedom" and "suppression," talk of tyranny and the Constitution, of war, of world economy and political theory.[31]

"Dialectical materialism by the pool . . . some of it was hilarious" is now a fairly routine way of viewing Hollywood radicalism, and we have no shortage of anecdotes contrasting people's vast personal earnings with their collectivist rhetoric. There are also plenty of stories about the phony prestige, the illusion of "substance," that the new activism seemed to carry with it. As Philip Dunne recalls:

> It started with fewer people in the Upton Sinclair campaign and then, in 1936, when the Spanish Civil War started, that was the catalyst. . . . All of a sudden people like Ernest Hemingway and André Malraux, who were gods, came to Hollywood and talked to screenwriters who were still partially despised.[32]

The truth is that those screenwriters who spent their evenings rushing about with pamphlets and petitions were, during office hours, almost powerless to "politicize" the movies they were being paid to write. Donald Ogden Stewart, at an April 1935 meeting of the League of American Writers in New York, told his audience: "Let us have no more million-dollar revolving staircases, no more star-filled symposiums of billion-dollar entertainment—but let us have some simple truths, against nothing but a plain background."[33] The screenwriters who listened to him that day must surely have been smiling to themselves: try telling *that* to Louis B. Mayer. Telling it to each other was difficult enough.

7

At a Screen Writers Guild meeting in 1935, the writer Mary McCall described how she had once been asked: "What can a writer, employed by a major studio, do to further the cause of the proletarian revolution?" Her response, she said, had been: "Aside from inserting one revolutionary sequence and perhaps one revolutionary line into a script, there is very little he can do. I was then engaged in constructing a starring vehicle for Miss Marion Davies. For the life of me, I couldn't find a spot in that script for 'up the workers.' "[1]

McCall was arguing at the time against the Guild's growing involvement in international politics: in her view, the "radicals" ought to have been concentrating on the labor union objectives that their guild had been founded to pursue. Dabbling in world politics, however good it looked and made you feel, would probably weaken the Guild's chances of achieving any local gains. Needless to say, she was denounced as a reactionary, with Donald Ogden Stewart expressing himself as painfully surprised that a Guild member could take such a low, self-serving line: "Miss McCall's indignation at the efforts of the organizers of the good causes sounds not so much like the desire of the true artist for the high lonely peak as the reminiscent whine of the well-fed [screenwriter] to be 'let alone' in her feather bed."[2] Stewart won the applause, but he was well aware that as a screenwriter during the years 1934–37, he had himself been able to do next to nothing in service of the beliefs he held most dear: *The Barretts of Wimpole Street, No More Ladies,* and *The Prisoner of Zenda* are listed as his total output for this period, and each of these is a collaboration. McCall might have been shouted down, but she had surely hit a nerve. The writer in Hollywood could never speak with any conviction about that "high lonely peak" until he could put his name to a film that he was proud of.

"If you've got a message, send it Western Union" was the time-honored Hollywood line on social consciousness, and indeed it must have seemed at moments that there was little or no scope for the writer to practice in his scripts what he preached at his Guild meetings. Although the Guild was supposed to be pressing for greater "creative control," few members believed that anything of the sort would ever be agreed to. There had of course been isolated silent films that could be thought of as "political"—von Stroheim's *Greed,* Chaplin's *The Gold Rush,* King Vidor's *The Crowd*—but each of these had been "authored" by a strong director. For the writer of talking pictures, the limits seemed more resolutely fixed—by the producers on the one hand and by the Hays Office on the other. The rule on both sides read: Thou shalt not rock the boat—not ours or theirs, whoever "they" might be. The serious filmwriter would need to be unusually cunning and determined if he wished to smuggle in some counterview. And yet it was possible, here and there or now and then, and surprisingly often, for the Hollywood screenwriter to persuade himself that he could "make a difference." If it hadn't been, few but the most cynically robotic would have been able to survive. There was always just enough scope for plausible rationalization: Look at this film or that film, the radical could say—untypical, perhaps, but significant. Who knows, perhaps next time . . .

And indeed there were stretches during the thirties and forties when the politicized screenwriter could believe in at least some of what he wrote. These stretches came and went according to the studios' reading of the political thermometer and could hardly be depended on to last. Every so often, though, it was good business to be socially aware, or good business to let a particular director have his head, or good business to permit a coincidence of ideology and entertainment. When the box office really is what matters most, all sorts of surprises are made possible. The skillful writer, the one who knew how to play the Hollywood game, could exploit this openness without, so far as anyone could tell, attempting to breach the formulaic boundaries. Or he could tell himself that he was trying to.

This in particular held true for writers hired by Warner Brothers. Historians find it hard to pinpoint how it was that Warners became the "political" studio during the early 1930s. It had to do, some say, with the studio's own underdog relation to the "majors." Warners was a precarious notch up from Poverty Row; they were obliged to work on low budgets without expensive stars, and their social-conscience movies were in part born of simple necessity: they were cheap to do. The "underdog" analysis is also used to account for Jack Warner's support for Roosevelt's New Deal (Jack helped to run FDR's West Coast campaign). Like most of the early moguls, the Warners were from a Jewish working-class background. Unlike the others, they never felt at home in their adopted empire:

> All their lives the Warners had been acutely aware of their status as outsiders, even within the relatively déclassé encampment of Hollywood and even after they had achieved success there. All of their lives they felt they had to fight. . . . "The fight has left its mark on the brothers," wrote one reporter as late as 1937. "They have not yet lowered their guard. They are neither in Hollywood nor of it."[3]

Some commentators recall the time when the Warners were thrown out of a Hollywood party by Louis B. Mayer; others point to Harry Warner's extreme touchiness on the matter of social prejudice. None of this matters much. What seems certain is that the brothers did not go political by accident:

> More and more is the realization growing that pictures can and do play an all-important part in the cultural and educational development of the world. I do not mean that we should strive for so-called intellectual films, but we should strive for pictures that provide more than a mere idle hour or two of entertainment.[4]

This was Jack Warner, speaking to the press. And on another occasion he is said to have said: "The country is in chaos. There is revolution in the air. We need a change." The change he had in mind was Rooseveltian, but even so, this was a studio chieftain and the very man who would shortly denounce the leaders of the Writers Guild as "communists, radical bastards and soap-box sons of bitches." (Brother Harry, it might also be noted, had to be helped from the room when the producers were eventually obliged to recognize the Guild. "They want blood," he screamed. "They want to take my

goddamn studio. . . . You goddamn Communist bastards! You dirty
sons of bitches! All you'll get from me is shit!"[5])

Darryl Zanuck, Warners' chief of production in the early 1930s,
was quite prepared to admit that social awareness was more than a
mere duty. It was suddenly good business: "You can't go on telling
the same story forever," he said. "The triangle is rusty." In 1930, it
was Zanuck who pioneered the Warners "headline" movie and with
it the notion of the filmmaker (in this case himself) as occupying "a
position similar to that of the editor of a metropolitan newspaper."
This was an entirely novel idea, and it fitted perfectly with the kind
of writing talent Zanuck had at his disposal: low-salaried ex-news-
men who were delighted to hear a movie executive speak of the
need for a story with "the punch and smash that would entitle it to
be a headline on the front page of any successful metropolitan
daily." The notion fitted also with the studio's disposition toward
quick production and was in line with its declared commitment to
"educational and cultural advancement." The Hays Code was not
yet in full force, and over the next four years, between 1930 and
1934, Warners released a body of films that now seem remarkable
for the bite and boldness with which they pondered the national
predicament. An article written by Zanuck in 1932 nicely captures
the studio's mix of commitment and opportunism:

Sometimes the story is a biography or an autobiography, like *I Am
a Fugitive from a Chain Gang.* Sometimes the story is that of a
fictitious character, based on headline incidents from the life of a
real character, such as *The Match King. . . .*

Sometimes the story is of an exposé nature, like *Grand Slam,*
which endeavors to tear the lid off the contract bridge racket. In
this case we use a formula that calls for a mixture of drama and
comedy, bordering slightly on satire. . . .

The success of the innumerable pictures along these identical
lines that we have produced in the past encourages us to continue.
The first of these productions was *Doorway to Hell* (1930). Then
came *Little Caesar, Public Enemy, Smart Money, Five Star Final,*
etc. We have touched on a great variety of subjects . . . a maternity
ward in *Life Begins,* labor problems of the new South in *Cabin in
the Cotton,* etc. etc.

Of the productions we are handling at the present time, the
most pretentious are *Silver Dollar* and Warden Lewis E. Lawes'

Twenty Thousand Years in Sing Sing. One deals with the spectacular rise and fall of Colorado's most famous silver mining character, and the other deals with Warden Lawes' greatly discussed
"honor system."

We have just completed a musical exposé, *Forty Second Street,*
which dramatically endeavors to lift the curtain and reveal the
strenuous, heart-breaking efforts of a well-known Broadway producer to stage a musical comedy in this year of depression.[6]

Zanuck was respected by most of the Warners writers (even those
who thought him a "tin-pot Mussolini"), because on the whole he
respected them; and the same was true of his successor (in 1933), Hal
Wallis. And although Jack Warner read neither books nor scripts and
thought writers were mere "schmucks with Underwoods," the atmosphere in the Warners Building seems to have been less lordly
and guilt-ridden than that at MGM or Paramount. The Warners
writers, like the Warners, were at the bottom of the Hollywood
heap. They were notoriously badly paid ("Why should I pay a writer
$1,000 a week when I can get four for that price?" was another of
Jack Warner's policy pronouncements), and they were treated like
mechanics, but they were let loose on subjects they could at least
have some genuine creative fun with: short, fast-paced, dim-lit
melodramas that centered on the urban proletariat or, as Neil Gabler has described it, "the prize-fighters, meat-packers, truck-drivers,
coal miners, cardsharps, gumshoes, racketeers, con artists, and the
rest of what might have seemed like the detritus of Depression
America." They were pioneering a filmic "vision of today's America," and they were helping to market a new style of movie hero:
the tough-guy city loner, victimized but not defeated by a society
that he has learned, firsthand, to think of as indifferent or corrupt;
his expectations are low, he is used to being pushed around, lied to
or preached at, or ignored—so what? That was what postwar America was like for most Americans. Sometimes the Warners hero is to
be admired for nothing more than his powers of survival; sometimes
he fights back—not on behalf of any political ideal, nor even because
he thinks he can win, but because his adversary has somehow gone
one step too far.

This step too far was what audiences waited for. They knew that
when it came, it would have something to do with personal honor,
with the hero's need to safeguard an inner, unbullyable self—and

this, finally, was heartening, if not exactly subversive. And audiences also knew, as the writers did, that they could trust the Warners actors to do the necessary in the circs. James Cagney, Edward G. Robinson, Humphrey Bogart, Paul Muni—these were Depression faces, and Warners knew how to bathe them in a menacing half light. They also knew how to tie up these actors in punishing long-term contracts and how to make them suffer some more if they made trouble.

Another advantage for the writers at Warners was that there was very little interference with their scripts. As Casey Robinson has testified:

> It was the greatest studio in town for a writer owing to some of Jack's characteristics that are not particularly admirable. He wouldn't pay for rewrites or for reshooting, so your stuff got shot as you wrote it. If it was good, you went up, if it was bad, you were out. It was as simple as that.[7]

Looking through a list of writers who got Warners credits during the 1930s, one gets an impressive sense of anonymity. No bought-in outside talent, no celebrated novelists or playwrights. There are perhaps four or five names that now figure in the film encyclopedias—and these names are known also for their involvement in Hollywood politics. Recruited for low wages to write tough-guy dialogue for the socially oppressed, a Warners writer naturally drifted to the left.

John Bright, for example, had a curriculum vitae that must have been much envied on the Warners lot. At thirteen he had been Ben Hecht's office boy in Chicago on the *Daily News*. From this, he graduated to soda-jerking for a pharmacist called Kubec Glasmon. Glasmon "would use prescription whiskey, which he got legally, then he cut it five or six ways, diluting it. He rebottled it and sold that to gangsters. I peddled the bottles around, to clubs and places." By this means, Bright came into contact with the Capone mob and was allowed to witness the odd gangland killing:

> I was present at a particularly dramatic incident in which [Capone] ordered the death of two Sicilians who were getting too big for their britches. They were illiterate Mafiosi. At the Commonwealth Hotel, Capone ordered them assassinated. And they were

beaten to death with baseball bats. Caved in their skulls. I was present at that time.

You saw it happen?

Mm-hm. I confess to being a little shocked.

With such knowledge in their possession, Bright and Glasmon got the idea of writing a novel about the underworld. They drifted to Los Angeles, and there

we rented a small house and went to work on the underworld book. We were running out of money and hocking everything when we were called on by some criminals we knew from Chicago.

They had a racket. They sold a lot of worthless property. They made a profit out of just the down payments. They collected $50,000 in down payments, which was a lot of money in those days. It was very colorful circumstances. They would look for suckers and their whole gimmick was getting a down payment for this worthless land on top of a mountain.

What did they want from you?

A "mooch cabin."

The mooch was the sucker?

Yeah. They wanted the little place we had as a residence, as a front for them. They'd bring the customers into the house and give them the pitch. They paid us six months rent, which enabled us to get by and for me to finish the underworld book . . . and they paid for a lot of booze and groceries and so on. The bunko squad came by, but they couldn't prove anything. (Laughs)[8]

Warners bought the book and turned it into *The Public Enemy*, and they hired both Bright and Glasmon as contract writers, at one hundred dollars a week. One might have thought that expertise of this caliber would have commanded a higher price. Certainly, Bright believed that he was worth more; he was one of the ten writers who met at the Knickerbocker Hotel to plan the relaunching of the Screen Writers Guild. He joined the Communist party in 1936; Glasmon joined the Screen Playwrights.

How much Party interest was there in influencing people through the scripts the writers wrote?

That was the absolute bullshit line. . . . It was impossible for any writer to have any influence at all in that respect. It was impossible to influence Hollywood movies in that way. The Party was interested in influencing society, people, not production.[9]

The movie most often cited as an example of Warners themselves seeking to influence society and people is their 1932 release *I Am a Fugitive from a Chain Gang,* an exposé of prison conditions in the South. It was one of Zanuck's most successful "headline" films, based on a book written by Robert E. Burns. Burns, having twice escaped from a Georgia chain gang, was actually on the run while the film was being made—although he was available, it seems, for fact-checking sessions and (later on) for brief publicity appearances. His case had had a lot of newspaper coverage, and it was widely believed that he should never have been imprisoned in the first place and that he had been tricked into giving himself up by a false promise from the Georgia parole authorities. (During his first stretch on the run, he turned himself into a respected member of the Chicago Chamber of Commerce; he went back to Georgia under the impression that he would be pardoned.) Burns, then, was an American victim—a World War I "forgotten man," he had done everything he could to "better himself," but society kept on kicking him in the face. Literally so, in the case of the sadistic Southern prison guards: both book and film gave graphic and horrifying accounts of the way things were done down there.

The film's original screenplay was in no doubt that Burns's predicament was representative. It proposed a scene in which, during a parade of returning doughboys: "A big American flag and a big American business man lean out the window. The Big American Businessman's paunch, grown huge on war profit, rests heavily on the window ledge. He waves his arms and cheers, and his paunch quakes with his tremendous fervor." In another scene, also not used in the film, a street corner orator tells his audience about the joys of life in the Soviet Union, where "Everyone is working—eating—living! Why? Because the country belongs to the people, that's why. Ten more years—mark my words, ladies and gentlemen—ten more years and Russia will be the greatest nation of all time."[10]

Darryl Zanuck took the view that scenes like these might somewhat clog the action. Three writers worked on three separate versions of the *Chain Gang* script. Zanuck, though, was in editorial control throughout, almost on a page-by-page basis. At the same time, he was having to fight off a growing feeling in the studio that the film would "lack box-office appeal . . . especially right now, when the whole public is depressed to the extent that many of them are leaping out of windows." Much dubiety centered on the film's now famous ending, in which the victim hero is *not* redeemed by the love of a good woman. On the contrary, he is shown to be condemned, against his will, to a life outside the law:

> HELEN (her voice choking): Jim! Jim—why haven't you come before?
>
> ALLEN: I couldn't. I was afraid to.
>
> HELEN: You could have written. It's been almost a year since you escaped!
>
> ALLEN (with a bitter laugh): I haven't escaped—they're still after me. They'll always be after me. I've had jobs but I couldn't keep them. Something happens—someone turns up—I hide in rooms all day and travel by night—no friends—no rest—no peace—
>
> HELEN (clutching him): Jim!
>
> ALLEN: Keep moving! That's all that's left for me.
>
> HELEN (cling to him): No—please! I can't let you go like this. It was all going to be so different. . . .
>
> ALLEN (with a hollow laugh): I hate everything but you. . . . I had to take a chance tonight to see you . . . and say goodbye. . . . (Helen gazes at him with tears streaming down her face; then she throws her arms about his neck impulsively and kisses him. They cling together fiercely. There is the sound of a police siren approaching, then fading away. Allen is startled, then starts away.)
>
> HELEN (following him): Can't you tell me where you're going? (He shakes his head.) Will you write? (He shakes his head.) Do you need any money? (He shakes his head, still backing away.) But you must, Jim! How do you live?
>
> (A car is heard approaching. Allen backs into the dark shadows of the alley.)
>
> ALLEN: I steal. . . .[11]

The words "I steal" issue from a totally black screen, and that's it: that's The End. It is one of the most joltingly effective moments in Hollywood cinema, and all the more so because audiences were so

thoroughly trained to expect an upbeat "resolution." Loose ends
were not allowed, certainly not loose ends like these: as Nick Roddick has commented, this was a clear case of "There but for the New
Deal. . . ."[12] Zanuck could get away with it because the real-life
Burns had not been caught. (Ironically, he was caught not long after
the film's release: excited by its success, he got careless. Eventually
a pardon was granted, and both he and the film were credited with
speeding up the reform of Georgia's prison system.)

We can learn a lot about the difficulties that face the film historian
by attempting to identify the "author" of this memorable scene. We
can learn a lot also about the astonishing speed with which these
Warner films were made. The first draft of the film's screenplay (the
one with the belly and the Russian propaganda) was written by
Brown Holmes (a twenty-three-year-old, seventy-five-dollar-a-week
novice) and Sheridan Gibney, an Amherst graduate and the author
of one or two opera librettos. Gibney was not much older than
Holmes and had just arrived in Hollywood (later on, he would
become a leading figure in the Guild). The pair of them were given
ten days to write a script based on Burns's book. This was mid-April
1932. This script was shown to possible directors and one or two
other studio people in preparation for a Zanuck story conference on
June 7. Zanuck turned up with six pages of "detailed and specific
changes" (the pro-Russian speech was changed to a speech expressing "sympathy for the poor and starving people of the Far East":
"We who live in the glorious land of the free must make them
human beings again"). The closing words of the film in the Holmes-
Gibney script were "I steal," but the writers wanted them followed
by a shot of the fugitive "sneaking across the border." Zanuck seems
to have approved this ending.

After the June story conference, Holmes and Gibney were
dropped and Howard J. Green, an ex-newsman and ex–vaudeville
producer, was given the job of incorporating Zanuck's changes.
Green was noted for his "matter of fact, realistic style." Within
twelve days, he delivered a new screenplay, which—after some
minor alterations—became the shooting script. Green's ending
reads as follows:

ALLEN: I steal. . . .
Helen stands watching, an expression of infinite suffering and
pity on her face, as Allen disappears into the darkness.
                                        DISSOLVE TO:

353: CLOSE-UP
of map as in previous scene with CAMERA jumping north,
south, east, west and finally

DISSOLVING INTO:

354: THE BROW OF A HILL AT DAWN
In the shot is a sign which reads

U.S. BORDER

The figure of Allen in silhouette is seen trudging slowly up and
over the brow of the hill, a broken, defeated, beaten figure of a
man, a hunted animal, a fugitive. Over this come the words:

THE END

On this evidence, either Holmes or Gibney should be given applause for having dreamed up one of Hollywood's most famous end-
ings: the "disappears into the darkness" was there from the beginning. But so, too, was the border crossing. At this point, we have to
introduce the evidence of the film's director, Mervyn LeRoy—evidence that we come to view with some suspicion, since LeRoy
makes a habit of pretending that everything that happens in his
films is his idea. In his account of the making of *Chain Gang*, there
is no mention of Holmes, Gibney, Green, or Zanuck. The picture
was LeRoy's from the beginning: "Once again, my insatiable appe-
tite for reading led to the picture. I had picked up an autobiography
by a man named Robert E. Burns. It fascinated me, with its details
of such sheer brutality as to be unbelievable—and yet all of it true."
In fact, the film was assigned to LeRoy by Zanuck. On July 23, he
was given the shooting script; production was scheduled to begin on
July 28. LeRoy was told to shoot "an average of thirteen and a half
scenes per day and finish the film in one month. The schedule had
been carefully arranged to make the most economical use of the
talent, most of whom were hired by the day or week and had to be
paid whether they worked or not." LeRoy delivered on time, and
then Zanuck supervised the editing. Back to LeRoy: *"Fugitive* was
a brutal picture, but here again I tried to show brutality without
being brutal. There was a scene of Muni [Paul Muni played the
Burns character] being flogged by sadistic guards. Instead of dwelling on the actual beating, I focused my cameras on the shocked and
horrified faces of the other prisoners who were witnessing the beating."[13] The script had instructed him as follows:

CAMERA MOVES UP past the other convicts, all staring towards
the empty doorway in morbid fascination. The crash of the
leather on bare flesh is heard as the CAMERA MOVES slowly
toward the open door. On the fourth crash of leather, just as
the CAMERA STARTS THROUGH THE DOOR, the scene . . . FADES
OUT.

On the matter of the film's ending, LeRoy wrote (in 1974) that he
had been taking bows for that scene for forty years but would now
like to confess that "it was achieved by sheer accident":

> That last shot had Muni, as the unfortunate Jim Allen, saying a last
> goodbye to his girlfriend. He knew that he would never be free,
> that he would have to spend the rest of his days running from the
> law. The two were in the mouth of an alley and, during their last
> two lines of dialogue, Muni backed away from her.
>   "But, Jim, how do you live?" she asked him.
>   As he edged deeper into the alley, the screen grew darker and
> finally was totally black. Then he whispered his last line—"I
> steal"—out of the darkness.
>   That wasn't the way I had originally planned it. As we were
> doing the last rehearsal, however, before we went into the take,
> the fuses on the big klieg lights blew out, just as Muni said, "I
> steal."
>   It was an accident, but I immediately recognized it as an acci-
> dent that worked. The boss electrician rushed over to me and
> apologized, and said the fuse was okay now. There would be no
> more trouble with the lights.
>   "Do it just that way when we roll," I told him.[14]

2

In the Depression, having a job could seem glamorous, and Warners
rather cleverly perceived that they could offer wish fulfillment and
social conscience in one package by putting together a cycle of
"worker films": thus the "mob" (as the mass audience was sometimes called in studio discussions) could get to watch oil drillers at
work in *Flowing Gold* and *Boom Town;* construction workers in
Steel Against the Sky; firemen in *She Loved a Fireman;* truck driv-

ers in *They Drive by Night;* fishermen in *Tiger Shark,* and so on. As Bosley Crowther noted in the *New York Times:*

> The Warner Bros., like Vulcan, know the pat way to forge a thunderbolt. They simply pick a profession in which the men are notoriously tough and the mortality rate is high, write a story about it in which both features are persistently stressed, choose a couple of aces from their pack of hardboiled actors and with these assorted ingredients whip together a cinematic depth charge.[15]

As always, the Warners watchword was "pace," and they didn't mind if their films seemed to have been "photographed by a newsreel cameraman with dyspepsia on an overcast day." In 1933, a busy year, the studio cranked out fifty-five feature films. A producer called Bryan Foy, known as the Keeper of the B's because of his low-budget assignments, recollects:

> In the old days at Warner, I made one picture eleven times. It started off with a picture called *Tiger Shark,* a fishing story, in which Edward G. Robinson lost his arm. I followed the script of *Tiger Shark* scene for scene and made the same thing as *Lumberjack,* only this time the guy lost his leg instead of his arm. Then I made it as *Bengal Tiger,* exactly the same, only now he was a lion tamer with a circus and lost his arm. The writers protested that he had lost his arm in *Tiger Shark* too; and I told them that he may have lost his arm in *Tiger Shark* too, but he's got two arms.[16]

A similar cycle was contrived on slum life and juvenile delinquency, with titles like *Hell's Kitchen, Boy Slaves, The Devil Is a Sissy,* and *They Made Me a Criminal.* After 1934, gangsters had to be deglamorized: one way of doing this was to shift the glamour across to the FBI sleuths who were hunting them; another was to portray the big-shot hoodlum as the victim of a disadvantaged childhood. *Angels with Dirty Faces* is a Cagney gangster pic, but it can also claim a public-spirited intent. With Roosevelt in the White House, Warners were no longer inclined to foster any *Chain Gang*–like despair or indignation. The new line was to present the federal government and its agencies as heroic and purposeful but in need of wholehearted public backing. A year after *Chain Gang,* Warners released *Wild Boys of the Road,* a Depression-linked juvenile delinquency melodrama. At the end of it, the judge frees the errant boys, saying: "I'm going to do my part if you do your part. Things are going to get better, not merely here, but all over the country. . . . I know your father will be going to work soon."

The Warners social-conscience phenomenon seems to have been watched with some bewilderment by the other studios. MGM and Paramount would not wish their films to look like cheapskate Warners quickies, but on the other hand, there was mounting evidence that Depression subjects were good box office. Interestingly, Irving Thalberg thought about bidding for the rights of *I Am a Fugitive from a Chain Gang* but was evidently dissuaded by a Hays Office memo that spoke of "southern sensitiveness" and therefore likely perils "from a business standpoint."[17]

An MGM approach to the Depression would look for ways of presenting it both as a lavish spectacle and as a star vehicle. If there really were millions of unemployed, Metro would spare no expense with crowd scenes. If the Depression truly was an evil to be vanquished, then surely an act of big-name individual heroism ought to bring it to its knees. In 1933, a curious film called *Gabriel Over the White House* was put out by MGM. In this, a weak, bumbling new president (played by Walter Huston) is transfigured by a visitation from the angel Gabriel. Overnight, he becomes a strongman head of state, decisive, ruthless, but essentially "simple and honest": he quotes Jefferson and signs things with Lincoln's own quill pen. "If he is mad," says his love-interest secretary, "it is a divine madness. Look at the chaos and catastrophe that the sane men of the world have brought about." Huston fires his cabinet, self-servers to a man, ignores Congress, and assumes near-dictatorial powers. At last "we have in the White House a man who is prepared to cut the red tape and get back to first principles—an eye for an eye, a tooth for a tooth, a life for a life." This is spoken as several bootleggers are shot by the president's personal firing squad, part of the gestapolike police force he has set up to see that things get done without any legalistic or bureaucratic interference. By sheer personality power, he solves the unemployment problem: the out-of-work millions are invited to sign up in the president's Army of Construction—army pay, army rations, army discipline. The army won the war; why can't it win the peace? Having fixed things at home, Huston turns his attention to the international scene. He persuades a gawping lineup of European statesmen that they should repay their war debts by cutting down on rearmament; in any coming war, navies would be obsolete: it would be a bombing war, and it would "depopulate" the earth. Even as his Lincoln pen scratches across the parchment of his epoch-making Peace Covenant, Huston slumps to his death: he, and the angel Gabriel, have done the job that needed to be done.

Preposterous, and faintly ugly. The screenplay for *Gabriel Over the White House* (based on "an anonymous novel") is credited to Carey Wilson, an Irving Thalberg protégé and former silent-picture scenarist. Later on, as executive producer of the Andy Hardy series, Wilson would be accused of claiming his writers' stories as his own. (When Louis B. Mayer was told of this, he is said to have retorted: "Sure he stole your story. He gets a $5,000 bonus for any original story he comes up with.") In the case of *Gabriel,* however, Wilson was not overanxious to pretend that it was all his own work. Although the film was distributed by MGM, it was actually produced (by Walter Wanger) for William Randolph Hearst's Cosmopolitan Pictures, an itinerant operation which at that point was enjoying a liaison with Louis B. Mayer—the deal being, roughly, that the Hearst papers would be friendly to MGM if MGM was friendly to Hearst's girlfriend, the actress Marion Davies. Hearst apparently took a keen interest in the making of *Gabriel Over the White House.* He was backing Roosevelt at the time, and he saw the film as a pungent way of telling the president how he should handle things: there was even a plan to release the film on Inauguration Day.

Darryl Zanuck might have seen himself as a news editor of film, following the headlines of the day, but Hearst was an editorialist. According to Carey Wilson, the magnate rewrote several of the film's more political speeches, paying particular attention to the Huston rhetoric. And the Hearst hand can surely be detected in one of the film's early speeches, delivered by an idealistic young reporter who is appalled by the President's pre-Gabriel dithering. At a press conference, Huston airily denounces the leader of the unemployed as a "dangerous anarchist" and claims that his party "has a plan. . . . My attitude is one of complete optimism. . . . America will weather this Depression. . . . America will rise again." The reporter refuses to buy this. Unable to contain himself, he blurts out the following carefully wrought editorial:

There is starvation and want everywhere, from coast to coast, from Canada to Mexico. Millions of dollars are poured into new

battleships, farmers burn corn and wheat, food is thrown away
into the sea while men and women are begging for bread. Millions are freezing without coats while cotton is rotting in the
fields. Thousands are homeless and there are millions of vacant
homes. . . . What does the new administration say to this? What
answer, what depthless plan does the government have for this
indictment, to this vale of misery and horror, of lost hope, of
broken faith, of the collapse of American democracy?

It is indeed an irony that this speech, which we might suppose was
penned in a moment of freedom by one of Hollywood's more fiery
radicals, was possibly the work of Citizen Hearst. Certainly, it would
not have been in the film if Hearst had not wished it to be there.

In 1935, MGM had plans to produce another political film—and
one that might have been a piquant follow-up to *Gabriel:* a movie
version of Sinclair Lewis's novel *It Can't Happen Here,* a somewhat
slapdash anti-Fascist fantasy, which had just reached the bestseller
lists. When the Hays Office saw Sidney Howard's faithful-to-the-
novel script, they became extremely nervous—especially, they said,
in view of an imminent presidential campaign. In December 1935,
Joseph Breen wrote a memo to Will Hays:

> The first question in my mind is whether or not the industry, as
> an industry, should sponsor a picture of this kind. You will have in
> mind that it is hardly more than a story portraying the Hitleriza-
> tion of the United States of America. . . . I think we should proceed
> with great caution before going too far with this story, having in
> mind our foreign markets. I am fearful that some of the European
> nations like England and France may not look with favor on this
> story; and the company may wake up to find its picture barred *in
> toto,* not only in these countries, but in a number of countries
> abroad.[18]

Like Germany and Italy, for instance. Both Lewis and Howard were
indignant: Howard spoke of "a fantastic exhibition of folly and cowardice," and in February 1936, Lewis announced to the *New York
Times:* "Today I have heard that the final decision has been made
to shelve the whole business . . . in fear of international policies and
threats of boycotts abroad." He went on, in a statement that must
have made uncomfortable reading for quite a number of Hollywood's screenwriting radicals:

The world is full today of Fascist propaganda. The Germans are making one pro-Fascist film after another, designed to show that Fascism is superior to liberal democracy. The Italians are doing the same. On the other side the Russians are making films to show that communism is superior to anything else.

I have yet to see Hollywood and its satellites threaten to ban all German, Italian and Russian pictures from the market on this ground. But Mr. Hays actually says that a film cannot be made showing the horrors of fascism and extolling the advantages of Liberal Democracy because Hitler and Mussolini might ban other Hollywood films from their countries if we were so rash.

Democracy is certainly on the defensive when two European dictators, without opening their mouths or knowing anything about the issue, can shut down an American film causing a loss of $200,000 to the producer. I wrote "It Can't Happen Here" but I begin to think it certainly can.[19]

3

Hollywood's "foreign policy" during the 1930s was marked by what now seems an almost contemptible timidity. Most studios managed to keep silent about Nazism until just before the outbreak of war in Europe, and even then they trod carefully. In 1934, Irving Thalberg returned from a trip to Germany and assured his Jewish colleagues that although "a lot of Jews will lose their lives . . . Hitler and 'Hitlerism' will pass; the Jews will still be there."[20] He believed that "German Jews should not fight back and that Jews throughout the world should not interfere." Hollywood's executives, most of whom "had spent the better part of their lives transforming themselves *from* Jews," were happy to concur. Adolph Zukor spoke for them when he declared: "I don't think Hollywood should deal with anything but entertainment. The newsreels take care of current events."[21]

Even when the Los Angeles Bund began pamphleteering against Jews in Hollywood, the moguls were reluctant to answer back; by sticking their necks out, it was argued, they would be providing anti-Semites in America with too visible targets. In the autumn of 1936, a gathering of four hundred Hollywood executives issued a statement committing themselves "to openly fight any cause that threatens our country," but they were careful not to center their attack on fascism. Communism was named as a similarly evil "ism," and for the next three years this was more or less the Hollywood position: "tentative and even-handed" has been one way of describing it. Even as late as 1940, however, many of the producers could be terrified when Joseph Kennedy (a former studio owner, then ambassador to Britain) warned them that "the Jews were on the spot" and would be "in jeopardy" if they used "the film medium to promote or show sympathy to the cause of the 'democracies' versus the 'dictators.' " According to Ben Hecht: "As a result of Kennedy's cry for silence, all of Hollywood's top Jews went around with their grief hidden like a Jewish fox under their gentile vests."[22]

Again, Warner Brothers were slightly to one side of the main tendency—to the extent, anyway, of allowing the political climate to impinge on their "pure entertainment." They steered clear of any anti-Hitler content until their own Jewish representative in Germany was murdered by a Nazi gang, and although their *Life of Émile Zola* (1937) had chiefly to do with the Dreyfus affair, the word "Jew" was never spoken in the film. But then the Warners "line" during most of the 1930s was dictated from the White House. In 1933, Roosevelt had offered Jack Warner a diplomatic post in gratitude for the studio's help in his California campaign. Warner had replied: "I'm very flattered, Mr. President, but I think I can do more for your foreign relations with a good film about America now and then."

An article on Warners' foreign policy by John Davis has traced in some detail the way in which Jack Warner carried out his promise.[23] Roosevelt, for instance, advocated a strong national defense: to help recruitment, Warner Brothers put out a series of "service" films—musicals and comedies—that promoted a virile but merry image of life in the ranks: *Sons o' Guns, Miss Pacific Fleet, Shipmates For Ever,* and so on. When Roosevelt was cross with the British (who in 1934 seemed to be flirting with the Japanese), Warners let loose a few devious screen limeys, diplomats and spies, and discovered a new interest in the Irish Question (in *The Key*). There was also a remake of *The Charge of the Light Brigade*—this time without Lord Tennyson's subtitles. Warners' in-house director Michael Curtiz seemed to have a particular taste for Anglophobic items (his *British Agent* and *Captain Blood* are cited by Davis, who also points out that Curtiz's sympathetic treatment of Leninist Russia in *British*

Agent immediately followed the United States' recognition of the Soviet Union).

The most obvious examples of Warners' obedience to White House thinking can be found in the studio's essays on the subject of America's attitude to the impending European war. The ploy here was to smuggle the presidential wisdom into historical costume pix, so that Robin Hood, for instance, can be made to denounce King Richard for having neglected his domestic responsibilities for the sake of wasteful adventuring abroad: "I blame King Richard, whose job was here at home, protecting his people instead of deserting them to fight in foreign lands." Similarly, in *The Private Lives of Elizabeth and Essex* (adapted from a play by Maxwell Anderson), the queen is portrayed as a Rooseveltian isolationist: "I've kept the peace and given my people happiness, relieved the poor and re-stored our coinage. . . . It takes more courage not to fight when one is surrounded by foolish hotheads urging wars in all directions." The hothead Essex is threatening to "drag down your country and drown her in a sea of debts and blood," and he must therefore die. As John Davis comments: "Before he mounts the execution block, Essex realizes that Elizabeth was right: war-mongers must be eliminated."

This was 1939, when Roosevelt was still telling Americans "again and again and again: your boys are not going to be sent into any foreign wars." A year later, things had changed. Warners, with an almost endearing lack of shame, consulted Queen Elizabeth once again. This time, in *The Sea Hawk*, she is having second thoughts. The black-shirted Philip of Spain cannot be reasoned with; he is set to destroy Elizabeth's "puny, rockbound island." "You know as well as I," Philip tells his aides, "that we will never keep Northern Europe in submission until we have a reckoning with England." The queen has done everything she can think of in the way of diplomacy, and now, egged on by Errol Flynn, she must acknowledge that

> a grave duty confronts us all—to prepare our nation for a war that none of us wants—least of all your queen. We have tried by all means within our power to avert this conflict. We have no quarrel with the people of Spain or of any other country. But when the ruthless ambitions of a man threaten to engulf the world, it becomes the solemn obligation of free men, wherever they may be, to affirm that the earth belongs not to any man, but to all men . . .

MED. SHOT. ELIZABETH AND ASSEMBLAGE

ELIZABETH (continuing): . . . and that freedom is the deed and title to the soil on which we exist. Firm in this faith, we shall now make ready to meet the great Armada which Philip sends against us. To this end I pledge you ships worthy of our seamen . . . a sturdy fleet hewn out of the forests of England. (Camera pans to the wooded shore that surrounds the harbor, and as we look, each tall pine becomes a ship's lofty spar—row upon row of them—a forest of mastheads, and each flying the British flag. Elizabeth's voice continues over scene.) A navy foremost in the world—not only in our time, but in generations to come.[24]

This rather lumpishly written speech was the work of a new Warners writer named Howard Koch, and he was much annoyed when it was cut from the U.S. version of *The Sea Hawk* (needless to say, it was allowed to be shown in Britain). Although, in 1939, Warners was prepared to concede that Britain could not avoid a war, but was not yet ready to provide all-out support. Koch's speech was "prematurely anti-fascist." When Koch complained about the loss of his big speech, Warner replied: "Dear Koch, this picture is costing us a million and a half. If you want to buy it for an extra million above cost, you can put on any ending you please."[25]

Koch was new to Hollywood, and he had already caused a minor stir by refusing tasks that seemed to him beneath his dignity. A former lawyer, he had worked in Federal Theatre projects during the thirties and eventually gained a modest stage success with a play called *The Lonely Man,* in which Abe Lincoln returns to "Depression-era America to confront slavery in its contemporary forms, such as racial discrimination and exploitation of industrial workers."[26] *The Lonely Man* was popular on the left-wing repertory circuits, and it brought Koch into contact with John Huston and Orson Welles. He also met John Houseman ("the pedestal on which the statue of Orson was erected"[27]) and was hired by him to work with Welles on a new radio series, "The Mercury Theatre on the Air." It was Koch's script for *The War of the Worlds* that caused the famous Halloween panic of 1938. On the strength of this success (and with the backing of John Huston), he signed with Warner Brothers in 1939.

When originally offered *The Sea Hawk* (which had been "developed" from a Rafael Sabatini novel by the playwright Clifford Odets), Koch was reluctant: "It posed a basic question; could I function in Hollywood on terms that I could live with?"[28] A very basic question, and it could only have been posed with such baldness by a writer who had not lived through the local feuds and enmities of the 1930s. Not until he was allowed to politicize the script did Koch agree to go ahead. As it turned out, he was not of course given the free hand he would have liked (for one thing, director Michael Curtiz had him banned from the set during shooting—the writer's "helpful" suggestions had become too helpful), but even so he was admired by many for his earnestness. Koch's subsequent "filmography" is remarkably uncluttered with the usual hack assignments, and his work on films like *Sergeant York, Casablanca,* and *Mission to Moscow* eventually made it inevitable that he would be targeted by the witch-hunters as one of Hollywood's key Reds. The irony is that in 1939, Koch and other radical playwrights were called to Hollywood precisely because they were radical: the treadmill would shortly be in need of trained anti-Fascist rhetoricians.

But not quite yet. The studios had their own brand of "premature anti-fascism": to them, it was known as forward planning. It would be a couple of years before the screenwriters would be given their heads on the matter of Hitler and Mussolini. At this stage, the best they could hope for was a bit more latitude than they had grown used to. And this, it must be said, was granted. Take, for example, the two films Hollywood produced on the subject of the Spanish Civil War: *The Last Train to Madrid* (released in July 1937) and *Blockade* (June 1938). *The Last Train* was never intended to be more than a lugubrious soap opera; even so, it was set in Spain and therefore had to be prefaced with the announcement: "We neither uphold nor condemn either faction of the Spanish conflict— This is the story of people—not a cause." It so happens that Paramount, on March 11, 1937, had been sent a letter from the Hays Office, saying:

we would recommend that great care be taken not to inject any material into your picture which might be offensive to either of the sides now fighting in Spain. This is important not only from the standpoint of your possible release in that country, but also in other countries in Europe, and throughout Latin America generally.[29]

The script was promptly submitted to Joe Breen and was found thoroughly acceptable: various love dramas are played out against a background of explosions and falling masonry; there are numerous uniformed requests for "your papers, please," but the incumbent regime has a sort of human face from time to time and is certainly no worse than whoever it is that's dropping all the bombs. A war is going on, that's all we know, and—since the last train runs from Madrid to Valencia—it has to be *that* war. But as one critic pointed out, the film's "sympathies, neither Loyalist nor Rebel, are clearly on the side of the Ruritanians." Nonetheless, the Hays Office had felt bound to point out that the enterprise called for even more timidity than usual:

> they [the filmmakers] must always keep this in mind: that Para-
> mount has recently been in trouble in Spain. The man responsible
> for this trouble was the ex-Minister of State, Gil Robles, who is the
> man who started the present revolution. Should the present revo-
> lutionaries win, this man will again be in power and if there is one
> thing in the whole picture on which he can lay a finger he will take
> a slap at it.[30]

Blockade is a good deal more purposeful, although here, too, the combatants are never named and we know that the film is set in Spain by means of a single caption: "Spain: the Spring of 1936." The writer of *Blockade* was John Howard Lawson, Hollywood's chief Stalinist, and there was little doubt that Marco, the film's close-to-the-earth hero (Henry Fonda), was on the Loyalist side, stirred into action by malign aggression from without. We never actually see the enemy: their representatives in the movie are spies and crooks, flagless international racketeers and corrupt local bureaucrats—none of them in it for anything other than the cash.

In between the massively virtuous Marco and the limitlessly evil "other side" is the seductive Madeleine Carroll, a pawn of the oppo-sition until she witnesses, firsthand, the suffering of innocent war victims and learns to reciprocate the love of Henry Fonda. The film as a whole is indeed (as one reviewer called it) a "Spanish omelette, with ham," but it is well paced and it has some affecting moments: in particular, the scene in which an outraged British journalist takes Carroll on a tour of a blockaded seaport: this is the heroine's mo-ment of enlightenment, and the film's director, William Dieterle, orchestrates the pageant of war horrors with a delicacy for which the rest of the film has little use. Also there is an Eisenstein-like power in the seafront crowd scenes: the starving townsfolk wait for the arrival of a supply ship, which will almost certainly be bombed before it reaches them. And the film ends vehemently, with Fonda—having routed the spies and saved the town—being congratulated by his general, who suggests that he has earned himself a furlough and some "peace." "Peace?" retorts Fonda, turning to the camera as it moves slowly in on him:

> Peace?—where can you find it? Our country's been turned into a battlefield. There's no safety for old people and children. Women can't keep their families safe in their houses. They can't be safe in their own fields. Churches, schools, hospitals are targets. It's not war—war's between soldiers. It's murder—murder of innocent people. There's no sense to it. The world can stop it. Where is the conscience of the world?

When Walter Wanger hired Lawson to write *Blockade,* each of them knew that he would be working within the usual Hollywood constraints. Lawson later recalled:

> We could not call the Loyalists by name, we could not use the actual Loyalists' uniform. This I accepted because it was the only way in which the picture could be undertaken. And there was complete understanding between Wanger and myself; there was no attempt on my part to introduce material without discussing it because I would consider that dishonest and would never attempt to do that with a film that I was making.[31]

When we call to mind that Lawson, when he was not writing *Blockade,* was spending his time organizing pro-Loyalist propaganda, this seems a bit too sanguine. Lawson, however, somehow managed to persuade himself that by offering "a simple message" by which the world might be made aware of "the horror visited on women and children by the bombing of cities and the starvation of civilian populations," he was achieving a near-alignment between his screenwriting duties and his political passions. It has been well pointed out that—so far as *Blockade* is concerned—"it made little difference whether the screenwriter, Lawson, was the head of the Hollywood

CP or a deacon in the First Presbyterian Church."[32]

Innocuous though it seems today, and even after last-minute cuts made by a nervous Wanger, *Blockade* caused a considerable uproar at the time. Roman Catholic groups were up in arms—in spite of the film's overstudious presentation of the suffering townsfolk gathering in church, lighting candles, sending up prayers. Boycotts were threatened; pickets were organized. Several theaters took fright and refused exhibition. The Knights of Columbus complained to the Hays Office; the Boston City Council introduced a ban. Walter Wanger's next project (also with Dieterle and Lawson) was to have been *Personal History,* a more explicitly anti-Fascist effort, based on the European reporting of the journalist Vincent Sheehan: "On the boat back to the United States, Joe [the character modeled on Shee-han] shows newsreels of the Austrian *Anschluss* to his fellow journalists and acts as narrator." At the end, the script calls for him to look directly into the camera for his final words. Where Marco's speech (in *Blockade*) was antiwar, Joe's was to be anti-Nazi: "In five hours it was all over but the shouting. The freedom of Austria was wiped out in five hours." The film was never made. According to John Howard Lawson: "Wanger was told that he would never get another loan to finance a picture if he made *Personal History.*"[33]

8

In 1916, the twenty-two-year-old Aldous Huxley went to see D. W. Griffith's film version of *Jane Eyre* and afterward pronounced: "The plot of the novel was absolutely destroyed . . . but that is of course of no importance." During the 1920s, Huxley liked to theorize about the movies, and he was not above using cinematic devices in his fiction. As his sight failed, though, his contempt for the "movie-going experience" seemed to harden. It was not so much the film medium that he despised; his disdain was focused rather on America and the Americans, their innate—as he perceived it—tendency to drag everything down to the "lower, animal levels."

In *Brave New World,* John and Lenina have a night out at the "feelies" (where they see "Three Weeks in a Helicopter. An All-Super-Singing, Synthetic-Talking, Coloured, Stereoscopic Feely With Synchronized Scent Organ Accompaniment"), and when, in *Eyeless in Gaza,* Anthony Beavis speaks of "the pitiable models on which people form themselves," it is Hollywood he has in mind, and the idea of audiences "sitting at a picture palace passively accepting ready-made daydreams." In 1926, the British poet Robert Nichols went off to try his luck in Hollywood (where, it seems, he rose to become a gagwriter for Douglas Fairbanks). Huxley wrote to him:

> A good subject to talk about, cinematography. But is it a good medium to work in? I say no, because you can't do it by yourself. You depend on Jews with money, on "art directors," on little bitches with curly hair and teeth, on young men who recommend

skin foods in the advertisements, on photographers. Without this co-operation your ideas can't become actual. You are at their mercy. What a disgust and a humiliation! It seems one worse, if possible, than the theatre. I shall stick to an art in which I can do all the work by myself, sitting alone, without having to entrust my soul to a crowd of swindlers, vulgarians and mountebanks. If one could make films oneself, I'd be all for the movies. But as it is—no. Surely Hollywood must have made you feel the same?[1]

Twelve years later, when Huxley was on a lecture tour in California, a Hollywood agent offered to sell his books for filming. Needing cash, Huxley agreed to work on the scripts of any novels of his own that might be bought, reckoning to make "tons of money" very quickly so that he could get back to that "art in which I can do all the work by myself." A familiar stratagem—with, as it turned out, familiar results. In Huxley's case, there were perhaps some compensations. Hollywood for him had more to offer than the movies. In Los Angeles, he discovered a "greater variety of the kind of people whose interests coincided with his own, at a time when he was turning away from literature as art and towards that world of metaphysics, decentralist politics and the marginal sciences in which his later life was mainly lived."[2] In other words, Los Angeles was full of cranks: it offered a new constituency to this author whose introverted style of pacifism was now being readily sneered at in Great Britain.

Huxley also valued the film community's willingness to supply him with the sort of uncomplicated sexual liaisons that best fitted with his work routines. These "dinner—and then bed" arrangements were fixed up by Huxley's wife, since he himself could not afford the time to go in for more than the most perfunctory types of courtship. Maria Huxley knew where to find the girls (she herself having found her niche in Hollywood's lesbian network), and she would also tidy up any loose ends when Aldous showed signs of getting bored; she wrote all his "goodbye letters," it is said. It seems likely that even if Huxley had been able to support himself on the earnings of his novels and essays, he would have chosen to settle in Los Angeles—in the film world but not of it. Unluckily, his British royalties were in decline, and in any case a large lump of them had been embezzled by his London agent. When Anita Loos suggested, in May 1938, that the time may have come for Huxley to confer with

MGM, he was not in a position to protest. Loos told Maria: "You will have enough to set yourself up for life, and I'll protect him at the studio."[3]

The deal offered by MGM was enticing: $1,800 a week for eight weeks to work on a film biography of Madame Curie. In two months, Huxley could earn more than he had made from his last two books, and he would earn it, moreover, by working on a subject that had some genuine appeal: as he saw it, here was a chance to transmit scientific know-how to a mass audience. He seems not to have suspected that for MGM the "science element" in the Curie saga was surely something that could be dealt with by flourishing a few test tubes and letting out the odd "Eureka!" Unquestionably the real point about the Curies was that they represented the ultimate marriage-partnership; they were codiscoverers, spurred on and strengthened by their decent love. When Huxley discovered that Madame Curie enjoyed performing infidelities in full view of her husband's portrait, the studio preferred to look the other way. And when the MGM brass received Huxley's finished treatment—145 pages of prose, instituting a sort of "hymn to scientism"—they fell silent. Huxley's contract quietly expired. The *Madame Curie* project trundled on, with other writers (including Scott Fitzgerald) brought in to work on it. As to Huxley's treatment, according to writer Salka Viertel "it was instantly forgotten. I was surprised that no one mentioned the Huxley script and on the next occasion I asked Bernie [Hyman] what happened to it. Embarrassed, he admitted that he had had no time to read it but had given it to Goldie, his secretary, who told him: 'It stinks.' "[4]

A year later, Huxley was given a second chance: an MGM assault on *Pride and Prejudice.* The money was not quite so good this time—$1,500 a week—and the employment would be on a week-to-week basis. On the other hand, the producer was the notoriously inaccessible Hunt Stromberg. Profitable weeks would pass between sightings of the man in charge. Hired in the autumn of 1939, Huxley wrote to his brother in January 1940:

No news here. Pee and Pee (as Jane Austen's masterpiece is called at MGM) drags on—not through any fault of writers and director, but because we cannot get to see our producer without whom nothing further can be done. If he does get round to seeing us, it will all be finished in a few days: if not, God knows.[5]

For *Pride and Prejudice,* Huxley was given a cowriter, Jane Murfin (an established pro, who had worked in Hollywood since 1917; she was married to the director-actor Donald Crisp, Griffith's assistant on *Birth of a Nation*). The collaboration seems to have worked well. Huxley knew that with *Pride and Prejudice,* he needed to prove his competence as a filmwriter. He also knew that fidelity to the original was hardly worth attempting:

> I work away at the adaptation of *Pride and Prejudice* for the moment—an odd, crossword puzzle job. One tries to do one's best for Jane Austen; but actually the very fact of transforming the book into a picture must necessarily alter its whole quality in a profound way. In any picture or play, the story is essential and primary. In Jane Austen's books, it is a matter of secondary importance (every dramatic event in *Pride and Prejudice* is recorded in a couple of lines, generally in a letter) . . . and the insistence upon the story as opposed to the dilute irony which the story is designed to contain, is a major falsification of Miss Austen.[6]

In spite of all this, the evidence suggests that Huxley took his task seriously; the rebuff over *Madame Curie* no doubt still rankled, and an original scenario he had written was being hawked around the studios with no success (the script was called *Success*). He seems not to have objected when the studio shifted Jane Austen's story forward by some forty years so that the film might have more "pleasing" costumes, a change that permitted the inclusion of lines like this (from Mrs. Bennet): "Five thousand pounds a year and not married. That's the most cheering piece of news since the Battle of Waterloo." Nor did he (or Miss Murfin) shrink from ironing out the Austen syntax, nor from slotting in this sort of signposting exchange between Elizabeth and Darcy:

> ELIZABETH: At this moment it's difficult to believe that you're so proud.
> DARCY: At this moment it's difficult to believe that you're so prejudiced.

At the end of the day (which lasted six months), Huxley felt—as we, too, largely feel—that the whole thing could have been much worse. *Pride and Prejudice* (1940) stands as one of Hollywood's most re-

spectful adaptations: some of Jane Austen's speeches survive more
or less intact, and one or two of the duets between Greer Garson and
Laurence Olivier come close to simulating the genteel fervor of the
novel. Huxley was considered by Hollywood to have scored something of a triumph, and his agent had no trouble arranging a follow-
up assignment—a 20th Century–Fox adaptation of *Jane Eyre.* This
project didn't reach the screen until 1944, and by then Orson Welles
and John Houseman had made it their own. Huxley's script was
completed in the spring of 1942.

Huxley's later adventures in Hollywood do not amount to
much—a failed collaboration with Christopher Isherwood on a
script about a faith healer, a rejected adaptation of *Alice in Wonder-
land* for Walt Disney, a saga of negotiations about a possible movie
of *Lady Chatterley's Lover* (with Isherwood, Auden, and even Samuel Beckett somehow involved as possible cowriters), a drawn-out
effort to make a film of his own *Brave New World* (which his crooked
British agent had sold off—for a song—to RKO in 1932). The *Brave
New World* discussions took place in 1946. By this time Huxley was
once again on the bestseller lists, with *Time Must Have a Stop,* and
the need for film gold was not quite so pressing.

Huxley lived on in California until his death, in 1963, and he
continued to dabble in filmwriting—*A Woman's Vengeance* (1948)
was shot from Huxley's screen adaptation of his story "The Gioconda
Smile"—but for him the struggle with Hollywood had taken place
in 1938–41, and he had good reason to believe that he had been the
victor. His credits are respectable, the getting of them involved very
little in the way of "disgust" or "humiliation," and there is no sense
in which the experience damaged or misdirected his best talents—
indeed, bits of it he turned to his advantage, in *After Many a Summer Dies the Swan* (based on his weekends chez William Randolph
Hearst), *Ape and Essence,* and *The Genius and the Goddess.*

In reflecting on the business of screenwriting, Huxley more than
once compared it to the making of a puzzle, crossword or jigsaw.
When he watched the final edit of *Pride and Prejudice,* he was
impressed by the way "Stromberg sat for weeks, night after night,
cutting here, putting in there, like a jigsaw puzzle." He told this to
a friend, who commented: "I should think he would go quite mad,
like taking Chinese water torture." "He *is* mad," said Aldous. "They
are all quite mad. You can't blame them when you see it done." To
view himself as a toiler in the company of eccentric puzzle-solvers

was much more congenial than having to confess that he had sold his literary gifts to a "crowd of swindlers, vulgarians and mountebanks."[7] Once the whole thing could be grasped as dotty, ingenious, obsessive, Huxley could live with it; indeed, he could regard it as a kind of challenge to his celebrated wits: "Aldous has learned," said his wife, "to do their kind of thing extremely well, as he does anything he really wants to."[8]

Certainly, after the success of *Pride and Prejudice* (which, unusually for a "prestige" adaptation, had been decently received by the critics), he could chuckle companionably when Selznick called him at 3 A.M., saying: "My car is at your door. Get right over to the studio." This was the way of cranks, of nocturnal puzzle freaks; it was not at all to be seen as an affront to the dignity of Aldous Huxley:

> The first thing a successful writer learns is to lose any self-conceit as to his abnormal abilities . . . when William Shakespeare, sitting in Bungalow No. 1, has sent in his story to the supervisor, the latter, if not immediately satisfied—a very, very rare occurrence—will pass it on to Ibsen in Bungalow No. 2 or Maeterlinck in Bungalow No. 6.[9]

Or Scott Fitzgerald in No. 29. Huxley and Fitzgerald crossed paths during the planning of *Madame Curie*, but aside from one unlikely anecdote, which has the pair of them chortling over the filmic possibilities of Madame's sexual peccadilloes, there is no evidence that a friendship developed between these two formerly bestselling novelists. A smart producer might have thought to team them up on *Madame Curie*, but it was not Hollywood's method to contrive such partnerships. The rule was that highbrow (and therefore "high risk") writers should be chaperoned by seasoned pros. Huxley didn't mind this; Fitzgerald minded it intensely, believing as he did that left alone, he would have had something splendidly original to offer.

2

In 1937, Fitzgerald was making his third visit to Hollywood. The second, in 1931, had been less stylishly madcap than the first; indeed, there were those (including Fitzgerald) who remembered it as an embarrassing fiasco. Hired by Thalberg to adapt a novel called *The Red-Headed Woman* (by Katherine Brush, a Fitzgerald imitator), Scott was fired after only a few weeks—for incompetence, or drunkenness, or both. His script was too glum, and so was he; almost from the first day he was drinking and making a fool of himself at parties. It had been a terrible year: in 1930, Zelda had had her first breakdown and was in a Swiss clinic until shortly before Fitzgerald set off, on his own, for Hollywood. In January, Scott's father had died of a heart attack; Zelda's father was to die in November 1931—just before Fitzgerald's MGM contract was torn up. It was hardly to be expected that an item like *The Red-Headed Woman* would bring out the best in him: frolicsome sexual comedy was never quite his sort of thing.

And yet, characteristically, he worked hard at the assignment—too hard, no doubt, and much too thoughtfully:

> I was jittery underneath and beginning to drink more than I ought to. Far from approaching it too confidently I was far too humble. I ran afoul of a bastard named de Sano, since a suicide, and let myself be gypped out of command. I wrote the picture and he changed as I wrote. I tried to get at Thalberg but was erroneously warned against it as "bad taste." Result—a bad script.[10]

The end had come after a party held by Mrs. Thalberg; in front of a roomful of "top-drawer" Hollywood personalities, Fitzgerald insisted on calling silence for a recitation, by himself, of some doggerel that he and Edmund Wilson used to have fun with in their college days. The response was icy: "as he finished, he had the sickening realization that he had made a fool of himself in view of an important section of the picture world, upon whose favor depended his career."[11] Thalberg in particular was not amused; soon afterward, *The Red-Headed Woman* was handed to Anita Loos.

A story by Fitzgerald called "Crazy Sunday," written not long after the event, describes the events of the Thalberg party but concocts a different outcome. The Thalberg character in "Crazy Sunday" (called Miles Calman) gets killed in a plane crash, and his wife turns to the delinquent screenwriter for solace: "Joel, I thought I could count on you. Miles liked you. He was jealous of you—Joel, come here." Joel would like to oblige, but his true spiritual attachment is to Miles:

Joel thought of Miles, his sad and desperate face in the office two days before. In the awful silence of his death all was clear about him. He was the only American-born director with both an interesting temperament and an artistic conscience. Meshed in an industry, he had paid with his ruined nerves for having no resilience, no healthy cynicism, no refuge—only a pitiful and precarious escape.[12]

This was written four years before Irving Thalberg's death by a writer whom Thalberg had just spurned. The need in Fitzgerald to conquer Thalberg, to make the man recognize their essential kinship, was mysterious and powerful enough to override even the most contemptuous rebuffs. Ernest Hemingway had a similar effect on Fitzgerald. Returning to Hollywood in 1937, a year after Thalberg's death but on the payroll of Thalberg's studio, Fitzgerald had a major score to settle—or rather a major ghost to be appeased.

The trouble was that, by 1937, Fitzgerald himself was something of a ghost. In *The Crack-Up*, a year earlier, he had published his own spiritual obituary, and it was now customary for people to think of him as "wrecked"—Hemingway's word for him in "The Snows of Kilimanjaro," also published (with typical Hemingway finesse) in 1936. Fitzgerald's stories were being turned down by the big-circulation magazines on which he depended for his income. His book earnings had dwindled to near-invisibility: the total royalties on all his books for the year 1935–36 amounted to a little over eighty dollars. His annual income from all sources was now lower than it had been in any year since 1919, when he had started out. In September 1936, his mother died, leaving him enough money to settle the worst of his outstanding debts. Although he had never liked her much ("my father is a moron and my mother a neurotic, half-insane with pathological nervous worry"), he was moved by what he saw as her "defiant . . . love for me in spite of my neglect of her . . . it would have been quite within her character to have died that I might live."[13] *The Crack-Up* was possibly the last of his works that she had read.

The timing of her death was eerie. Fitzgerald was now a forty-year-old orphan. His fortieth birthday was on September 24, and the next day a front-page article appeared in the *New York Post*. It was headed:

THE OTHER SIDE OF PARADISE
SCOTT FITZGERALD, 40, ENGULFED IN DESPAIR
BROKEN IN HEALTH, HE SPENDS BIRTHDAY REGRETTING
THAT HE HAS LOST FAITH IN HIS STAR

The article, by Michael Mok (Fitzgerald would soon be calling him "Muck"), told of a visit to the "jittery . . . restless . . . trembling" novelist, whose "twitching face" bore the "pitiful expression of a cruelly beaten child":

> The poet-prophet of the post-war neurotics observed his fortieth birthday yesterday in his bedroom at the Grove Park Inn here [Asheville, N.C.]. He spent the day as he spends all his days— trying to come back from the other side of Paradise, the hell of despondency in which he has writhed for the last couple of years.
>
> . . . with his visitor [i.e., Mr. Mok], he chatted bravely, as an actor, consumed with fear that his name will never be in lights again, discusses his next starring role.
>
> He kidded no one. There obviously was as little hope in his heart as there was sunshine in the dripping skies, covered with clouds that veiled the view of Sunset Mountain.

This, to Fitzgerald, had seemed "about the end"; he swallowed four grains of morphine, "enough to kill a horse." He then saved his life by vomiting and afterward "felt like a fool."

Less than two years earlier, in January 1935, Fitzgerald had been invited to Hollywood to write a screenplay of *Tender Is the Night*. He had refused, he said, because "I hate the place like poison with a sincere hatred It will be inconvenient in every way and I should consider it only as an emergency measure."[14] That December, he turned down another offer. His agent had written to him:

> I am sure that if you live quietly there and work hard and make a business of saving money that you could do a lot to get yourself out of the hole you are now in . . . there is no reason why you shouldn't get enough money ahead to write a novel when you get ready to write one.[15]

To this, Fitzgerald answered, with what is probably his most neutral and considered judgment of the matter:

I don't think I could do it now but I might. Especially if there
was no choice. Twice I have worked on other people's stories,
with John Considine [his producer on *Lipstick,* in 1927] telling
me the plot twice a week and the Katherine Brush story—it simply fails to use what qualities I have. I don't blame you for lectur-
ing me since I have seriously inconvenienced you, but it would
be hard to change my temperament in middle-life. No single
man with a serious literary reputation has made good there. If I
could form a partnership with some technical expert it might be
done. . . . I'd need a man who knew the game, knew the people,
but would help me tell and sell my story—*not his.* This man
would be hard to find, because a smart technician doesn't want
or need a partner, and an uninspired one is inclined to have a
dread of ever touching tops. . . . I'm afraid unless some such
break occurs I'd be no good in the industry.[16]

By the end of 1936, Fitzgerald could no longer afford to hesitate,
or to dream of "touching tops." The movies, in whatever guise, now
seemed to be his only hope. In order to stomach this realization, he
was obliged to refashion his theoretical approach. Looking back, he
claims to have perceived some time earlier, albeit grudgingly,

that the novel, which at my maturity was the strongest and sup-
plest medium for conveying thought and emotion from one
human being to another, was becoming subordinated to a mechanical and communal art that, whether in the hands of Hollywood merchants or Russian idealists, was capable of reflecting only
the tritest thought, the most obvious emotion. It was an art in
which words were subordinate to images, where personality was
worn down to the inevitable low gear of collaboration. As long past
as 1930, I had a hunch that the talkies would make even the
best-selling novelist as archaic as silent pictures.[17]

There is self-pity here, and bitterness, and the usual Fitzgerald
compulsion to think in terms of apocalyptic fracturings, epochal
dislocations, but even as he concedes the future to the movies, he
is preparing the ground for his own transforming intervention: he
may be a washed-up novelist, but what if the novel—that is to say,
The Novel—was itself washed up? As Gore Vidal observed: "He
realized that the novel was being superseded by the film; he also

realized that the film is, in every way, inferior as an art form to the novel—if indeed such a collective activity as a movie can be regarded as an art at all. Even so, Fitzgerald was still enough of an artist or romantic egotist to want to create movies. How to go about it?"[18]

First of all, he had to get a contract, and this was not as easy in 1937 as it had been in 1931. Reports of his alcoholism had put a stop to negotiations with RKO in the autumn of 1936—and here, too, the publication of *The Crack-Up* hadn't helped. His agent, Harold Ober, was now warning him: "I think the days are over when an author with a good name can go out to Hollywood for a week or two and pick up a sizable amount of money."[19] He might have written *"even an author with a good name,"* but he didn't. Luckily, Fitzgerald still had one admirer left in Hollywood—a high-up MGM functionary named Edwin H. Knopf. Knopf had even, a year earlier, recorded his admiration on celluloid, in a film called *The Wedding Night;* directed by King Vidor from a story by Knopf, this "two ton dud" had Gary Cooper playing big-time novelist to an admiring Anna Sten. Fitzgerald, who had known Knopf in the twenties, seems to have been in no doubt that the Cooper character was based on him. But even the ardent Knopf had trouble persuading MGM to take a gamble on Fitzgerald. Months passed without a final yes or no; Fitzgerald grew more agitated: "I'm anxiously waiting for news—no news is no doubt bad news. *Why don't I just go to the coast and let them see me?* I haven't had a drop in two months and I feel fine. There's nothing I'd like better for immediate cash and a future foothold."[20] The deal came through in June 1937: one thousand dollars a week for six months, with a renewal option. In July, Fitzgerald wrote to his daughter, Scottie:

> I must be very tactful but keep my hand on the wheel from the start—find out the key man among the bosses and the most malleable among the collaborators—then fight the rest tooth and nail until, in fact or in effect, I'm alone on the picture. That's the only way I can do my best work. Given a break I can make them double this contract in less than two years.[21]

Checking into the four-hundred-dollar-a-month Garden of Allah was one way of recapturing the old days, although his agent no doubt pulled a face, and it was not long before he was ebulliently dropping names: "I have seen Hollywood, dined out with March, danced with Ginger Rogers . . . wisecracked with Montgomery." He was even allowing Dorothy Parker to take him to meetings of the Anti-Nazi League. He was once more a star dwelling among stars. And this time he was determined not to mess it up. Having listed all his glitzy chums, he adds: "the work is hard as hell."[22]

The "work" at this point was to tinker with a script based on John Monk Saunders's "idea" for *A Yank at Oxford.* Fitzgerald's rewrites were rewritten (some by George Oppenheimer, so ubiquitous a script doctor that many people thought his first name was really And), and he received no credit: in this case a relief, perhaps, since the movie was widely derided for its misty-eyed approach to Merrie Oxforde—"made by Metro in England and in awe" was Alistair Cooke's kindly verdict.

Fitzgerald's next assignment was the one that scholars have been poring over for three decades: an adaptation of *Three Comrades,* a novel by Erich Maria Remarque (of *All Quiet on the Western Front*). The reason for the close scrutiny is threefold: *Three Comrades* turned out to be the only film on which Fitzgerald got a credit, and it so happened that the quarrels he had with his producer were heavily documented, showing Fitzgerald desperately fighting to preserve *his* film against the interference of the MGM know-nothings. There is also a political dimension. *Three Comrades* the novel is an explicitly anti-Nazi text, and although the MGM version took care not to mention the word "Nazi" and to cut out any references to Jews, book-burnings, Nazi insignia, and the like, there were such vehement protests from the German consulate that Louis B. Mayer urged on by Breen tried to have the film's rampaging street gangs identified as Communists ("it might be as well to make the communists the 'heavies' "). The producer, Joseph Mankiewicz, threatened to resign if this was done. Fitzgerald, on hearing about this, embraced Mankiewicz in the MGM commissary.

Alas, this was one of the few moments of harmony between them. As Fitzgerald saw it, Mankiewicz had from the start been needlessly tampering with Fitzgerald's "personal" understanding of *Three Comrades.* First of all, he had saddled Fitzgerald with a cowriter— one E. E. Paramore, a writer whom Fitzgerald had known slightly in New York and always thought of as inferior. This was the first "insult": after all, had not Mankiewicz promised Fitzgerald that he would be left alone? Fitzgerald set to quarreling with Paramore about "the terms of our collaboration"—and poor Paramore is now fixed in literary history as the man who was hired to interfere with Scott Fitzgerald's screenplay. Joe Mankiewicz would be similarly fixed if he had not gone on to become the author of two stylishly written films: *All About Eve* and *A Letter to Three Wives.* The second "insult" also came from Mankiewicz, when the Fitzgerald-Paramore screenplay was handed in. Mankiewicz began making cuts. Even the most rabid admirer of Fitzgerald would have to agree that some of these cuts were, shall we say, essential. For example, this scene by Fitzgerald presents the film's two lovers arranging their first date, by telephone. A split screen shows Robert Taylor nervously picking up the phone and asking to be put through to Margaret Sullavan, who is sitting demurely in her apartment. And then:

54: A SWITCHBOARD
with a white winged angel sitting at it.

Angel (sweetly): One moment, please—I'll connect you with heaven.

CUT TO:

55: THE PEARLY GATES
St. Peter, the caretaker, sitting beside another switchboard.

St. Peter (cackling): I think she's in.

56: BOBBY'S FACE
still ecstatic, changing to human embarrassment as Pat's voice says:

Pat: Hello

Bobby: Hello.[23]

It should be said that apart from this sequence, the film's method is entirely naturalistic: the celestial machinery makes no other appearance in the script—and this is just as well, because Pat is suffering from terminal tuberculosis. "What the hell does he think he's writing about? How do you photograph *that?*" was the MGM response. The pearly gates were cut. And so, too, was an ambitious

opening montage explaining the economic plight of Germany in
1928. After much business with bronze eagles dissolving to a pile of
rifles dissolving to queues outside food depots, we are shown:

9: A GRAPH
to show the passage of ten years. A line drawn from the upper
left to the lower right of the graph, is marked "National
Wealth of Germany." A moving pen draws another line which
crosses the first line and moves always upward. This line is
marked "Cost of Living." As this insert is primarily for a time
lapse, the dates on the graph should be very large. When the
pen stops under 1928—

                                                    DISSOLVE TO:

10: A SIGN READING "GASOLINE, 1M 40PFG."[24]

Other Mankiewicz excisions involved the removal or altering of
scenes, the dilution of the hero's drinking problem, and the polishing—more usually the unpolishing—of dialogue. Later on, Mankiewicz would say:

I personally have been attacked as if I had spat on the American
flag because it happened once that I rewrote some dialogue by F.
Scott Fitzgerald. But indeed it needed it! The actors, among them
Margaret Sullavan, absolutely could not read the lines. It was very
literary dialogue, novelistic dialogue that lacked all the qualities
required for screen dialogue. The latter must be "spoken." Scott
Fitzgerald wrote very bad spoken dialogue.[25]

According to Mankiewicz, Fitzgerald had been put on the film because of his supposed "feel" for Europe in the twenties (he did not
say that *Three Comrades* might have had a special meaning for
Fitzgerald because it ends with the heroine languishing in an Alpine
sanitarium). It was never considered that his dialogue would reach
the screen intact, nor—presumably—that his feelingful scene setting would be of much use to the film's director, Frank Borzage, "a
glorified cameraman," according to Fitzgerald, but perhaps not
sufficiently glorified to do full justice to the following:

From the other side of the Buick there has appeared a lovely
girl. Patricia Hollman is in her middle twenties, stylish and

beautiful—and something more. She seems to carry light and music with her—one should almost hear the music of the "Doll Dance" whenever she comes into the scene—and she moves through the chaos of the time with charm and brightness, even when there are only sad things to say.[26]

Comparing the Fitzgerald script with the film that eventually reached the screen, it is hard now to see what the fuss was all about. Now and again, Mankiewicz's dialogue is a good deal more wordy and pretentious than the Fitzgerald original. Mostly, though, there is not much to choose between the warring pens. For example, here is a love scene written by Fitzgerald:

Pat: I don't think. I don't think about anything—except about us and the sun and the holiday and the sea. (She tickles his nose with an anemone.)
Bobby: Take away that rose, woman.
Pat: It isn't a rose.
Bobby: Violet, then.
Pat: Isn't a violet.
Bobby: Then a lily—it better be—those are the only names I know.
Pat: Not really?
Bobby: I've always got by with those three. More oil.
Pat: No more. You just like the rubbing.[27]

And here is the Mankiewicz scene that replaced it:

Erich [a late name change for the hero]: There, you see. I was afraid of that. You're bored—
Pat: No, I'm not.
Erich: You will be, soon. What on earth are we going to talk about for the rest of our lives?
Pat (turns back, smiling now): You—
Erich: Twelve minutes, by the clock—
Pat: Me, then—
Erich: We couldn't talk. We'd have to sing—
Pat: Darling. Books and music. They're always safe.

Erich: I don't know anything about books, and I don't know anything about music.

Pat: I'll teach you. It's time you went to school—[28]

Well, we can take our pick. By the time Fitzgerald read Mankiewicz's new version of the scene, he was already involved with the columnist Sheilah Graham (their romance had blossomed at a dinner given by the Screen Writers Guild). Graham also knew nothing of books, and Fitzgerald enrolled her in what she called a "College of One," supplying her with reading lists ("I'll teach you. It's time you went to school"). In a letter to Mankiewicz, which he may or may not have sent (Mankiewicz says he never received it), Fitzgerald picks out the books-and-music banter as a particularly obvious example of the Mankiewicz insensitivity:

You are simply tired of the best scenes because you've read them too much. . . . You are *or have been* a good writer, but this is a job you will be ashamed of before it's over. The little fluttering life of what's left of my lines won't save the picture.

. . . Pat on page 72—"books and music—she's going to teach him." My God, Joe, you must see what you've done. This isn't Pat—it's a graduate of Pomona College or one of [the] more bespectacled ladies in Mrs. Farrow's department. Books and music! Think, man! Pat is a lady—a cultured European—a charming woman. And Bobby playing soldier. . . . Recognizable characters they simply are not, and cutting the worst lines here and there isn't going to restore what you've destroyed. It's all so inconsistent. I thought we'd decided long ago what we wanted Pat to be![29]

It is a long letter, a sad confusion of pedantry and paranoia ("For nineteen years . . . I've written best-selling entertainment, and my dialogue is supposedly right up at the top"), and it ends with a burst of almost pitiable vehemence:

My only hope is that you will *have a moment of clear thinking. That you'll ask some intelligent* and *disinterested* person to look at the two scripts. Some honest thinking would be much more valuable to the enterprise right now than an effort to convince people you've improved it. I am utterly miserable at seeing months of work and thought negated in one hasty week. I hope

you're big enough to take this letter as it's meant—a desperate
plea to restore the dialogue to its former quality . . . all those
touches that were both natural and new. Oh, Joe, can't producers
ever be wrong? I'm a good writer—honest. I thought you were
going to play fair.[30]

The wonder is that Fitzgerald should have cared so much, or
believed that the movie, in either version, would rise above the level
of box office kitsch. And it is not as if, having sounded off and sobered
up, he was able to leave the thing alone. When *Three Comrades* was
previewed for exhibitors, there were objections to the ending. Fitzgerald's ending runs as follows (Pat has died, "quite full of love—like
a bee is full of honey when it comes back to the hive in the evening,"
and one of the three comrades has been killed by a sniper because
of his commitment to a "cause"):

367: FADE IN: A SNOW-COVERED CEMETERY ON A HILL IN THE
CITY—EVENING
Bobby and Koster, their eyes straight before them, are walking
down a broad path. There is a faint glow in the sky and far
away the unmistakable tp! tp! tp! of a machine gun.

Koster: There's fighting in the city. As they continue on, they
are suddenly four instead of two—the shadowy figures of Pat
and Lenz, grave and tender, walk beside them toward
whatever lies ahead.[31]

In the screen version, the four of them are setting off for South
America (which, throughout the film, has been oddly represented as
a kind of far-off Utopia). They are walking away from the "fighting
in the city." When he saw this, Fitzgerald was distraught. He rattled
off a letter to the MGM top brass, hoping to save them from themselves. Again there is the dreadful boasting: "In writing over a hundred and fifty stories for George Lorimer, the great editor of the
Saturday Evening Post, I found . . ." and again the tone is life or
death:

To every reviewer or teacher in America, the idea of the comrades
going back into the fight in the spirit of "My Head is Bloody but
unbowed" is infinitely stronger and more cheerful than that they
should be quitting—all the fine talk, the death of their friends and

countrymen in vain. All right, they were suckers, but they were
always that in one sense and if it was despicable what was the use
of telling their story?

The public will feel this—they feel what they can't express. . . .
The public will be vaguely confused by the confusion in our
mind—they'll know that the beginning and end don't fit together and when one is confused one rebels by kicking the thing
altogether out of mind. Certainly this step of putting in the "new
life" thought will not please or fool anyone—it simply loses us the
press and takes out of the picture the real rhythm of the ending
which is:

*The march of four people, living and dead, heroic and uncon-
querable, side by side back into the fight.* [32]

The South American reference was allowed to stand—although
the ending is more ambiguous than Fitzgerald believed it to be:
there *is* just a chance that the comrades will change their minds
once they have fully registered that "There's fighting in the city."
But in this mood, there was no deflecting Fitzgerald from his conviction that something very precious and profound had been despoiled.
Sheilah Graham recalled:

When *Three Comrades* opened, Scott and I drove into Hollywood
to see it. "At least they've kept my beginning," he said on the way.
But as the picture unfolded, Scott slumped deeper and deeper in
his seat. At the end he said, "They changed even that." He took
it badly. "That s.o.b.," he growled when he came home, and furi-
ously, helplessly, as though he had to lash out at something, he
punched the wall, hard. "My God, doesn't he know what he's
done?"[33]

What Mankiewicz had done was nothing much, because the film
was nothing much, with its ludicrously faked-up studio settings,
mawkish lighting, stop-go sense of rhythm, and a dreadful, "Have I
remembered my lines?" performance from the chief male star, Robert Taylor. For Fitzgerald, though, it was necessary to pretend that
great issues were at stake: artistic integrity under threat from the
uncaring philistines. To have seen it as it was would have been to
concede that he was not much good at a job he now depended on
and, worse, had come to think of as an elevated sort of "challenge";

it would have been to agree with those in Hollywood who, on the strength of the Mankiewicz set-to, were beginning to believe that "he had simply wandered away from the field where he was a master and was sludging around in an area for which he had no training or instinct."[34] No training? Had he not sat for hours watching all of MGM's hit movies from the last fifteen years; had he not collected hundreds of file cards listing tricks of the trade, noting the strengths and weaknesses of individual stars, itemizing well-tried "plot-lines"? Writing to a friend about *Three Comrades* after its release, he advised her to "credit me with the parts you like."[35]

All that had gone wrong could readily be blamed on Mankiewicz. When Fitzgerald, for his next task, was assigned to the more senior Hunt Stromberg, he was almost snobbishly relieved. Stromberg, a tall man with a professorial demeanor, was suddenly "the best producer in Hollywood," "a sort of one-finger Thalberg, without Thalberg's scope, but with his intense power of work and his absorption in the job."[36] In spite of everything, Fitzgerald's credit on *Three Comrades* had enhanced his local reputation: the film was a 1938 box office hit. Stromberg also had high hopes; he was old enough (two years older than Fitzgerald) to remember *The Great Gatsby*, which had been published when Joe Mankiewicz had barely turned sixteen.

Both parties were soon disillusioned. There were no confrontations, just a gradual loss of confidence all around, with Fitzgerald eagerly, and then less eagerly, turning in his lines and Stromberg becoming ever more silent and unreachable. It is hard not to feel sorry for Fitzgerald as he labors to convince Stromberg of his masterful professionalism:

So much for the story. Now, will the following schedule be agreeable to you? The script will be aimed at 130 pages. I will hand you the first "act"—about fifty pages—on March 11th, or two weeks from Friday. I will complete my first draft of the script on or about April 11th, totalling almost seven weeks. This is less time than I took on *Three Comrades,* and the fact that I understand the medium a little better now is offset by the fact that this is really an original with no great scenes to get out of a book. Will you let me know if this seems reasonable? My plan is to work about half the time at the studio but the more tense and difficult stuff I do better at home away from interruptions. Naturally I'll always be within call and at your disposal.[37]

Fitzgerald's first assignment for Stromberg—called *Infidelity*—collapsed under pressure from the Hays Office; the second—an adaptation of Clare Boothe's play *The Women*—was almost insultingly pedestrian: Fitzgerald was expected to clean up the Boothe dialogue but otherwise leave it pretty well untouched. *The Women* was passed to Jane Murfin and Anita Loos, who got the credits. A week was spent tinkering with *Marie Antoinette;* after that, Fitzgerald was switched to the intractable *Madame Curie.* If it was to Hunt Stromberg that he sent the following character sketch, perhaps Stromberg's deepening silence becomes less difficult to understand:

We must be true to Mme Curie, who did not like fools—in high places or low. We must dramatize the fact that much of the great work of the world is done in loneliness and neglect—and to do that we must concentrate, as she did, upon the work itself, and its glory. We must see her as a gorgeous instrument of human achievement. We must not ape the public that she ran away from by making a goddess of her—a great impossible close-up of a monster, what the public calls a genius. No, we must pull aside a curtain and let others see as individuals what they would like to have seen in Marie's life-time—what it is that made her so great and fine and good, so that those who came to adore remain to love.[38]

Again Fitzgerald was taken off the film—which did not get made until 1943. A brief loan-out to David Selznick on *Gone With the Wind* (on which he was "absolutely forbidden to use any words except those of Margaret Mitchell") presaged the end. Fitzgerald's contract with MGM was not renewed: "Why I don't know, but not on account of the work. . . . Baby, am I glad to get out! I've hated the place since Monkeybitch rewrote 3 Comrades."[39]

Dismissal from MGM was of course a mortifying blow. Fitzgerald had lasted eighteen months on a huge salary, and he had worked extremely hard, approaching each new project with obsequious solemnity. Whenever he had seen a chance, he had given lavishly of his most valuable obsessions: superior drink-problem heroes, beautiful doomed girls, dreams squandered or destroyed—in his single day on *Marie Antoinette* he had come up with a speech on the mystique of kingship, and on *Infidelity* he is thought to have been seeking to defend his adulterous relationship with Sheilah Graham. And apart from one or two binges, he had kept the alcohol at bay. Fitzgerald was convinced that he had honored the terms of his probation, or parole: he had been *good*.

And yet from MGM's point of view, he wasn't good enough: investmentwise, Fitzgerald had failed to deliver. By renewal time, Stromberg had come to believe, with Mankiewicz, that Scott just didn't have "the knack." A significant aspect of this judgment was that Fitzgerald's contract placed him near the top of the MGM pay scale for writers. Had he been on $500 a week, or even a bit less, the studio might have been content for him to jog along doing rewrites or high-sounding treatments, or to settle down as a "corpse-ranger," nursing other people's ailing scripts. For $1,250 a week, the moguls expected more than this—and Fitzgerald himself believed that he was worth more than he was being paid. As Nunnally Johnson analyzed it: "His biggest misfortune, which I doubt that he ever realized, was that they paid him fat money at the very beginning. And even though he blew his chances with inadequate work he believed that he should continue to draw such salaries or even larger ones."[40]

And so, in February 1939, Fitzgerald went free-lance. He was now asking $1,500 a week, and it might have been better for him if there had been no takers at this price. As it was, he was insufficiently surprised when Walter Wanger hired him, almost immediately, to write a film called *Winter Carnival*—a college love story, to be set in Dartmouth, Wanger's own university. The twenty-five-year-old Budd Schulberg, another Dartmouth graduate, had written a first draft, but Wanger was unhappy with it; Fitzgerald would inject some class. What happened next has been told a dozen times. Fitzgerald and Schulberg set off on a research trip to Dartmouth, much drinking took place on the journey, and it all ended in humiliation and disaster, Fitzgerald's "biggest, saddest, most desperate spree." Sacked by Wanger, Fitzgerald finished up in a New York hospital. Schulberg, who has written the story more than once (most notoriously in a novel called *The Disenchanted*), somehow kept his job—a young lad, son of B.P., led astray.

For Fitzgerald it was "one of the silliest mistakes I ever made."[41] *Winter Carnival* was his last big-money job in Hollywood. After this, he was reduced to picking up any bits and pieces that might come his way—a few days on *Air Raid,* a brief encounter with *Honeymoon in Bali,* a rewrite job on *Raffles,* a much-rejected proposal for an "original," *The Feather Fan:* "The real lost generation of girls were those who were young right after the war because they were the ones with infinite belief. The sanitariums are full of them and many are dead." The drinking continued. Harold Ober refused to advance him any further cash: in 1938, only ninety-six copies of Fitzgerald's books were sold; in 1939, his book royalties had dropped to a miserable thirty-three dollars. The only reliable source of income was from *Esquire,* for a series of "Pat Hobby" stories. Slight and would-be slick, these chronicled the doings of a hack screenwriter. For each Hobby story, Fitzgerald collected what poor, failed Pat was paid each week—$250. On the face of it, a rock-bottom situation: "I don't know what the next three months will bring further, but if I get a credit on either of these last two efforts things will never again seem so black as they did a year ago when I felt that Hollywood had me down in its books as a ruined man—a label which I had done nothing to deserve."[42]

Fitzgerald, when he wrote this to Zelda, had eighteen months to live, months in which he wrote six chapters of *The Last Tycoon* and attempted a screen version of his "Babylon Revisited"; by any reckoning, an impressive output for a sick man who was spending a lot of his time and energy touting for movie work and agonizing about his status at the studios. In 1940, the "big one" seemed yet again to be in sight, with the twelve-year-old Shirley Temple dithering over whether or not to star in Fitzgerald's *Cosmopolitan* (the title of his "Babylon Revisited" screenplay). Miss Temple was in fact twenty-seven by the time this "poignant story of a father's lonely love for his little girl" finally got filmed; it was by then called *The Last Time I Saw Paris,* and needless to say, there was no credit for Fitzgerald, who had been dead for fourteen years.

In the autumn of 1940, some money relief came in the shape of an offer from Darryl Zanuck at 20th Century–Fox. Zanuck wanted an adaptation of Emlyn Williams's play *The Light of Heart;* the money was good—seven hundred dollars a week for ten weeks ("a fairly nice price," confessed Fitzgerald)—and the subject could hardly have seemed more approachable: the travails of a onetime celebrity stage actor now brought low by liquor. The actor is briefly rehabilitated, but when his adored clubfooted daughter goes off to get married, he botches the big "You are men of stone" speech in a comeback performance of *King Lear,* gets very drunk again, and kills himself.

On reading all this, in Fitzgerald's downbeat version, even Darryl Zanuck fell silent. Fitzgerald's script was passed to Nunnally Johnson (who knew nothing of Fitzgerald's involvement) for "brightening." Johnson tagged on a happy ending and changed the title to *Life Begins at 8:30.* Fitzgerald had once again entertained high hopes, worked hard, and put a lot of himself into the assignment; like the actor in Williams's play, he had sorted himself out, and things were looking good:

> CAMERA FAVORS Mackay who sits with a magazine on his knee.
> He looks ten years younger; his hair is cut, his suit is new, and
> he wears horn-rimmed spectacles. Now that he is neither
> drunk nor suffering from after effects, his true manner emerges
> for the first time—shy, good-humored and unpretentious. After
> eight years of desperation . . . this journey into the world of
> country houses, leisure, and luxury is a great adventure.[43]

And once again Fitzgerald couldn't understand what had gone wrong. Shortly after being taken off the picture, in November 1940, he had what he called "a cardiac spasm"—a blackout in Schwab's drugstore, of all places. In December he had a second heart attack, which killed him. "Poor son of a bitch," said Dorothy Parker at his funeral. Not many in Hollywood knew that she was quoting from *The Great Gatsby.*

3

The day after Fitzgerald's death, on December 22, 1940, Nathanael West and his wife, Eileen, were killed in a car accident as they traveled back from a hunting weekend in Mexico. The "world's worst driver," West had over the years been involved in many an auto wreck—he habitually drove fast, was known to make U-turns across six lanes of rush-hour traffic, and was more or less color blind. He was also famous for daydreaming at the wheel; several of his friends refused to drive with him. When "bluntly warned" by one of them that "some day he would be killed if he did not keep his eyes on the road ahead, his answer was always the same scornful laughter."[44] On the day of his death, West skidded out of a side road onto the main northbound boulevard and hit the first oncoming car: he had not noticed a red light, or he noticed it too late and was traveling too fast.

West was thirty-seven, and his wife was ten years younger. They had been married for eight months—his first marriage—and had just moved into a new house in North Hollywood. For once, things were looking up for "Pep," as he was known; he had recently teamed up with Boris Ingster—who had been an assistant to Eisenstein on the Mexico project and was now a skilled Hollywood operator—and between them they had sold a couple of treatments to Columbia and RKO. West, who was accustomed to life at the very bottom of the screenwriters' pay scale, could now start thinking about putting up his price. At least one commentator has suggested that West had curtailed his Mexican weekend and was hurrying back to Los Angeles because he had heard about Fitzgerald's death. The two had never been close friends, but Fitzgerald had once or twice gone out of his way to praise West's fiction, and West was grateful to him.

Although obituarists knew little about Nathanael West—"he was said to have written such books as *The Day of Locusts* and *Miss Lovely Hearts* or he was characterized as a Hollywood scenarist"— he was a revered figure in the sections of literary Hollywood that centered on Musso and Frank's, Stanley Rose's bookstore, and the offices of the Screen Writers Guild. "He was one of the few men I met in Hollywood who filled me with a sense of awe," said Milton Sperling, "for he knew he had something to write about."

> He affected fellow writers as Bogart did actors, with his reserve and rock-like integrity. He threatened them with his avoidance of both scorn and enthusiasm for movies, since he regarded them as an immense fountain pen, as an adding machine, a vehicle whereby to sustain his own real interest in creative writing. He was ahead of his time in knowing that Hollywood was impermanent and literature lasting, and in never confusing the two.[45]

In *The Day of the Locust,* the painter Tod Hackett (named after West's friend Albert Hackett, scenarist—with his wife—of *The Thin Man*) has been bought by Hollywood, to do "set and costume designing." His friends from the Yale School of Fine Art, where he studied, chastise him for selling out, but Tod needs the money, and he's curious. When he gets to Hollywood, he finds rooms in a sleazy neighborhood near Hollywood Boulevard and discovers, with some glee, the "other Hollywood"—a Hollywood peopled by failures, drifters, and grotesques, a parasite culture that feeds off the Big Dream of movieland but is also weirdly self-sufficient. Bit players, extras, washed-up comics, dumb blondes, dwarfs, con artists—they all at one time gravitated to Hollywood to try their luck, to make it in the movies. Their luck has long ago run out, but by the time they acknowledge this they have already become citizens of their own unreal metropolis—a metropolis so rich in disappointment and mad self-delusion that it can sometimes make the center it aspires to seem suburban. On good days, when a big film is in production, Tod's neighbors can get to spend a day fighting the Battle of Waterloo, or steam down the Mississippi in full evening dress, or loaf against the bar of a cowboy saloon. On bad days, they can pimp or be prostitutes or push drugs or play the horses or pick fights or just stand around. Tod Hackett is particularly fascinated by those who stand around:

> Scattered among these masquerades were people of a different type. Their clothing was somber and badly cut, bought from mail-order houses. While the others moved rapidly, darting into stores and cocktail bars, they loitered on the corners or stood with their backs to the shop windows and stared at everyone who passed. When their stare was returned, their eyes filled with hatred. At this time Tod knew very little about them except that they had come to California to die.[46]

West had not come to California to die, but he did a lot of standing around. He lived in Hackett's neighborhood and was admired by his writer friends for having a wide circle of acquaintances in what Lillian Hellman called Hollywood's "whorish, drunk dope-taking world." Even a tough guy like John Bright was impressed by West's easy relationships with "bums and derelicts and criminals." One evening, West might be found hanging around the homicide division of the Los Angeles Police Department; another night, it would be heard that he was smuggling guns across the Mexican border with a different set of pals. A lot of the time, though, he spent "people-watching":

I can see Pep now, as I not infrequently encountered him on Hollywood Boulevard after dinner, standing in front of Musso and Frank's eating place, frequently alone, idly chewing a toothpick and eyeing his surroundings.[47]

West quit Hollywood in 1933, and his fortunes had deteriorated. He had published *A Cool Million* in 1934, and it had failed to sell. He was turned down for a Guggenheim grant (which Fitzgerald tried to help him get). The magazines were rejecting his short stories. In the summer of 1935, he returned to Hollywood, penniless but hopeful that he could pick up more or less where he had left off. He took a room downtown, in a seedy apartment hotel, and—living on money borrowed from Sid Perelman—he set about looking for screenwriting jobs. Nothing was offered—and this was maybe just as well, because West was soon laid low by a nasty bout of gonorrhea and then by a congested prostate gland ("brought on," he joked, "from a lack of intercourse"). Both ailments were extremely painful, and West needed regular morphine shots to keep him going: "Even if I got a job now I couldn't accept it. I can't walk and am in continuous pain.... I can't work during the day; I can't sit in a chair for more than ten minutes at a time, and at night I can't sleep."[48] It was during this black period that West began shaping *The Day of the Locust.* It was also around this time that he met the hugely successful Dashiell Hammett at a party and asked him if he could fix up a job at MGM:

> [Hammett] made me eat plenty of dirt.... I sneaked out early and spit all the way home to get the taste of arse out of my mouth. I couldn't drink and had a miserable time of course, drinking wouldn't have helped and he did his best to rub it in. One of the girls there tried to make up to me and for some reason or other he said, "leave him alone he hasn't got a pot to piss in." Another time when I tried to talk to him about Stromberg and a job, he made believe he didn't understand what I was saying and called out in a loud voice so that everyone could hear, "I haven't any money to lend you now, but call me next week and I'll lend you some."[49]

It was not all that long ago, West must have mused, that he was giving Hammett cheap-rate accommodation at the hotel he used to manage in New York. West had helped a lot of other writers at that time. Now he was writing to his agent: "I'll work for as low as $50 a week, anything, even a reader's job." His "people-watching" had assumed a new intensity—a sort of fellow feeling and a sort of paralyzing horror: "I have deteriorated mentally. I have nothing to say and no talent for writing."[50]

In January 1936, West finally landed a contract, at $250 a week, with Republic Pictures, a studio that had by now assimilated its Poverty Row neighbors—outfits like Monogram, Mascot, and Majestic—and was toying with the idea of edging into the A-picture market. It was known around town as Repulsive Pictures because of the stunningly cheapskate look of most of its productions: it was the cheapest of the cheap, its output "geared mainly for small-town and neighborhood reception." Serials, Westerns, melodramas, and the odd musical were Republic's specialties. Their stars tended to be ex-stars or—rather more rarely—stars whose hour had not yet come (John Wayne was a Republic stalwart until he made his name in *Stagecoach,* and Rita Hayworth, or Rita Cansino, had put in some time at the studio, in "other woman" roles). Republic's shooting schedules were so tight that fluffed lines quite often made it to the final cut, and it was not unusual for action sequences to be lifted out of stock and dusted down for a second or third life in some new cheapie. "You'd think someone was *waiting* for this," said one veteran B-picture director to his weary crew after a fifteen-hour day of hectic shooting, and this seems to have summed up the cheerful view of all concerned. It was certainly West's view; he liked B-picture people, and he enjoyed the company of other bottom-of-the-scale screenwriters—he shared an office with Lester Cole and co-wrote with Samuel Ornitz, two of Hollywood's busiest Reds.

These two were, of course, active in the Screen Writers Guild, which in 1936 was approaching its first major showdown with the studios. Again, in this most political of years, West was both taking part and standing back. He was a Guild sympathizer; he joined early on and for a time served on its committee. He also attended the odd pro-Communist lecture or discussion group, signed petitions, and collected money for the Republicans in Spain. But the hard left thought him irresponsibly bohemian: although he supported many of the left's stated objectives, he was sardonic about their day-to-day solemnities. He had much in common here with Perelman, who has recalled:

I well remember West's feelings about the current political activity in Hollywood. The noble piety of the Hollywood folks, as they immersed themselves in the plight of the migratory workers and the like, was pretty comical. One couldn't fault them for their social conscience, but when you saw the English country houses they dwelt in, the hundred-thousand-dollar estancias and the Cadillacs they drove to the protest meetings, it was to laugh.[51]

In West's two years at Republic, he wrote or had a hand in over a dozen screenplays: comedies, melodramas, and even (with Cole and Ornitz) a musical called *Follow Your Heart.* He put in uncredited stints on sundry other projects, from *Gangs of New York* to *Ladies in Distress.* These were all routine hack assignments, and West made no claims for them. It did amuse him, though, that two of his pictures—*The President's Mystery* and *It Could Happen to You*—were singled out by left-wing reviewers as courageously political. *The President's Mystery* was based on a series of features that had been running in *Liberty* magazine. *Liberty* invited a number of writers to answer a question put by FDR: "What if a millionaire, having seen the Rooseveltian light, decides to give away his money?" The theme of Rich Man Transfigured by Direct Contact with the Poor was a favorite in Hollywood in 1936 (*My Man Godfrey* and *Mr. Deeds Comes to Town* were two popular benefactor movies of that year), and it seems that West, together with cowriter Lester Cole, took advantage of the climate. They dreamed up a yarn in which a corrupt lobbyist happens to visit a town brought to its knees by the effects of his Washington machinations. The local canning factory is at a standstill: "Men loiter about in idleness and over them rumbles the distant thunder of mob rule and violence." The lobbyist is made to think, and then: "By fearlessly risking his own happiness and doing what he believes right, he quells the forces of capitalistic greed . . . as well as winning the heart of [the canning plant's] young owner."

Meyer Levin praised *The President's Mystery* as "the first Hollywood film in which a liberal thesis is carried out to its logical conclusion," and other accounts suggest that it was indeed grittier—and duller—than either *Godfrey* or *Mr. Deeds,* with the lobbyist (presalvation) portrayed not as a lone shyster but as one of a crowd. The film also made use of newsreel footage and vox pop. interviews to enforce a clear editorial polemic: "Let's hear now from the man in the street." M in the S: "I'm the man in the street all right, that's the trouble. And I gotta get off the street and back in that factory if I'm gonna keep these kids fed and get 'em back to school."

It Could Happen to You seems to have projected a Fascist take-over of the United States, along the lines of *It Can't Happen Here.* West wrote the screenplay with Samuel Ornitz, but the film flopped badly at the box office, and according to its producer, "Only about three people in the world ever saw it." This may well be true, since Fox two years later released a nonpolitical comedy-drama under the same title. Both *It Could Happen to You* and *The President's Mystery* are now extremely difficult (if not impossible) to view, like many other Republic productions, but from the evidence available it would appear that West, along with his two Marxist colleagues, did manage to "politicize" these humble B scripts in a way that would have been impossible at MGM. Donald Ogden Stewart's *Keeper of the Flame* (an explicitly anti-Fascist effort and one in which Stewart took much pride) did not appear until 1942, and even Warners' *Confessions of a Nazi Spy* was not released until May 1939.

In January 1938, West quit his job at Republic, perhaps in the hope that he could break into a higher salary bracket at some other studio. He was out of work for a few months, but the gamble just about paid off. In June, he signed with RKO—not for more money (they offered him the $350 he had finally been earning at Republic) but for the prospect of more money. RKO was a "major" studio, albeit a precarious one, and a solo credit there could lead to bigger things. RKO, of course, signed West because of his B-picture flair. They wanted him for one picture only, an air-crash/jungle-survival parable called *Five Came Back,* which he worked on for eight weeks. He was then "released," his script was rewritten, and he ended up with one-third of the credit.

Out of work again, West was not too downcast. *Five Came Back* had won him a few marks, he had sold a treatment to MGM, and he had a play scheduled for Broadway production in the autumn. And he was almost ready to hand in *The Day of the Locust* to his publisher. There were *prospects.* Unhappily, none of them quite worked out as he'd have wished. The MGM treatment was never used; the money West was paid for it had to be invested in the play, which was six months behind schedule, and the play—an antiwar satire—folded after two performances. September 1938 was the wrong month in which to chortle over the grotesque errors of the

British High Command. As to the novel, Random House offered a cautious five-hundred-dollar advance. By the end of 1938, West was back at work in Hollywood, this time at Universal, hired to work on a film called—of all things—*The Spirit of Culver,* a celebration of life at the well-known military academy, with Jackie Cooper and Freddie Bartholomew learning to love war. The Universal executives were full of praise for West's mastery of this important subject. He was rehired to write *I Stole a Million,* which had George Raft trying to go straight and earned West not only a solo credit but also an extraordinary tribute from Joe Breen of the Hays Office. Breen wanted it to be known that out of the 3,600 scripts and stories submitted during the year, "it is our unanimous judgment, here in this office, that this new treatment by Mr. West is, by far, the best piece of craftsmanship in screen adaptation that we have seen." West laughed at this letter, but he made several copies of it, just in case.

The reviewers of *I Stole a Million* seemed to agree with Breen. Many of them made a point of praising the film's "pithy dialogue," "valid character development," and "legitimate" plotting. It was doubtless this success that led West to promise Sid Perelman that his next film would be "a real guzma about aviators, lost cities, jungles, and such guzmarie. Right now, my agent tells me, escape literature is the thing and so the one I am concocting touches the earth nowhere and is spun out of pure, unadulterated bubameiser."[52] In November 1939, West was invited back to RKO to work on a screen version of Francis Iles's mystery *Before the Fact.* This was the beginning of his partnership with Boris Ingster, and although *Before the Fact* was eventually appropriated by Alfred Hitchcock and filmed as *Suspicion,* West and Ingster had quickly evolved a working method that appealed to each of them. Ingster's English was imperfect, but he was good at thinking up the stories. "With Ingster setting out a straightforward plot, West would take up the story and characters, elaborating them and giving them uniqueness. Talking, improvising, tossing ideas about, they found that they could turn out commercial screen treatments with ease. It was, as Ingster says, 'no sweat.' "[53] With Ingster at his side, West made more money in Hollywood in 1940 (from the sale of treatments rather than from finished screenplays) than he had ever made before, and his weekly rate had at last risen—to six hundred dollars a week, which was about twice what was earned from sales of *The Day of the Locust.*

West's remarkable Hollywood novel had appeared in May 1939, and it was well received by the literary press. West hoped for sales of around five thousand and was appalled to hear from Bennett Cerf at Random House that "the total sale from June 1st through June 13th was exactly 22 copies, bringing the total to 1486—[the] outlook is pretty hopeless."[54] "Thank God for the movies," West replied. And when Edmund Wilson wrote to him in 1939, "Why don't you get out of that ghastly place? You're an artist and really have no business there," West patiently explained:

I once tried to work seriously at my craft but was absolutely unable to make even the beginning of a living. At the end of three years and two books I had made a total of $780 gross. So it wasn't a matter of making a sacrifice, which I was willing enough to make and will still be willing, but just a clear cut impossibility.[55]

9

At the end of John Ford's *The Informer* (1935), the wretched Gypo Nolan gets what's been coming to him. Traitor, drunkard, wastrel, overactor, he meets his Maker with a smile because his victim's mother has decided to forgive him: "Gypo shivers from head to foot. A great joy fills his heart. Mercy and pity are upon him at last. He turns towards the front of the church and cries out in a loud voice of joy: 'Frankie! Frankie! Your mother forgives me!'"

Mary of Scotland (1936), also directed by Ford, ends—as it surely has to—with the execution scene: "CLOSE UP Mary as she lifts her head, listening." (There is Scottish music playing, somewhere.) "Then courage seems to flood into her heart as the pipes swell louder, and her heart lifts, and strength surges into her and a great joy. . . . Mary's body straightens with joy and as the pipes grow louder until they fairly thunder with joy and jubilation she goes up on the steps with the lightness of faith and a great happiness."[1]

In *This Land Is Mine* (1943), directed by Jean Renoir, the scene is France under the Nazi occupation. A cowardly schoolmaster is rescued from the shame of collaboration when he sees his admired, freethinking headmaster gunned down by a firing squad. The schoolmaster (played by Charles Laughton) is on trial for his own life and has been offered a deal by the Nazis. In earlier days, he might have accepted some arrangement. But now: "He opens his eyes and looks, the frenzy going from his face which seems to fill with strength and resolution. It is as if the explosions of their rifles had smashed through a window in his mind, and now he sees a new and

1. C. Gardner Sullivan,
the highest-paid screenwriter
of the silent era.

2. *Above:* Anita Loos with director John Emerson. **3.** *Below:* John Monk Saunders and F. Scott Fitzgerald with a still from *Wings.*

4. Charles MacArthur and Ben Hecht.

5. *Above:* Edward G. Robinson, W. R. Burnett, and Mervyn LeRoy on the set of *Little Caesar*. 6. *Below:* Harry Cohn and Frank Capra.

7. Irving Thalberg.

8. Lillian Hellman and Dorothy Parker
at a Spanish Refugee Appeal Campaign dinner, 1945.

9. *Above:* Donald Ogden Stewart, Lewis Milestone, Walter Wanger, and Herman Mankiewicz.   10. *Below:* Dudley Nichols.

11. William Faulkner.

12. Nunnally Johnson,
who adapted *The Grapes of Wrath*
for the screen.

13. *Above: The Road to Glory* set, with Lionel Barrymore, Howard Hawks, Gregory Ratoff, and Fredric March. 14. *Below:* "Mr. Deeds" the dachshund and Robert Riskin, working on the script of *Meet John Doe.*

15. *Above:* A barefoot Preston Sturges coaching a scene from *The Power and the Glory.* **16.** *Below:* Philip and Julius Epstein at work on the final script of *One Sunday Afternoon.*

17. Charles Brackett
at the First Annual
Screen Writers Guild
Awards, 1948.

18. Raymond Chandler.

19. John Howard Lawson.

20. Members of the "Hollywood Nineteen." *Front row, left to right:* Lewis Milestone, Dalton Trumbo, John Howard Lawson, and attorney Bartley Crum. *Center row, left to right:* Gordon Kahn, directors Irving Pichel, Edward Dmytryk, and Robert Rossen. *Top row, left to right:* Waldo Salt, Richard Collins, Howard Koch, Albert Maltz, director Herbert Biberman, Lester Cole, Ring Lardner, Jr., and attorney Martin Popper.

21. Bertolt Brecht testifying
before the House Un-American Activities Committee.

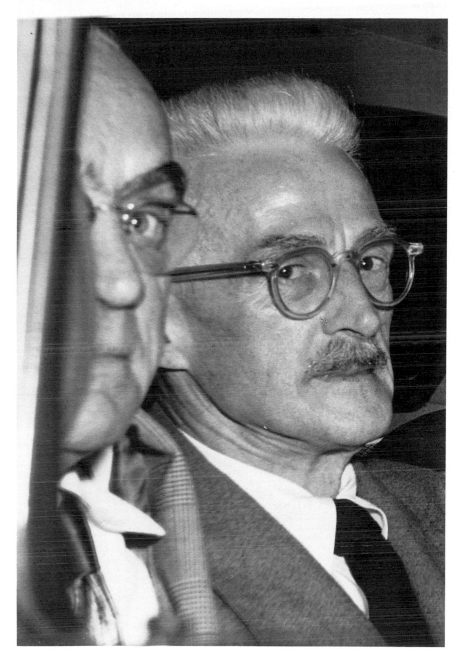
22. Dashiell Hammett
being driven to jail.

23. Gloria Swanson and William Holden in *Sunset Boulevard*.

unknown world." It is indeed a new and unknown world: a world of syntax and vocabulary and high-sounding abstract nouns. Suddenly, Laughton has become a compelling orator, a master of alliteration ("The hard truth is that the hungrier we get the more we need our heroes"); he has learned how to "look around the room with compassion," to "touch his heart" at moments of emotive emphasis, and to have his "eyes glow with his belief"—all sorts of little courtroom touches that even the most skilled advocate might envy. Like Gypo Nolan, like Mary, Queen of Scots, Laughton has peaked—but just in time. This is his last and finest hour:

> The whole crowded room sits spellbound, in hushed silence, as he sits down. Here and there we see people crying.

> CLOSE SHOT—Louise and Mrs. Lory. Mrs. Lory is weeping hopelessly and silently while Louise watches Albert with a transfigured face and tears of joy in her eyes, loving him as she has never loved any human being.[2]

A bit later, after Albert (the Laughton character) has been acquitted—a meaningless reprieve, since this is a civil court and the storm troopers are waiting for him at the door—Louise's face is once again "transfigured." This time she is "bursting with pride of Albert, who is equally proud of her—his face glowing with joy and pride and dignity." Soon after this, he, too (still glowing with J, P, and D), is led off to meet the firing squad.

These three sequences were written by Dudley Nichols, Hollywood's most earnestly respected screenwriter, and there can be little doubt that they were written "from the heart." They are sheer Hollywood, mawkish, melodramatic and oh-so-cozily attached to the concept of "transfiguration"—the redemptive personality change, instantaneous, visible, and putatively cleansing for those who get to witness it. Such moments crop up time and again in films written by Nichols, and since he was so stunningly successful—top of the pay scale, solo credits, not tied down to any studio—they also crop up in films written by dozens of his colleagues. Anyone who has seen more than half a dozen Hollywood films will have viewed at least one transfiguration, one moment in which hate turns to love, bad turns to good. Such moments do not have to be fatal (although Nichols happened to be keen on firing squads: see *The Fugitive*), but they

do have to be sudden and before our very eyes. We remember the
prostitute Dallas, in *Stagecoach* (another Nichols–John Ford collaboration). On the journey from Tonto to Lordsburg, Dallas helps to
deliver a copassenger's baby. The copassenger, it so happens, has
been mercilessly snubbing Dallas since the film began. It is Dallas,
though, who is "transfigured" by the birth:

> The last trace of hardness has vanished from Dallas as she
> holds the infant in her arms, and there is a glow of wonder in
> her face. She stands a moment in the doorway, a smile in her
> eyes. . . . Her experience of the last few hours has deeply
> affected her, taken all the defiance out of her face, and
> softened it into beauty.[3]

Hollywood transfigurations are more biblical than Shakespearean,
small remakes of The Greatest Story Ever Told. Dudley Nichols, in
an article called "The Writer and the Film," acknowledges his ante-
cedents:

> Jesus of Nazareth could have chosen simply to express Himself in
> moral precepts; but like a great poet He chose the form of the
> parable, wonderful short stories that entertained and clothed the
> moral precept in an eternal form. It is not sufficient to catch man's
> mind, you must also catch the imaginative faculties of his mind.[4]

It is not difficult to see why Dudley Nichols was a Hollywood
success: he seems to have had precisely the right combination of
innocence and guile. He was heavily serious about his craft, and yet
he also understood that in Hollywood, compromise was unavoidable. "Real screen-writing is something new under the sun of literature and in Hollywood one seldom gets a chance to practice it. It is
only by continual striving, driven by the urge for quality, only by
leaguing oneself with film-makers in other departments who have
a similar urge, that one can begin to find out what screen-writing
should be." Nichols spoke of himself as "a master craftsman in the
factory system" and talked of the need for writers to involve themselves in the filmmaking process, to think visually, and to acknowledge that the script is a mere blueprint, a pointing of the way. More
humbly placed writers could observe that when Nichols wrote this,
he was lucky enough to have had a dozen of his screenplays directed

by John Ford. Nichols was always careful, though, to balance his disclaimers with a fair amount of rhetoric on behalf of the Screen-play as a Work of Art. With John Gassner, he pioneered the publish-ing of filmscripts, and he was not in the least shy with his advice on visual matters:

> Does one write for the camera? Of course. One is not a screen-writer until one writes "*as* a camera." You key your visualizing faculties to all the possibilities—and limitations—of the camera. Hence one must understand the camera thoroughly. Too fre-quently writers check their imaginations by not knowing the cam-era's infinite possibilities; too often through ineptitude they write beyond its limitations. There are a thousand forms and a thousand styles for photographing a drama; if you thoroughly understand the complex business of film-making, the form and style will be determined during the writing of the first draft. I see no way to gain this understanding save by experience; and it must be written against the film monopoly that it has made little or no effort to enable writers with ability and an inclination to work in film to gain the necessary experience. If entrepreneurs would make the same effort to bring in new writing talent and to understand the needs of such writers once they have arrived, as they have given to bringing in new acting talent, the business of film-making would be much further advanced. For I devoutly believe it is the writer who has matured the film medium more than anyone else in Hollywood. Even when he knew nothing about his work, he brought at least knowledge of life and a more grown-up mind, a maturer feeling about the human being.[5]

This is cleverly put, suggesting as it does that screenwriters are not really to blame for being less successful than Dudley Nichols. But Nichols evidently meant what he said: he took seriously his responsibilities as the industry's top writer. As we have seen, he refused an Oscar for his script of *The Informer* rather than give the impression that he was running out on his Guild colleagues—in Hollywood terms, this, too, must have seemed like a transfiguration. He remained intelligently active in the Guild long after his own earnings had made him the envy of most of his comembers, and throughout the quarrels of the thirties he could be depended on to take a decent, moderate position on most of the key issues—neither leftist nor producer's pet. Directors liked Nichols because he seemed to agree with them that dialogue ought to be kept down to less than the bare minimum; other writers liked him because his high earnestness helped to dignify their calling; producers liked him because he did not secretly yearn to be doing something else—and because his films now and then made money.

Nichols's background and his various apprenticeships might now seem to have offered a model preparation for a Hollywood career. Born in 1895, in the Midwest, he was trained as a radio operator, and in World War I he invented a technique for the "electrical protection" of U.S. Navy minesweepers. He also did a bit of minelaying in the North Sea, and in 1920 he was awarded the Distinguished Service Medal. His first published work had appeared in the *New York Times* a year earlier; it was called "The Art of Sweeping Up Mines."

On the strength of this, he was tempted into journalism and worked for ten years on the *New York World*, first as a courtroom reporter and later as a theater critic. Heavily dramatic courtroom scenes crop up in Nichols's scripts wherever possible. In 1929, with the Great Talkies Panic, he was invited to Hollywood by Winfield Sheehan, an ex–*World* reporter who had become a high-up executive with Fox. Nichols's credentials could hardly have been more promising. He was a word-spinner, but he knew about sound transmission; he was a theater buff, but he had served time in the "real" theater of the courthouse; he was a war veteran, an expert on neutralizing enemy bombardment, especially the sneaky sort. Sheehan offered him double the salary he was earning at the *World:*

> I knew nothing about films and told him so. I had seen one film I remembered and liked, Ford's *The Iron Horse.* So I arrived rather tentatively and experimentally, intending to leave if I found it dissatisfying. Sheehan assigned me to John Ford. . . . Working with Ford closely, I fell in love with the cinema.[6]

His first film with Ford was *Men Without Women* (a five-men-trapped-in-a-submarine drama). "From then on," Ford would say, "we worked together as much as possible, and I worked very closely with him. He had never written a script before, but he was very good, and he had the same idea I had about paucity of dialogue."[7] This association with Ford immediately separated Nichols from the main pack of contending scribes. Together, he and Ford worked on

fourteen films—several of them adaptations of stage plays and novels (Nichols rarely wrote anything "original"), and the idea seemed
to be that Ford's flair for the grandiose might derive intellectual
nourishment from Nichols's more ponderous imagination. According to Ford's grandson, Dan, they "made an ideal team":

> Dudley Nichols was the butterfly, John the bull. John was bursting
> with enthusiasm and energy while Nichols was subtler, more con-
> trolled. His were the Athenian qualities of logic and grace, while
> John's were the Spartan ones of raggedness and perseverance. In
> the years ahead, Dudley Nichols would have a great influence on
> John, implanting in him the seeds of social consciousness and col-
> oring the director's cinematic style.[8]

Nichols was admitted to Ford's inner circle of hard drinkers—
John Wayne, Ward Bond, and other cowboys—but even here he
seems to have served in a kind of butterfly capacity. Ford and his
cronies used to drink in a room above the Hollywood Athletic Club.
As show biz folk, they were not allowed to join any of the smart Los
Angeles country clubs, so they decided to form a club of their own.
In fact, it was something of a fashion in Hollywood at the time to set
up these mock clubs. Ford's was called the Young Men's Purity Total
Abstinence and Yachting Association, and it described as its chief
purpose the determination to "promulgate the cause of alcoholism."
One of the club's running gags, says Dan Ford, had to do with
Dudley Nichols's application for membership: this, it seems, was
"repeatedly denied because his liberal politics were deemed 'socially reprehensible.' Although Nichols liked to claim that he was a
big drinker, and loudly boasted of his alcoholic exploits, he really
drank very little, at least when compared with the likes of Messrs.
Wayne, Bond and Ford." John Ford was in charge of keeping the
club's minutes, and in one of these he records a dramatic new development in Nichols's relations with the group:

> At the last meeting of the Young Men's Purity Total Abstinence
> and Yachting Association, Mr. Ward Bond was summarily dropped
> from our rolls for conduct and behavior which is unpleasant to put
> in print. Mr. Dudley Nichols, the well known Irish-American
> screen writer, was elected in his place.
> Mr. Nichols' first action on becoming a member was to put

forward a motion changing the name of the Association from
the YOUNG MEN'S PURITY TOTAL ABSTINENCE AND YACHTING
ASSOCIATION to THE YOUNG WORKERS OF THE WORLD'S ANTI-
CHAUVINISTIC, TOTAL ABSTINENCE LEAGUE FOR THE PROMUL-
GATION OF PROPAGANDA CONTRA FASCISM. This motion was defeated. Then Brother Nichols arose and presented each member
with an autographed copy of his brochure thesis on the "Origin,
Development and Consolidation of the Evolutionary Idea of the
Proletariat" which he has recently sold to Sam Briskin to do as a
musical with the Ritz Brothers. The copies of the pamphlet were
refused by members.[9]

The team of Ford and Nichols scored its first big success with *The
Informer,* a film much praised at the time for its visual symbolism.
Nichols, in particular, was commended for his contribution; for
once, people said, the screenwriter was making no effort to push his
literary wares. The famous symbolism now seems pretty leaden,
more to do with Nichols than with Ford (fog = "groping primitive
mind"; blind man = "brute conscience," and so on), but some of the
dialogue is admirably terse. Here, too, Nichols seemed to be attempting something new. In fact, Ford later claimed that the dialogue in one of the key scenes—a Nichols-style trial setup—was
largely improvised by the performers:

> the whole thing was extemporaneous, made right on the set. I said
> "Victor [McLaglen], interrupt—say "You're a liar, you're a liar"—
> you know, interrupt whenever you want to. There are no lines in
> the script I can give you, but just realize they've got you and try
> to lie your way out of it." Preston Foster's a pretty good actor and
> I told him, "Help Victor all you can, ad lib a little bit, throw him
> a few lines, interrupt *him."* It went pretty well.[10]

Another account of the making of the script also somewhat
reduces Nichols's input and gives us another telling glimpse of the
Ford-Nichols working partnership:

> Dudley Nichols was first to bear the brunt of John's enthusiasm for
> *The Informer.* They worked on the script in the living room of
> John's Odin Street house, where John, dressed only in a bathrobe

and chomping on endless cigars, dictated the script scene by scene. Nichols often found himself standing up and shouting to make himself heard. John's typical response if they didn't agree was that Nichols didn't "understand the Irish temperament" or that he had "no firsthand experience with the Irish people." When that didn't work, John exploded in a tirade of personal insults, calling the writer a "supercilious egghead" who wanted to write "a doctoral dissertation on the origins of the Irish proletariat." When they finally did agree on a scene, Nichols would write it down and John would go over it, making brutal cuts in Nichols' dialogue.

When the first draft was completed, Nichols typed it up and the whole process began again. Only after countless rewrites and the most intense effort did John consider the script ready. By then Nichols was so exhausted from the work and from John's bullying that he vowed never to work for him again.[11]

But of course he did, and the work methods seem to have remained pretty much the same. Another story, told by John Wayne, has Ford hacking away at Nichols's script for *Stagecoach:* "He would . . . just reach down and take a line out of this one, and then three lines out of all this wonderful writing, but flowery language of Dudley Nichols—he'd just go right to the valuable thoughts."

On the documentary *The Battle of Midway,* Ford had Nichols work day and night for two days on a commentary. Nichols turned in his script and waited for the customary comeback; he was "anxious to do anything Ford wanted—revise, rewrite, start over—anything." Ford took the script and told Nichols to go off and get some sleep. He then telephoned James Kevin McGuinness, the archreactionary and thus, in Ford's view, Nichols's "opposite," and persuaded him to drop everything: a commentary was needed for this important patriotic film—a film, Ford said, "for the mothers of America." McGuinness set to work. When Ford had *his* contribution, he combined bits of it with bits from the Nichols draft and recorded the narration himself. He then disappeared to Washington, leaving both writers to toil on "revisions" that he knew would not be needed. Neither writer knew that the other was involved. Later, when the film was completed, Ford asked the editor how Nichols and McGuinness had reacted when they learned the truth.

"I said McGuinness was upset but that Nichols was philosophical and had said, 'Ford probably knows what he's doing.' 'He probably does,' said Ford."

Ford also probably knew what he was doing when, during a marathon poker session on board his yacht, the hapless Nichols delivered a new script:

> "Be careful with it," Nichols said, "I don't have a copy." "You bet," Ford replied. According to Ward Bond, Ford then leafed through the script, weighed it in one hand, and pitched it through an open porthole into the ocean. There were too many pages in the script, which meant that there was too much dialogue. Nichols returned to his work and made it shorter.[12]

In stories like these, Nichols is presented as a rather craven yes-man, a minor functionary in the Ford wagon train, and there surely was a sense in which he was suited for that role: middlingly Irish, middlebrow and politically middle of the road, a drinker who didn't drink too much, a navy man who was a bit nervous of the sea. It was Ford's habit with actors to bully the ones he was most fond of, and so it may have been with Nichols. Nichols in his turn did have an influence on Ford's choice of subjects: the Ford screen versions of plays by O'Casey and O'Neill might well not have happened without Nichols's guidance, and *Stagecoach,* for example, might not have achieved its mythic status had it not been so solemnly schematic.

Nichols, whatever he pretended about the high dignity of his screenwriter's calling, was—like so many of his colleagues—a playwright manqué: his one Broadway effort, a play called *Come Angel Band,* had been savaged by the critics not long after Hollywood offered him an Oscar for having written *The Informer. Come Angel Band* closed after a month, leaving Nichols with the nagging feeling that success in Hollywood was second-rate: however many Oscars he received, he would still rather be Eugene O'Neill. Indeed, it was a meeting with O'Neill in 1940 that almost persuaded Nichols to cut loose from Hollywood. Nichols had persuaded Ford that four of O'Neill's short plays—each of them set on a freighter during World War I—could be turned into a perfect Ford scenario: the Irish angle, the navy angle, the men-without-women angle, etc. He and Ford visited O'Neill in California, and Nichols came away transfigured: a *real* writer, he perceived, would not be wasting his precious time getting yelled at by John Ford. The film was completed—under the title *The Long Voyage Home*—and Nichols set off for his remote farmhouse in Connecticut. From there he delivered his farewells to Ford:

> I got a terrific belt out of the film. I know you've got a magnificent picture, and I think you know it too. Another 16-inch shell into the MGM glamour empire . . . all you need is the phone book and the contents of the office wastebasket—then get on the set. I didn't think any picture could ever be as good as "Grapes," but I have a feeling that this one is better. . . .
>
> I shan't be doing any more Hollywood work for a long time, and it's a fine thing to be connected with a picture like "Voyage" on going away. It leaves a sweet taste in the mouth. You're a thorny guy, but a grand thorny guy, the O'Neill of the picture makers. Trouble is, that nobody who works with you ever wants to work with anyone else. In that sense, you've deprived me of an easy living. I can no longer sit on my ass with a fat contract and turn out crap. I don't want to be a screenwriter any more—I want to be a writer.
>
> I want to thank you for many things, you will know what; and not the least is for what I've learned about screenwriting. You're so far ahead of the rest of Hollywood that they'll never catch up. Good luck and God bless you.[13]

In the following year, Nichols was back in Hollywood, and it was probably around this time that he began setting down his theories about the Art of the Screenplay and to talk of the screenwriter as if he, too, might become an "O'Neill of the picture makers." Apart from a spell of cowriting with Lamar Trotti during the early thirties, Nichols tended to work without interference from cowriters, and by the forties he was a powerful figure in Hollywood, well placed to try out a few of his own theories. Film, he liked to say, was the medium of *re*action (the stage being the medium of action); film dialogue ought to be "synoptic," terse and bare; ideas should whenever possible be rendered pictorially: "ideas need words for their expression," but "words are not entertaining to the mass, who need simpler images." In all his musings on the high possibilities of the screenwriter's craft, Nichols tended to measure filmwriting against theater writing: in doing so, he built up the impression that the best screenwriter is the one who most effectively subordinates himself to a director. Whether this is true or not, it hardly amounts to the bracing aesthetic that Nichols, on his own behalf, was so anxiously in search of.

In 1943, Nichols was teamed with Jean Renoir to make a film for RKO. The film would be *This Land Is Mine:*

> RKO has given us absolute freedom for the making of a film, and if we fail it will be our own fault. Under such circumstances, it is important not to fail, not only to make a significant film but a successful film; and were it not for my own conviction that a really fine film can also be a highly successful film with the public, I should have fled Hollywood long ago.[14]

This Land Is Mine was not a "highly successful film with the public." Indeed, it was a commercial flop, possibly because of its overzealous pursuit of the "significant." It is a worthy attempt to explore a community's response to the perils and temptations of an enemy occupation. The occupier is glib, pretending a distaste for many of his tasks, and yet superficially persuasive in his belief that the present conflicts will in time resolve themselves into a larger good. Here is the head Nazi, von Keller, chatting with a French collaborator, George Lambert:

> VON KELLER: . . . I have many ears, as you know, and you are in touch with all the men who work here.
>
> GEORGE *(bitterly):* You think they'll tell *me* anything? No. I'm the man who gives orders around here—and they regard anyone who gives orders as an enemy.
>
> VON KELLER *(nods thoughtfully):* I can remember the time when we had the same problem in Germany—during the Republic, under capitalism. I fought in the streets for our Führer, Lambert—I killed workers with my own hands. For my class it was either kill or be killed. But we won, and now we are brothers. Absolute obedience!
>
> GEORGE *(with bitterness):* I, too, fought the unions—right in this yard. *(Shows a scar on his temple.)* I was nearly killed. But you had a leader, and you were many. We had no leader and we were few. That's why you're here.

VON KELLER: But not as your enemy, Lambert.

GEORGE: If I thought you were I wouldn't be doing what I am.

VON KELLER: I know that. We're here to help men like you rebuild your own country. Remember what my country was before our Führer. A country without food, without arms, without honor. But the people were not bad, they were only waiting to be told the truth. It's the glory of the Third Reich that we have shed German blood to give that truth not only to your people but to the Aryans of the whole world.

GEORGE: Your ideas are exactly my ideas. I saw how our country was destroyed. False democratic ideas—women refusing to have children—strikes in all our factories for a 40 hour week while your people were working 70 and 80 hours a week. I want the new order for my country. I work for it. But I know we can't have it till this war is over. I must tell you the truth—I don't like the Occupation.

VON KELLER: Neither do I.

(GEORGE *stares at him curiously.*)

VON KELLER (continues): I'm glad we understand each other. We are both working for this war to be over. Only then can we have a peaceful and united Europe. And only then can your country—and men like you—regain their dignity and honor. *(Extends his hand.)* Let us both work for that day.

(GEORGE *grips his hand with emotion.*)

DISSOLVE.[15]

This is meaty material for Hollywood, and Nichols is surely to be praised for attempting to get beyond the propagandist's clichés—although von Keller does have a thick accent and George does speak perfect English (well, perfect for a Frenchman). The trouble is that on the screen this whole exchange seems wordy and static, as do several other important stretches of the film—the stretches, unhappily, in which "ideas" are most keenly being aimed for: the headmaster's long speech on the necessity of "moral resistance," the coward's transfiguration address (which runs to two pages of close print), the final scene in the schoolroom, when the torch of liberty is being handed to the young. In each of these sequences, it is Nichols the literary sage rather than Nichols the elliptical screen craftsman who is on display. Nichols is of course writing down to his audience, but he is also writing with one eye on the intelligentsia, an elite who will admire him for his "content":

> These books must be burned. Very well, we must burn them.
> We can't resist physically. But morally, within us, we can resist.
> We contain those books, we contain truth, and they can't
> destroy truth without destroying each and every one of us. We
> can keep truth alive if the children believe in us and follow
> our example. Children like to follow a leader—and they have
> two kinds of leaders today: We seem weak, we have no
> weapons, we don't march—except to air-raid shelters—and our
> leaders have guns, tanks, parades, uniforms, they teach
> violence, self-love, vanity, everything that appeals to the
> unformed minds of children—and their criminals are called
> heroes. That's a lot of competition for us. . . . Love of liberty
> isn't glamorous to children. Respect for the human being isn't
> exciting. But there's one weapon they can't take away from us
> and that's our dignity.[16]

This is the proud headmaster addressing the cowardly Charles Laughton, who has been observed by his pupils blubbering with terror in the corner of the school's shelter during a British air raid. On hearing the headmaster's speech, Laughton, or rather Laughton's face, becomes "illuminated," and when the headmaster hands him his prized copy of Juvenal (the classics "quiet the mind"), we know that the coward is well on course for his transfiguration. It has been pointed out that when *This Land Is Mine* was made, Dudley Nichols had more clout in Hollywood than did Jean Renoir: on this project there was no John Ford to terrorize him. Even so, when given a free hand, Nichols opted for words rather than pictures. The playwright in him could not resist this opportunity to show what he could do. At the same time, he badly wanted this film to succeed at the box office. As Richard Corliss has remarked: "No wonder the mass rejected *This Land Is Mine.* Nichols' attempts to bring an adult idea to the cinema ended in his treating his audience like children."[17]

In 1943, Nichols was perhaps unusually sensitive about his reputation in literary circles. A year earlier, he had been severely chastised by Ernest Hemingway over his script for *For Whom the Bell Tolls.*

Hemingway complained that Nichols had "botched everything up," and he listed "instance after instance of material that was ridiculous or incredible." When Hemingway threatened to give a press interview repudiating the screen version of his novel, Nichols hurriedly incorporated most of his suggestions. Paramount was not so amenable and proceeded to edit out almost every use of the word "fascist" from the revised Nichols script, using "nationalist" instead. According to the film's director, Sam Wood (shortly to emerge as a leading, some would say fanatical, Hollywood right-winger): "It is a love story against a brutal background. . . . It would be the same love story if they were on the other side."

The politics of the novel are reduced to a single speech by Robert Jordan (played by Gary Cooper), in which he nicely blurs the issues by opining: "The Nazis and Fascists are just as much against democracy as they are against the Communists. They're making your country a proving ground for their new war machinery . . . so they can get a jump on the democracies." James Agee commented, in his review:

> When f-sc-sts are actually mentioned, the one time they are, the context makes it clear that they are just Italians who, in company with German Nazis and those dirty Russian communists, are bullyragging each other and poor little Spain, which wants only peace and quiet. In the same speech, if you are not careful, you may easily get the impression that Gary Cooper is simply fighting for the Republican Party in a place where the New Deal has got particularly out of hand.[18]

There were rumors that Paramount had been got at by the State Department, which in turn had been got at by the Franco government and by the Catholic Church. Adolph Zukor issued a spirited denial: "It is a great picture, without political significance. We are not for or against anybody."[19] Although Nichols was exonerated in most discussions of the film, it was well known that he had been trampled on—"occupied," one might say. Not for the first time, this anxious writer had been forced to set aside the "one weapon they can't take away from us."

2

When Nunnally Johnson was hired to write a screenplay based on John Steinbeck's *The Moon Is Down,* he wrote to the novelist asking if he had any hints on how the story should be developed for the screen. Steinbeck's reply was: "Tamper with it." After all, had not this same screenwriter already tampered with *The Grapes of Wrath,* cutting out the interchapters, losing the last third of the novel, and in general toning down the book's political vehemence? Johnson's view on adaptations was straightforward; the screenwriter's duty, he believed, "is not to the book. Whenever I work on these things, my eye is on the audience, not on the author."

With *The Grapes of Wrath,* Steinbeck had gone to great lengths in an effort to ensure that Darryl Zanuck's production would be faithful to his text. The $75,000 he had collected for the screen rights Steinbeck placed in escrow until the movie was completed, so that he would be free to sue Zanuck if he wanted to. The film's deviations and dilutions have been extensively chronicled and must have been obvious to Steinbeck at the time. When he saw the film, though, he was thoroughly delighted, announcing that "Zanuck has more than kept his word":

> He has a hard, straight picture in which the actors are submerged so completely that it looks and feels like a documentary film and certainly it has a hard, truthful ring. No punches were pulled—in fact, with descriptive matter removed, it is a harsher thing than the book, by far. It seems unbelievable but it is true.[20]

Steinbeck was shrewd enough to see that Hollywood had here given of its best: John Ford's direction, Gregg Toland's cinematography, Darryl Zanuck's editing, Henry Fonda's acting. No shame would come of this; indeed, if anything, the book's "classic" status would be enhanced by the event. And sure enough, not long afterward, the *New York Times*'s notoriously hard-to-please Frank Nugent had no complaints about the way Steinbeck had been softened up: "In the vast library where the celluloid literature of the screen is stored, there is one small, uncrowded shelf devoted to the cinema's master-pieces. To that shelf of screen classics, 20th Century Fox yesterday added *The Grapes of Wrath.*" (Zanuck, it might be noted, signed

Nugent as a screenwriter soon after this review appeared. Nugent had been needling the moguls for some time, and this seemed like a good moment for him to be neutralized: "Zanuck told me he didn't want me to write . . . he just thought the studio would save money if I criticized the pictures before they were made." In fact, later on, Nugent did write—and rather well, especially for John Ford: *Fort Apache, She Wore a Yellow Ribbon, The Quiet Man,* etc.)

The Grapes of Wrath was indeed softened up for the screen, and so, too—well before the film went into production—was John Steinbeck. At an early point in their discussions, he fell victim to Nunnally Johnson's seemingly formidable Southern charm. According to Mrs. Johnson, "Nunnally and John got along beautifully; their sense of humor meshed perfectly, and they fed each other lines and anecdotes all evening. The wine flowed and spirits ran high, and there was a lot of singing. . . ." By the end of the evening, Steinbeck was ready to tell Johnson: "A novel and a screenplay are two different things. Do whatever you wish with the book. I've already made my statement. Now it's up to you to make yours."[21]

In fact, Johnson—unlike Dudley Nichols and a few other of his colleagues—had no "statement" up his sleeve: his job was to turn Steinbeck's dangerously socialistic novel into something that Hollywood could stomach. Populist sentimentality was acceptable, so if—for example—you take Ma Joad's speech from the middle of the book, the speech about "Can't nobody lick us. We'll go on forever. . . . We're the people," and move it to the end of the film, and snip off the subversive punch line, the bit that says, "A different time's comin'," and then fade out with a purposeful long shot of Tom Joad setting off to a new dawn . . . well, essentially, what have you lost? What harm is there in highlighting those themes in the book—"love of the land, the family and the nobility of the human spirit"—with which Hollywood feels a natural affinity? Even the most fiercely programmatic novelist likes to be told that his work has made contact with the universal: when a fact becomes a legend, print the legend.

Johnson was a Southern conservative of liberal inclinations, an ironist rather than an ideologue, and he had a nicely sardonic understanding of the limits of his craft. He knew very well, with *The Grapes of Wrath,* that John Ford would need to discover in the script something that reminded him of his "Irish tradition—the idea of this family going out to find their way in the world" and that

Zanuck would insist on an uncluttered narrative with some Americanist uplift at the end. Johnson's own "statement," had he been disposed to make one, would have needed to be ready to adjust itself: this being so, why not make the adjustments in advance?

It was a policy that worked well for Johnson during his long and extremely successful career in Hollywood (he eventually became his own producer and director), and he pursued it with a relaxed stylishness that marked him out from the hustlers and go-getters with whom he had to deal. "Nunnally rendered himself no threat to anybody," wrote Alistair Cooke, "by adopting, as a second nature, the air of a bewildered mouse in a world of tigers and jaguars." When pressed, Johnson would say that the screenwriter's craft was on a level maybe with that of a good cabinetmaker, and he was always ready to downplay the "message" potential of his films. On one occasion, he wrote to the critic Walter Kerr, praising him for having understood "what I was trying to say" in a movie called *Along Came Jones:*

> Almost without exception, the critics took it to be simply another account of some people trying to shoot the ass off Gary Cooper. Actually, as you saw at once, I was again using the cold, unflinching eye of the camera to probe a sick society.

On another occasion, Johnson wrote to George S. Kaufman about the forthcoming *Letter to an Unknown Woman* (written by Howard Koch, a writer who almost always had a message). The picture, Johnson says,

> is about a girl who falls in love with another of those God damned pianists (CLOSE UP of fingers on keyboard sort of fellow) and nuzzles around him until, finally, what the hell, he gives her a bang. Next week he goes to Milano to play a concert and that's the last she sees of him—for ten years. By then she has a nine year old boy that looks like the pianist and she is married to another fellow, no musician, but what does she do now but go for this piano player again. And to her horror, what do you think? He doesn't remember her! Right in the middle of this nuzzling, it dawns on her that he doesn't know who the hell she is and, frankly, doesn't seem to care so long as she gets those clothes off in a hurry. So out into the snow she runs and that's the way the thing straggles to its tragic conclusion.

In case the film becomes a hit, Johnson has taken the precaution of preparing a sequel. This, he claims, will be an altogether bigger affair than the original:

> It's called *Collected Correspondence of an Unknown Woman* and instead of one incident I have something like a dozen. In other words, the piano player knocks her up regularly every five years and never DOES recognize her. Every semi-decade around she comes again, with another new kid tagging on behind, and every time he throws her on the bed and marks up another score. Once or twice he says "Your face certainly does look familiar to me" but that's all. Of course she does everything she can think of to get out of him some further recognition than that, but nothing doing. Even when she lines up eight children behind her, every one of them the spitting image of him, all he says is: "Jesus Christ, have we got to have that mob around while we're doing it?" Finally, and this is the fade out, he's a real old bastard, can't hardly play Chop-sticks, much less cross-handed stuff, and around comes this old bag again, a dozen little illegitimates trailing along behind, and nuz-zles up feebly, still hopeful but much too proud to tip him off who she is, and after some heavy preliminary work, he manages to ring the bell again, possibly for the last time in his life, and as he is leaving the house and putting his hat on, we go to a CLOSE SHOT of him and he shakes his head and quavers, "I don't care what ANYBODY says, I've seen that broad somewhere before!" FADE OUT[22]

This was the Hecht-Mankiewicz, sub-Algonquin school of Holly-wood humor, but with a gentler edge. After his first Hollywood sortie in 1926, Johnson had been happy to get back to his journalism and short story writing, but he took a modest view of his own talent; he was not itching to write a major novel, but he did have a fund of back-home anecdotes that he enjoyed turning into stories. Born in Columbus, Georgia, in 1897, Johnson had been a reporter on the *Savannah Press* before joining the army during World War I. A corporal in his regiment (Johnson was a lieutenant) gave him a contact on the *New York Herald Tribune,* and when the war ended he served a brief stint on that paper before joining the *Brooklyn Daily Eagle* as a "light-hearted" columnist. This led to his recruit-ment by Herman Mankiewicz for his celebrated Paramount "Fresh Air Fund for Reporters."

After that first, six-week brush with Hollywood, Johnson changed
newspapers again and during the late twenties became moderately
well known as the "Around the Town" columnist for the *New York
Evening Post* and as a story writer for the *Smart Set* and then the
Saturday Evening Post. In 1931, he published a collection of short
stories called *There Ought to be a Law*. At first, the *Saturday Evening Post* outlet was hospitable enough for Johnson to believe that
he could live quite well on his short story earnings. He sold the
magazine dozens of lightweight but well-crafted items about small-
town life down South and was being paid one thousand dollars for
each of them; there was a tale circulating among the envious that
Johnson had never had a rejection from the *Post*.

In 1932, though, the magazine was forced to cut its size, from 210
to 102 pages, and its fees also were slashed, plummeting to less than
four hundred dollars for a story. Meanwhile, as Johnson has observed, the competition was getting more intense: he was up against
some "fast company," in the shape of Ring Lardner, Sr., Scott Fitzgerald, J. P. Marquand, and other then popular, prestigious names.
By mid-1932, his own "personal market" had shrunk by 75 percent.
It was at this point that Merritt Hulberd, a former *Post* editor and
now in charge of the story department at Paramount, invited Johnson to make a second trip to Hollywood.

Johnson joined Paramount as a junior writer at three hundred
dollars a week and was put to work on the assembly line under
producers who put their own names on the scripts they supervised,
or who insisted that their movies had at least one barbershop sequence so as to make use of an existing set, or who doled out drama-
tis personae, one each to a team of five writers—the writer was then
instructed to supply "his" character with lines of dialogue but to
avoid consultation with other members of the team: the idea, so far
as anybody understood it, was that the producer would "assemble"
the five contributions, jigsaw style, into a final script. On this last
assignment, Johnson considered himself fortunate to be given "a
sailor with a parrot": at least *his* character had someone to talk to.

All this was comically absurd, but Johnson was fairly sure that he
would soon be moving on. In the six years since his last exposure to
Hollywood, he had been doing some homework on the techniques
of screenwriting. His first wife has recalled:

Nunnally had been studying pictures for several years. We had
gone to many. When I was caught up in the story, the romance,

with tears, with fear, Nunnally was studying exits, entrances, build-up, story-climax, hurdles, interruptions, let-downs, false motivations.[23]

One of Johnson's more important first assignments with Paramount was to work with Arthur Kober (Mr. Lillian Hellman at the time) on a B picture called *Mama Loves Papa.* Johnson was assigned to the dialogue, and Kober was in charge of continuity. According to Johnson, this meant that Kober "every now and then wrote 'Cut,' 'Fade in' or 'Fade out' or something like that." When, having taken note of this imbalance, Johnson discovered that Kober was being paid more than he was, his effort on the homework was redoubled.

Mama Loves Papa, a Charles Ruggles vehicle, turned out to be a remarkable success for a low-budget picture—"audiences savored each witty line and plot twist"—and Johnson was no longer anonymous. Darryl Zanuck had by now left Warners to run 20th Century Pictures (a production company housed with United Artists), and Johnson was one of his earliest recruits. Johnson's first task under Zanuck was to inject some "elegance" into a comedy-suspense script called *Bulldog Drummond Strikes Back,* and he seems to have enjoyed the challenge: later on, he would name *Bulldog* as his favorite screenplay. In the same year, Zanuck handed him a somewhat less enticing subject: *The House of Rothschild,* planned as one of a series of great-figures-in-history pix of the sort that Warners had released with some success during Zanuck's reign there: *Alexander Hamilton* (1931), *Voltaire* (1933), etc. George Arliss, who had been known as Warners' "house impersonator," was lined up to play the starring role of Nathan Rothschild.

The House of Rothschild was Zanuck's most successful film during his first year as an independent, and Johnson's screenplay was voted one of 1934's "six best" by the Screen Writers Guild. Johnson was pleased—a solo credit of this caliber immediately propelled him to a higher pay bracket—but he couldn't understand why Zanuck had assigned him to the picture in the first place ("my characters are liable to fall into flour barrels and such things. I write kind of low comedy"), and he certainly did not expect a movie about the heroism of bankers to make much headway during the worst year of the Depression. Nonetheless, and with a straight face, Johnson arranged for a twinkling but steel-willed Nathan Rothschild to rescue Europe from Napoleon by sheer force of accumulated funds. And he does not mean us to laugh when he has Metternich and Talleyrand come knocking on the door of Rothschild's ghetto birthplace to ask if he could perhaps see his way to sparing a few million for the war effort. In the film's big "story-climax," the British stock exchange is about to collapse; Nathan has been single-handedly keeping it open, but now even he is beginning to feel the pinch. Just in time, he receives word—by carrier pigeon—that Wellington has won the day at Waterloo. Cheers and pandemonium break out on all sides, but Nathan stays cool, ruminatively fingering his lucky boutonniere—he had left it at home by mistake, but Mrs. Rothschild had sent it after him (not by pigeon), with a message to the effect that, rich or poor, stock exchange or no stock exchange, her love would never die.

The junior love interest is also unblushingly contrived: Wellington's Gentile ADC falls in love with Nathan's blond, headstrong daughter. Nathan opposes the match, having just suffered the anti-Semitic lash at a meeting of top bankers. A scene in which Johnson has Nathan arguing against the marriage on the grounds that so many Gentiles "have that terrible grasping spirit . . . All they ever think of is money, money, money" is somehow missing from at least one print of the film in current circulation.

The film's most solemn and most admirable scenes are those set in the Rothschilds' "Prussian" ghetto at the end of the eighteenth century, with old Amschel Rothschild educating his five sons on how to prosper in a racist Europe. For the Rothschilds, he says, money is "the only weapon the Jew has to defend himself"; it gives him the power to insist that his people are free to "trade with dignity, to live with dignity, to walk in the world with dignity." Cut to: thirty years later—a montage of Rothschild brass plates on the fronts of deluxe buildings in London, Paris, Rome. Cut to: Nathan, grown up but with his top hat the wrong way round—human dimension still thoroughly intact. Darryl Zanuck, Hollywood's one non-Jewish mogul, wanted his 1934 audience to take note of Hitler's rise to power. *The House of Rothschild* now stands as a lone, rather eccentric-looking effort to respond to a subject that the rest of Hollywood would soon be making great efforts to ignore.

For all its absurdities, Johnson's script for *The House of Rothschild* is constructed with considerable skill, so that floating a loan is made to seem a heroic, suspenseful undertaking: a shoot-out, really, with the virtuous little guy pitted against a gang of big-league international financiers. This fantasy might have carried a special excitement for Darryl Zanuck in 1934. He was himself on the brink of pulling off a megadeal that would amalgamate his small, twelve-pictures-a-year operation and the giant Fox, still a major Hollywood power, with (in Zanuck's view) "the best distributing organization in the world." As Zanuck's biographer describes it, the deal was pushed through with a zeal that would have warmed the heart of Nathan Rothschild:

> The net worth of Fox was $36 million, the net worth of Twentieth only $4 million, but the earning power of the respective companies was $1.8 million and $1.7 million. Twentieth received only 130,000 shares of preferred stock, which would earn about $200,000 a year, but half of the common stock. Fox had not really swallowed Twentieth. As it developed, it was really the other way around. Significantly enough, when it came time to discuss the name of the new combined organization, the Fox forces wanted Fox–Twentieth Century, and recalls Zanuck: "I insisted on Twentieth Century–Fox."[24]

After the triumph of *The House of Rothschild* and with Zanuck installed as head of a new empire, he and Nunnally Johnson seem to have become dazed with mutual admiration. Zanuck speaks of Johnson as "a Rock of Gibraltar. If he thought something stank, it stank," and Johnson says of Zanuck: "If he'd asked me to jump off the bridge for him I'd have done it." Johnson admired Zanuck's skills as a story editor, and Zanuck, in turn, valued Johnson's unfussy professionalism:

> Zanuck was, you might say, happy as a lark with me. He saw he had to get thirty or forty pictures a year and he delegated authority in a way, but he kept a tight rein on everybody. . . . To be able to make thirty pictures, he must have about ninety sets of people engaged on this script or that script. So, better or worse, he liked me, because he'd hand me the stuff, and he didn't have to see me again for ten or twelve weeks. He didn't have to bother about that at all.[25]

This close relationship with Zanuck meant that Johnson could afford to distance himself from the directors of his scripts. Indeed, more than once he let it be known that in his view the director's role was seriously overrated. He believed that a "well-executed, literate screenplay lies at the heart of any good movie" and that

> The director deserves little more credit than, say, the engineer who brings the Twentieth Century Limited from Chicago to New York. There's very little he can do except stay on the track and come into New York. He didn't create the track. He has no choice about which way he was going.[26]

When Johnson was quoted in *Time* as having said of director Stuart Heisler that his "chief contribution [to *Along Came Jones*] seemed to be that he kept the actors from going home before six o' clock," Mervyn LeRoy proposed a resolution at the Screen Directors Guild that no director should ever work with Johnson again. Johnson claimed that he had been misquoted. When Johnson himself was given the chance to direct his own films, Henry Hathaway warned him that he would be no good at it because he was "not a bastard. Look at the big directors, all of them bastards, John Ford, George Stevens, Fritz Lang, Willie Wyler." Johnson, Hathaway believed, would "compromise." Johnson more or less agreed: "I don't think it matters enough," he said, "and besides, I'm not that dedicated. I'm not going to spend my life arguing with people when I don't think it makes that much difference."[27]

Paradoxically, it was this intelligent and detached *placing* of his craft, this seeing it for what it was, that enabled Johnson to amble up the Hollywood ladder as he did. By 1940, he was able to pick his subjects in a way that even John Ford, when under contract, was not able to. Under Zanuck's patronage, Johnson progressed to associate producer, then producer, and in the end he was in a position to produce, direct, and write films of his choice. When his friend Harold Ross of *The New Yorker* upbraided him for wasting his gifts "sucking around the diamond merchants of Hollywood," Johnson could afford to smile. As he saw it, the lightweight, craftsmanlike, commercial sort of writing that Hollywood required just happened to be the sort of writing he was good at. And being good at something mattered to him, just enough; in the end, his own cabinetmaking analogy seems well chosen.

Johnson was admired in Hollywood for his equable approach to the local jaguars and tigers, but he was essentially loyal to his paymasters: he didn't mind people chuckling about Tinseltown, but he could get ruffled when he heard it denounced as a cultural disease. For example, he readily waxed indignant when it was said that the movies had destroyed F. Scott Fitzgerald. Johnson liked Fitzgerald well enough (the novelist had once told *him*: "Listen, Nunnally, get out of Hollywood. It will ruin you. You have a talent—you'll kill it here"), but he believed him to be "next to useless" as a screenwriter:

> [Fitzgerald] was immensely proud of a script he did from his short story "Babylon Revisited," one of the very best he or any other American short story writer ever wrote, but I read it a few years ago and to me it is unusable. To me he managed to destroy every vestige of all the fineness in his own story. He had padded it out with junk and nonsense and corn to an unbelievable extent.[28]

Johnson said this in 1952, just after the appearance of the Andrew Turnbull biography of Fitzgerald, in which Hollywood—and Joe Mankiewicz in particular—is represented as a destructive villain. According to Johnson, Fitzgerald's "failure here was no miscarriage of justice."

In his long career in Hollywood (about forty years), Johnson was involved in the writing of some fifty movies. Of these, only two were original screenplays. One of the two, *Prisoner on Shark Island,* was the story of a persecuted Southerner (Dr. Samuel A. Mudd, the physician who—unknowingly—treated the injured John Wilkes Booth after he shot Lincoln), and the other was in praise of *Jesse James*—another Southerner, who, according to this version, stood out in defense of the small farmer against the railroad shysters who were trying to steal his land. Both men, Mudd and James, were victimized, displaced, reviled—but each of them was portrayed as a more than competent professional, pretty good at what he did. The speech Johnson gives to Major Cobb, in homage to the murdered Jesse James, says plenty about Johnson and his hero, Darryl Zanuck, and it also has in it just a trace of self-esteem:

> There ain't no question about it. Jesse was an outlaw, a bandit, a criminal. Even those that loved him ain't got no answer for that. . . .
> I don't know why, but I don't think even America is ashamed

of Jesse James. Maybe it was because he was bold and lawless like we, all of us, like to be sometimes. Maybe it's because we understand a little that he wasn't altogether to blame for what his times made him. Maybe it's because for five years he licked the tar out of five states. Or maybe it's because he was so good at what he was doing. I don't know.

10

"Are you Mr. Johnson?"

"I am. Are you Mr. Faulkner?"

"I am."

There was an awkward silence. During this silence, Faulkner fished into his hip pocket, took out a pint of whiskey and began uncorking it. This act was complicated by the fact that the bottle had been sealed with heavy tinfoil. Bill dropped his hat on the floor and went to work with both hands. In the process, he cut his finger on the tinfoil. He attempted to staunch the flow of blood by wetting the wound with his tongue, but it was too deep a cut for that. Next, he looked around for a suitable drip pan. The only thing in sight was the hat at his feet. Holding the bleeding finger over the hat, he continued to work, methodically and silently, until the bottle was finally uncorked. He then tilted it, drank half its contents, and passed it to Johnson.

"Have a drink of whiskey?" he offered.

"I don't mind if I do," said Johnson, finishing off the pint.

This, according to the legend, was the beginning of a drunk which ended three weeks later, when studio sleuths found both Faulkner and Johnson in an Okie camp, sobered them up, and got them to work.[1]

Do we believe this? Almost certainly not. Most Hollywood "legends" were the work of screenwriters trained in the manufacture of big scenes: the two taciturn Southern gentlemen bonded by the bottle, the blood dripping into the hat, the half pint knocked back in a few swallows, the three weeks (three *weeks*) in an Okie camp, the "studio sleuths" whose mission it was to track down recalcitrant employees, and so on. And all this—at around three thousand a week—to launch the writing of a film for Darryl Zanuck?

Maybe because he didn't say much or because not many people understood him when he did decide to speak, William Faulkner is at the center of quite a few well-known filmland anecdotes, each of them with a grain of truth but mostly adaptations or remakes. Consider the famous "working at home" story, which is so often taken as the perfect summing up of relations between writers and the movies. Faulkner's own version places it in 1932, during his first-ever year of Hollywood employment. He had worked for MGM for six weeks, been laid off and had just wired a "director friend," asking for another job:

> Shortly after that I received a letter from my Hollywood agent enclosing my first week's paycheck. I was surprised because I had expected first to get an official notice or recall and a contract from the studio. I thought to myself the contract is delayed and will arrive in the next mail. Instead, a week later I got another letter from the agent enclosing my second week's paycheck. That began in November 1932 and continued until May 1933. Then I received a telegram from the studio. It said: *William Faulkner, Oxford, Miss. Where are you? MGM Studio.*[2]

In fact, during November 1932 and May 1933, Faulkner was commuting between Hollywood and Oxford, working on a film version of one of his own stories. Howard Hawks, his "director friend," had persuaded MGM to allow Faulkner to do some of his work in Mississippi: Faulkner's father died in August 1932, and his affairs needed to be "straightened out." By May 1933, the Hawks project was completed, and the studio wanted Faulkner back in Hollywood full-time. When he refused (his wife was expecting a child in June), MGM politely wired him:

OWING TO NECESSITY BROWNING SCRIPT BEING COMPLETED HERE AT STUDIO AND YOUR INABILITY TO RETURN HERE I BELIEVE IT BEST WE RELIEVE YOU OF YOUR ASSIGNMENT STOP MANY THANKS FOR ALL YOU HAVE DONE STOP STUDIO FEELS THIS METHOD OF

WORKING IS NOT FEASIBLE CONSEQUENTLY WE WILL BE MOST
HAPPY TO CONTINUE YOU ON STAFF HERE AT ANY TIME YOU WILL
COME TO CALIFORNIA STOP I HAVE ASKED HOWARD HAWKS TO
WRITE YOU. . . .[3]

Faulkner, in a 1956 interview, pretended that the telegram was
addressed not to him but to Tod Browning, the director he was by
then supposed to be working with: "the telephone rang. It was
Browning. . . . He had a telegram. It said: *Faulkner is fired. MGM
Studio.*"[4]

Two years later, Faulkner was back in Hollywood, reporting for
duty (with his whiskey bottle) to the office of Nunnally Johnson at
20th Century–Fox. Darryl Zanuck's biographer reports:

> Zanuck hired Faulkner at Hawks' suggestion, set him up in a
> bungalow on the studio's writers' row. About five days later he
> walked into Zanuck's office, and announced, "I can't work in my
> office. It's driving me crazy. Would you mind if I worked at
> home?" Zanuck agreed. Faulkner left, and to Zanuck's amaze-
> ment went home to Oxford, Mississippi. "I thought home meant
> where he was living in Beverly Hills!" recalls Zanuck.[5]

In fact, having completed his first assignment, Faulkner was given
leave by the studio in January 1936, "temporarily due to illness."
Howard Hawks had asked him to stay sober during the writing of
the film. By January, the script was done and Faulkner had also
managed to complete (in his Beverly Hills hotel room) the manu-
script of *Absalom, Absalom!* His celebrations had brought on the
temporary illness. By February, he was recovered and made his way
back to Hollywood—not all that reluctantly, it should be said, since
he had begun an affair with Hawks's secretary, Meta Carpenter.
After a five-week separation, he was "seized with a consuming sexual urgency" and for that spring remained thoroughly obsessed with
"my heart, my jasmine garden, my April and May cunt; my white
one, my blonde morning, winged, my sweetly dividing, my honey-
cloyed, my sweet-assed gal."[6]

But the "working at home" legend continued to gain ground. In
the 1940s, Faulkner was at Warner Brothers, where he worked with
Hawks on *The Big Sleep* and *To Have and Have Not.* In Jack
Warner's autobiography (published in 1965), we read:

Jerry Wald brought him to Burbank, and I gave him a sumptuous office with two attractive secretaries, and I said: "No one's going to bother you here, Mr. Faulkner. Your time will be your own."

"Thank you, Mr. Warner," he said, "but if it's all the same to you, I'd rather work at home."

"Now, we don't expect you to punch any clocks, Mr. Faulkner," I said. "You can come and go as you please."

"I would prefer *not* to work in an office," he said stubbornly.

Some weeks later, when something urgent arose in connection with the script, I asked Bill Schaefer to call Faulkner.

"You know he works at home," Bill said.

"Of course. Call him at home."

"This is long distance. We're ready on your call to Mr. Faulkner."

"Long distance?" I almost yelled.

"Yes, sir," the operator said. "He's in Oxford, Mississippi."

"Mr. Faulkner, how could you do this to me? How could you leave town without letting me know? You said you'd be working at home."

"This is my home," Faulkner said patiently, "I live in Mississippi."[7]

In December 1935, Faulkner would have been glad to suppress this legend, along with a few others. He was broke, he badly needed his contract with 20th Century–Fox; it was not at all in his interests to be portrayed as a misfit or a drunk. On the other hand, when he walked into Johnson's office his life *was* something of a mess: his younger brother had just been killed in a plane crash, his marriage was wretchedly unhappy, he was in debt to his publisher, and *Pylon*, his most recent book, had not done well. "I don't care how I get a contract," he had written, "just so I do." More than likely, he and Johnson did bury a few drinks. They may even have stayed up all night.

Faulkner had been hired by Fox to write a screenplay for *The Road to Glory*, a World War I romance conceived by the studio as a means of using up some war footage that Zanuck had purchased from the French. Nunnally Johnson would be the film's associate producer, and Howard Hawks would direct. It was Hawks who had suggested Faulkner, and Zanuck had agreed to pay the novelist a thousand dollars a week, a high rate of pay considering the status of the Faulkner legend at that time. Zanuck, it seems, had needed some persuading. Faulkner was already notorious in Hollywood for his epic drinking bouts and for his almost total lack of interest in the cinema. In addition to the "writing at home" business, several other stories had been spun out of his year at MGM in 1932–33. It was said that Faulkner had reported to the studio a week late, drunk, with a bleeding head wound, and had instantly made it clear to the story editor, Sam Marx, that he knew nothing of the movies: "Why don't I write newsreels for you? Newsreels and Mickey Mouse are the only movies I like." Marx had it in mind to assign Faulkner to a wrestling picture, called *Flesh,* with Wallace Beery in the lead. Faulkner claimed not to have heard of Beery, so Marx arranged a special screening of *The Champ.* After watching for a few minutes, Faulkner walked out—out of the projection room and out of the studio's main gate. A week later, given up for lost, Faulkner reappeared; he said he had been wandering around in Death Valley: "The truth is that I was scared. . . . I was scared by the hullabaloo over my arrival, and when they took me into a projection room to see a picture, and kept assuring me that it was going to be very easy, I got flustered."[8] The "Death Valley" story could well be the source of the "three weeks in an Okie camp" story of 1935; like the "writing at home" story, they are tales of truancy.

After Death Valley, Faulkner was rehired by MGM and set to work on various treatments. None of these reached the screen; indeed, an MGM reader described one of them as "an evil, slimy thing, absolutely unfit for screen production."[9] At the end of his six-week trial period (at five hundred dollars a week), he would certainly have been "given the air" had it not been for Howard Hawks, his "director friend." Hawks had bought the rights of Faulkner's story "Turn About," and he persuaded MGM that Faulkner ought to be given the task of adaptation. Far from sitting in Mississippi counting unearned checks, Faulkner seems to have applied himself with some resolve: in five days he prepared a draft screenplay, which so impressed Irving Thalberg that he told Hawks to "shoot it as it is" (the film was released under the title *Today We Live*).

Faulkner was back on contract until his dismissal in May 1933, still sneaking off to Mississippi when he could do so and still protesting that he knew nothing about writing for the screen. This know-nothing image was mostly fabricated, and Howard Hawks liked to help it along with a few stories of his own. Hawks is, for instance, the

source of another well-known Faulkner anecdote, the one that tells
of his meeting with Clark Gable. "Mr. Faulkner, do you write?"
asked Gable. "Yes, Mr. Gable, what do you do?" said Faulkner in
reply. Hawks wished to demonstrate that Gable never read books
and that Faulkner never watched movies. Scholarship now seems to
have established that Gable and Faulkner knew each other reasonably well and that the exchange, if it took place, was whimsical.[10]

Most of Faulkner's misfit-in-Hollywood stories date from his first
visit, which—with interruptions—lasted but a year. He had gone to
Hollywood because he could not live on earnings from his six novels—two thousand copies was his average sale. From MGM he took
about six thousand dollars, and he was well pleased. His only worry,
after his dismissal, was that he had not given value for money. He
had learned—he thought for good—that screenwriting "ain't my
racket" ("I can't see things . . . I can only hear"), but even so he
would have wished to "do an honest day's work according to what
the man said." In spite of the legend, Faulkner seems genuinely to
have done his best: for MGM, he worked on ten different projects
and turned in about six hundred pages of typescript.

But there had been binges and disappearances, and in twelve
months he had notched up merely one half-credit (on *Today We
Live*). After he'd gone, the Hollywood verdict pretty well tallied
with his own: pictures were just not his "racket." Howard Hawks
thought differently. The two men had become friends; they saw
themselves as "broken down aviators" and shared a love of drinking
and hunting. Most important of all, perhaps, was that each of them
had a younger brother who had been killed in a plane crash. Dean
Swift Faulkner had crashed in his own plane, bought for him by
brother Bill, just one month before Faulkner clocked in at 20th
Century–Fox. During that first-day binge with Nunnally Johnson, he
talked about his brother with remorse: after all, it was he who had
taught the kid to fly. Some of his Hollywood money would go to
supporting Dean's widow and child. Hawks's brother Kenneth had
died five years earlier, stunt flying for a film called *Such Men Are
Dangerous.* Damaged tough-guy buddies tend to appear in the films
Hawks and Faulkner made together. A cowriter of Faulkner's has
recalled:

> Howard Hawks was always trying to give Faulkner work. And
> Faulkner didn't do anything with Hawks, really. Bill's contribution

would be little bits here and there. But the continuity of a script, he couldn't do it. The screenplay form was alien to him. He was muscle-bound with his talent. He needed prose so he could run off with it.

He loved Hawks, though, got along with him very well. You know why? Because they could sit there together and not say anything. Commune in silence. Hawks would ask a question and they'd have a few drinks. Faulkner would be "thinking" and after a long while he'd finally nod his head and say "Uh-huh."[11]

Hawks, when asked to explain his professional attachment to Faulkner, would say pious things about the novelist's "inventiveness, taste and great ability to characterize and the visual imagination to translate these qualities into the medium of the screen," but now and then he would admit that the real reason for hiring Faulkner was that he liked "having him around." Nunnally Johnson's theory was that perhaps Hawks "simply wanted his name attached to Faulkner's. Or since Hawks liked to write it was easy to do it with Faulkner, for Bill didn't care much one way or the other."[12]

For Hawks the would-be writer there was never any question of surrendering narrative control, and it was his method, anyway, to do a lot of improvising on the set: having Faulkner around to throw in lines of dialogue or to suggest a way around some foul-up in the plot would have suited him perfectly. "Bill could fix a scene," he'd say. And it suited Faulkner too. He always liked to describe himself as a "script doctor" rather than a screenwriter: "When they run into a section they don't like I rework it and continue to rework it until they do like it." He was wont to end his screen treatments with flourishes like "Lana tells Mary whatever sappy stuff they need here about love conquers all things etc."

The Hawks working arrangements did not at all suit Darryl Zanuck, who liked to consult with his writers and then tell the director what to shoot. On *The Road to Glory,* Nunnally Johnson was meant to be the link between Zanuck in his office and Hawks-Faulkner on the set, and Zanuck covered himself further by installing a cowriter, Joel Sayre. This move was heartily welcomed by Faulkner—he and Sayre became good friends. In any event, Johnson himself ended up writing nearly all the dialogue, or so he said.

Actually, no one knows for certain who wrote what. There is

evidence that Faulkner worked hard on the screenplay in its early
stages, and perhaps a "Faulkner touch" might be discerned in the
character of the cognac-swilling, aspirin-crunching captain
("twisted . . . but not dead inside"), who loses his girl, his sight, and
then his life for the sake of nothing very much and who is saddled
the while with a garrulous, bugle-blowing father who, although evidently nudging sixty-five, refuses to be discharged from the army.
The best moment in the film comes right at the end, when Fredric
March, the captain's victorious rival in love, takes over command of
the regiment after the captain has been killed. March has the captain's girl, he has the captain's regiment, and now he delivers, word
for word, the captain's routine speech to a new intake of recruits,
just before leading them off to the front. As March concludes the
speech and turns away, we notice that he is knocking back a handful
of the captain's aspirins. More than likely, this ending came from
Hawks, with his noted fondness for "plot circularity," but perhaps
Faulkner mixed the cocktails.

To a professional like Nunnally Johnson, Faulkner's presence in
the studio was something of a joke—a Howard Hawks foible that had
to be put up with. But without Hawks, Faulkner was an expensive
luxury. After *The Road to Glory,* Hawks was anxious to get away
from Zanuck, but Faulkner stayed on and was put to work on *Slave
Ship, Splinter Fleet,* and, more promisingly, *Banjo on My Knee:* for
this Deep South item he composed several long speeches, but it
turned out that the performers couldn't speak them, and eventually
they were cut.

Faulkner's pay was also cut (to $750 a week), and he was loaned
out to RKO to work on *Gunga Din.* At 20th Century–Fox he was
given credits on *Slave Ship* and *The Road to Glory,* bringing his
grand total up to three. Not that Faulkner cared much about that,
either; although this was 1936, he showed no interest in the doings
of the Screen Writers Guild. By 1937, he had had enough, and so had
his employers. Faulkner's affair with Meta Carpenter was over, or
so he believed. She had lost patience with his inability to break free
of his marriage and had herself got married—to a young concert
pianist who had been pursuing her for several months:

On her wedding day, [Faulkner] went on a nonstop binge . . . out
of control, spinning into an inner midnight of hallucination and

terror. He awoke in the Good Samaritan Hospital, suffering from an acute alcoholic condition. When he left in late April and returned to the studio, people talked about him: he was "skin and bones, and hardly recognizable." A colleague urged him to see a psychiatrist, but Faulkner refused. He distrusted psychiatrists even more than regular doctors. Outside his fiction, he didn't trust anyone.[13]

Three months later, 20th Century–Fox declined to take up an option on Faulkner's contract, and he returned to Oxford, drunk and depressed but certain that this time he really was finished with the movies. It seemed like a bonus when in 1938 he sold the screen rights of *The Unvanquished* to MGM for $25,000 (it appears that the MGM people were anxious to acquire an interest in the distribution of *Gone With the Wind,* which David Selznick owned, and—as a bargaining lever—were threatening a Deep South epic of their own).

For a couple of years after this, Faulkner was not too badly off. But his extended family was a considerable burden. He was "the sole, principal and partial support—food, shelter, heat, clothes, medicine, kotex, school fees, toilet paper and picture shows—of my mother, an inept brother, and his wife and two sons, another brother's widow and child, a wife of my own and two stepchildren, my own child," and he had also inherited his father's debts. He wrote this to Random House in 1940. The film money had run out, and the book money was not getting any better. In his good year of 1939, he had raised a six-thousand-dollar loan to help an old friend and to do this had had to borrow from Random House and sell his life insurance; "I have known him all my life . . . never any question of mine and thine between us when either had it." By 1941, he was writing again to Random House:

I have 60¢ in my pocket, and that is literally all. I finished a story and sent it in yesterday, but with no real hope it will sell. My local creditors bother me, but so far none has taken an action because I began last year to give them notes for debts. But the notes will come due soon and should I be sued, my whole house here will collapse: farm, property, everything. . . . I have reached the point where I had better go to Cal. with just r.r. fare if I can do no better.

He would take anything Hollywood had to offer, he said, anything above one hundred dollars a week: "Once I get away from here where creditors cannot hound me all the time, I think I can write and sell again."[14]

Another important factor in his thinking was that Meta Carpenter was back in Hollywood. Her marriage had failed: the concert pianist was not what he had seemed. Faulkner had been in touch with Meta over the years. They had met once in New Orleans and slept together, and he had been helping her with money. To him, the idea of reliving their spring of 1936 seems to have been irresistible. His own marriage, he said, had burned out long ago and his attempts to get himself a girlfriend (or, as he put it, "a physical spittoon") had not worked out. According to a recent biographer: "Faulkner needed Meta in the worst possible way. . . . His head swam with erotic thoughts."[15]

Without the Meta incentive, so to speak, Faulkner would still have been in a hurry to arrange a job in Hollywood. It is possible, though, that he might have paid more attention to the contractual negotiations. As things turned out, he allowed himself to be trapped into a dreadful deal: three hundred dollars a week from Warner Brothers. The contract had been signed on his behalf by a new, inexperienced agent who was somehow working at cross-purposes with Faulkner's usual representative. At first, Faulkner, believing that the arrangement was for thirteen weeks, was happy to accept. He then discovered that he had been signed up for an extraordinary *seven years*. He refused to sign, but the agent assured him that he was already committed: committed both to Warner Brothers and to paying the agent an annuity of fifteen hundred dollars. Faulkner signed.

Three hundred dollars a week was, of course, less than he had been getting from MGM ten years before: it marked him, at the age of forty-five, as one of the studio's most lowly hacks. And it was not as if Faulkner was generally held to be in decline. As Hollywood saw it, his books may not have reached the bestseller lists, but his face had been on the cover of *Time* magazine. Jack Warner later boasted that he had bought America's best living novelist "for peanuts," and friends of Faulkner believed that something punitive was in the air: as if Hollywood was making him suffer for that "legend." The work-at-home genius who despised the movies was now a seven-year Warner Brothers property, a bargain.

Another view was that "he'd been drunk so often that no producer would look at him," and certainly there were no signs of Faulkner easing up in that department. His day-to-day off-duty life in Hollywood was fairly grim. Meta had wanted him to live with her, but he wouldn't. He was anxious to preserve, he said, "The mystery of each other, mainly mine for you, if I have any." This meant that when he wasn't seeing her, he did a lot of hanging out in bars and cheap hotels. The Faulkner-drunk stories were no longer told for laughs or for the legend. For a time, he moved in with one of his Warners writer colleagues, A. I. ("Buzz") Bezzerides (later to be canonized by French cineastes on account of his screenplay for *Kiss Me Deadly* but in the 1940s known mainly for two "trucker" novels—bought, also for peanuts, by Warners and filmed as *Thieves' Highway* and *They Drive by Night*). Bezzerides has recalled:

> I'm at Warner Bros. and I'd been there a few months when who do I see coming down the aisle between the secretaries but Faulkner. He had a pipe in his mouth and he had a way of walking leaning backwards. Well, I see him and he sees me. I say, "Do you remember me?" He says, "Yes, suh, I do. What are you doing here?" I said, "I'm a writer." (Laughs) I said, "What are you going here?" And he said, "Uh, I'm a writer, too."
>
> We talked. I asked him where he was staying. He was living at a hotel. He was going to catch a cab home and I said I'd take him home. And then we went to the endless places where he went to get drunk. And he could get *drunk*, man. I had to take him to the hospital, to dry out. Then I'd take him home, and he'd be very shaky. . . . He was making $300 a week and he was starving on it. He was sending the money home. That was one of the reasons why he stayed with me.[16]

As to Faulkner's work for Warners, Bezzerides believed that, essentially, "He had contempt for it. Get the paycheck that's all. Sometimes he'd think he would do it for the art. He wanted to do *Pickwick Papers*. And he wrote *The De Gaulle Story*, at 400 pages. And that was a bunch of shit." Bezzerides goes on to describe a more routine assignment:

> Faulkner and I were put together on a script at Warners, to polish a picture called *Escape in the Desert*. We sat in the office and sat

and sat and sat. I didn't want to start writing for fear of embarrassing him. I wanted him to start and then we could pitch in together.
But he didn't say a word. Finally, I got exasperated and I said:
"Hey Bill, we got to write!" And he turned and looked at me and
said, "Shucks, Buzz, it ain't nuthin' but a *movin' picture.*" So,
screw him, I decided to start trying to write. And I started and
finally he began to think of things. There was a scene in there
where the Nazis are in the desert and he thought of a bit where
a rattlesnake jumps out and frightens them. That was Faulkner's
scene. And Warner read it and didn't want to shoot the scene. He
said it would frighten pregnant women and give them spontane-
ous abortions. I said to Warner, "If you can guarantee *that,* you'll
have a big hit." Jack didn't get it. He said, "No, no, they'll sue us."[17]

The De Gaulle Story was never made and may well have been a
"bunch of shit," but Faulkner took it seriously for a time as a possible
contribution to the war effort. He had tried to join the air corps in
the spring of 1942 but had been turned down, and this rankled. One
way of dignifying his situation in Hollywood might be to find in it
some propagandist usefulness. Tom Dardis has quoted a speech
from *The De Gaulle Story* as evidence that Faulkner put at least
something of himself into this screenplay. The speaker is a French
resistance worker who is "trying to talk her lover into joining the
Underground." The Nazis, she tells him, are not invulnerable:

> it's like those little ants in the jungle that nothing can stand
> against—not the biggest and fiercest and the most powerful—
> nothing. You can kill them by the millions just by stepping on
> them, but they keep coming because they are so little. That's the
> mistake they made. They tried to force the little people. And
> there are too many little people. There are so many of them
> because they are small. All they have to threaten us with is
> death. And little people are not afraid to die. The little people
> and the very great. Because there is something of the little peo-
> ple in the very great. . . .

Dardis comments: "This passage shows pretty clearly what Faulkner
would do as a screenwriter when left entirely on his own: he simply
wrote as the novelist he actually was. What he wrote was often very
good, even wonderful, but this dialogue is really close to a form of
incantation, and although it might work in a film of the seventies,

it was quite impossible in the Hollywood of the thirties and forties."[18] Well, was it? Surely it could be argued that in this speech (which apparently goes on for two full pages) Faulkner was aiming not for originality but for conformity. Lengthy harangues on the subject of "the little people" were the stock-in-trade of the hugely successful screen parables of Frank Capra and his two top writers at Columbia, Sidney Buchman and Robert Riskin. In *Mr. Smith Goes to Washington,* it is insisted ad nauseam that "there is something of the little people in the very great," and in 1941 this same populist sentimentalism was given a war-preparation slant in *Meet John Doe*—with a script by Riskin, a $2,500-a-week man whose performances Faulkner might well have noted with some care. Doe tells the mob:

> I know a lot of you are saying, What can I do, I'm just a little punk, I don't count. Well, you're dead wrong. The little punks have always counted because in the long run the character of a country is the sum total of its little punks. But we've all got to get in there and pitch. We can't win the old ball-game unless we have team-work, and that's where every John Doe comes in. . . .

And so it goes on. Perhaps Faulkner's error was in seeing his little people as ants rather than as backyard baseball players. Robert Riskin's personal letters (recently quoted by his widow Fay Wray in her autobiography) make it clear that he actually *meant* the things he made his film characters say to one another. Writing home from London during the Blitz, Riskin says:

> the moment the siren started, I was no longer alone . . . thousands . . . millions of other hearts stirred simultaneously . . . skipped a beat just as mine skipped. At that moment, they were in the room with me . . . and I was with them . . . in a million homes . . . in a million cellars. At times like that, no matter how impoverished you might feel . . . in worldly goods or in the spirit . . . you are lifted to a level of equality with the most blessed of human beings . . . all are one . . . of which you are an equal part.[19]

As in a Capra movie, the "preachment" is completely genuine. With this kind of competition, Faulkner in Hollywood really didn't stand much of a chance.

Even so, when Howard Hawks interrupted Faulkner's work on

The De Gaulle Story to recruit him for a big Warners propaganda film called *Air Force,* the novelist was pleased. Hawks's morale-builder had War Department cooperation, it was almost "official," and although Faulkner would later sneer at "the frantic striving of motion pictures to justify their existence in a time of strife and terror," he was caught up in Hawks's enthusiasm for the project: the broken-down aviator having his say on the matter of Pearl Harbor. The script for *Air Force* had been written by Dudley Nichols, but Hawks wanted some rewrites on a deathbed scene. Nichols, it seems, had been up to his transfiguration tricks again and had made the dying of Captain Quincannon too wordily protracted. In Faulkner's abbreviated version, Quincannon's last thoughts are for the *Mary Ann,* the broken-down bomber plane that is the true hero of the film:

292B: CLOSE SHOT: WHITE
his face contorted with repressed anguish

QUINCANNON (imperatively, as White is silent): Tell me, Robbie, what's wrong with her?

WHITE: Props. Gear. One wing tip. That's all.

292C: GROUP SHOT
Quincannon very feeble but agitated, his eyes wide open now.

QUINCANNON: That's all. Just a wing gone. Gone.

WHITE (in protest): No, I tell you. Just a tip. What's a wing tip? Just a couple of days.

QUINCANNON (blurrily): Two days?

WHITE: Yes, sir. *Sure.* (Looks around at the others; then, emphatically) Two days!

QUINCANNON (feebly; with a kind of panic): Wait a minute . . . don't go . . . don't go . . . wait for me, fellows.

His fingers relax and the toy rattles to the floor as his whole excited body relaxes and his eyes close. The doctor steps in quickly and stoops over him, masking his face from camera. None of the men moves but there is an agony of questioning in their faces as they watch the doctor.

WHITE (choking): Doctor!

The doctor straightens up, still masking Quincannon's face from camera, and lays Quincannon's limp arms across his chest without replying to White. The big guns go on thudding as we

FADE OUT[20]

Air Force was a triumph, both commercially and with the critics. Dudley Nichols won an Oscar nomination for his screenplay, and Faulkner's stock moved up a notch or two. People knew that he had had "something" to do with the writing of this winner, so it was relatively easy for Hawks to arrange for him to work on his next war epic, to be titled *Battle Cry*. Faulkner had high hopes for *Battle Cry* and was even heard to speak of it with some fervor as an important piece of war work. He hoped also that if *Battle Cry* was a success, Warners would at least modify his contract: they had already raised his paycheck to four hundred dollars. There was even a plan for him to set up with Hawks as a free lance—a plan that might well have made him rich. But *Battle Cry* was never produced: the studio refused to sanction Hawks's giant budget. For Faulkner, it was back to the assembly line.

During 1943, Faulkner worked on two other "properties" that failed to reach the screen: *Country Lawyer* (racial and other tensions in small-town Mississippi) and *Life and Death of a Bomber*, a war picture, which Faulkner, in his treatment, divided into three big sequences: "It Is Going to Be Too Late"; "It Is Too Late"; "It Was Too Late." Bruce F. Kawin, the leading authority on Faulkner's film work, has said that the treatment, an original, was directly inspired by *Air Force* and was Faulkner's "own vision of the war," built around "the history of a single plane":

> *The Life and Death of a Bomber* follows its plane from factory to combat, and emphasizes the conflict between the self-sacrificing attitude taken by American workers and soldiers, and the undermining of their efforts by greedy corporate management. The bomber, constructed improperly to save money, becomes the symbol of a value-system that must be reexamined if America is to succeed in not only a military but also a cultural sense. This treatment was, of course, not approved for expansion or production.[21]

Again, though, it was Hawks to the rescue. In February 1944, he asked Faulkner to help him revise Jules Furthman's adaptation of Hemingway's *To Have or Have Not*. The Furthman script was already a travesty of the book, so Hawks was exaggerating when he said that "Faulkner enjoyed changing Hemingway's material because it was Hemingway's." *To Have or Have Not* was conceived as a follow-up to *Casablanca*, Warners' big hit of 1943, and it lifts many

bits and pieces from that model, but most people now think of it as
the movie that sparked off the Bacall-Bogart romance—and, praise
be, sparked it off on camera. When Faulkner joined the team, Hawks
was in something of a panic. The Furthman screenplay, like the
Hemingway novel, was set in Cuba, and Jack Warner had received
strenuous objections from the Office of the Coordinator of Inter-
American Affairs: Batista must not be embarrassed; the Cuban setting had to go. Faulkner, it seems, suggested changing it to Mar-
tinique, a French territory, because this would give him scope to
make use of some of the anti-Vichy material he had worked up for
The De Gaulle Story. Faulkner started writing on February 22 and
Hawks started shooting on March 1. "Since then," Faulkner said, "I
have been trying to keep ahead of him with a day's script. I should
be through about May 10–15." According to Humphrey Bogart, the
script more or less evolved, with Faulkner toiling away in Hawks's
office (sometimes only one page ahead of the action) and then a
combination of Faulkner, Hawks, and Bogart "devising new scenes,
dialogue and gags as they went along, on the set." Faulkner is now
given credit for a general tightening and reshuffling of Furthman's
script and for throwing in a few misogynistic touches of his own, but
he probably had little to do with the remarkably likable flavor of the
finished film—this was all to do with Hawks and his relationship with
his performers. But then, so far as Faulkner was concerned, the film
was nothing special. Howard Hawks was simply "making a picture
at our shop. As usual, he had a script, threw it away and asked for
me."[22]

For the next six months of 1944, Faulkner returned to the usual
studio hackwork, writing treatments for *God Is My Co-Pilot* and *The
Damned Don't Cry,* revising a screen version of *The Adventures of
Don Juan,* tinkering with a projected remake of *The Amazing Dr.
Clitterhouse,* introducing the rattlesnake into *Escape in the Desert,*
and polishing dialogue in Nunnally Johnson's script for Jean Renoir's
The Southerner. He also had a hand in revising the endlessly revised
script of *Mildred Pierce,* although here Faulkner's input has been
faulted for its obsession with "the contractual arrangements" involved in the setting up of Mildred's restaurant; his "only other
significant contribution seems to be in casting Lottie, Mildred's
maid, as a black woman."

The next summons from Howard Hawks came in September: he
wanted Faulkner to work on a film adaptation of *The Big Sleep,*

Raymond Chandler's first novel, written when he was fifty. It was an unusual assignment for Faulkner. For once he was in at the beginning of the scripting process, and for once he had a collaborator whose salary was lower than his. Leigh Brackett had written a thriller called *No Good from a Corpse* and a "ten-day wonder at Republic"—*The Vampire's Ghost* was the title, "and very horrible it was." Aged twenty-nine, she was brought in by Hawks to write tough dialogue for Bogart, who nicknamed her Butch:

> I went to work in a daze. A great Chandler fan, a great Bogart fan . . . I couldn't believe it. All this, plus one hundred and twenty five separate and distinct dollars per week, all the money in the world even with take-outs. I'd have done it for nothing.
>
> And there was William Faulkner. *The* William Faulkner. How was I, a nowhere writer with four years of pulp behind me, going to collaborate with him?
>
> I needn't have worried. The morning I checked in, Mr. Faulkner, immaculate in country tweeds, greeted me courteously, handed me a copy of the book and said, "We will do alternate sets of chapters. I have them marked. I will do these, you will do those."[23]

And so it was: she had no further dealings with Faulkner on the script. Some of Faulkner's nastier scenes for *The Big Sleep* were cut, by the Hays Office or by Hawks, and neither Faulkner nor anybody else could work out who killed the Sternwoods' chauffeur (when Chandler was consulted, he answered: "I don't know"). In the end, Jules Furthman was brought in for a rewrite, and he supplied some of the wittiest Bogart-Bacall exchanges. After a bit, Faulkner simply wanted to be finished. He had a new arrangement with Warners that permitted him six months leave (unpaid) each year, and he had begun work on *A Fable*, an overambitious novel that had at first been thought of as a screenplay. In December 1944, still jotting down notes for *The Big Sleep*, he caught the train for Oxford. From home, he sent the studio a memo:

> The following rewritten and additional scenes for *The Big Sleep* were done by the author in respectful joy and happy admiration after he had gone off salary and while on his way back to Mississippi. With grateful thanks to the studio for the cheerful and

crowded day coach which alone saved him from wasting his time in dull and profitless rest and sleep. With love, William Faulkner.[24]

Faulkner was not yet free of Hollywood. Six months later, he was back again, working with Bezzerides on a version of his own "Barn Burning" and completing a screenplay based on the novel *Stallion Road,* by Stephen Longstreet—the only other Warners writer Faulkner could actively get along with. But by the summer of 1945, he was writing about Hollywood with a new resentment, edgier and more venomous. He was sick of California—"one day one leaf falls in a damn canyon up there and they tell you it's winter"—and the studio drudgery was even harder to return to now that he was half free of it:

> I think I have had about all of Hollywood I can stand. I feel bad, depressed, dreadful sense of wasting time. I imagine most of the symptoms of blow-up or collapse. I may be able to come back later but I think I will finish this present job and return home. Feeling as I do, I am actually afraid to stay here much longer.[25]

The relationship with Meta Carpenter had reached another impasse; soon she would remarry the piano player—again unhappily. After his 1945 stint was completed, Faulkner wrote a letter to Jack Warner, more or less begging to be let off the remainder of his contract:

> Dear Colonel Warner,
>   . . . I still feel that I should not . . . commit myself further to studio work, and that if possible I should sever all my existing studio commitments. . . .
>   I feel that I have made a bust at moving picture writing and therefore have mis-spent and will continue to mis-spend time which at my age I cannot afford. During my three years (including leave-suspensions) at Warners, I did the best work I knew how on 5 or 6 scripts. Only two were made and I feel that I received credit on these not on the value of the work I did but partly through the friendship of Director Howard Hawks. So I have spent three weeks doing work (trying to do it) which was not my forte and which I was not equipped to do, and therefore I have mis-spent time which as a 47 year old novelist I could not afford to spend.

And I don't dare mis-spend any more of it.

For that reason, I am unhappy in studio work. Not at Warner's studio; my connection with the studio and all the people I worked with could not have been pleasanter. But with the type of work. So I repeat my request that the studio release me from my contract. . . .

Waiting to hear from you, I am
Yours sincerely,
William Faulkner [26]

Colonel Warner handed this letter to the studio's legal department, which at once wrote to remind Faulkner that under the terms of his contract, *all* his writing was the property of Warner Brothers. In other words, the novel he was writing actually belonged to them. Bad things would happen to him if he tried to sell his work to anybody else—to his publisher, for instance. It took a few months for Random House and Harold Ober (Faulkner's New York agent) to persuade Warners that even worse things might happen to them if they insisted on pursuing this extraordinary line. The studio backed off. Faulkner was never officially released from his contract, but it was allowed quietly to lapse—on the vague understanding that when his novel was completed, he would come back of his own accord.

And so he did—sort of. Eight years later, as a favor to Howard Hawks, the Nobel Prize winner agreed to serve time on an Egyptian epic called *Land of the Pharaohs*. Puzzling over the question of "how a pharaoh talks," Faulkner asked Hawks: "Is it all right if I write him like a Kentucky colonel?" Hawks told him to go ahead, it didn't really matter, since the whole thing would surely be rewritten on the set.

11

In September 1941, a Senate subcommittee was convened to investigate the motion picture industry's alleged dissemination of "propaganda for war," its "premature interventionism." The committee, headed by Senator Gerald P. Nye, was abandoned three months later, with the Japanese attack on Pearl Harbor, but in any case, things had been going rather badly from Nye's point of view: he simply couldn't remember the names or plots of the pictures he wanted the committee to condemn. "It is a terrible weakness of mine," he said, "to go to a picture tonight and not be able to state the title of it tomorrow morning." It was not as if there were many such pictures to remember: not until 1940 had it been considered "safe" in Hollywood to take sides on the subject of the European war. Even so, Nye had his way:

> At least twenty pictures have been produced in the past year all designed to drug the reason of the American people, set aflame their emotions, turn their hatred into a blaze, fill them with fear that Hitler will come over here and capture them, that he will steal their trade. . . . [The movies] have become the most gigantic engines of propaganda in existence to serve war fever in America and plunge the Nation to her destruction.[1]

The films Nye could not remember would certainly have included Howard Hawks's *Sergeant York,* in which Gary Cooper sets aside his

Christian scruples and—after much anguished deliberation on a hill-top—proceeds to render unto Caesar a record number of dead Germans. *Sergeant York* was Hollywood's most unambiguous call to arms, and its huge commercial success during the summer and fall of 1941 probably had a lot to do with the setting up of Nye's committee.

Another film not recalled by Senator Nye would have been Hitchcock's *Foreign Correspondent,* which showed Joel McCrea combating a foreign spy ring that had been using an international peace movement as its front. The film ends with McCrea broadcasting to America from London, during an air raid: "The lights have gone out in Europe! Hang on to your lights, America—they're the only lights still on in the world! Ring yourself around with steel, America!" *Foreign Correspondent* was in fact a cleaned-up version of Walter Wanger's abandoned *Personal History*—all references to Spain and to German anti-Semitism were now removed—and the Hays Office had been pleased to find that the Hitchcock version bore "little resemblance to the story we were concerned about two years ago." Two years ago, Wanger was warned that his script's "pro-Loyalist propaganda, pro-Jewish propaganda and anti-Nazi propaganda . . . would inevitably cause enormous difficulty."

A similar nervousness had been evinced when, in December 1938, Warner Brothers announced its intention to make a film about a real-life Nazi spy ring that had been operating in the U.S.A. This is how Harry Warner described the film's origins to the Nye subcommittee:

> The plot was not the creation of a fiction writer. Nor did we sit down to devise a story to show the dangers of Nazi espionage. *Confessions of a Nazi Spy* correctly portrays the operation of a Nazi spy ring in this country, as this operation was disclosed at a Federal trial which convicted the conspirators.

The trial had begun in New York in October 1938. In that month, an item in the *Hollywood Reporter* noted that Milton Krims, a Warners contract writer, had been commissioned by Warners to "cover" the proceedings. A letter was then sent to the Hays Office by the German consul in Los Angeles:

My dear Mr. Breen:

   Will you kindly see to it that the matter, which is mentioned in the enclosed clipping of the "Hollywood Reporter" of October 27, 1938 will not result in difficulties such as we have unfortunately experienced before.

                    With best regards, I remain,
                    Very truly yours, George Gyseling

Breen stalled, but in December the consul wrote again. This time Breen penned a (possibly unsent) letter to Jack Warner, to raise "for your serious consideration, the question of whether or not your studio, and the industry as a whole, should sponsor a motion picture dealing with so highly controversial a subject." For some reason, in the same Hays Office file, there is a December 1938 letter to Joe Breen from one Luigi Luarischi, head of Paramount's censorship department, and the line it takes is worth noting, since it is typical of much Hollywood thinking at the time. Luarischi refers to Charles Chaplin's proposed "burlesque of Hitler" as an attempt to apply "his moneymaking talents to a film which could only have horrible repercussion on the Jews still in Germany." Luarischi goes on to assert that Warners, if they proceed with their spy-trial movie, will be exposed to a similar charge: "Warners will have on their hands the blood of a great many Jews in Germany."[2]

   Warners proceeded with the film. *Confessions of a Nazi Spy* was released in April 1939 and was hailed by the *Hollywood Reporter* as "unique . . . in the annals of screen entertainment":

   It may well lay the foundations for new and broader adventures in dramaturgy. It will unquestionably sound out the efficacy of a new approach to purposeful entertainment and in so doing, pave the way for the absorption of more daring and presumably fertile sources of material.[3]

The newspaper of the German-American Bund called it a "nightmarish concoction," drawing on "the choicest collection of flubdub that a diseased mind could possibly pick out of the public ashcan." The *New York Times* called it "childish." Certainly there is nothing much to tax the intelligence in the film's hammer-blow style of delivery: a bullying March of Time narrator and high-speed montages depicting Hitler rallies, swastikas encircling the globe, subversive leaflets skimming off the presses, and so on. The German conspirators are too heavily caricatured, full of accented talk about the need to liberate "unter Amerika" from the dire constraints of "democracy and racial equality." The decent folk are a bit too feeble and unknowing, and in spite of Edward G. Robinson, the FBI sleuthing is ponderously done. What matters is the Message, and there's no escaping it: Beware—this, very easily, *could* happen here. And there is, throughout the film, an urgency in the telling that still comes across today: "America is not just one of the remaining democracies," announces the trial prosecutor. "It *is* democracy," and then (with a shot of the White House to reassure us, or to remind us where we are); "When our basic liberties are threatened, we wake up."

Harry Warner ended his address to the Nye subcommittee on a similarly rousing note:

> In conclusion, I tell this committee honestly, I care nothing for any temporary advantage or profit that may be offered to me or my company. I will not censor the dramatization of the works of reputable and well informed writers to conceal from the American people what is happening in the world. Freedom of speech, freedom of religion and freedom of enterprise cannot be bought at the price of other people's rights. I believe the American people have a right to know the truth. You may correctly charge me with being anti-Nazi. But no one can charge me with being anti-American.[4]

Of course, from the radicalized screenwriter's point of view, *Confessions of a Nazi Spy* was the sort of explicitly anti-Fascist script he had been yearning to work on for five years. Understandably, the man who got the job, John Wexley, was reeling somewhat from the shock, calling *Confessions* "the most exciting and exhilarating work I had ever done in Hollywood." The film would, he said, "prove a turning point in the motion picture industry," and "aside from any question of its merit," he believed that exhibitors around the country would "spring upon the prints of *Confessions of a Nazi Spy* as manna from heaven."[5]

This is not quite how it worked out. The box office returns on *Confessions* were disappointing enough for Jack Warner to take temporary fright (he also had to contend with a hefty libel suit from the German-American Bund). In October 1939, he announced that Warners would be making no more propaganda movies; from now on, they would increase "production of light comedies to counter the effects of war." And in the first half of 1940, there was indeed a lull. Hollywood was waiting to see who came out on top in Europe. As *Variety* explained in April: "Stories with European background are being shunted to the sidings by studios in favor of domestic locales. Inasmuch as it is impossible to tell which way the war wind is blowing, producers don't want to be left out on a limb. Writers have been instructed to steer clear of war-ridden countries in treatments."

By the summer of 1940, though, American films had been banned in Germany—the half-expected outcome of a process that *Variety* had been tracking with some care throughout the year: "The German sweep through Central Europe this month represents a loss of 2½%–3½% of total income." With no customers to lose, a number of movies that had been kept on hold during the first half of 1940 now began to trickle out. MGM made its first anti-Nazi statement in *The Mortal Storm* (released in June 1940), 20th Century–Fox weighed in with *Four Sons* (June 1940), and Paramount contributed *Arise, My Love* (November 1940). And it was this trickle that culminated in Gary Cooper's momentous change of heart in *Sergeant York* (September 1941).

Although York in the movie is a Tennessee hillbilly, he could in some respects just as easily have been a certain sort of thirties intellectual, moving from pacifism to a reluctant acceptance of the necessity of fighting this just war. The screenplay for *Sergeant York* was coauthored by Howard Koch. In *The Sea Hawk,* as we have seen, Koch had Queen Elizabeth declare that "freedom is the deed and title to the soil on which we exist." This was in 1939, and the speech was not used in the United States version of the film. In 1941, Koch—himself a former pacifist—contrives an echo of that earlier call to arms: "By our victory in the last war, we won a lease on liberty, not a title to it."

2

With Senator Nye and his supporters silenced by Pearl Harbor, Roosevelt was free to set up a direct line of communication between

Hollywood and the White House: no one could any longer complain about presidential pressure, or say "that, in some mysterious way, the government orders us to make this or that picture," which is how Harry Warner paraphrased what he took to be the Nye committee's central grievance. A coordinator was appointed to advise the filmmakers on how they might most effectively contribute to the war effort. As usual, the producers flinched at the idea of an outsider telling them what to do, but these were special circumstances, and they offered no immediate resistance. The President's appointee was a man named Lowell Mellet, an ex–newspaper editor who had been advising Roosevelt on media relations, and he got off to a good start by praising (with no apparent trace of irony) Hollywood's splendid efforts so far in the struggle against fascism: "You couldn't have done more," he said, "in your efforts to educate people." The producers meanwhile had set up their own War Activities Committee to think up how best to "emotionalize and glorify the blood, sweat and tears of war, the sacrifices demanded and the ends for which America and her allies were fighting." And within a week of Pearl Harbor, the screenwriters had formed the Hollywood Writers Mobilization and vowed to "dedicate their talents to furnishing morale-building material."

At first, the liaison between government and studios ticked over quite nicely. Although by December 1941 most of the studios had one or two war films in production, it was too early for Mellet's large staff of propaganda analysts and "reviewers" to be set to work, just as it was too late for the studios to cancel items like *Honolulu Lu* (a cheerful Hawaiian comedy released on December 11, 1941), or to do more than tag on a grim "So they bombed Pearl Harbor, did they?" to the end of *Yank on the Burma Road*. This MGM film, about a taxi driver who ferried medical supplies to the Chinese, was released in January 1942 and was prefaced with the printed message: "On December 7, 1941, Japan attacked the United States of America and engaged it in war. This is the story of one American who tackled Japan a little before the rest of us—and what he started, the rest of the Yanks will finish."

It would be several months before Hollywood could give full voice to the nation's sense of outrage. John Huston's *Across the Pacific* has Humphrey Bogart foiling a sneaky Japanese attempt to blow up the Panama Canal, but in the first half of the film (a follow-up to *The Maltese Falcon*) the Japanese conspirators are differentiated—some small effort has gone into equipping them with tics and traits, and Fat Man Sydney Greenstreet delivers lectures on their culture. In one extraordinary scene, Greenstreet tries to explain Japanese poetry to Bogart and Mary Astor: "Your occidental poem . . . is wont to describe grand passions and events . . . not so with the Japanese. Their emotions are stirred by some tiny fragment of life possessing the quality of beauty. . . . This they would reduce, extract, distill, as it were, down to its purest essence." Mary Astor's eyes widen: "So they do have emotions, like us . . .?" to which an attendant Japanese replies: "We are taught not to [show our feelings] . . . it is our way of life . . . we must not show too much sadness or too much joy . . . if you praise what we have we say it is nothing, if you admire our sons, we must say they are unworthy."

We are also shown a jujitsu contest; at the end of it, the contestants perform a sort of prayer ritual, and Bogart asks: "What's that all about?" Greenstreet explains that judo is "more than a mere contest—it's a devotee's form of brotherhood, similar in many respects to our Western freemasonry. It too has its secrets, as well as its religious or should I say philosophical background." "Come again," says Humph. Greenstreet: "It's an Oriental concept that destructive force acts upon itself and there you have the principle of jui-jitsu, to turn the power of one's antagonist upon himself and by so doing . . . vanquish him! That's the art of the thing." "How would that stack up against a right cross?" asks Bogie.

Greenstreet is, of course, a spy, and the message seems to be that we should beware smooth-tongued Orientalists. And we should beware, too, of those seemingly Americanized, second-generation Japanese, like Greenstreet's sidekick, Joe. Joe doesn't go in for the inscrutable stuff; he's a "live wire, born in the good old U.S.A." He talks side-of-the-mouth Brooklynese, he likes card games ("Let me get at those pasteboards"), drinking ("What's that you're knocking yourselves out with? . . . Waiter, I'll have one of those!"), Mary Astor ("a swell dish"), and Humphrey Bogart ("You sure are a fast worker, Rick"). Joe is projected as seductively, treacherously one of the boys; all the more reason to cheer when eventually Bogart pumps him full of lead. By the time *Across the Pacific* was released, Californians who looked like Joe had been "evacuated" in their thousands to local assembly centers, en route to internment camps. In the words of General DeWitt, head of the Western Defense Command: "The Japanese race is an enemy race and while many second- and third-generation Japanese born on United States soil . . . have become 'Americanized,' the racial strains are undiluted . . . a Jap is a Jap."

Across the Pacific was in production before the Japanese attack on Pearl Harbor—hence the unevenness of tone, the shift of gear. In the semiofficial *Air Force,* there is no effort to humanize the enemy or to puzzle over his differentness. By now—late 1942—a Jap *was* just a Jap, a "buck-toothed little runt." The crew of the *Mary Ann* hear the news of Pearl Harbor over the radio, and they are themselves the victims of a cowardly surprise attack:

> Listen, any buck-toothed little runt can walk up behind Joe
> Louis and knock him cold with a baseball bat—but a clean man
> don't do it. Your Uncle Sammy is civilized: He says, "Look out,
> you sneaks, we're gonna hit above the belt and knock the
> daylights outa you!"[6]

We hear Roosevelt's "date which will live in infamy" speech, and there is much bitter talk about "fifth column work" and the *"friendly* Japanese" of Honolulu:

> BAGLEY (his eyes are bitter): . . . If we'd had our twelve
> fighters up, we'd have smeared them on that first attack. But
> we were listening on the shortwave to Tokyo telling about Mr.
> Saburo Kurusu's peace mission to the United States. (Quietly)
> I've studied all the wars of history, gentlemen, but I've never
> come across any treachery to match that.[7]

This echoes the words of Cordell Hull, U.S. secretary of state, who was "negotiating" with Kurusu even as news of the attack was made public: "In all my fifty years of public service I have never seen a document that was more crowded with infamous falsehoods and distortions on a scale so huge that I never imagined until today that any Government on this planet was capable of uttering them."

The script for *Air Force* was completed in July 1942. By that time, Lowell Mellet's Bureau of Motion Pictures had been given a fair taste of what Hollywood meant when it vowed to "emotionalize" the "blood, sweat and tears of war." Mellet's office took a dim view of *Air Force,* in spite of its presidential echoes and its close involvement with the military, but had to admit that there were far worse examples of hate rhetoric to choose from. Analyzing the seventy-two war pictures released between December 1941 and July 1942, the BMP reviewers were shocked to find so many of them disfigured by a bloodcurdling racism—a near-hysterical "Beast of the East" approach, typified by *Menace of the Rising Sun, Secret Agent of Japan,* and *Little Tokyo, USA* (the title "Remember Pearl Harbor" had been instantly copyrighted by Republic, which was then temporarily stuck for a story to go with it).

Little Tokyo, for instance, called itself "a film document" and was offered to the American people as "a reminder to a nation which until December, 1941 was lulled into a false sense of security by the mouthings of self-styled patriots whose beguiling theme was: it can't happen here." The BMP reviewer denounced the film for its "rabidly unbalanced racism" and its clamorous suggestion that all Japanese-Americans should be viewed as likely traitors. "That's for Pearl Harbor, you slant-eyed . . . ," says the tough Los Angeles police detective as he drags a spy suspect off for questioning, and a radio commentator comments: "Unfortunately, in time of war, the loyal must suffer inconvenience with the disloyal. Be vigilant, America!" *Little Tokyo* was actually shot in L.A.'s Chinatown: the real-life Little Tokyo, stripped of its evacuees, was now a sort of ghost town. No one seemed to care that in the film the Japanese street signs were written in Chinese. No one, that is, except Lowell Mallet's analysts, who seem to have been quite overwhelmed by this "invitation to a witchhunt."

At this stage, the BMP had virtually no powers of "prior restraint." They could advise and criticize, but by the time they had a chance to do so, it was usually too late. The producers submitted scripts to the Hays Office, as always, and even to the War Department (whenever they needed to borrow equipment and manpower), but they drew the line at giving real power to the Bureau, whose reviewers—they believed—were in the main liberal or leftist intellectuals of the sort that in peacetime would be writing supercilious film reviews in papers like the *New Republic.* The BMP, on the other hand, soon began to feel that without teeth, it might as well not be involved at all. In the view of Mellet and his representative in Hollywood, Nelson Poynter, another ex-newsman, it was not the war propagandist's job merely to whip up hatred against the enemy. There were other, more positive objectives, objectives that had their roots in prewar political idealism.

To clarify matters, the BMP compiled a manual, which asked

filmmakers to ponder their responsibilities in these momentous times.[8] A good propaganda film, according to the manual, should attempt to explain why the war was being fought, and it should also convey some vision of the "new world" that victory would bring about. In the BMP vision, this would be a sort of liberal paradise, a League of Nations "dedicated to the free flow of trade, ideas and culture." To promote such a vision, the responsible propagandist should eschew racial stereotypes and should make it clear that wars are waged not by satanic "other races" but because ordinary people are misled by evil rulers. American propaganda should keep alive the possibility of dealing with those ordinary people once again, after their bad leaders had been vanquished.

Propaganda should, of course, also assist in the winning of the war. Again, though, its contribution should be positive. Home-front morale building was of vital consequence: civilians should be shown, wherever possible, in harmonious war-effort situations, accepting shortages with a smile, purchasing war bonds, not cheating on their taxes, toiling happily on the production lines, accepting with fortitude the loss of loved ones, and so on. There should also be some effort to portray the fighting services as exemplary social units; army platoons should be "multi-ethnic," and care should be taken to provide soldiers with "names of foreign extraction." Finally, the BMP wanted the filmmakers always to ask themselves: "Does a picture tell the truth or will young people of today have reason to say they were misled by propaganda?"

At first, the producers were happy enough to be preached at in this way, and from time to time they succeeded in offering films that the BMP heartily approved: *Mrs. Miniver*, for example, or *Since You Went Away*. The vicar's sermon in *Mrs. Miniver* was ordered by Roosevelt to be dropped as leaflets on occupied territories, and Frank Knox, secretary of the navy, declared: "God bless the men and women who made this film; its effect in these trying days will be miraculous." Nelson Poynter considered it a model for other propaganda films to follow, and so, too, did the reviewing press, the Academy Awards judges, and almost everybody else except the *New Republic*'s Manny Farber, who found this tale of British home-front pluck phony and artificial; he cited Will Hays and Little Lord Fauntleroy as the film's dominating influences. Actually, *Mrs. Miniver* was released before the BMP became fully active in Hollywood, and it had begun production two weeks before Pearl Harbor. In the planning of the film (with a nervous L. B. Mayer at his elbow), director William Wyler had had to exercise restraints, which paid off after he no longer needed them: the bad German could be worse, that is to say, and the sermonizing might have spread itself around a little more. The script was concocted at high speed by a team of four writers, including James Hilton, but Wyler later claimed much credit for the composition of that vicar's speech:

> this is not only a war of soldiers in uniform, it is a war of the people—of all the people—and it must be fought, not only on the battlefield, but in the cities and in the villages, in the factories and on the farms, in the home and in the heart of every man, woman and child who loves freedom. Well, we have buried our dead but we shall not forget them. Instead, they will inspire us with an unbreakable determination to free ourselves and those who come after us from the tyranny and terror that threaten to strike us down. Fight it, then! Fight it with all that is in us! And may God defend the right.

Mrs. Miniver, viewed now, seems an absurdly sugary confection, as does its American home-front counterpart, David Selznick's *Since You Went Away,* but each of them accorded perfectly with the BMP recipe. In both films, middle-class complacency adjusts itself to emergency conditions: genteel wives take factory jobs ("I love it so!"), rent out spare rooms, cut down on the petrol and the sugar, and make sympathetic contact with the lower orders. "Not what we are used to at the country club," says Claudette Colbert when she meets one of her co-welders at the shipyard, a Polish refugee who, when Colbert is nice to her, mists over and says: *"You* are America!"

Tears are shed in private, anxieties are well suppressed. Bereavements, when they happen, as they must, are viewed as worthwhile sacrifices. Petty domestic and social enmities are seen for what they are, yet decent peacetime standards are maintained. The family unit is made all the stronger by this temporary fragmentation: "In years to come, this will be the greatest adventure we ever had, though we had it separately." Wives are grippingly faithful, young lovers cling to each other as they contemplate their higher duties, crusty old-timers learn to give a little, and even the domestic animals seem to sense an alteration in the scheme of things.

The violence of the war is elsewhere but omnipresent. The

enemy, when briefly glimpsed or described, is brainwashed, fanati-
cally misguided. The home-front male, if for some good reason not
in uniform, is finding ways to lend a hand. "You don't need to be an
officer, strutting in gold braid," Jennifer Jones tells her shamefaced
boyfriend, of grand military stock but unlikely to be offered a commission. "Gee," he whimpers, "I'm so glad you feel that way." There
are no seriously bad home-front baddies, no slackers or profiteers,
no good-time girls, no wacko dropouts, no mean-mindedness that is
not instantly corrected: as with the overfastidious Mrs. Hawkins in
Since You Went Away, who wonders if nursing is the correct sort of
job for a nice girl to be doing. "Please don't worry," she is told, "if
our precious well-bred hands come in contact with their mangled
bodies. We'll survive, even if they don't." In *Mrs. Miniver,* a pimply
Oxbridge radical stops griping about social injustice and becomes a
Spitfire pilot, and even the monstrously posh Lady Beldon ends up
running an air-raid shelter. When the bombs come, they are greeted
with disdain. "Um—bit of a mess," grunts Mr. Miniver as he inspects
his gutted house. And in *Since You Went Away,* war shortages are
almost welcomed. "Suits me if they tax me one hundred percent"
say the wealthy. Discomforts are laughed off with a patriotic jest: "I
wouldn't wish this on a Japanese."

Mrs. Miniver and *Since You Went Away* were both box office hits:
well-crafted schmaltz that happened to fit the BMP's criteria. More
contentious by far was King Vidor's *An American Romance,* a three-
million-dollar, all-Technicolor glorification of America's industrial
might. Vidor's hero is an illiterate but lionhearted immigrant
worker who claws his way to the top of the capitalist heap. It took
weeks of negotiation with BMP functionaries before MGM could
supply the film with an acceptable labor-relations policy. In Vidor's
original version, either the hero inspires mute awe in his work force
or—if it steps out of line—he swiftly brings it to heel. The BMP was
not happy with this. It liked the film's Americanism, its endless
boasting about productivity levels and war readiness, and it liked the
land-of-opportunity go-getting of the hero ("Is that why you left the
old country? To dig in a hole? I thought you wanted to climb to the
sky"). But when this same hero, now an automobile tycoon, was all
set to disperse a sit-down strike with tear gas, the BMP broke into
a sweat: "This is a fascist tactic pure and simple, tending to divide
one group of Americans from another." Vidor might have argued
that the tear gas scene was set in the 1930s, but the BMP was not

interested in the airing of old grievances. For war purposes, it wanted an "affinity of man and machine" and a joint labor-management commitment to a single goal: the making of steel planes that would wipe out the enemy. Vidor's capitalist hero is forced to make a deal: the workers, who loved him all along, cooperate, and it's all roses among them by the film's end. Warplanes lift off from a factory floor that now has women workers assisting a merry, moderate trade union.

MGM had protested throughout that the BMP was pushing them to make a "New Deal picture . . . Metro doesn't want to make controversial subjects," but in the end *An American Romance* was fake enough to satisfy both sides: a lumbering compromise between BMP liberalism and MGM mogulism that had little in it of Vidor's original inspiration—little, that is, except his long-held enthusiasm for the technicalities of steel production.

King Vidor's first script for *An American Romance* (the work of some twelve writers, with Vidor's very much the guiding intelligence at first) was read by the BMP in November 1942. Over the next few months, the Bureau became even bolder and more pretentious in its efforts to control "motion picture content," its dictates wobbling always between the visionary and the priggish, the theme and the detail. The reviewers had no particular love of the movies, nor any real taste for "entertainment," and were on the whole grindingly humorless in their appraisals. Licensed as they were by the objectives of the war effort, these liberal apparatchiks could get their revenge on a Hollywood that had been eating away at America's finer sensibilities for three decades: this certainly is how many producers viewed the Bureau's "interference."

When the BMP began to insist on vetting scripts in advance of production and then threatened to seek backup from the censorship authorities whenever their "advice" was disregarded, the studios got nervous. And when Bureau officials took to rewriting scripts, adding their own creative flourishes (after all, were they not writers too?), there was a feeling in the air that seemed familiar. By May 1943, Roosevelt's enemies in Congress were alerted to the growing power of Mellet's liberals, and they struck back with resounding force: the BMP budget was slashed from $1.3 million to a humiliating $50,000. This meant the end for Mellet and his men, the end of what had all along been a most peculiar arrangement.

For almost a year, the studios had been obliged to defend themselves against just the sort of moral and ideological critique that had been swept aside so contemptuously in 1936. The producers could live with the Hays Office; it advised on what the market, or markets, could or couldn't stand. It had its Roman Catholic reflexes, but these were in any case powerfully echoed in the marketplace; and it was politically conservative, but then so, too, by instinct, were most of the producers. What the Hays Office never did was to tell the studios that they ought to make better pictures, pictures that were more serious, responsible, or subtle. It never talked the way screenwriters always talked. The BMP did, and that is why it had to be shut down.

Lowell Mellet's replacement, amusingly enough, was the chairman of Paramount's executive committee, and this new man instantly declared that "his main objective was to protect the industry." The demise of Mellet's operation—the "domestic" branch of the Office of War Information's Hollywood liaison—meant that from now on the government would be advising the moviemakers merely on overseas affairs. In other words, the OWI provided a sort of Hays Office in uniform. The producers didn't mind this sort of control; indeed, they welcomed it as useful "market research." If a movie had to be altered in order to get an export license from the OWI, then so be it. In the words of two recent commentators:

> Each mile of territory recaptured in Europe and Asia by the Allied armies brought the interests of the government and Hollywood closer. The government was eager to use approved films as a weapon in its cultural reoccupation of Axis-held countries—and audiences in those nations were eager to see American movies again. . . . OWI's help was invaluable. It exhibited films which had its seal of approval and held the money in trust for the companies. . . . The shakeout in OWI in mid-1943 had brought a rapprochement between businessmen and bureaucrats.[9]

3

By 1943, over two hundred screenwriters were serving in the armed forces. A few others were with the OWI or with film units covering the war. Of those who stayed in Hollywood, the majority was over-age (i.e., older than thirty-eight), but several of the thirty-five who were "vulnerable to the draft" had asked to be deferred on the grounds that "war writing" was an exempt occupation. To test this claim, a joint writer-producer committee was set up, and it proposed "a tentative outline of writer categories for war-production." The categories were:

1. capable of translating complex technical information into screen terms (technical)

2. adept at dramatizing socio-historical information (educational films)

3. adept at giving emotional power to ideological concepts (morale)

4. physically equipped to accompany film-making units into action (combat films)[10]

One or two writers were so sickened by the qualification process that they enlisted immediately. Some, though, were not allowed a choice. Maurice Rapf, for instance, had applied to join the navy, the OSS, and then the Marine Corps photographic unit, but "I always got turned down. They'd always say it was my eyes or something. But we knew it was political. And they always asked me the question, 'Are you a member of the Communist Party?' and I always denied it, which I shouldn't have done."[11] The same applied to several other prominent Hollywood "progressives"—although Budd Schulberg, Rapf's companion in conversion back in 1934, somehow achieved a commission in the navy. Dorothy Parker was refused a passport when she tried to become a war correspondent. Ring Lardner, Jr., and John Bright also had their enlistments blocked: each of them was the subject of an FBI dossier stamped "PAF"—Premature Anti-Fascist. Later on, the Hollywood Nineteen would have one thing in common—none of them served in the armed forces during the war.

They served in Hollywood instead. For the first time, the American film industry needed its "politicals," writers "adept at dramatizing socio-historical information" and at "giving emotional power to ideological concepts"; for the first time, the left-leaning screenwriter felt his objectives to be in tune with those of his employers. By seeing to it that the leftists stayed at home, the FBI had of course prepared the ground for later probes and persecutions. In 1942, though, a rare harmony prevailed in Hollywood, with Communists seeking to protect the interests of "our Russian ally" and the liberal democrats seeking to perpetuate America's New Deal: for all parties, the first objective was to win the war. There was disagreement about how this should be done, and there were continuing squabbles over local issues, but all in all there was an impressive rallying to the common cause.

Even at meetings of the Screen Writers Guild there was a burying of hatchets, and it was during this pull-together period that the screenwriter's minimum wage (of $125 a week) was finally conceded by the producers:

> we walked into the producers' meeting and let them talk first. And [Eddie] Mannix said, "We've been screwing around long enough. We won't give them the world, but let's give them the minimum wage" . . . and Mannix then said, "There's a war on. So let's sign this goddamn contract and make pictures for the boys."[12]

With this long-pursued contract settled, the Writers Mobilization became the center of activity in the literary war effort, and there was plenty to be done: commentaries for documentaries and propaganda shorts, war bond speeches for the radio, scripts for psychological testing films, pamphlets, instructional brochures, and so on. And all this without credits. "The writers in Hollywood were amused at the sudden paradox. Never had their services been so highly valued, and never had they been so anonymous."[13]

Writers of the left were also amused to find themselves considered the "right men" for any feature films that had political content, and in particular for movies that celebrated the United States alliance with the Soviet Union. Howard Koch and director Michael Curtiz, fresh from some stylish work on *Casablanca*, were recruited to pump badly needed zest into a film called *Mission to Moscow*, to be based on the bestselling memoirs of Joseph E. Davies, U.S. ambassador to Russia from 1936 to 1938. *Mission to Moscow* is now seen as a notorious Hollywood disaster, and there are several conflicting accounts of its genesis. What seems clear is that Roosevelt wanted a pro-Russian picture and suggested the project to Jack Warner, that Davies badly wanted to see himself in a movie (so badly that when he complained that Walter Huston did not look like him, the producers were forced to let the real Davies perform an on-screen prologue to the film), and that Howard Koch—according to the producer who

hired him—"was a capable screenwriter, following orders, but with
no clear knowledge of the truth or falsity of the issues involved."
This same producer, Robert Buckner (himself a former Warners
screenwriter), later described the whole enterprise as "an expedient
lie for political purposes, glossily covering up important facts with
full or partial knowledge of their false presentation."

The most repugnant distortion of the facts was in the film's account of the Moscow trials of 1936–38. According to Ambassador
Davies, these trials (presented in the film as one trial) were fairly
conducted and entirely just in their conclusions:

207: CLOSE SHOT: AMBASSADOR DAVIES
at his desk in the embassy, dictating his communication to the
State Department. As he dictates, the CAMERA PULLS BACK to
include the embassy secretary who is taking down the message.
DAVIES: . . . There is no longer any question in my mind that
these defendants, under the leadership of Trotsky, Bukharin,
and Tukhachevsky, were guilty of a conspiracy with the
German and Japanese high commands to pave the way for an
attack upon the Soviet state.

208: STOCK SHOT: WASHINGTON
(Shot should include the State Department building)
DAVIES' VOICE (OVER SCENE): Consequently all of the trials,
purges, and liquidations which at first seemed so violent and
shocking to the rest of the world . . .

209: FULL SHOT: THE CODE ROOM, WASHINGTON
showing about eight code machines, each with its own
operator. Surrounding the machines is heavy wire grating. An
armed guard stands at the only entrance. During the decoding
of the message two or three messengers deliver other
communications to the operators.
DAVIES' VOICE (OVER SCENE): . . . are now seen clearly as part
of a vigorous and determined effort by the Stalin government
to protect itself from not only revolution from within, but from
attack from without. They went to work thoroughly and
ruthlessly to clean out all treasonable elements—fifth
columnists—within the country.

210: CLOSE SHOT: A MACHINE
over the shoulder of the operator, who is decoding the Davies
communication. First we see the message in its code form;

then as it comes out of the machine we read the words of
Davies that we hear OVER SCENE

DAVIES' VOICE (CONTINUING OVER SCENE): When I asked Mr.
Litvinov whether the government now felt positive it could
rely upon the support and loyalty of the Red Army, he assured
me that the army is unquestionably loyal and that the position
of the Soviet government is actually strengthened by the purge
of its traitors.[14]

Advising on *Mission to Moscow* was one of the very last jobs
undertaken by Lowell Mellet's BMP reviewing staff in Hollywood.
The verdict was as follows:

Mission to Moscow is a magnificent contribution to the Government's motion picture program as a means of communicating
historical and political material in a dramatic way. As the picture
unfolds the whole field of international relations, Axis intrigue and
the shameful role of the appeasers of the Axis in the past decade
is illuminated for us. The presentation of the Moscow trials is a
high point in the picture and should do much to bring understanding of Soviet international policy in the past years and dispel the
fears which many honest persons have felt with regard to our
alliance with Russia.[15]

There were other pro-Russian films in 1943, though none so solemn and shameless as *Mission to Moscow*. Communist screenwriters Paul Jarrico and Richard Collins penned *The Song of Russia*, in
which Robert Taylor plays an American musician—actually a genius conductor—who finds himself trapped in Russia after the German invasion. He falls in love with a girl from the darling little
village of Tchaikovskia ("I thought Russians were a melancholy
people. You might be an American girl") and eventually escapes
with her, aided by the gallant locals and with their words ringing
in his ears: "Tell them what you have seen. . . . Tell them that we
will hold on. . . . We will feel you fighting side by side with us."

Rather more ambitious was *The North Star*, a Goldwyn picture
directed by Lewis Milestone, scripted by Lillian Hellman, and
"based on a suggestion by" F. D. Roosevelt. This one opens on a
Goldwynized collective farm, with cheery peasants singing folk
songs composed by Aaron Copland, doing hankie dances and braid-
ing flowers into one another's golden hair. ("Patches by Irene" was

one wag's suggestion for the credits.) It is "the last day of peace": not knowing this, a group of beaming villagers sets off on a day trip to Kiev. On the way, their caravan is knocked off the road by Nazi bombers. The invasion has begun. The rest of the film (and we are about halfway through by now) portrays the villagers' resistance to their Fascist occupiers. The old tell the young: "We are a people with a noble history. You must carry on that history with complete dedication and self-sacrifice." The villagers burn their own houses, and the young men swear an oath: "I am a guerrilla of the Soviet Union and ready to die to keep my people from fascist slavery." Even the Germans are impressed: "A strong people. A hard people to conquer," they are heard to murmur as they go about their workaday atrocities.

The dialogue throughout *The North Star* is stiff and literary, the characters are pasteboard, the locations are prettified, and the propaganda is breathtaking in its simplemindedness. And yet, such was the climate, the film was respectfully reviewed: *Time* magazine called it a "cinemilestone," and Mellet's analysts adored it. Lillian Hellman said she hated it, claiming that Milestone had turned her script into a "big-time, sentimental, badly acted mess," and she paid Goldwyn $27,500 to be released from her contract.[16] The Russian-born Milestone retorted that "Lillian knew *nothing* about Russia—especially the villages." He had asked for script changes, but Hellman had been too grand to take advice. It is certainly true that Hellman had been pampered by Sam Goldwyn from the beginning of her screenwriting career and had mostly worked on adaptations of her own plays. She was not accustomed to directors restructuring her plots and dreaming up new characters. It would be pleasant to believe that she walked off *The North Star* because of the film's trashiness; it seems more likely, though, that she was piqued because Goldwyn did not this time take her side. The text of her script does not encourage any notion that a different director would have made much difference.

Other pro-Russian touches appear in John Howard Lawson's *Action in the North Atlantic* and *Counter-Attack,* but with *Life* magazine naming Stalin as its "Man of the Year" for 1943 and describing the Russians as "one hell of a people . . . [they] look like Americans, dress like Americans and think like Americans," it is perhaps surprising that the leftist screenwriters were so restrained. The wily Lawson was ever careful to check his scripts against the BMP criteria and to bear in mind that the tide would surely turn. Thus in *Action in the North Atlantic,* when the Russians greet the heroic Humphrey Bogart with cries of "Tovarich! Tovarich!" Humph lets his men respond in kind, but he himself falls silent. What's the matter? he is asked. "I'm just thinking about the trip back," says Bogart. The line is in character, because the trip back will be tough, but it is also patriotic: This "Comrade" stuff is all OK but I can't wait to get back home.

But then John Howard Lawson had all along played a cunning game in Hollywood—not asking too much and not taking too much when it was offered and always managing to have work. He knew that even in a period of license, the screenwriter could do little more than slip in the odd line here and there, or at best attempt a civilizing scene or two.

When Lester Cole and Alvah Bessie were set to work on the screenplay of *Objective Burma,* they protested that "there are no American troops in Burma." The producer Jerry Wald replied: "So what? It's only a moving picture." Wald probably said much the same thing when the British refused to screen this account of Errol Flynn almost single-handedly "liquidating Japs so thoroughly that not one survives to shoot back, or even squirm." In the course of the film, a war correspondent inspects the remains of a Jap-conquered village and then gives voice to what has been described as "the most vindictive film speech of the war":[17]

> I thought I'd seen or read about everything one man can do to
> another, from the torture chambers of the middle ages to the
> gang wars and lynchings of today. But this—this is different.
> This was done in cold blood by people who claim to be
> civilized. Civilized! They're degenerate, immoral idiots.
> Stinking little savages. Wipe them out, I say. Wipe them off the
> face of the earth.

In Cole and Bessie's script, Errol Flynn replies: "There's nothing especially Japanese about this. . . . You'll find it wherever you find fascists. There are even people who call themselves American who'd do it, too." Jerry Wald cut the reply. If Cole and Bessie had succeeded in preserving Flynn's retort—and they tried hard to make Wald change his mind—they would no doubt have spoken proudly of their "contribution." The film's larger dishonesty was not thought

to be worth combating: to insist that Errol Flynn did *not* win the war
in Burma would have been like asking for the film to be closed down.

It is easy to find something pitiable in the way such solemn trifles
are advanced by screenwriters as evidence of their clandestine
power for good. In the case of Cole and Bessie and *Objective Burma,*
the power for good was rumbled, sabotaged. Sometimes it struggled
through. Albert Maltz, for instance, wrote a movie called *Destina-
tion Tokyo,* in which Cary Grant's ship is almost blown up by an
enemy bomb marked "Made in the USA." Grant comments: "Ap-
peasement has come home to roost, men." And Maltz has added his
own footnote: "It is true that weapons that came back, and shells
that came back on Pearl Harbor came from scrap iron that we had
sent. Now this was a straight political comment, but this was something that delighted Jerry Wald. And Cary Grant was delighted to
say it. And audiences accepted it, and it gave the film some intellectual content." The *Daily Worker* was alone in detecting "the hand
of Maltz" in this "courageous" scene that "aims a two-ton bomb at
the heart of the American fifth column."[18]

With this sort of appreciative audience to keep in mind, the wartime screenwriter was easily tempted into self-importance. Scripts,
although more "serious" than most of what had gone before, were
also by a margin duller, more self-conscious, more anxious to put
their credentials on display. Pauline Kael has said that "the writing
that had given American talkies their special flavor died in the war,
killed not in battle but in the politics of Stalinist anti-Fascism." This
is histrionically put, and yet it is not hard to see how such an impression could be formed. Kael no doubt had in mind the sort of piety
that lured a witty writer like Donald Ogden Stewart into declaring
that "the one film I am proudest of" is the turgid *Keeper of the
Flame,* the only anti-Fascist movie Stewart got the chance to
write—and then as late as 1942. Kael might also have been thinking
that it needed the wartime atmosphere to create a reputation for
the likes of Dalton Trumbo: that is to say, for expert providers of the
sort of souped-up inspirational rhetoric that such an hour seemed to
demand, or was ready to forgive.

Dalton Trumbo, from his earliest days as a hack writer for almost
every studio in town, was famous for the speed with which he came
up with so-called quality material, and there is indeed a sort of
automatic feel to what he did. The more portentous the theme, the
more accelerated seems the manner of delivery. In 1938, the near-

pacifist Trumbo wrote a novel called *Johnny Got His Gun,* which foresaw with horror "starved cities black and cold and motionless and the only things in this whole dead terrible world that made a move or a sound were the airplanes that blackened the sky and far off against the horizon the thunder of the big guns and the puffs that rose from barren tortured earth when their shells exploded." Unluckily, the book did not appear until 1939, in the middle of the Hitler-Stalin pact phase of leftist thinking, and this meant that Trumbo was at first labeled as a faithful party-liner. After Hitler's invasion of Russia, he was relabeled—by the right—as a hero of isolationism. The book then fell foul of army censorship, and Trumbo was showered with "fiercely sympathetic letters denouncing Jews, Communists, New Dealers and international bankers, who had suppressed my novel to intimidate millions of true Americans who demanded an immediate negotiated peace." Trumbo asked his publisher to keep the book out of print for the duration of the war. Although prepared to argue that *Johnny* was actually in favor of a "good and worthy war," he could also see that not many readers would instantly glean this from the text. He himself was now pro-war. Within two years, his book had become something that even he could not bring himself to read:

> if all the little people all the little guys saw the future they would begin to ask questions. They would ask questions and they would find answers and they would say to the guys who wanted them to fight they would say you lying thieving sons-of-bitches we won't fight we won't be dead we will live we are the world we are the future and we will not let you butcher us no matter what you say no matter what speeches you make what slogans you write.[19]

Yes, it's those "little guys" again. Substitute "quit" for "fight," and you have the makings of a terrific post–Pearl Harbor screenplay or one of the many speeches that Trumbo would soon be writing for the government. The substitution was made with admirable fluency, and by 1942 Dalton Trumbo was acknowledged to be one of Hollywood's most sonorous word warriors.

In Trumbo's *A Guy Named Joe,* we find Hollywood's inspirational war rhetoric pumped up to bursting point—perhaps beyond that point, depending on your mood. Spencer Tracy is a daredevil air ace who gets himself killed in a near-kamikaze assault on an enemy aircraft carrier. Translated to heaven, and ankle-deep in wispy clouds, he is brought before a postmortal Chief of Staff (Lionel Barrymore), who briefs him on his next assignment. Spencer must return to earth, where comely young Van Johnson needs instruction in the basic air-ace skills. Unluckily, Van falls for Spencer's girlfriend (Irene Dunne): she is loyal to Spencer's memory, but only just. Invisible to them but not to us, Spencer has to watch as Van, through sheer force of niceness, begins melting her resistance. Furious, Tracy stalks off back to heaven—if this is immortality, the C of S knows where he can shove it. The great Chief is of course all-wise; he understands the wayward passions—even the wayward passions of a dead guy. Reaching for his trusty Trumboid cadences, he tries to explain a few heavenly home truths to his by now somewhat shamefaced messenger:

CHIEF: It's hard for me to put it into words if you don't feel it.

Tracy: I think I understand, sir.

CHIEF: No, I don't think you understand at all. Let's put it this way. Have you ever been up in your plane, alone, at night, somewhere 20,000 feet above the ocean?

Tracy: Yes, sir.

CHIEF: Did you ever hear music up there?

Tracy: Perhaps.

CHIEF: No, if you've heard it you'll remember it. It's the music man's spirit sings to his heart when the earth is far away and there isn't any more fear. It's the high, fine, beautiful sound of an earthbound creature who grew wings and flew up high and looked straight into the face of the future and caught just for an instant the unbelievable vision of a free man in a free world. But if you haven't heard it there's no way I can talk to you.

Tracy: I've heard it. I *have* heard it, sir. I used to try to explain it to some kids but I could never find words. . . .

CHIEF: O, children would understand I'm sure because the future belongs to them. They're going to climb out of the dust and the muck and lift up their heads and see the sky. They're going to fly like a generation of angels into the free air and the sunlight. O, children will always understand. "Free as the air." Men have said that ever since they crawled out of caves and

came down from the trees. That's what we're fighting for. The
freedom of the very air we breathe, the freedom of mankind
rushing to greet the future, on wings. Can you understand that,
can you?

Tracy: Yes, sir, I do.

CHIEF: No man is really dead unless he breaks faith with the
future. No man is really alive unless he accepts his
responsibilities to it. That's the chance we're giving you
here—the opportunity to pay off to the future what you owe
for having been part of the past. It's just another way of saying:
I'm glad I was alive. Let me give you a hand. You thought you
were choosing between life and death when you flew in over
that carrier. But you weren't. You're choosing between 'em
now. It's up to you, Pete.

Tracy: If you please, sir, I'd like to go back. I think I can do
my job now. Thank you, sir. [Muzak of spheres takes over.]

4

In October 1943, over thirteen hundred people attended a three-
day Writers' Congress at UCLA to discuss "the social obligations of
the mass media during and after war-time." Organized by the Writers' Mobilization in an attempt to forge links with the local academic
community, the Congress laid on a series of seminars and general
meetings with subject headings like "The Responsibility of the Industry," "The Nature of the Enemy," and "The Problems of Peace."

It was all a bit abstract and self-congratulatory, endorsing —more
or less—the BMP guidelines and in general basking in the new order
of things: an order in which screenwriters could be heard urging
their colleagues not "to raise any issues whatsoever here at home as
between any race or creed or class" (with Russia in peril, this was
do-not-rock-the-boat time on the left), while Darryl Zanuck, arch-
tycoon, was declaring just the opposite. You writers, Zanuck said,
should be dealing with "the causes of wars and panics, with social
upheavals and depression, with starvation and want and injustice
and barbarism under whatever guise."[20] Seriousness was the new
orthodoxy, and to most of those present at the Congress, it really did
seem as though they might be witnessing a sort of revolution. When
the *New York Times* came to review the book of the proceedings,

they interpreted the whole event as follows: the writers, they said, had "made a solemn declaration of their responsibilities and in effect served notice on the entertainment industry that they are about to take over Hollywood."[21]

And this was exactly how it was perceived by observers from the right. The House Un-American Activities Committee had been sniffing around Hollywood for years. In 1938, its chairman, Martin Dies, had conducted hearings in Los Angeles to test the "loyalty" of various film personalities (including the ten-year-old Shirley Temple), and in 1940, he had announced that there were "forty two or forty three" Communists "active in the film colony." Now, in 1943, the California State Un-American Activities Committee, headed by Senator Jack Tenney (a former leftist but now a rabid disciple of Dies), declared that the Writers' Congress was being "promoted and controlled by the communists" and that innocent, state-funded academics were being led astray. Through the press, and by direct threats to the university, Tenney did his utmost to have the event canceled. He did not succeed, but Tenney "was a man who didn't take defeat lightly. He now began his investigation of the Hollywood Writers' Mobilization in earnest."[22]

And Tenney was not the only hostile observer at the Congress. The old Screen Playwrights were now out in the cold, but their spirit lingered on. Early in 1944, they got together to form a new organization, calling it the Motion Picture Alliance for the Preservation of American Ideals and boasting among its supporters quite a few big names: Walt Disney, Gary Cooper, King Vidor, Victor Fleming, Clarence Brown. The Alliance screenwriters included James K. McGuinness, Morrie Ryskind, Rupert Hughes, and Casey Robinson. "We resent," said the Alliance, "the growing impression that this industry is made up of, or dominated by Communists, Radicals and crackpots . . . we want only to defend against its enemies that which is our priceless heritage: that freedom which has given man, in this country, the fullest life and the richest expression the world has ever known." The president of the new body was Sam Wood, the director who had expunged the Fascists from his film of *For Whom the Bell Tolls*.

In March 1944, the Alliance went to Washington to complain formally about "totalitarian-minded groups" at work in the film industry. A month after this visit, Martin Dies and his sleuths reappeared in Hollywood, this time to denounce the making of pictures which extol a foreign ideology—propaganda for a cause which seems to spread its ideas to our people and the "leftist" or radical screenwriters. . . . Many of them, perhaps in the belief they are aiding a cause they could not give an intelligent explanation of if called upon to do so, slyly and cleverly insert these "leftist" ideas into their screenwritings. . . . In my opinion, if it is worth anything to the [motion picture executives] they will do well to halt the propaganda pictures and elminate every writer who has un-American ideas.[23]

12

Under the 1941 contract agreed upon between the producers and the Screen Writers Guild (and finally signed in 1942), the writers were given the responsibility for allocating their own credits. Disputes between scenarists would be presented to a three-member arbitration panel, which would base its findings on an inspection of the paperwork (the treatments, drafts, revises, and so on). If the panel's decision was appealed, further evidence would be listened to: from the appellant writers themselves, or from producers and directors. Credits would be divided into "top" credits, "joint" credits, and "additional" credits. The top credit would usually go to the first writer hired. If a second writer wanted a half share, he would have to prove that he had written 50 percent of the material that reached the screen. To bid for an "additional" credit, he would have to establish a 30 percent input. The new arbitration system did not suit everybody, but it did go a long way toward eliminating the old "son-in-law" abuses of the past and on the whole made it more difficult for writers to go around boasting about their secret authorship of this or that successful film. In theory, film history became a shade more checkable.

And yet people are still arguing about the true authorship of film "classics" like *Citizen Kane* and *Casablanca;* indeed, one could say that the more successful the film, the more lingering the doubt about who wrote it. *Citizen Kane* was almost one of the Guild's first arbitration "cases" (although the producer-writer contract was drawn up in 1941, the credit arbitration clause had been agreed in

October 1940). The credits went to Herman J. Mankiewicz and Orson Welles. This sounds simple, and according to the evidence, it was entirely just. But the issue remains just a bit uncertain, slightly blurred. Orson Welles let it be known that the original script for *Kane* was his and that Mankiewicz merely contributed one or two important scenes. And Mankiewicz said that 99 percent of the finished screenplay was by him. And then there was a third claimant, the Mercury Theatre producer John Houseman, who asserted that it was he and Mankiewicz together who did most of the work. To this and other Housemanisms, Welles answered: "I have only one real enemy in my life that I know about, and that is John Houseman."[1]

The probable sequence of events is that the idea for *Kane* was chanced upon by Welles and Mankiewicz or by Mankiewicz and Welles or by a solo Mankiewicz as just one of many plot ideas for Welles's Mercury radio scripts. Welles had given Mankiewicz a job as a radio scriptwriter at a time when Hollywood was trying to disown him and his "orbit was smaller, his word carried less weight, his reputation was increasingly 'Ho, Ho, here comes crazy Mankiewicz.' " It was not just the drinking or the gambling or the ever more erratic delivery of screenplays that had damaged him; it was also his politics, which had been becoming right-wing, almost Lindberghian—at least that's what they sounded like when he had had a few drinks and was surrounded by radicals. Although in the early thirties he had raged against Hitler, he was now more interested in raging against the reds who ran the Anti-Nazi League. "The more Herman believed that communism was mobilized in Hollywood, the more outrageous he became."[2] In 1939, outrageousness was seriously out of fashion.

Mankiewicz was therefore grateful to be taken up by Welles the boy wonder, even at $200 a script and even though the deal at the Mercury was that all the writing credits went to Welles—it was part of the boy-wonder myth that every show should be "produced, directed, and written" by O. Welles. At this early stage of the *Kane* saga, Mankiewicz would not have been thinking about credits. For Welles, though, they were important, because the myth was under threat. He was disliked and envied in Hollywood on account of the contract he had been handed by RKO—a contract that paid him $100,000 a year "to write, direct, produce and perform in 4 movies, one per year." Welles also had choice of subject and the promise of no interference. He was twenty-four, and he had grabbed a deal that most of the old pros would have killed for. And to make things worse, he didn't seem to appreciate his luck: "This is the biggest electric train a boy ever had," he was reported to have said. Hollywood was praying for Welles to fail, and by the end of 1939 the omens were beginning to look good. His first project for RKO had been shelved, and his second was not looking healthy; he had fallen out with John Houseman, who was thought by some to be the brains behind the throne, and his Mercury stage productions had been getting poor reviews. In September 1939, Mankiewicz was hospitalized after a road accident; Welles came to visit him and offered him the job with Mercury: "I felt it would be useless," Welles later explained, "because of Mank's general uselessness many times in the studios. But I thought, 'We'll see what comes up.' " From their very different standpoints, both men at this time badly needed something to "come up."

The idea of a script about William Randolph Hearst was a natural for both Mankiewicz and Welles. Mankiewicz had been a fascinated student of the news tycoon for several years, and Welles knew Hearst as an old friend of his father's. Mankiewicz insisted later that he "told Welles that I would be interested in doing a film based on Hearst and Marion Davies. I just kept on telling him everything about them." Welles has said that he couldn't remember who first thought of it but that "I suppose I would remember if it had been me." To him, it did not greatly matter, since "I had no intention of Mank being the coauthor. None. Rightly or wrongly, I was still without self-doubt in my ability to write a film script. I thought Mank would do that anecdotal kind of thing about Hearst, give me a few ideas, fight me a little. . . . But I didn't know how *not* to let him in since the essential idea of the many-sided thing had arisen in conversations with him."[3]

With the idea established, the pair began arguing about angles of approach, and in January 1940 it was agreed that Mankiewicz should go into retreat at a ranch near Victorville, California, and get to work. He could take with him a secretary and a nurse, but no alcohol. Mankiewicz said he also wanted John Houseman in attendance to edit whatever he came up with (Houseman had edited Mankiewicz's scripts for Mercury). It is at this point that the reminiscences diverge. According to Mankiewicz—and he is supported by testimony from his secretary—he wrote a 325-page script called *Ameri-*

can, with valuable if marginal assistance from John Houseman. According to Houseman, *American* was a joint endeavor, with him and Mankiewicz laboring together on almost every aspect of "their" script: "We started with the image of a man—a giant, a tycoon, a glamour figure—we asked each other how this man got the way he was. . . ." After twelve weeks of disciplined if sometimes quarrelsome collaboration, Houseman says, the pair of them had completed a script for Welles to shoot from. According to Welles, Mankiewicz and Houseman already had a script—*his* script—before they went to Victorville: "Though everything was reworked, that contained the script as it developed. But apparently Mank never showed it to anybody." Welles also claimed that it was he who had sent Houseman to Victorville, so as to keep Mankiewicz from drinking.

After Victorville, the story becomes slightly clearer. The *American* script was cut from 325 pages to 156 pages, with Welles doing most of the cutting and Mankiewicz doing a lot of rewriting and protesting. "Revised pages were passed back and forth between the two, Welles changing Herman, who changed Welles—'often much better than mine,' says Welles," who also modestly avowed: "I didn't come in like some more talented writer and save Mankiewicz from disaster." When Mankiewicz was difficult, Welles was able to blame this on the malign influence of Houseman, who he believed had spent the whole time at Victorville "arousing Mank's latent hatred of any body who wasn't a writer—and directing it at me." Welles's assistant Richard Barr believes the real work on *Kane* was done post-Victorville: "I know Orson touched every scene, and I don't mean cutting a word or two. I mean some serious rewriting, and in a few cases he wrote whole scenes. I think it's time history balanced this situation."[4]

Some would say that it was Welles who first did the unbalancing, by tending always to blur Mankiewicz's contribution, saying things like: "Without Mank it would have been a totally different picture. It suits my self-esteem to think it might have been almost as good but I could not have arrived at *Kane* as it was without Herman." This sounds generous until you read it through a second time. When pressed, Welles would give the impression that Mankiewicz's portrait of Hearst came out of knowledge that was "journalistic, not very close, the point of view of a newspaperman writing about a newspaper boss he despised," whereas he—Welles—had a much surer grasp of the man's "inner corruption."

In August 1940, Welles told Louella Parsons (Hearst's gossip writer, as it happened): "and so I wrote *Citizen Kane.*" It was a casual remark, and possibly misquoted. Mankiewicz, however, was enraged. In the view of Welles's biographer Barbara Leaming, the "real" cause of Mankiewicz's ire was that he realized, when he viewed the film's rushes, that *Kane (a)* was going to be a great picture and *(b)* was going to be a great picture because of what Welles the director had made out of his/their script. "Whatever he had contributed to the film—and it was a great deal—it had already become something different."[5] It had become the work not of a words man but of a pictures man: this was a distinction that Orson Welles had only lately come to fathom, and rejoice in. Mankiewicz could see for himself that Welles had indeed appropriated the essence of the thing. Hence his excessive indignation.

And the indignation was excessive, because at this stage of the drama Welles had actually set aside his original plan to claim sole credit. Any hesitation about saying so had to do with his contract with RKO, which insisted that he be represented as the sole author of everything he did. The studio was looking for an excuse to break the contract, and Welles's lawyer did not want to yield even the tiniest opening. And Mankiewicz, in his contract, had signed away all claims to a credit—and for a fee of around $23,000, he had not minded doing so.

But now, egged on by his wife—and possibly also by Houseman and Ben Hecht—he decided to lodge a complaint with the Screen Writers Guild. He wished to claim sole credit. Since it was Guild policy to look with disfavor on producers who claimed writing credits, there is just a chance that Mankiewicz's claim might have prevailed. Welles struck back: now *he* wanted sole credit and, according to one story, offered Mankiewicz $10,000 to drop his claim. Ben Hecht's advice to Mankiewicz: "take the money and screw the bastard." So far as we know, Mankiewicz did not take the money, but he did withdraw his Guild complaint. The credit proposed by RKO was "Screenplay by Herman J. Mankiewicz and Orson Welles," and in the end this was accepted by both parties.

Mankiewicz's supporters continued to feel that their man had been ill-used, and Welles never quite shook off the feeling, or the accusation, that he might have been a little greedy. As for Mankiewicz, Hollywood's "own resident loser-genius," this was the high point of his career. The more it dawned on him that *Citizen Kane* was a film masterpiece, a movie that would last, the more he yearned for that sole credit. He was forty-four, and in his and everybody else's view he had misspent half his writing lifetime. To be acknowledged as the originating author of *Kane* would make sense of all the waste; to have to share the credit with the film's innovative director left too many question marks hanging in the air. After all, the whole world knew that Mank was brilliant at one-liners: the doubt was that he had much to offer in the way of vision or design. When the RKO publicity men took to trumpeting *Kane* as a one-man show, a film by Orson Welles, Mankiewicz wrote to his father: "I'm particularly furious at the incredibly insolent description of how Orson wrote his masterpiece. The fact is that there isn't one single line in the picture that wasn't in writing—writing from and by me—before ever a camera turned."[6]

At the 1941 Academy Awards, Hollywood made a point of not honoring Orson Welles. *Citizen Kane* got one nomination—for the screenplay. Neither Welles nor Mankiewicz attended the ceremony. Welles was in Mexico, and Mankiewicz believed he was being set up for a humiliation: "He thought he'd get mad," his wife said, "and do something drastic if he didn't win." He did win, and when the award was announced: "Herman J. Mankiewicz," the "and Orson Welles" got "drowned out by voices all through the audience calling out 'Mank! Mank! Where is he?' " Mank was at home, listening to it all on the radio, already composing—for dining-out purposes—the speech he would have made if he had been there: "I am very happy to accept this award in Mr. Welles's absence because the script was written in Mr. Welles's absence." And Orson Welles was already devising this letter to "Dear Mankie":

Here's what I wanted to wire you after the Academy dinner:
                "You can kiss my half."
I dare to send it through the mails only now that I find it possible to enclose a ready-made retort. I don't presume to write your jokes for you, but you ought to like this:
                "Dear Orson: You don't
                know your half from a
                whole in the ground."[7]

2

The Mankiewicz-Welles dispute over the credits for *Citizen Kane*
has been kept simmering over the years by opponents of *auteur*ism:
to root for Mankiewicz has been to strike a blow against all arrogant,
proprietorial directors. In the case of *Casablanca,* the squabbling
sets writer against writer—although never face to face. Ordinarily,
such a dispute would be of little interest; with *Casablanca,* though,
it bears somewhat on the character and quality of a movie that most
of us now know, or think we know, by heart. One of the charms of
Casablanca is its awkwardness, its fresh-seeming uncertainty about
the kind of film it wants to be. The politics and the romance sit side
by side, half pretending to care about each other and in the end
stirring themselves into a state of conflict, but actually quite self-
contained. So it is with the film's two or three contrasting manners
of address—the comic-cynical, the soppy-elegiac, and the solemn-
propagandist: they jostle each other in a chummy sort of way but
only because none of them knows where it's going. The whole thing
has an anthology air to it: not so much a story as a stringing together
of great moments to remember. How, and in what order, we remember them is left to us, and this is part of why we like the film
so much: it never bullies us.

At least four writers have a claim to be thought of as the "true"
author of *Casablanca.* In his autobiography, which he took care to
call *As Time Goes By,* Howard Koch claims that he was responsible
for the film's treatment of "the political intrigues with their rele-
vance to the struggle against fascism." Koch was brought in to work
on a script already drafted by Julius and Philip Epstein, and he saw
it as his task to "shape the film's politics." When pressed, he could
not recall which lines, precisely, were by him.

According to Julius Epstein, Koch's "stuff was not used. . . . I've
always liked Howard . . . he is thinking the wishful thought." Philip
Epstein, Julius's twin brother, died in 1952, and we do not have his
testimony, but another Warners writer, Casey Robinson, believes
that he himself first had the idea of making a film out of a "lousy
play" called *Everybody Comes to Rick's.* He persuaded Hal Wallis
to buy the rights, and then:

> Pretty soon I hear that he [Wallis] has put the Epstein brothers to
> work on it, and I'm furious! Here's my pal! Something I've found!

And he's given it away! . . . The next thing I hear is that the Epsteins have finished, and they have a man named Howard Koch on it. I don't know him, but he's a pretty fair writer, I believe.

So they started shooting, and Hal comes to me and says, "We need some help. There's a little trouble." I found out shortly that the little trouble was big trouble because Bogart had said, "I won't shoot this————; and he had used a very nasty word and gone home.[8]

This coincides with an account by Ingrid Bergman:

every day we were shooting off the cuff; every day they were handing out the dialogue and we were trying to make some sense of it. No one knew where the picture was going and no one knew how it was going to end. . . . Every morning we said, "Well, who are we? What are we doing here?" And Michael Curtiz would say, "We're not quite sure, but let's get through this scene today and we'll let you know tomorrow."

It was ridiculous. Just awful. Michael Curtiz didn't know what he was doing because he didn't know the story either. Humphrey Bogart was mad because he didn't know what was going on, so he retired to his trailer.

And all the time I wanted to know who I was supposed to be in love with, Paul Henreid or Humphrey Bogart?

"We don't know yet—just play it well—in between."[9]

According to Casey Robinson, this is where he stepped in and sorted out the love interest, arranging for Bergman to love Bogart but to fly off with Paul Henreid:

Frankly, I never read the script, because I had already written this script in my mind. I do know that the [Epstein] boys wrote the police stuff and the comedy, and they wrote it very well. And the breaking into and closing down of the club—they wrote that. So what it came to was I wrote the love story. I wrote the scene where she came to him ("I hope you enjoyed it, it's over . . ." and so on), the scene where the husband comes to Rick, and the finish of the thing.[10]

The problem seems to have been that the Epsteins, originally hired by Warners to do the screenplay, had gone off to Washington to work for Frank Capra on one of his "Why We Fight" documentaries. The studio tried to stop them, but in the end it was agreed that they would send back the *Casablanca* script as they wrote it, page by page. And so they did. In the meantime, though, as a precaution, Howard Koch had been brought in, and he promptly began mixing his "political" interpretation of the story with the Epsteins' comedy material. After a bit, two scripts were in the making, and neither of them was sufficiently concerned with the love angle. Enter Casey Robinson, the love machine: "There was, incidentally, never any question about the way the story would end. . . . The ending was clear as far as I was concerned . . . once I was on the picture."[11]

According to Julius Epstein, this Robinson claim is preposterous: "He wrote some test scenes for the actors, which we rewrote to fit the script. The only line of his that remains that I can remember is, 'A franc for your thoughts,' which I always thought was a terrible line. We fought to get it cut. Let me just say this . . . the studio knows who did what. They made us producers right after *Casablanca*. . . . They gave us a new contract. They gave us a whole bungalow with fireplaces." As to the Koch claim that it was he who shaped the politics: "If there was an arbitration panel in those days—if such a thing had existed—Howard Koch would not have received a credit. Because you have to have at least 30 per cent of a script to get credit. He never would have come close. No way." Of course, there *was* an arbitration panel in 1942, but none of the four claimants thought to make use of it. This could be because none of them knew that he was working on a movie that would turn out to be something to boast about: all the signs were that *Casablanca* was a stinker. The credits went to the Epstein twins and Howard Koch. Why didn't Casey Robinson complain?

> . . . about that credit. I am angry still. I was pretty smart-assed in those days, too. I wouldn't put my name on the screen with another writer. I was very proud of the fact of my solo screenplays . . . to go on the screen with three other writers with my piece— because I regarded it as *my piece!* And I wouldn't put my name on the screen. It was a very bad mistake, because the boys proceeded to earn an Academy Award.[12]

Perhaps history should record that in addition to the four main contenders, there are one or two minor claimants to a piece of *Casablanca*. The film uses several lines from the play *Everybody*

Comes to Rick's, by Murray Burnett and Joan Alison, including the line "Then play it . . ." and the song "As Time Goes By." In the flashback scene (which Koch wanted to show Bogart fighting against the Fascists), Casey Robinson was helped by Albert Maltz. The line "Louis, I think this is the beginning of a beautiful friendship" was, says Robinson, dreamed up by Hal Wallis, the producer. And of course some of the script was dictated by the Hays Office, where Joe Breen was much exercised by the suggestion that "Renault is an immoral man who engages himself in seducing women to whom he grants visas": to placate Breen, lines like "Another visa problem has come up"; "Show her in" were cut, and "At least your work keeps you out of doors" was changed to ". . . gets you plenty of fresh air."[13]

Howard Koch was happy enough to be remembered as the man who wrote *Casablanca:* after all, the alternative was to be remembered as the man who wrote *Mission to Moscow.* Julius Epstein, though, claims to be sick of the *Casablanca* tag. Nobody ever seems to ask him about *The Male Animal,* or *Mr. Skeffington,* or any of the other fifty or so scripts he penned between 1934 and 1983. *Casablanca* he came to speak of as "slick shit":

> *Casablanca* is one of my least favorite pictures. I'm tired of talking about it after 30 years. I can explain its success only by the Bogie cult that has sprung up after his death. I can recognize that the picture is entertaining and that people love it. But it's a completely phony romance, a completely phony picture. For instance, nobody knew what was going on in Casablanca at the time. Nobody had ever been to Casablanca. The whole thing was shot in the back lot. There was never a German who appeared in Casablanca for the duration of the entire war, and we had the Germans marching around with medals and epaulets. Furthermore, there were never any such things as letters of transit around which the entire plot revolved. . . . The movie is completely phony![14]

Even so, try telling him that it was written by Casey Robinson and Howard Koch. Epstein says that he had defended his credit because he was "forced" to do so by his children, who were "outraged" by the claims of others: "If it wasn't for the pressure from my kids and from my friends, I wouldn't have even been interested."[15]

3

Neither *Citizen Kane* nor *Casablanca* went to arbitration at the Screen Writers Guild, but even if they had, people would still be quarreling today about where the "real" credit should have gone. One film that famously did have to seek a ruling from the Guild (in 1943) was *Hangmen Also Die;* the Guild made its ruling, but the arguments go on. *Hangmen* is still chewed over with some passion as the film for which Bertolt Brecht received no screenplay credit and the one that taught him a few ugly lessons about Hollywood.

Brecht arrived in Los Angeles in 1941, after seven years of "changing countries more often than our shoes." His passage and his immigration papers had been arranged by leading figures in Hollywood's émigré community—principally the director William Dieterle. Brecht also received help from Fritz Lang, and when, in 1942, Lang invited Brecht to collaborate with him on an anti-Nazi picture, it seemed an almost perfect match. Lang had refused Goebbels's offer of the directorship of the German film industry; he had fled Germany in 1933, leaving his Nazi wife behind, and had withstood a fair amount of neglect at MGM before delivering a hit with *Fury* (1936), an intermittently stirring polemic against mob prejudice. Brecht knew him as the director of esteemed German classics like *Metropolis, M,* and *Dr. Mabuse;* Brecht's actress wife had appeared in *Metropolois,* and Peter Lorre, one of Brecht's best friends, had played the murderer in *M.* Brecht and Lang had met a few times in Germany during the twenties.

Brecht's first few months in Hollywood had been frustrating: he did not fit easily into the émigré social whirl that centered on Sunday-afternoon tea parties at the home of writer Salka Viertel. (Later on, he did try to organize screenplay collaborations with Salka, whose close friendship with Greta Garbo gave her some influence at MGM, and also with her son Hans: "As I knew English," said Hans, "and he really didn't, he asked me to collaborate with him. I would put our work into English as we went along.") From the week of his arrival, Brecht declared himself uncomfortable in Hollywood, this "Tahiti in metropolitan form." He was, he said (somewhat obscurely), like a "chrysanthemum in a coal-mine." He hated the climate, the food, and a good number of the people—especially those émigrés who tried to Americanize him.

Brecht was forty-three, well known in Europe but with no reputation to speak of in Amerca. Hollywood people vaguely knew that he wrote plays: Donald Ogden Stewart, for example, was not aware of Brecht's European fame—although he, like a few others, believed that there was a connection with Kurt Weill, by then a Broadway presence of some note. In Hollywood, Brecht was an obscure, non-English-speaking writer with no money and with no known background in the movies. And Brecht's demeanor did not help to break the ice. He was, said John Houseman, "absolutely open in his contempt for the movies as a medium for *him* to work in." As to screenwriting: it "was a kind of racket, and he hoped he could collect some dollars."[16] Brecht's own theories about drama were utterly opposed to what he saw as Hollywood's "narcotic" approach to its huge audience: all around him he heard people talk of the need for pictures to "grip," to "involve," and even to "knock out" the masses. All this was repugnant to him, and yet he was fascinated by the potential of the medium—those vast audiences could surely be "taught to think": taught to think, that is to say, by Bertolt Brecht. After all, had he not himself, in 1931, written, directed, and produced a movie *(Whither Germany)* in which his theories about Epic Theater had not been compromised? After a year in Hollywood spent trying to sell "serious" film stories, Brecht was beginning to learn what émigrés like Lang and Dieterle already took for granted—that the Hollywood system had to be joined before it could be beaten. But, being Brecht, he was learning this only in theory. When Lang invited him to work on a film based on the May 1942 assassination of Reinhard Heydrich, the Nazi Reichsprotektor in Czechoslovakia, he entertained cautiously high hopes of the collaboration. Lang, it is true, was a haughty Viennese bourgeois of suspect politics; even so, on a subject like this, there was every reason to suppose that they could together achieve something that might rise an inch or two above the "sewer" (one of Brecht's several names for Hollywood). And in any case, by the time Lang made his offer, Brecht was desperately short of money.

Lang and Brecht began work on the Heydrich treatment in June 1942. The joint idea at this stage was to make a film that portrayed the German response to the assassination of one of their top men. They would be shown rounding up hostages, terrorizing the community, testing the will and solidarity of the Resistance. So far, so good. By the end of June, however, Brecht was beginning to mutter into his diary about Lang's obsession with box office expectations:

> I work with Lang usually from nine in the morning until seven in the evening on the hostage story. A remarkable period during which it emerges that the logic of a process or a development under discussion is: "The public will accept that." The mastermind of the underground movement hides himself behind a curtain when the Gestapo searches the house—the public will accept that. Also the commissar's corpse falling out of the closet. Also "secret" meetings at the time of the Nazi terror. Lang "buys" things of that sort. Interesting also that he is far more interested in surprises than in tension.[17]

The real division that had emerged between the two of them was that Brecht wanted to make the film a sort of hymn to the possibilities of mass resistance (his working title for the script was *Trust the People*), whereas Lang saw it as a manhunt melodrama, an individual on the run protected by an occupied community. By August the strain between these two interpretations had become difficult to handle. Lang began to feature in Brecht's journal as Hollywoodized, corrupt, a judgment that would later flower into the following description:

> He sits with the bearing of a dictator ... behind the executive desk, full of drugs and prejudices against every good idea, gathering "surprises," little tensions, dirty sentimentalities and inauthenticities, and taking "licenses" for the box office.[18]

Lang, for his part, seems to have decided that the time had come for Brecht to be outgrown, or somehow marginalized. In August, without Brecht's knowledge, he approached John Wexley with a commission to write the screenplay of the Heydrich film. From Wexley's point of view, so he has said, this was a straightforward proposition: he did not see it as a co-writing assignment. Brecht, after all, spoke no English and seemed to know little about assembling a film script. As Wexley saw it, Brecht and Lang had outlined the "original story," and now it was his job to write the script— assisted, if so it happened, by further suggestions from Brecht-Lang. Brecht saw it very differently. He had the story laid out in all its

essentials, and Wexley had been hired to do the Englishing. Lang
certainly allowed Brecht to believe that Wexley had been brought
in to help rather than to take over, and he privately trusted that
Wexley's left-wing pedigree *(Confessions of a Nazi Spy)* would
soften any Brecht objections—as at first it did: "very leftist and
decent" was Brecht's first verdict on his partner. Brecht was also
gratified to learn that Wexley shared his view of the way the movie
should proceed: "Above all, I have won [Wexley] over to writing
with me at my house in the evenings a completely new ideal-script
that will be submitted to Lang. Naturally I lay the heaviest weight
upon those scenes that involve the people." (This "ideal-script" has
been lost, and in any case was a bit of a fantasy: it seems that as well
as writing the real script, Brecht and Wexley amused themselves by
compiling an alternative dream script, made up of scenes and lines
that Lang, for one reason or another, would reject or had rejected.)

The two worked together fairly harmoniously for some ten weeks.
From Wexley's account, the real work was done by him during the
day. In the evenings he would visit Brecht at home because, as an
alien, the German was subject to a curfew. They would talk about
the real script, to be sure, but they would also chat about the theater
or have fun messing about with the "ideal-script." We get the sense
that Wexley believed he was humoring Brecht, keeping him involved but not taking him at all seriously as a cowriter. Brecht, on
the other hand, saw it quite straightforwardly: the German-speaking
Wexley wrote down the script in English, and then "I correct his
work." Brecht was, it is true, slightly bothered by Wexley's habit of
writing "John Wexley" at the top of every piece of paper that was
used, and he was disconcerted also to discover that his collaborator
was being paid $1,500 a week (Brecht's own arrangement was for an
overall fee, which eventually came to between $8,000 and $10,000,
for five months work). There were also a few clashes involving Wexley's heretical attachment to the concept of "catharsis."

Even so, by October there existed a "real" screenplay of some 280
pages, which Brecht was actually quite proud of, calling it "no run-
of-the-mill thing":

> the film is constructed on epic lines, employing three stories that
> alternate: the story of an assassin; the story of a girl whose father
> is taken hostage; and the story of a quisling who is hunted down
> by an entire city. That, for example, is not bad. Not bad either, that

the underground makes mistakes, which the people at large correct, etc.[19]

This bulky, possibly unfinished script was delivered to Fritz Lang,
and here Brecht's direct participation ended. Lang, in the meantime, had been told by his producer (an independent, Arnold Press-
burger) that "pressure from the banks" had ordained an earlier
shooting date than had been planned. Wexley was ordered to cut the
script in a hurry, bringing it down to conventional length—around
150 pages. Lang stood over him as he worked, to make sure that the
manhunt theme took precedence over Brecht's mass resistance line.
Wexley later on grumbled about Lang's timid approach, his "fear of
being taken as a Communist," and his nervousness about tackling
the issue of anti-Semitism. ("John, don't politicize this," was, Wexley
says, the Lang refrain.) Nevertheless, Wexley did what he was told.
    Brecht knew nothing of all this, although when he bumped into
Wexley at a dinner, the American wore the appearance of "a living
bad conscience." Shooting of *Hangmen Also Die* began in early
November 1942, and Brecht went along to watch. At first, he was
impressed by the spectacle of Lang at work. He spoke of the "dignity and respectability of craftwork" and discovered "something
almost resembling art" in the director's handling of one of the nastier fight scenes: "Artistically, it's not uninteresting how precisely
and elegantly a prostrate man is kicked in the chest and then the
ribs." It soon dawned on him, though, that many of the scenes being
shot were scenes that he and Wexley had eliminated from "their"
screenplay. "I was able to remove the main stupidities from the
story," Brecht wrote in his journal. "Now they're back in." He also
observed that Lang was not even sticking to the script that he had
butchered: he was making things up as he went along, now and then
consulting Wexley but ignoring Brecht. And when Lang came to
edit the film, Brecht's material suffered further damage, or so it is
believed. All in all, Brecht's verdict was that his screenplay had been
mutilated by "criminals."[20]
    But he did not disown it. On the contrary, when he learned that
he was to receive no credit as author of the screenplay but merely
a joint credit, with Lang, for the original story, he demanded an
arbitration hearing at the Guild. For all his rage against Lang's
treatment of his script, he knew that "credit for the film would
possibly put me in a position to get a film job if the water gets up

to my neck." At the Guild hearing, though, he discovered why Wexley had been so busily autographing all those bits of paper. Wexley turned up with "half a hundred-weight of manuscripts," said Brecht, "and claimed he had hardly spoken with me." Brecht had only a few pages to exhibit, together with a report on the "discussions and writing sessions" he had had with Wexley. The Guild gave the solo credit to Wexley, even though Fritz Lang spoke up for Brecht. Lang later said that Wexley won

> despite the fact that [Hanns] Eisler, the composer, and I both went in front of the Screen Writers Guild and swore that many, many scenes—obviously—were written by Brecht and that nobody else in the whole world, certainly not Mr. Wexley, could have done them. But they said, "Well, Mr. Brecht will go back to Germany but Mr. Wexley will stay here. Mr. Wexley will need the credit much more than Mr. Brecht."[21]

He might have added that while Wexley was popular with most of his colleagues, Brecht made no secret of his contempt for the Hollywood screenwriter as a species. Of the Guild panel, he opined: "the sight of intellectual deformity makes my physically ill. I can scarcely stand to be in the same room with these intellectual cripples and moral casualties."[22]

Hard-line Brechtians, it is said, do not admit *Hangmen Also Die* into the canon, presumably because of the risk of attributing to the Master lines that might turn out to have been written by John Wexley. One can sympathize with their predicament. For example, in the film there is a jail scene, during which a leading Czech poet is approached by one of his cohostages, an ordinary peasant sort of fellow:

> ORDINARY FELLOW: I happened to scribble down today—just a few lines for a song, maybe; and I thought that you being such a big writer, and if you had the time, you could please look it over and fix it up a bit?
> POET: My friend, I have all the time in the world. . . .

Why not read it aloud? says the poet. The other hostages shuffle into position, and all listen, with feeling, as the ordinary fellow reads:

Fellow patriots, the time has come.
Fellow patriots, there is work to be done.
Raise the invisible torch and pass it along.
Keep it burning, keep it burning.
Forward on that road that has no turning.
Die if you must
For a cause that's just
But shout to the end: "No surrender."
Ever onward, no returning
Till the senseless butcher will be learning
That his war isn't won
Until the last battle's done.
Carry on when we are gone.
No surrender.

"Of course," he adds, *"you* could make it a lot better." "No," says the poet. "No, my friend, let's have it just as it stands."

Brecht wrote all this in German and was then most displeased to find that Lang had hired a songwriter named Sam Coslow ("Cocktails for Two") to put it into English. Coslow's rendering Brecht described as "incredible filth": "invisible torch," it seems, should have been "invisible flag," and "Fellow patriots" was originally "Comrades." Both mistranslations were, in Brecht's view, cowardly evasions of the known fact that 95 percent of the Czech underground's leadership was Communist. Later in the film, the doomed hostages defiantly set the poem to music by Hanns Eisler. Eisler saw to it that part of his "Comintern" tune was woven in. As James J. Lyon comments:

> Unwittingly, millions of American movie-goers who saw this resistance film heard Czech hostages in a Nazi prison singing a few bars from a political song well known in the Communist movement throughout the world. Brecht must have smiled.[23]

Writing about screenwriting, one would like to be able to report that *Hangmen Also Die* is the only example of a poet-turned-screenwriter seizing the chance to put one of his own poems on the screen. But even here, it transpires, the "onlie begetter" was obliged to share his credit.

13

In his book *Billy Wilder in Hollywood,* the entertaining Maurice Zolotow tries to explain why Charles Brackett and Billy Wilder wrote *The Lost Weekend* "with their blood"—an odd phrase to use of a movie about alcoholism. Wilder, he says, had a special interest in the subject because he had just emerged from cowriting *Double Indemnity* with the alcoholic Raymond Chandler. Brackett also had strong views on the booze; no drinker himself, he was married to an alcoholic, had alcoholic relatives, and over the years had been the caring friend of several celebrity drunks like Scott Fitzgerald, Robert Benchley, and Dorothy Parker:

> She had become a lush—but there was in Charlie some compassion for the lost souls of the world that compelled him to succor them. It was Charlie Brackett, as Lillian Hellman tells us in her memoirs, who nursed Dashiell Hammett through many of his drunks in Hollywood. And in 1937, it was Brackett who phoned Hellman in New York and told her how sick Hammett was and put him on a plane to her.[1]

In Diane Johnson's life of Dashiell Hammett, this 1937 incident takes place in 1938. Johnson tells how Hammett was discovered lying on his bed at the Beverly Wilshire Hotel, "pale and grey-skinned and thin." In her version, though, he is discovered not by Charles Brackett but by Albert Hackett and his wife, France Goodrich Hackett, coauthors of three screenplays based on Hammett's

1934 novel, *The Thin Man.* According to Johnson, it was the Hack-ctts who airmailed Hammett to Hellman in New York—and then had to pick up an eight-thousand-dollar tab on the hotel room.[2] We might expect to find Johnson's account confirmed in another Ham-mett biography: *Shadow Man,* by Richard Layman. But no; it turns out that Mr. Layman has a third version of the event, in which the Hacketts are turned into the Bracketts:

> As quickly as the money came, the money went. Hammett saw no reason to save. In a 1969 interview, Lillian Hellman told about visiting Hammett while he was living at the Beverly Wilshire, apparently in 1936. His unpaid hotel bill was $11,000, he owed the pharmacy where he bought his liquor $1,300, and he was broke. When he fell ill, his friends the Charles Bracketts paid his bills and sent him to New York to recover.[3]

Diane Johnson's source is not identified but was probably the Hack-etts; her story, it should be said, carries far more circumstantial detail than the others. Both Zolotow and Layman refer us to Lillian Hellman, whose stories about Hammett and herself are now listened to with caution. ("Did anyone ever see them together?" was Gore Vidal's memorable summary of their romance.)

Hacketts and Bracketts: it sounds like an error anyone could make—anyone, that is, who was not in the movies in 1938 (or '36 or '37). By the end of the 1930s, Brackett-Wilder and Goodrich-Hackett were two of Hollywood's most celebrated duos: Brackett and Wilder for comedies like *Midnight* and *Ninotchka;* the Hacketts for their *Thin Man* scripts. Couplings like theirs seemed to give credence to the studios' fetish for collaborative composition.

The Brackett-Wilder combination was the more mysterious: seen together, the two looked like something out of vaudeville—a routine based on comic incongruities. Wilder was all boulevardier impu-dence and bounce; Brackett was courtly and reserved. Wilder, a UFA screenwriter before he fled Berlin in 1933, spoke an American based on boyhood movie-watching and listening to dance songs (asked on the boat over if he missed his homeland, he is said to have replied, "Gee, but I'd give the world to see/That old gang of mine"). Brackett was a former East Coast lawyer and *New Yorker* drama critic, fourteen years older than Wilder, admired for his elegant syntax, courtly epigrams, and three-piece suits. In terms of Hollywood culture, it was a meeting between Salka Viertel's salon and the Algonquin Round Table. The smart-arse and the gent, Wilder and Brackett made a perfect movie-writing team: even when they were off duty, their casual conversations were, so to speak, in dialogue.

And this, it seems, could also have been said about the Hacketts. Two former stock-company performers, they had come to Hollywood in the middle of the Talkies Panic, after selling to the movies a play they had written about the "marital complications of a two career family." An MGM contract followed, and between 1933 and 1939 they got their names on thirteen films. In their *Thin Man* scripts, the banter between William Powell and Myrna Loy is witty enough, line by line, but what makes it unusual is its deeply companionable spirit: the barbs and counterbarbs add up to a sort of ardently literate love talk, a sustaining of the relationship's vitality and edge—and its equality. And if we count the number of drinks downed by William Powell in the course of a *Thin Man*'s ninety minutes, we can tell it wasn't easy. The Nick and Nora Charles partnership was Dashiell Hamett's invention, but Albert and Frances Hackett knew it from within and added much that was their own. Film actors, it is said, liked to perform scripts by the Hacketts; for some reason, they always ended up getting praised for the *intelligence* of their interpretations.

In 1940, then, not even the most heavily Benzedrined tycoon would have hired Bracketts when he wanted Hacketts (nor would he even in 1944, when Leigh Brackett—no relation—came to Hollywood to work on *The Big Sleep*). Some Hollywood historians, however, do not seem to mind a few minor confusions of this sort. In the Hammett story, what matters is that someone put the drunk author on a plane to his celebrity companion in New York, and someone paid a huge bill for his luxury hotel accommodation. In the end, it is a Hammett story (or a Hellman story), not about the likes of Hackett and Brackett; also, it is a nicely made scandalous set piece, a scene out of a movie: print the legend. Stories about Hammett in Hollywood are often like this, and so, too, are stories about Raymond Chandler, Scott Fitzgerald, William Faulkner, and the other big-name wrecks. They are stories that sound as if they have been improved many times in the retelling, and they are very often stories about drink. This might explain why they sometimes mix up the Hacketts and the Bracketts.

In the case of Chandler, there are two oft-told tales: the *Blue*

Dahlia story and the *Double Indemnity* story. Each of them has at its center a moment when Chandler formally challenges the system and comes out on top, but each of them also carries a strong whiff of drink and desperation. On *The Blue Dahlia,* Chandler had to write the script in a hurry because Alan Ladd was about to be called up to the military. John Houseman, producer of the picture, has told and retold how Chandler, behind schedule, decided that he would only be able to complete his duties if he could get and remain very drunk throughout the writing process. On this basis, Chandler drew up a new contract for himself:

> The studio was to provide two Cadillac limousines, constantly on call outside Chandler's house to fetch the doctor, take the script to the studio, drive the maid to the supermarket and anything else which might arise. Six secretaries, in relays of two, were to be available at all hours for dictation and typing. Nurses to administer vitamin shots were also required as Chandler never ate when on a bender. Finally, he wanted a permanently open telephone line to the studio.[4]

And so it was. For the next week, Chandler stayed drunk. The picture was finished on time and was a vast commercial triumph. A perfect Hollywood story, even down to the P.S., which reveals that the Navy Department (this was 1944) forced Chandler to change the murderer from a war-damaged navy man to a . . . well, for a time nobody could think of who else might have done the killing. In desperation, Chandler pinned it on a minor character of such implausibility that the poor fellow had to be given a speech in which he could *explain* why it was he. Chandler, whose own tales about Hollywood are as suspect as most other people's, claimed that because of this and other distortions, he threatened to walk off the picture. On this one, the *Blue Dahlia* director, George Marshall, has spoken with some scorn:

> He was in no shape to walk anywhere—certainly not from the studio because he wasn't there and certainly not from home because at the time John Houseman, the producer, was either sitting on him or locking him in the closet to try to get the script finished.[5]

By 1944, it had become Raymond Chandler's habit to write embittered pieces about the plight of the Hollywood screenwriter without ever quite admitting that he was one; it was as if he wished to combat a sense of developing entrapment, a feeling that (in Billy Wilder's words) he would "never find his way back to novel writing":

> He found it very difficult, I guess, to go back to a lonely life with just a wife and a typewriter and to switch back again to a completely different medium. And he was making exceedingly good money, not the sort of money you have to wait for while you are writing a novel—this was instant weekly money.[6]

Wilder was responsible for bringing Chandler into the studios in the first place. He had read *The Big Sleep,* and when Charles Brackett, on grounds of moral repugnance, refused to work on *Double Indemnity,* Wilder sent for the author of this tough-guy, L.A. novel from which he had no doubt already culled a few new hints on the demotic: "How often," he asked later on, "do you read a description of a character who says that he has hair growing out of his ear long enough to catch a moth?" But when the fifty-five-year old Raymond Chandler appeared at Paramount dressed in English tweeds, talking with an English accent, and sucking a foul-smelling pipe, it was—for both of them—"hate at first sight":

> [Chandler] didn't really like me, ever . . . to begin with, there was my German accent. Secondly, I knew the craft better than he did. I also drank after four o' clock in the afternoon and I also, being young then, was fucking young girls. All those things just threw him for a loop. . . . He would just kind of stare at me. I was all that he hated about Hollywood. He'd never seen an animal like this before. . . . And he was kind of bewildered, you know; and I was much more at ease with the medium because this was the first piece of pottery he'd ever done and by this time I had done thousands of pieces of pottery—pots to piss in, pots with Mexican designs, every kind of pot went through my hands. But for him, it was a new medium.[7]

And it was also a medium for which Chandler at first had nothing but disdain. He despised the work of James M. Cain, whose novel he was being hired to adapt ("the offal of literature," he called it), and he thought Billy Wilder a typically souped-up filmland clown, with his baseball hat and his riding crop and his boorish straightforwardness. But Chandler needed the money, and after five weeks he turned in a script full of long speeches, heavy descriptions of L.A. locales, and an excess of briskly abbreviated camera directions: "DOLLY IN FOR CU," and so on—"the usual ploy of the neophyte," says Zolotow. Wilder threw the script back at him:

> yes, *hurled it*—right at Chandler. It hit him in the chest and fell on his lap. "This is shit, Mr. Chandler," he said, amiably. He suggested that Chandler use it as a doorstop or contribute it to the scrap paper drive. "I think I have to teach you the facts of life, Mr. Chandler. We are going to write this picture—*together.* We are going to lock ourselves in this room and write a screenplay. It is going to take us a long time. You will be on salary even if it takes a year to write this picture."
>
> Chandler said he had never written in the same room with another person. Wilder said that was how he did it. Chandler had signed the contract. Those $750 checks looked real tasty. He sighed. He frowned. He twitched. He agreed to endure the collaboration.[8]

The description here is by Zolotow, Billy Wilder's worshiping biographer, many of whose anecdotes are set up to provide Wilder with a masterful last word. Even Zolotow, however, concedes that what happened next must be chalked up as a victory for Chandler. After several weeks of face-to-face collaboration, Chandler one day failed to show up at the office. Tracked down at home, he produced a list of reasons why he could no longer tolerate his work companion: "Mr. Wilder frequently interrupts our work to take phone calls from women. . . . Mr. Wilder ordered me to open the window. He did not say please. . . . He sticks his baton in my eyes. . . . I can't work with a man who wears a hat in the office. I feel he is about to leave momentarily." Unless Wilder apologized for these various discourtesies, Chandler would resign. Wilder, somewhat to his own astonishment, apologized. The moment has gone down in history: "It was the first—and perhaps the only—time on record in which a producer and a director ate humble pie, in which a screenwriter humiliated the big shots."

"Chandler gave me more aggravation than any writer I ever worked with," was Wilder's final verdict on the team-up, and Chandler even managed to improve on this. His verdict was politer, but more deadly:

Working with Billy Wilder on *Double Indemnity* was an agonizing experience and has probably shortened my life, but I learned from it about as much about screenwriting as I am capable of learning, which is not very much. . . . Like every writer, or almost every writer, who goes to Hollywood, I was convinced in the beginning that there must be some discoverable method of working in pictures which would not be completley stultifying to whatever creative talent one might happen to possess. But like many others before, I discovered that was a dream. Too many people have too much to say about a writer's work. It ceases to be his own. And after a while he ceases to care about it. He has brief enthusiasms, but they are destroyed before they can flower.[9]

The screenplay of *Double Indemnity* is stylish and tightly constructed, and the finished film turned out to be a model for dozens of wicked-blonde-meets-fatal-flaw murder movies of the late 1940s. It was a happy accident, perhaps, that Chandler and Wilder, as they wrote it, were jointly engrossed by the technicalities of their own unhappy partnership. In the movie, the murderous collaboration of Fred MacMurray and Barbara Stanwyck is gradually eaten into by the investigation of Edward G. Robinson, MacMurray's office colleague. Like Wilder and Chandler, MacMurray and Robinson sit, figuratively, across the desk from each other, on the lookout for dubious plot angles, fake motivations, implausible interventions of fate. In the film, the twist is that MacMurray's criminal accomplice has filed a bogus claim on the life insurance of the husband he and she have murdered. Edward G. takes a bit longer than usual to sniff out the culprits because in this case one of the accomplices is also *his* accomplice. MacMurray sweats as Robinson ruminates.

Murder is never perfect. It always falls apart sooner or later. When two people are involved, it's usually sooner. Now we know the Dietrichson dame is in it *and* the somebody else. Pretty soon we'll know who that somebody else is. He'll show. He's got to show. Sometime, somewhere, they've got to meet. Their emotions are all kicked up. Whether it's love or hate, it doesn't matter. They can't keep away from each other. They may think it's twice as safe because there're two of them. But it isn't twice as safe. It's ten times as dangerous. They've committed a murder. And it's not like a trolley ride together where they can get off at different stops. They're stuck with each other and they've got to ride all the way to the end of the line and it's a one-way trip and the last stop is the cemetery.

When MacMurray is finally rumbled and lies dying, he tells Robinson why the investigation has been so troublesome and slow: "The guy you were looking for was too close, right across the desk from you." And Robinson replies (as police sirens wailing in the background): "Closer than that." It's the last line of the film, and very touching, but one has to wonder which of the cowriters wrote it.

Wilder never worked with Chandler again. After *Double Indemnity,* he was more than ready to patch up his differences with Brackett, and Brackett was by now huffily waiting for his call. "So now," Wilder announced, "we're back together again, and we're Hollywood's happiest couple." In their next movie, *The Lost Weekend,* the writer hero's only collaborator is the bottle.

2

Raymond Chandler's grumbles about those "brief enthusiasms" that are "destroyed before they can flower" could have been spoken by Billy Wilder himself a few years earlier. The director of *Double Indemnity* had served his time as a lowly writer of B pictures; in 1935, Wilder's one writing credit was *Lottery Lover,* for which he was paid two hundred dollars a week for five weeks work. Everything else he wrote that year was ghost work. In 1936, he joined Paramount, where his hero, Ernst Lubitsch, was the star director, but he got no easy favors. At first, he was just one of the studio's 104 staff writers, put to work on frothy musicals like *Champagne Waltz* and *Rhythm on the River.* It was 1937 before the Lubitsch connection yielded a result: Wilder was teamed with Charles Brackett to write *Bluebeard's Eighth Wife.* Their task was to aim for a high erotic input without troubling the Hays Office. Wilder has spoken of the experience with pride:

> we had to operate cunningly to outwit the censors and this made us write more subtly. It was not permitted to have a character speak even a puny little curse like "you bastard" or "you son of a bitch." Once Charlie and I figured out this substitute: "if you had a mother, she would bark."

You couldn't show on the screen a man fucking a woman to whom he was not married, or even fucking a woman to whom he was married. For that matter, you couldn't even show a couple occupying the same bed at the same time. As far as the Hays Office was concerned, every bedroom in the whole goddam world had twin beds. So, the problem is, how do you show that man and woman making love?

Someone figured out a *shtick* like the maid is making up a man's bed the next morning; on the pillow she finds a hairpin. Lubitsch was the genius of what I call the hairpin-on-the-pillow tricks. He wants to show you, let us say, a man and a woman in a passionate affair. First a scene in which they are kissing ardently the night before. Then . . . dissolve to the following morning. . . . We see them at breakfast. Ah, but regard how they are sucking their coffee and how they are biting their toast. This leaves no doubt in anybody's mind that other appetites have been satisfied. In those days, the butter was on the toast and not the ass, but there was more eroticism in one such breakfast scene than in all of *Last Tango in Paris*.[10]

Bluebeard led to the marvelously complicated comic jigsaw *Midnight* and then to *Ninotchka,* a Lubitsch comedy, which was remarkable in 1939 for its jaunty anticommunism. Luckily for Wilder's standing in the eyes of Hollywood's radical community, the Hitler-Stalin pact fell neatly between the end of shooting and the film's release date. *Ninotchka* was a great popular success, and not just because "Garbo Laughs" in it. Audiences, it seems, enjoyed reencountering the old anti-Bolshevik stereotypes and were comforted by the knowledge that an embrace from Melvyn Douglas and a rooftop view of Gay Paree could undermine even the stoniest political convictions.

After *Ninotchka* came *Hold Back the Dawn* (1940). In this, Wilder and Brackett devised a scene in which the hero, played by Charles Boyer, is stranded in a Mexican flophouse, waiting for his entry papers to the United States. Lying on his bed, the Boyer character spots a cockroach on the wall and starts to poke at it with his cane, saying: "Where you going? What is the purpose of your trip? Let's see your papers." Wilder greatly enjoyed writing this scene because he himself a few years before had been obliged to serve time in Mexico before getting his U.S. immigration visa. This was real writing from experience. The scene was thrown out of the film by the director, Mitchell Leisen, because Boyer refused to speak the words. Said Boyer: "One does not ask a cockroach for his passport. You wish to make me look *stupide?*"[11]

Wilder was furious, raging against Boyer and Leisen (whom he loathed anyway, after working with him on *Midnight*). When the credits were allocated, with "Screenplay by Charles Brackett and Billy Wilder," he crossed out "Screenplay" and put "Written by" instead. And this, we are told, was the moment when Billy Wilder decided that he would become his own director: from now on, he would decide about the cockroach. Paramount did not like the sound of this, nor did Brackett, who believed that Wilder was too crazily irascible to handle actors. Wilder persisted; he agreed to one more writing-only job, on *Ball of Fire,* on condition that he could be on the set each day to watch Howard Hawks at work. After that, no more.

In the end, after more nagging, Paramount agreed to let him direct one of his own script ideas, *The Major and the Minor,* in which a buxom Ginger Rogers character had to pass herself off as a thirteen-year-old girl. The Hays Office failed to spot the script's powerful strain of pedophilia, and the Paramount executives believed that, with Ginger Rogers so disfigured, the whole thing was a surefire failure—a lesson for Wilder that he ought to stick to writing. On the day before shooting began, Wilder was "literally crapping in his pants." He confided his fears to Lubitsch, who decided that a bit of German-American solidarity was called for. On the first day, he turned up on Wilder's set with a small army of émigré directors, "to lend Billy support and technical advice." William Wyler, Michael Curtiz, William Dieterle, and others were in attendance as Wilder launched into his Scene One. To start the picture, Brackett had written one of his best-ever lines: "Why don't you get out of that wet coat and into a dry martini?" The assembled geniuses, we might surmise, took this advice to heart: Day One was "a shambles," yielding not "a single foot of usable film."[12]

One of the onlookers that day was the man who had made it possible for screenwriters like Wilder to dream of directing their own scripts. Three years before, in 1933, Preston Sturges had forced through a deal with Paramount that had Hollywood murmuring with admiration and unease. For a token ten-dollar fee, he had sold the studio a screenplay called *The Great McGinty* on condition that he be allowed to direct the film himself. Paramount was tempted: after all, it normally paid this writer up to $2,500 a week. And they no doubt recalled that Sturges had set Hollywood talking once before, in 1933, when—uncommissioned—he had turned in a "perfect" (said Jesse Lasky) shooting script for a film called *The Power and the Glory*. That was the first time, so far as anybody knew, that a one-time Broadway playwright had shown any real commitment to playwriting for the screen. It was also the first time, said Sturges, that a script had been sold "on a royalties basis, exactly as plays and novels are sold."[13]

The Power and the Glory was filmed, shot by shot, as Sturges wrote it, without any of the customary rewrites and excisions. The film was not a great commercial success, but over the years it had come to be recognized as a pioneering work. Its use of "narratage," for instance, was innovative: "That is, the author's voice describing events carried out by the actors and the author's voice speaking the dialogue while the actors only moved their lips. Strangely enough, this was highly effective and the illusion was complete."[14] Even as Sturges bargained for control of *The Great McGinty*, Orson Welles was taking note of this early voice-under study of crumbling tycoonery and would later half acknowledge the influence, on *Citizen Kane*, of Sturges's method of cine-narration.

The evidence of *The Power and the Glory* and of the dozen or so other scripts Sturges had written since coming to Hollywood in 1932 was enough to soothe Paramount's more extreme terrors about handing him control of his own movie, although there was of course a residual anxiety. Sturges wanted to direct because he thought screenwriters should not be treated like low-level factory hands, and this was a heresy that the producers, by 1939, believed they had stamped out. On the other hand, they could not reasonably brand Sturges as a radical: he had all along refused to join the Screen Writers Guild, preferring instead to protect the membership of his own dotty gatherings at the West Side Riding and Asthma Club (later the Corned Beef, Cabbage and Culture Circle). He spent most of his spare time, and spare money, starting up expensive restaurants and inventing curious machines—a bantam automobile, a machine for projecting ticker tape onto a screen, a canned-laughter box, and other follies. In his youth, he had been in charge of his mother's Paris cosmetics business and had marketed a kissproof lipstick. Sturges was a spendthrift capitalist, who had run through one or two fortunes before even getting to Hollywood. Paramount decided to take the risk—although, just in case, they insisted on appointing an assistant director, George Templeton, to take care of scheduling and budgets: "The production office called me down and said: 'Look, Preston Sturges, who's a kook and very difficult in many ways and doesn't know his ass from a hot rock, is making a picture. . . . You have to stay with him all the time.' "[15]

The risk turned out to be no risk at all. *The Great McGinty*, an amiable comic study of political corruption, was a spectacular triumph, commercially and with the critics. Sturges picked up an Academy Award for the year's best screenplay and all in all could not have asked for a more clinching vindication of his eight-year boast that his writing had been diminished by indifferent translation to the screen. After *McGinty*, there was no stopping him. He had a trunkload of accumulated story ideas and knew that he could not afford to pause. He followed up with *Christmas in July* (1940), an adaptation of one of his own stage plays, *The Lady Eve* (1941), and *Sullivan's Travels* (also 1941). In 1942, the year of Billy Wilder's directorial debut, he was delivering his fifth big hit, *The Palm Beach Story*. Five winners in two years: this was the stuff of a "phenomenon." Paramount was thrilled, or had to pretend it was. These movies were not only making money; they were also perceived to be original: fast, edgy, and sardonic, they combined farce and slapstick but maintained a coherent, if rather hectic story line. And they were cheap to make. On the whole, Sturges did not depend on stars: he had assembled his own stock company of bit-part actors, and his audience was forming an attachment to unlikely characters like William Demarest and Robert Grieg. The major worry was that Sturges seemed to be getting a number of his laughs at Hollywood's expense: a certain disrespectfulness was in the air. In many of their aspects, these were movies about movies. It was as if Sturges, while waiting for his opportunity, had assimilated all the current moviemaking styles and genres and was now respinning them at his own chortling, frenetic pace.

Thus, in *The Great McGinty*, Sturges teases Frank Capra in the idiom of a Warner Brothers politico-gangster pic. *McGinty* tells how a "little punk" is plucked from nowhere and, by intimidation and vote rigging, gets installed first as mayor, then as governor. In office, he is meant to look after the interests of his hoodlum backers. We wait for a Capraesque transfiguration. When it comes, with McGinty—aided by a woman at his side—declaring that from now on he will serve the interests of "the people," the boss retorts: "The people! Are you sick or something?" And when McGinty persists with his Jimmy Stewart talk, vowing to "put in a child labor bill ... stamp out the sweatshops ... banish the tenements," he is at once farcically bundled out of office, then into jail, and from there he is returned to his original bum's status. McGinty is a pawn, made use of and then dumped: once a little punk, always a little punk.

In *Christmas in July,* another little punk is briefly hoisted up the ladder. Penniless Jimmy, who dreams of shiny cars and trips to the Grand Canyon, is hoaxed into believing that he has won a huge cash prize in an advertising slogan competition. For a brief moment, he "becomes" a rich man. The slapstick finale of the film portrays a streetful of irately clamoring shopkeepers demanding their goods back: Jimmy's checks have bounced, and his big break has turned into a maddening ordeal. Again, the message is: big breaks don't just happen, they are organized. Sturges's treatment of the deluded or manipulated little punk is never gloating or sadistic. His real target is the rhetoric that promotes fantasies of cheaply won success. The pratfall, the custard pie, the Big Mistake: these are components of an essentially generous worldview. In the end, Jimmy's pathos is more affecting, and more genuinely "populist," than the sentimentally calculated growth-into-grandeur of a John Doe or a Mr. Smith. Manny Farber has brilliantly, if overexcitedly, characterized the Sturges little punks as creatures who live in busy terror of the Big Banana Skin, creatures who

> work feverishly as every moment brings them the fear that their lives are going to pieces, that they are going to be fired, murdered, emasculated, trapped in such ridiculous situations that headlines will scream about them to a hooting nation for the rest of their lives. They seem to be haunted by the specters of such nationally famous bone-heads as Wrong-Way Corrigan, Roy Riegels, who ran backward in a Rose Bowl game, or Fred Merkle, who forgot to touch second base in a crucial play-off game, living incarnations of the great American nightmare that some monstrous error can drive individuals clean out of society into a forlorn no man's land, to be the lonely objects of an eternity of scorn, derision and self-humiliation.[16]

Hollywood, of course, has encouraged such nightmares by pretending that the banana skins can be skirted, the derision and the scorn transcended by the merely pure of heart. Sturges found it hard to think about life without thinking about life as it had been misrepresented by the movies. There is always a touch of film criticism in his films, a showing how it should be done. In *Sullivan's Travels,* a celebrated comedy director suffers pangs of social guilt. His next movie, he says, will be "a document. I want to hold a mirror up to life. I want this to be a picture of dignity . . . a true canvas of the suffering of humanity." He proposes this to his producers:

MR. HADRIAN: How about a nice musical?

SULLIVAN: How can you talk about musicals at a time like this? With the world committing suicide . . . corpses piling up in the street, grim death gargling at you around every corner . . . people slaughtered like sheep. . . .

MR. HADRIAN: Maybe they'd like to forget that.

SULLIVAN (jerking his thumb toward the screen. He and the producers have been watching a new message pic): Then why do they hold this over for a fifth week at the Music Hall—for the ushers?

MR. HADRIAN: It died in Pittsburgh.

MR. LEBRAND: Like a dog.

SULLIVAN (contemptuously): What do they know in Pittsburgh?

MR. LEBRAND (mildly): They know what they like.

SULLIVAN: If they knew what they liked they wouldn't live in Pittsburgh! If you pandered to the public you'd still be in the horse age. . . . I wanted to make you something you could be proud of, something that would realize the potentialities of film as the sociological and artistic medium it is. . . . Something like . . .

MR. HADRIAN: Something like Capra. I know.

SULLIVAN: What's the matter with Capra?

After some further banter of this sort, the executives agree. Sullivan will be given a million to make *Oh Brother, Where Art Thou?* (based on the novel by "Sinclair Beckstein"). LeBrand will "take it on the chin. I've taken it before." "Not from me," says Sullivan.

MR. LEBRAND: Not from you, Sully, it's true. Not with pictures like "So Long, Sarong," "Hey, Hay in the Hayloft," or "Ants in

Your Plants of 1939" . . . but they weren't about *tramps,* and lockouts, and sweat shops, and people eating garbage in alleys and living in piano boxes. . . . They were about nice, clean young people who fell in love, with *laughter* and *music* and . . . *legs* . . . you take that scene in "Hey, Hay in the Hayloft" . . .

SULLIVAN: Yes, but you don't seem to understand, conditions have changed. There isn't any work . . . there isn't any food . . . these are troublous times. . . .

MR. HADRIAN: What do *you* know about trouble?

And this is the key question. Hadrian persists: "What do you know about garbage cans . . . when did you eat your last meal out of one?" Sullivan rethinks: Hadrian is right, of course. In order to make a decent job out of *Oh Brother, Where Art Thou?* Sullivan must discover, firsthand, what trouble really *feels* like. He decides to dress as a tramp and take to the road with but ten cents in his pocket: "I don't know where . . . and I'm not coming back till I know what trouble is." LeBrand and Hadrian promptly insure the director for a giant sum and then arrange to squeeze maximum publicity out of his lonely trek: "It'll break the front page of every newspaper in the country . . . *the world!* It'll put the war back . . . with the want ads . . . right next to the lost dogs." And Sullivan's trek will not be as lonely as he thinks. He will be followed "at a discreet distance" by "that lovely land-yacht De Mille used in 'Northwest Mounted,'" and there will be constant supplies of hot coffee and sandwiches and even "a little bar in the back":

MR. CASALSIS: It's connected directly to the studio by short-wave and it carries also . . .

MR. JONES: . . . a hot shower and a secretary . . .

MR. CASALSIS: . . . a physician . . .

MR. JONES: . . . and two strong arm guys . . .

MR. CASALSIS (triumphantly): . . . all dressed like tramps! What a novelty! You see, we have thought of everything.

SULLIVAN: Look, I'm looking for trouble and I'm not going to find it with six acts of vaudeville on my tail . . . at least not the kind I'm looking for . . .

MR. LEBRAND (gently): Be reasonable, Sully.

Sullivan eventually, after much knockabout, shakes off his entourage. The first lift he hitches takes him back to Hollywood. He tries again, this time with Veronica Lake in tow, and there follows a sequence of farcical adventures in freight trains, flophouses, railroad yards, and so on. The world of poverty turns out to be more mean and menacing than Sullivan had dreamed: cheated and double-crossed, he finds himself serving six years hard labor and looking like a fugitive from *I Am a Fugitive from a Chain Gang.* By now, he has had enough of his experiment and wants to go home. But the studio has long ago given him up for dead, and nobody in the jail believes that he is a Hollywood director. In a nearby Negro church, the preacher puts on a picture show for the jailbirds—a big event that the despairing Sullivan does not appreciate:

> The wriggling beam of light shoots PAST US from the projector. Suddenly there is a yell of laughter from everybody except Sullivan. He looks to his left, up at the screen, then to his right and glumly up at the screen.
>
> THE SCREEN—PAST SOME SILHOUETTES
> On it we see a silent comedy, possibly Chaplin in "The Gold Rush," possibly a Laurel and Hardy two-reeler. As each funny thing happens, we hear a roar from the audience. After a while—
>
> SULLIVAN—AMIDST THE LAUGHING AUDIENCE
> Alone he is glum.
>
> CLOSE SHOT—SULLIVAN
> Imperceptibly, as he watches the screen, his expression softens and he smiles very faintly.
>
> A VERY FUNNY BIT ON THE SCREEN
>
> CLOSE SHOT—SULLIVAN
> As if it pained him, he snorts a couple of times.
>
> ANOTHER FUNNY PIECE ON THE SCREEN
>
> SULLIVAN
> He laughs outright. Now there is a roar from the audience; Sullivan throws back his head and laughs with them.
>
> A GOOD PIECE OF THE FUNNY BUSINESS ON THE SCREEN
> A FULL SHOT OF THE AUDIENCE LAUGHING

DISSOLVE THROUGH:

SUPERIMPOSED CLOSE SHOT—BIG HEAD OF SULLIVAN
LAUGHING SEEN THROUGH THE ENTIRE AUDIENCE

DISSOLVE TO:

THE LITTLE CHURCH REFLECTED IN THE LAGOON
We hear the music and the distant laughter.

FADE OUT: END OF SEQUENCE "J."[17]

The film Sullivan and his coprisoners get to see is actually a
Mickey Mouse cartoon. What matters is, it makes them laugh, even
though they have every reason to despair. Sullivan, when he is freed,
determines to stick to what he knows: He has suffered, certainly, but
"I never *will* have suffered enough to make 'Oh Brother, Where Art
Thou?' "

SULLIVAN (gently): And I'll tell you something else: there's a lot
to be said for making people laugh . . . did you know that's all
some people have? It isn't much . . . but it's better than
nothing in this cockeyed caravan. (He shakes his head
reminiscently.) Boy!

The screen is then filled with images of laughing convicts, then
laughing soldiers. Then:

We see a HOSPITAL WARD with the patients laughing at a
Punch and Judy show. We see children in a BOMBED STREET
laughing at an organ grinder's monkey. To this the PREVIOUS
MONTAGE SHOTS ARE ADDED: SOLDIERS, REFUGEES, CONVICTS,
WOUNDED CHILDREN AND NEGROES SHARE THE SCREEN. The
sound builds into wild and deafening laughter. ON THE SCREEN
appear the words: "The End."

By entering this rather hefty plea for the social usefulness of
laughter, Sturges is doing what he often does: softening his own
satiric edge by means of some final palliative flourish. His admirers
have learned to blink a lot during the closing one or two minutes of
his movies. As Sturges admitted more than once, *Sullivan's Travels*
is concerned with the laughter of ridicule rather than the sort of
laughter that soothes and distracts. In a press interview in 1942, he

called Sullivan "a composite of some of my friends who tried preaching from the screen. I thought they were getting a little deep-dish and wasting their excellent talents in comstockery, demagogy and plain dull preachment." And five years later, writing to Bosley Crowther (to whom he earlier admitted that the ending of *Sullivan* "wasn't right"), he is still complaining about the lack of artistry for its own sake in the usual Hollywood product of the day:

> All my director friends loathed *Sullivan's Travels* but I saw it again about a year ago and liked it. If allowed only one I would be willing to hang my hat on this one. . . . Incidentally, I wish you would write a piece sometime on the growing ponderosity of picture making which is getting to resemble the building of a suspension bridge, rather than the gathering together of a few strolling minstrels to spout the words of some local poet.[18]

As if to cover himself against the possible failure, or offensiveness, of *Sullivan's Travels,* Sturges immediately followed it with *The Palm Beach Story,* a thoroughly escapist comedy-romance about the love tangles of the idle rich. Escapism, however, was no longer the best medicine in town. The war propaganda reviewers were scandalized, calling the film "a fine example of what should *not* be made in the way of escape . . . a libel on America at war." "We are shown," they said, "only unbridled extravagance, fantastic luxury, childish irresponsibility and silly antics on the part of those who should, by virtue of wealth and position, be the economic leaders of a nation at war." One scene in particular irked the BMP's "deep-dish" analysts. Traveling to Florida by train, several drink-maddened members of the Ale and Quail Club (all of them millionaires) engage in a bit of berserk target practice; their private carriage is wrecked as they blast away at crackers thrown into the air by trembling waiters. The analysts reported: "This is 1942, we are at war, there is an acute rolling stock shortage, and there's nothing funny about the misuse or destruction of a war essential. . . . Furthermore, useless civilian travel has been abandoned for the duration." The whole film, they said, would surely "gladden Hitler's heart."[19]

A bit later, Sturges got another BMP reprimand, when he was warned that the screeching of car tires in *The Miracle of Morgan's Creek* would encourage people to waste rubber. (An amusing study could be made of the impact on the movies of war shortages: fewer bullets, fewer balsa-wood barstools to break on people's heads, no stepping on the gas.) In this same movie, Sturges also fell foul of the Hays Office; Breen and his boys were outraged by the portrayal of a small-town girl made pregnant by an itinerant, and anonymous, GI. Although the whole plot turned on the girl's need to marry a local "little punk" in order to legitimize her child, Sturges was forced to change things around so that she somehow *married* the mysterious GI before letting him seduce her. Sturges got his revenge by calling the girl Trudy Kockenlocker.

And with *Hail the Conquering Hero*, in 1944, he almost got his own back on the BMP. Woodrow Lafayette Pershing Truesmith, son of World War I hero Sergeant "Hinky-Dinky" Truesmith, has been rejected by the army, 4-F, on account of his hay fever. Woodrow, ashamed to face his mother—who has a candlelit Hinky-Dinky shrine built in her living room—pretends to her that he is fighting overseas: actually he is in a San Diego factory. Then, in a bar, he meets a group of battle-scarred marines, former comrades of his father: to them, he confesses all. The marines are greatly moved: a mother's love must at all costs be nourished and sustained, and so, too, must the memory of Hinky-Dinky. They telephone Woodrow's mother: her son, they tell her, has indeed performed miracles of bravery at Guadalcanal, and now he is returning home—plus friends. By the time Woodrow and his new buddies get there, the whole town has readied itself for the arrival of a "conquering hero." Brass bands wait (Sturges style, they are trying to drown each other out by playing different tunes), a monument fund has been set up, and the townsfolk have agreed to pay off Mrs. Truesmith's mortgage. When Woodrow tries to tell his assembled admirers that "I really don't deserve it" or "I'm no hero," the cheers get louder: he is modest too. "Woodrow for Mayor" becomes the cry, and soon Woodrow has been taken up by one of the town's political factions (the town is, of course, full of shysters, tax evaders, profiteers, etc.). And so it goes on, the deception getting deeper and more complicated as Woodrow tries to wriggle out of it. And then, of course, there is the local beauty: would she still love him if she knew he was a fraud?

If the film had dared to carry Woodrow's deception to the limit, the BMP would indeed have had something to complain about. Again Sturges falters in the end. The film closes with Woodrow at last able to persuade the mob that he is a dissembler: "I've told you all this because too many men have died for you and for me to use this lie any longer." The flags are lowered, his mother weeps, and Woodrow wishes he were dead. At this, the marine sergeant leaps to the fore: "What that kid done takes *real* courage," he declares (the standard Hollywood line when cowardice has been confessed). The townsfolk rally: at last, an *honest* political contender, a John Doe. "Woodrow for Mayor" sounds out a second time, and as the marines leave town, mission accomplished, Woodrow stares after them and silently mouths the marine motto: *Semper fidelis.* For them, it's back to business, fighting business.

Once more we get the sense of Sturges copping out—or having to, since it is unlikely that any other resolution would have been allowed to reach the screen. Even as it stood, Sturges got no real backing from Paramount, and the OWI refused the film for distribution "in liberated areas." After all, the first two thirds of *Hail the Conquering Hero* are unlike anything else that came out of Hollywood in the war. A 1944 letter from Dudley Nichols reminds us of the terms in which Sturges's creative courage should be measured:

> Dear Preston: I saw Hail the Conquering Hero the other night and at once came home and ordered the firing of twenty one guns. You are an original, you have done that amazing thing—created a new style, out of the best of the past in film plus 1000 units of Sturges vitamins and a dash of pure courage. It's amazing how you keep the ball in the air all the time. I swore three times it was going to lob to the ground but each time you picked it up and sent it higher.[20]

Sturges's later years—from around 1948 until his death, in 1959—are sad to contemplate. After finishing *Hail the Conquering Hero,* he resigned from Paramount and formed a partnership with Howard Hughes. Nothing very good came of this "independent" venture, and by the time it was dissolved Sturges had gone three years without scoring a success—he who was accustomed to turning out two hits a year. The word in Hollywood, needless to say, was that the genius had finally "burned out."

Perhaps he had. In 1947, Sturges joined Zanuck at 20th Century–Fox to make a film called *Unfaithfully Yours,* in which Rex Harrison, famous conductor, wrongly believes his wife has been unfaithful; he dreams up—and for us acts out—methods of revenge, all of them borrowed from the movies. Nowadays the film is hard to watch. All the Sturges ingredients are there but not fully under control, as if some central spring had snapped. The film trudges, then leaps about, then tries to stroll, but the governing rhythms are all wrong. With Sturges at his best, the pace—the "graphic velocity," as Bosley Crowther called it—is what matters most, and although there is often an excess of slapstick, an overindulging of some favorite set piece, Sturges rarely seems tired or uncertain. He larks about because there is time to spare, or so it seems, and when he moves quickly it is to do with ebullience, not haste. In *Unfaithfully Yours,* he is looking for laughs that earlier he took for granted, or could do without.

According to Darryl Zanuck, Sturges was "at the end of his career" when he joined Fox (Sturges was fifty, Zanuck forty-six): "He had a restaurant, and it was losing a bloody fortune, a boat company which was losing more and more. He was brilliant in conversation but he was drinking like mad. I got him at the end of his career." It has been suggested that perhaps Zanuck admired and liked Sturges too much, giving him total control when perhaps he was in need of guidance, and allowing him "300% more time to edit than any director in Fox history." But from the picture we get of Sturges from Rex Harrison, it sounds rather as if he was beyond welcoming even benevolent interference:

> a most extraordinary and ingenious creature. The whole thing was like a party. He directed in a red fez. He would have a Doberman pinscher on set with him. Before he would start, he would stuff a handkerchief in his mouth to stop from laughing.[21]

Unfaithfully Yours was a box office disaster, and Sturges was no longer in demand. Between 1948 and 1949, he made one or two comeback attempts, mainly in Europe. None was successful. He was broke, out of work for long periods, and "full of ideas . . . too many ideas," said an actress who worked with him on one of the several projects that collapsed under him during these years. "In a way, his spirit seemed doomed and broken almost. I think by then he had had many reversals, but I never talked to him about it." In Hollywood, there were still loyal supporters, but the general feeling was that Sturges had had his day, that his imaginative world was distinctively prewar, his style a sort of post-Depression mania, and that the times now required something weightier, more grave: in other words, precisely the sort of "deep-dish" movies that he had ridiculed so lovably in 1941. In the words of screenwriter Earl Felton:

> He was too large for this smelly resort and the big studios were scared to death of him. A man who was a triple threat kept them awake nights, and I'm positive they were waiting for him to fall on his face so they could pounce and devour this terrible threat to their stingy talents. They pounced and they got him, good. But he knew the great days when his can glowed like a port light from their kissing it.[22]

14

At the 1943 Writers' Congress at UCLA, there was much looking forward to Hollywood's postwar role. Darryl Zanuck spoke ardently about the need for filmmakers to assist the healing process: "We have radiated sweetness and light since the advent of motion pictures and we have carefully refrained from even remote contact with the grim and pressing realities before us in the world."[1] And shortly afterward, addressing his troops at 20th Century–Fox, Zanuck spelled out his new commitment:

> The war is not yet over but it soon will be. And when the boys come home from the battlefields, you will find they have changed. They have learned things in Europe and the Far East. How other people live for instance. How politics can change lives. . . . Oh yes, I recognize that there'll always be a market for Betty Grable and Lana Turner and all that tit stuff. But they're coming back with new thoughts, new ideas, new hungers. . . . We've got to start making movies that entertain but at the same time match the new climate of our times. Vital, thinking-men's blockbusters. Big-theme films.[2]

There was something of this mood running throughout the Congress's deliberations: things would be different after the war, but different in an elevating sort of way. An abstract sincerity was in the air, with ancient Hollywood prognoses tricked out in a new disguise: out of hate comes love, out of destruction comes rebirth, out of spiritual struggle comes . . . well, sweetness and light, maybe, but from now on radiance would have to be, or seem to be, hard-won, world-comforting—that's to say, big-theme.

Robert Rossen, offering the Congress an "Approach to Character, 1943," struck a similarly high-pitched note. He told a story about a screenwriter of his acquaintance who was famous for writing "quick, slick, breezy stuff that's a carbon copy of every other picture that's ever been made." This writer used to mock Rossen as a "socially significant Joe." Nowadays, however, it was different. The writer, having served his time in wartime documentaries, had drastically altered his position: "Rossen, you're a dead duck," he would now say. "After the war is over, writers who remain in Hollywood won't have a chance."

> I asked him what he meant.
>
> "It's simple," he said. "You think pictures are going to stay in a groove. Well, they're not. They're going to change. If you think an audience is going to accept the kind of pap you screenwriters have been dishing out . . . you're crazy. If you think they're going to accept characters that are as phoney as a quarter watch, you're even crazier.

Rossen's writer friend had discovered, in documentaries, the attractions of the "real": real sweat, real speech, real danger, and so on. Most important of all, perhaps, he had come in contact with some real members of his audience, the fighting men who would soon be coming home:

> Two things have happened to them. The first is that they've been dealing with too much reality to be taken in by what we think is reality. The second is that they've gotten to know more people than they ever knew before, and to know more about them. And what's more important, you can't sell them on the idea that you have to be a special kind of guy to be a hero. You know, the kind of heroes we've always been writing, handsome, tall and cool— special people. They will have seen too many ordinary people become heroes, and by ordinary, I mean everybody from a banker's son to a ditch digger, and very few of them will be handsome, tall and cool. They'll be all sizes and shapes and they won't be cool at all. They'll be mad and sweaty and dirty and the gals they meet and know, they'll be different too.

Interestingly, Rossen does not construe from all this that postwar pictures will be sour or unillusioned, or that the new heroes will show signs of having been damaged by the war. On the contrary, he expects that—because of wartime solidarity against fascism—the ordinary man will have discovered a new sense of his own dignity:

> He knows much more about what's going on and he's more and more convinced that he can handle whatever comes his way. . . . This country needs him. There's a place for him, and he has a sense of his own importance. He has pride now and courage and belief that he and a lot of other people like him can work it out. . . . I'm not trying to be Pollyannish about this, I'm not trying to say that all's lightness and sweet. What I'm trying to say is that people have found dignity, they've appraised its worth, and they'll live for it, or die for it.[3]

Sweetness and light; lightness and sweet. On the international front, a brotherhood of nations; domestically, a continuation of wartime heroism by a unified, patriotic proletariat. Working on documentaries certainly gave Hollywood filmmakers a few lessons in realism, but it also gave them an inflated idea of their own educative capacities and duties.

When Zanuck spoke at the Writers' Congress, he was already at work on "the most important event in fifty years of Motion Picture Entertainment"—a giant screen biography of Woodrow Wilson. Zanuck, a colonel in the Signal Corps for part of the war, believed that World War II had come about because of the failure of President Wilson's efforts to set up a League of Nations. *Wilson*—to be billed as "The Movie to Prevent World War III"—would seek to revive the Wilson dream (or the Wendell Willkie dream, as it might now be called). Screenwriter Lamar Trotti, emerging from a crash course in Wilson studies, wrote to Ray Stannard Baker, the former President's biographer, expressing

> our earnest hope that the men and women who see this picture [will understand] that here was a great man who fought and died for a great ideal—a world united at peace through a League of Nations and that they will be awakened to the issues at stake, to the dangers of indifference, isolation and reaction, so that the tragedy of the present war which the Wilson dream might have prevented, may never again be permitted to occur.[4]

Wilson, released in 1944, was a two-and-a-half-hour, three-and-a-half-million-dollar spectacular, as earnest in its "showmanship" (Wilson at play, Wilson in love, Wilson attending a grand ball, etc.) as in its pursuit of global rehabilitation. The press received the film with reverence, and for a brief moment Zanuck, who had vowed never again to make a film without Betty Grable in it if this, the big one, flopped, seemed to have good reason to believe that "he had a masterpiece, a movie to stake a career, and perhaps a civilization on."[5] In Los Angeles, San Francisco, and the East Coast cities it was a box office success, but in Middle America it ran out of steam. When Zanuck took a print of *Wilson* to his hometown of Wahoo, Nebraska, for a special showing, a public holiday was declared, and everybody went to see the film. He then previewed it in Omaha, and again the house was packed. "The next day there were only seventy-five people in the audience. Zanuck was shocked. The family doctor set him straight on the arch-conservatism of the natives: 'Why should they pay seventy-five cents to see Wilson on the screen when they wouldn't pay ten cents to see him alive?' "[6] Overall, *Wilson* did not recoup the studio's huge outlay: worse than that, it made a net loss of around two million dollars. Zanuck's second "big theme" project, a film version of Wendell Willkie's book *One World,* was abandoned in 1945.

With the war over, Zanuck and his covisionaries had to revise their notions of what the new, changed audience might swallow in the way of entertainment. It seemed clear that the returning veteran—not to speak of those to whom he was returning—might not, after all, wish to be preached at by morale-builders or urged to fight the peace as heroically as he had fought the war. Closer to his mood, it seems, were films like *Pride of the Marines,* in which Al Schmid, a blinded war veteran, tries to adjust to civilian life, or *The Story of G.I. Joe,* a flat, semidocumentary tribute to the men who died.

Pride of the Marines was written for Warner Brothers by the Communist screenwriter Albert Maltz and would soon be cited as an example of Red propaganda. In the hospital with other returning GIs, Schmid listens to a discussion about postwar readjustment. One of the GIs declares: "Now that I'm going home, I'm scared. I wasn't half as scared on Guadalcanal as I am now. If a man came along—anybody—and told me I'd have a decent job for the rest of my life, I'd get down on my knees and wash his feet." At this, some of the others chime in with memories of prewar deprivations, but their point of view is balanced by one or two optimists, who voice a line not dissimilar to Robert Rossen's: "I'll tell you what happens—we're part of the People, that's what happens. You think because we done the front line fighting we can take a free ride on the country for the rest of our lives? There's no free candy for anyone in this world. . . . Don't tell me we can't make this country work in peace like it does in war. Don't tell me we can't pull together. Don't you see it, you guys, can't you see it?" To this Al Schmid retorts: "You askin' me? I don't see a thing," and he leaves the room.

Later on, back in America, Schmid is rescued from self-pity and general disaffiliation by the love of a nice girl and by a society that, although insensitive from time to time, is fundamentally decent. But when the film appeared, in August 1945, it was the blamelessly liberal hospital debate that attracted the attention and lodged in the memories of Maltz's enemies in the Motion Picture Alliance. (Ironically, before Maltz was called to account by the right, he had to stand trial before the bosses of his own CP. In 1946, he published an article called "What Shall We Ask of Writers?" in which he suggested that "an artist can be a great artist without being . . . a progressive thinker in all matters." For this lapse of concentration, he was denounced by Mike Gold in the *Daily Worker*: "Albert Maltz seems to have let the luxury and phoney atmosphere of Hollywood at last poison him." Maltz apologized in public for his "one-sided, non-dialectical treatment of complex issues"—it should have been clear to him, he said, that talent could always be wrecked by a "poisoned ideology.")

Pride of the Marines was one of the first Hollywood movies to attempt a reckoning of the war damage. In *The Story of G.I. Joe*, based on the writings of Ernie Pyle, an intrepid war journalist who was killed in 1945 at Okinawa, the tone is somber and unsparing: the war that Pyle reports has little to do with glamorous heroics, or antifascism, or the League of Nations. It is dirty, frightening, and sad. When a soldier says to Pyle, "If only we could create something good out of all this energy," the journalist does not reply. When the soldiers lose their much-liked Captain Walker, Pyle's commentating voice is heard: "In the end we will win. I hope we can rejoice in our victory, but humbly. . . . As for those beneath the wooden crosses, we can only murmur: thanks, pals, thanks."

The Story of G.I. Joe has a few passing references to "lousy kraut swine" and the like, but the hate angle is downplayed throughout.

The question of what to do about the enemy after the war had from the beginning been a preoccupation of the BMP, but from mid-1944 it was beginning to show itself in pictures. Striking the right balance was not easy. When Alfred Hitchcock addressed the topic in *Lifeboat,* he was attacked for portraying his German character as a "virtual demigod." Adapted by Jo Swerling from a John Steinbeck story (distorted, Steinbeck would complain), *Lifeboat* is a "cross-section" movie of the type that had by 1944 become fairly routine. Instead of a multiracial platoon, we are given a small boatload of American survivors from a torpedoed freighter: a rum crew, by any reckoning, it includes a reporter, an immigrant, a Negro, a leftist, a business tycoon, a little-punk crewman, a couple of Brit allies, and so on. Adrift on the ocean (with no musical accompaniment; an inspired omission), the Americans pick up another survivor: the captain of the German U-boat that had sunk their ship.

What to do with him? The Allies take a vote ("Do I get a vote too?" asks the Negro) and decide to hold him as a POW. In no time at all, the German's natural leadership qualities emerge, along with other useful skills. The humble crewman (poor old William Bendix, who else?) falls sick. The German turns out to be a surgeon in civilian life and deftly amputates a Bendix arm. He is also the only one on the boat who knows anything about navigation: who but he can guide the survivors to the safety of Bermuda? The Americans are confused and panicky, quarreling among themselves, developing love interests (Tallulah Bankhead is on board); the German is cool and resourceful, outsmarting them at every turn. How does he navigate without a compass? How does he anticipate their every move without knowing any English? How does he maintain his wonder strength on short water rations? "It's the master race, the *Herrenvolk,*" seems to be the only explanation. But then . . . it turns out that the cunning fellow *does* speak English; not only that, he has a secret compass and a secret water supply and a secret stash of vitamins. The Americans, scandalized, set upon him "in an orgasm of murder" and throw him overboard. What now? Aha! *Another* wreck, another German survivor, and an Allied ship on the horizon. One of the Americans asks: "What are you going to do with people like that?" Should they kill this one too ("Exterminate him! Exterminate them all!" is one proposal), or have they learned mercy from their savage treatment of the captain? "Unless we had seen it with our own eyes," wrote Bosley Crowther in the *New York Times,* we would never in the world have believed that a film could have been made which sold out democratic ideals and elevated the Nazi superman. Mr. Hitchcock and Mr. Steinbeck failed to grasp just what they had wrought. They certainly had no intention of elevating the superman ideal. . . . But we have a sneaking suspicion that the Nazis, with some cutting here and there, could turn *Lifeboat* into a whiplash against the "decadent democracies." And it is questionable whether such a picture, with such a theme, is judicious at this time.[7]

Hitchcock believed that he had made a film exhorting the Allies to pull together against a formidable foe. Watching it now, one can readily understand how the film might have seemed somewhat perverse at the time: the hard-to-ignore suggestion is that if the Americans were half as intelligent, dedicated, and well-trained as the Germans, they might—just might—have half a chance of not losing the war. "When we killed the German, we killed our motor," says the tycoon. The Negro replies that they still have a motor, and points to the sky. This seems to have satisfied the Hollywood powers that Hitchcock's heart was where it should be. To others, it said: We will need a miracle to win this war. Hitchcock's interest in the superman ideology would resurface most explicitly in *Rope*, which was released in 1948. In 1944, *Lifeboat* was about as near as he could get to exhibiting an unhealthy interest in such matters.

Lifeboat, The Pride of the Marines, and *The Story of G.I. Joe* were war films that, in one way or another, seemed ready to prepare themselves for peace. *The Best Years of Our Lives,* released by Sam Goldwyn in 1946, was a peacetime film suffused with nostalgia for the intense certitudes of war. Three returning GIs struggle to reinstate themselves as small-town American civilians, and the first two thirds of the film betray an almost vengeful distaste for the tedium and complacency of the noncombatant routine and for the ignorance and wrong opinions of those whose lives were not essentially altered by the war. An infantry sergeant returns to his post as a bank manager, to his loyal wife and lovely children, but he is drinking too much, his mind is not really on the job. In a moment of remembered comradeship, he grants an unsecured loan to a GI and is scolded for doing so by the fat cats who run the bank. At a welcome-home dinner, he comes close to the breaking point but is restrained by Myrna Loy, once more starring as "the perfect wife." The bank manager, Al Stephenson, is superbly played by Fredric March. His predicament is both delicate and explosive: he loves his loved ones and they in their turn are supremely understanding and "supportive"; he is good at his job and he is reasonably prosperous; he had "a good war"—what's wrong with him?

Of the three returning buddies, Al suffers the most troubling malaise. Homer Parrish has lost his arms: surely his girlfriend will be repelled by his prosthetic hooks—after all, even his mother flinches when she sees them. Fred Derry, a commissioned bomber pilot in wartime, must return to his poverty-line background: parents half-senile, wife callously unfaithful, job prospects zero. He ends up taking his old job as a soda jerk. The travails of Homer and Fred are unsparingly portrayed; in each case, though, romance will provide reintegration. Hollywood knows how to handle them. With the character of Al, however, we feel that William Wyler and his writer, Robert Sherwood, have evoked a restlessness that cannot be assuaged by any of the usual unguents: apart from halfheartedly suggesting that Al might find greater job satisfaction by fighting for special bank treatment for GIs, the filmmakers leave him as he is.

The Best Years of Our Lives was a record-breaking triumph, winning seven Oscars and cleaning up at the box office. There was a note of gratitude, almost, in the praise that came pouring in—as if something disorderly in the nation's psyche had been tidied up. Even the toughest critics, like James Agee, found themselves vulnerable: "It is easy, and true, to say that it suggests the limitations which will be inevitable in any Hollywood film, no matter how skillful and sincere. But it is also a great pleasure, and equally true, to say that it shows what can be done in a factory by people of adequate talent when they get, or manage to make themselves, the chance." *The Best Years of Our Lives* is not a vindication of Hollywood formulas; nor does it seek to repudiate them. Somehow it touches with genuineness conventions that had seemed worn out by automatic usage.

And now and then, the film has moments of inspiration. There is cameraman Gregg Toland's deep-focus scene in the bar—the focus used not as a visual decoration but because we really need, at that second, to see two things happening at once. And there is the famous sequence in the aircraft graveyard. William Wyler has described its origin:

When Fred decides to leave town in defeat, unable to get a job, no longer married and at odds with Peggy, whom he loves, he goes to the airport to hitch a ride on an army plane. While he waits, he wanders around among endless rows of junked combat fighters and bombers. In long moving shots, made on location at the Army scrapheap at Ontario, California, we found Fred Derry as he moved through the gigantic graveyard. At once the parallel was apparent: for four years Fred was trained, disciplined and formed into a precise human instrument for destruction. Now his work is done, and he, too, has been thrown onto the junk pile.[8]

In neither of these fine sequences, it might be said, are we at all keenly aware of the screenwriter's contribution. Indeed, when Fred Derry climbs into the cockpit of one of the junked B-17s, Robert Sherwood writes in his screenplay: "and here Mr. Wyler will have to invent something cinematic."

2

Wilson, The Pride of the Marines, and *The Best Years of Our Lives* were named on a list of so-called subversive movies drawn up by the Motion Picture Alliance and offered for scrutiny to J. Parnell Thomas when, in May 1947, that congressman brought his House Un-American Activities Committee to the Biltmore Hotel in Los Angeles to begin what he called "preliminary hearings" into the infiltration by Communists of the motion picture industry. HUAC's arrival in Hollywood was not unexpected. The California state committee had been running its investigations for years, and for several months the Hearst press and the *Hollywood Reporter,* egged on by the MPA, had been railing against Hollywood's radicals and hinting that some sort of federal intervention might be called for. And the radicals had been railing back, at anticensorship meetings and in the columns of their own periodicals.

The Motion Picture Alliance for the Preservation of American Ideals had, since its inception, been angrily analyzing the content of movies as they appeared and monitoring the studios for news of any sinister-sounding projects that were being scheduled. From the Alliance point of view, all this talk of "big theme" pictures and of an audience that had changed its taste in entertainment was itself subversive. As they saw it, a leftism that had grown powerful during the war-propaganda period was now being given its head, as radical screenwriters returning from the war found a Hollywood grown used to accommodating themes to do with antifascism, ordinary-Joe solidarity, and fighting for a better world. There were signs in the studios of influential left-wing team-ups. It was rumored that RKO's team of producer Adrian Scott and director Edward Dmytryk was planning a series of films on the subject of racial prejudice and that one of these—*Crossfire*—would actually portray a returning veteran as an anti-Semitic murderer. Darryl Zanuck was backing Elia Kazan's *Gentleman's Agreement,* also on the theme of anti-Semitism, and Sam Goldwyn had it in mind to produce *Earth and High Heaven,* about a Jewish-Gentile marriage. Communist screenwriter Abraham Polonsky's *Body and Soul,* with left-wing actor John Garfield playing a Jewish boxer seduced by the big-money ethos, would be directed by near-Communist Robert Rossen, author of the antilynching picture *They Won't Forget.* In the boom year of 1945–46, the studios were getting careless and overconfident. There was even talk of Lester Cole becoming a producer at MGM. Dalton Trumbo was already that studio's highest-paid screenwriter and—in 1945–46—editor of the Screen Writers Guild's official magazine, which had been pushing for the establishment of something called the American Authors Authority. (This so-called AAA proposed that screen authors should retain copyright of their work and should lease, not sell, it to the studios, thus getting a stake in what are now known as "residuals." This proposition was believed by the right to be a plot to win control of screen content. In many ways, the AAA campaign was a rerun of the 1936 dispute, with Louis B. Mayer once again declaring that he had twenty years' worth of old screenplays in his cupboard. Paradoxically, the SWG, by claiming author ownership, would be jeopardizing its status as a labor union, and it was on this technicality that the scheme eventually foundered.)

All in all, so far as the Motion Picture Alliance could interpret it, the situation was getting out of hand. In 1947, emboldened by the Republicans' recently won control of Congress and heartened enormously by the passing into law of the Taft-Hartley Act (which required union officials to take a non-Communist pledge), the Alliance stepped up its propaganda. In 1947, it issued a *Screen Guide for Americans* (composed by the majestically anti-Soviet novelist Ayn Rand), in which filmmakers were provided with a list of Dos and

Don'ts, along the lines of the very first Hays Code: "Don't Smear the Free Enterprise System"; "Don't Deify the Common Man"; "Don't Glorify the Collective"; "Don't Glorify Failure"; "Don't Smear Success"; "Don't Smear Industrialists"; and so on. "It is the *moral* (no, not just political but *moral*) duty of every decent man in the motion picture industry," said the pamphlet, "to throw into the ashcan where it belongs, every story that smears industrialists as such."[9]

During his May–June visit to Hollywood, J. Parnell Thomas heard testimony from fourteen witnesses, all of them sympathetic to the aims of his committee: Alliance stalwarts like Sam Wood and Rupert Hughes, as well as a sprinkling of big-name actors, for headline-grabbing purposes. Adolphe Menjou, Gary Cooper, and Robert Taylor were interviewed, and Taylor told the committee that his entry into the navy had had to be delayed so that he could spout Red propaganda in a film written by two party members (Richard Collins and Paul Jarrico: *Song of Russia*). Ginger Rogers's mother famously testified that her daughter refused to portray the pinko *Sister Carrie* but had been forced to speak subversive lines in films by Dalton Trumbo. For example? Mrs. Rogers cited a line from *Tender Comrade*: "Share and share alike—that's democracy."

On the basis of what these witnesses told him—"hundreds of very prominent film capital people have been named as communists for us"—and of his own reading of the various attacks made on HUAC during its Hollywood sojourn, Thomas began issuing subpoenas. His friends of the Alliance had so far testified in closed session; now they would be required to repeat their allegations at a public hearing, scheduled to take place in Washington in October 1947. Also subpoenaed were nineteen of the individuals who had been named as Communists in the course of the May hearings. The nineteen were: directors Herbert Biberman, Lewis Milestone, Robert Rossen, Irving Pichel, and Edward Dmytryk; producer Adrian Scott, actor Larry Parks, and writers Alvah Bessie, Bertolt Brecht, Lester Cole, Richard Collins, Gordon Kahn, Howard Koch, Ring Lardner, Jr., John Howard Lawson, Albert Maltz, Samuel Ornitz, Waldo Salt, and Dalton Trumbo.

At first, the response of Hollywood to the subpoenas was indignant—in some quarters, even buoyantly so, as if here at last was the Big Showdown. Protest meetings were held, Howard Koch convened a Thought Control Conference at the Beverly Hills Hotel, and a Committee of the First Amendment was set up; the Nineteen, as they were referred to, had decided that their strategy at the hearings would be to invoke that amendment, which guarantees freedom of belief (the actual word it uses is "religion"). When put on the stand, they would refuse to answer "yes" or "no" to the inevitable question: "Are you or have you ever been a member of the Communist party?" They would then attempt to use the hearings as an opportunity to denounce the activities of the committee.

This second strategy was not wholly approved by the liberals who set up the Committee for the First Amendment: John Huston, William Wyler, Philip Dunne. They believed that the Nineteen should certainly refuse to answer the committee but that they should then, in Wyler's words, "go before a judge, or the press, or something, and answer the questions." In this way they would challenge the legality of the House committee's procedures but would not seem as if they had anything they wished to hide. Despite this disagreement, John Huston organized an airlift of celebrities to Washington for the October hearings. The idea was that stars like Humphrey Bogart, Lauren Bacall, Frank Sinatra, Henry Fonda, Katharine Hepburn, et al. would be seen around the courtroom evincing solidarity with the accused Nineteen and would thus stir up press backing for their cause.

Just before the hearings began, J. Parnell Thomas told the press that for all the semblance of big-name support for the Nineteen, the facts were that the producers had already agreed to institute an anti-Communist blacklist throughout the industry. Lawyers for the Nineteen demanded that the producers make their collective position clear. As a result, Eric Johnston, president of the Motion Picture Association, made the following statement:

> As long as I live, I will never be a party to anything as un-American as a blacklist, and any statement purporting to quote me as agreeing to a blacklist is a libel upon me as a good American . . . tell the boys not to worry. There'll never be a blacklist. We're not going to go totalitarian to please the committee.[10]

The "boys" were reassured. At the moment, with a planeload of movie stars speaking out on their behalf and with the producers more or less guaranteeing that their jobs were safe, they could afford to strike a defiant posture at the hearings—better than that, they might emerge as heroes to the nation as they spoke out against the neo-Fascist, totalitarian threat. By this stage, they were spoiling for a fight.

And at first, as Thomas wheeled in the "friendly witnesses," the Nineteen had every reason to feel that compared to the opposition, they themselves would come across as men of intelligence and decency. Thomas's May informants repeated the claims they had made in secret, although Gary Cooper looked, or tried to look, bewildered as he did so. Ginger Rogers's mother repeated her "democracy" line and Robert Taylor his story about *Song of Russia*, adding that "if I were given the responsibility of getting rid of them [the Reds], I would love nothing more than to fire every last one of them and never let them work in a studio or in Hollywood again." Writer Morrie Ryskind got a laugh when he said that "if Lester Cole isn't a communist, I don't think Mahatma Gandhi is an Indian," and so, too, did Rupert Hughes when he boasted that he could "smell" a Communist if one came near him.

Adolphe Menjou came to the stand bearing dossiers representing his own research in the field of Communist infiltration, and to some extent his pseudo-academic bearing compensated for the sad spectacle of Gary Cooper, who mumbled shyly about unpleasant things he may have overheard at cocktail parties. The producers were then called—Louis B. Mayer and Jack Warner—and they put on a lamentable show. Mayer named a number of screenwriters, but when asked about their motivation, he blurted out: "In my opinion, Mr. Congressman, I think they are cracked." Jack Warner—producer of several of the films under attack—told the committee that "communists injected 95% of their propaganda into films through the medium of writers" but then denied that his own films had been contaminated. Asked specifically about *Pride of the Marines*, he explained: "Some of these lines have innuendoes and double meanings and you have to take eight or ten Harvard law courses to find out what they mean." And anyway, he himself had now "cleaned out" his studio: "You have been doing exactly the same thing in your business that we have been attempting to do in ours," he said. (In this connection, Warner claimed that he had fired Howard Koch, now notorious as the author of *Mission to Moscow*; Koch later took out advertisements in *Variety* explaining that it was he who had paid Warner ten thousand dollars to be released from his contract.)

The Nineteen were not too worried by any of this. The only troubling moment for them came when Emmett Lavery, president of the Screen Writers Guild, declined to adopt the First Amendment strategy. Lavery, a Catholic of mildly liberal inclinations and a former lawyer who had recently won a libel suit against Lela Rogers—she had denounced him as a Communist—did not wait for the Big Question to be asked. Authorized by the Guild to act as its official spokesman, he was anxious not to run afoul of a contempt-of-court citation, and declared:

> I have a piece of information that I would like to put in the record on my own motion, and on my own volunteering, because I am not sure as a student of constitutional law whether the committee does have the authority to demand it of me, but let me break the suspense immediately and tell you that I am not a communist.

This was the first formal intimation that the Guild might wish to distance itself from the predicament of the Nineteen: to them, Lavery's statement felt like a betrayal.

Even so, when the Nineteen began to take the stand, they were still in a fighting mood. John Howard Lawson got them off to a vigorous beginning:

> HUAC: Mr. Lawson. Are you a member of the Communist Party? Or have you ever been a member of the Communist Party?
> LAWSON: It's unfortunate and tragic that I should have to teach this committee the basic principles of Americanism. . . .
> HUAC: That's not the question. The question is—Have you ever been a member of the Communist Party?
> LAWSON: I am framing my answer in the only way in which an American citizen can frame his answer to a *(overlap)* question which invades his absolutely invades his rights.
> HUAC: Can you deny—can you deny—you refuse to answer that question is that correct?
> LAWSON: I have told you that I will . . . my beliefs, my affiliations and everything else to the American public and they will know where I stand as they do from what I have witnessed.
> HUAC: Stand away from the stand. . . .
> LAWSON: (OVERLAP) . . . Americanism for many . . .
> HUAC: Stand away from the stand!
> LAWSON: . . . fight for the Bill of Rights . . .
> HUAC: Take that man away from the stand. *(Audience noises)* There will be no demonstration.

Add to this snatch of dialogue the raised voices, the pounding of Thomas's gavel, the audience commotion that went on throughout, and then the sight of stewards bearing down on Lawson so as to drag him from the stand, and we get some idea why, seated in the hall, the Committee for the First Amendment was already beginning to feel hesitant about its all-out support for the Nineteen. The Huston-Wyler-Dunne road show was, after all, a troupe of high-ranking show biz personnel, and each of them could tell a bum performance when it happened. Simply in theatrical terms, Lawson was striking the wrong note, and it may be as well that he did not get to read out the prepared statement he had brought with him into court. In this, he denounced the friendly witnesses as "stool pigeons, neurotics, publicity-seeking clowns, Gestapo agents, paid informers and a few ignorant and frightened Hollywood artists." As to the committee itself, its aim, he said, was "to cut living standards, introduce an economy of poverty, wipe out labor's rights, attack Negroes, Jews and other minorities [and] drive us into a disastrous and unnecessary war."

The Dalton Trumbo testimony at first looked more promising. He arrived carrying boxes of scripts and cans of film and invited the committee to pinpoint the subversive content. Parnell Thomas was having none of this: he wanted a "yes" or a "no" to the Big Question. Trumbo contemptuously declined to answer: "Very many questions can be answered 'yes' or 'no' only by a moron or a slave." Like Lawson before him, Trumbo was cited for contempt. Eventually he was dragged from the witness stand, yelling: "This is the beginning of an American concentration camp."

Herbert Biberman, when it came to his turn, tried a different approach. When asked: "Are you or have you ever been . . .?" he whispered that he "would like to reply to this very quietly." His exchange with the committee turned into the noisiest so far:

BIBERMAN: If I will not be interrupted, I will attempt to give you a full answer to this question. It has become very clear to me that the real purpose of the investigation . . .

HUAC: That is not the question . . . (Bangs gavel)

BIBERMAN: . . . is to try . . . (OVERLAP)

HUAC: . . . THE QUESTION! THE QUESTION! (Bangs gavel)

BIBERMAN: . . . of the motion picture industry . . .

HUAC: Ask him the next question, ask him the next question . . . ask him the next question.

BIBERMAN: (OVERLAP) . . . I am defending . . . not only of ourselves but of the future . . .

HUAC: Are you a member of the Communist Party or have you ever been a member of . . . Are you a member of the Communist Party? Are you now or have you ever been a member of the Communist Party?

BIBERMAN: It is perfectly clear to me gentlemen that if you continue in . . .

HUAC: (OVERLAP) . . . answer the question . . . you are excused . . .

BIBERMAN: . . . in the industry . . . in the industry . . .

HUAC: . . . ANSWER THE QUESTION . . .

And so it went on. Biberman did not answer the question and when removed from the stand wished "to apologize for one thing and that is raising my voice." The succeeding witnesses performed no more impressively. When Albert Maltz was asked if he belonged to the Screen Writers Guild, he refused to answer because "Next you are going to ask me what religious group I belong to," and Alvah Bessie won a laugh or two when he reminded the committee that "General Eisenhower himself has refused to reveal his political affiliations and what's good enough for General Eisenhower is good enough for me." Parnell Thomas told him: "If you want to make a speech go out there under a big tree." Samuel Ornitz, Adrian Scott, and Edward Dmytryk tried to focus attention on the committee's racist tendencies: in the case of Scott and Dmytryk, the contention was that they had been subpoenaed specifically because they were the makers of *Crossfire*. Each of them had a statement that he wished to read, but neither was permitted to get much beyond the first half sentence. Ring Lardner, Jr., turned in perhaps the wittiest performance, although he, too, was refused permission to read out the text in which he asserted that "Under the kind of censorship this inquisition threatens, a leading man wouldn't even be able to blurt out the words 'I love you' unless he had first secured a notarized affidavit proving she was a pure, white, Protestant Gentile of old Confederate stock." When asked, not for the first time, "Are you or are you not?" Lardner actually grinned as he explained: "It depends on the circumstances. I could answer it, but if I did, I would hate myself in the morning." The audience let out a big laugh at this, and Parnell Thomas became apoplectic. "Leave the witness chair! Leave the witness chair!" he yelled.

The tenth witness to be called was Lester Cole, and when he, too, began hedging—"I would like to answer that question, I'd be very happy to. I believe the reason the question has been asked is to—" Parnell Thomas interrupted him in tones of what can only be described as anguish: "NO NO NO NO NO NO NO NO NO NO NO NO NO"—thirteen "No"s, each of them accompanied by a huge thump of the gavel. "I hear you, Mr. Chairman," said Cole, and shortly thereafter he, too, was ushered from the stand, cited—like the others—for contempt.

There were still nine witnesses to be called, but Thomas seemed to be heading for a crack-up. In the end he called only Bertolt Brecht, who had already agreed with the others that he would not pursue the common plan. As an alien, he believed that he did not enjoy the protection of the First Amendment. When asked the Question, he contrived a weird echo of Thomas's anguished response to Cole. Had he ever applied to join the Communist party? "No, No, No, No, No, Never!" he replied. Nor was he in any sense a Communist. The committee congratulated him on his performance: "You are a good example to the witnesses." Lester Cole said later:

> I was the tenth witness called up, and Brecht was the eleventh. I stayed throughout his testimony, and we drove back to the hotel in a cab. Naturally we talked about the ordeal we had just been through, and he was in tears because, as he said, he had wanted to take the same position as the rest of us had and refuse to answer the Committee's questions. But he thought there was nothing he could do but cooperate with the Committee and answer questions. But still, he felt he had betrayed us by taking a different position. He didn't want to stay in this country another minute.[11]

On the day of his testimony, Brecht drove to New York, and the following day he took a flight to Paris, never to return to the United States. On the plane he wrote in his journal:

> The hearing is unfailingly polite and ends without accusation; it is to my advantage that I had practically nothing to do with Hollywood, that I never mixed in American politics, and that my predecessors on the witness stand had refused to reply to the Congressmen. The 18 are very satisfied with my testimony and also the lawyers.[12]

Certainly, there is no evidence to suggest that anyone at the time thought his testimony was excessively shaped by self-interest. One bit of it, though, must have been noted with amusement by John Wexley. Asked about his employment in the motion picture business, Brecht replied: "I sold a story to a Hollywood firm, *Hangmen Also Die,* but I did not write the screenplay myself."

Brecht, it so happened, was the only witness to be called who was not and had never been a member of the party. After his testimony, the exasperated Parnell Thomas called a "temporary suspension" of the hearings. Thus, the Nineteen became the Ten: Biberman, Dmytryk, Scott, Bessie, Cole, Lardner, Lawson, Maltz, Ornitz, and Trumbo. (The remaining eight were not called to testify—although when the hearings were resumed, four years later, Robert Rossen and Richard Collins appeared as "friendly witnesses" and named names to the committee. They were not alone in this.) The Ten announced their intention of appealing the contempt citations.

For a week or two after the hearings closed, it appeared that a sort of victory had been achieved: the press, although it was caustic about the antics of the Ten, seemed on the whole relieved that Thomas had been given pause. The Ten themselves began organizing victory rallies and civil rights gatherings to celebrate the suspension and to declare war on the contempt citations. On returning to Los Angeles, they were greeted at the airport by "five hundred cheering partisans" and delivered speeches dedicating themselves to the struggle against HUAC.

As they remembered it, most of Hollywood was on their side. They had had formal support from the Motion Picture Association and celebrity backing from the Committee for the First Amendment; mildly martyred now, they seemed well set to strike back at Parnell Thomas's unpopular committee. Further rallies were scheduled; radio broadcast slots were booked. The fight was on. Albert Maltz summed up their mood when he wrote to their lawyer: "I think we have *done magnificently . . .* we have *fundamentally* challenged the Thomas Committee and the entire reactionary movement of which it is the spearhead."

This confidence soon began to crumble. Within days, it became evident that the atmosphere in Hollywood had changed. Nobody at all had been much impressed by the Ten's conduct on the witness stand. Even the staunchest of their liberal allies had quit Washington with a sense of disillusion: the show had flopped, the notices were bad. "It was a sorry performance," said John Huston. "You felt your skin crawl and your stomach turn. I disapproved of what was being done to the Ten but I also disapproved of their response. They had lost a chance to defend a most important principle."[13] And Philip Dunne agreed: "If they'd gone on the stand and answered with dignity: we respectfully decline to answer your questions on the ground that no Committee of Congress has a right to inquire of the citizen's political beliefs or associations. If they'd said something like that, we'd have applauded it. Without applauding them in particular but saying that is the correct stand. But this blustering and shouting—getting in the gutter with the committee, and it was a gutter committee: counter-productive is the kindest word I could find for it."[14]

The stars who had gone to Washington with Huston and Dunne were also beginning to wish they had not made the trip. There was news that an audience in North Carolina had been throwing stones at the screen during a Katharine Hepburn movie. Humphrey Bogart had been heavily tipped off that he had better distance himself from the Ten if he knew what was good for his career. Bogart took heed, claiming that he and others had been duped. "An American dope" was how he styled himself in a *Photoplay* article; "you fuckers sold me out" was how he addressed the lefties who had got him into it. The Committee for the First Amendment had gone to Washington in support of what had seemed a glorious cause, the cause of free expression, and had found themselves lined up with a group of writers who had come across as shifty, ill-mannered, fanatical, and—well, frankly, un-American.

The studio bosses had of course been quietly speaking to their stars. They themselves were already regretting their earlier brave stand against the committee's "totalitarianism." Nineteen forty-seven was the first year of what would become a serious slump in attendance at movies (between 1946 and 1948, they dropped from eighty to sixty-two million a week). Wall Street, with $60 million already invested in Hollywood, did not feel confident about supplying further funds in a climate of political controversy. The prospect of an ongoing confrontation with Washington (not to mention the American Legion and other boycott-threatening bodies) was unpalatable. Almost immediately after the hearings closed, plans were being made to dump the Ten and to protect Hollywood against any possible future probes. "Wall Street jiggles the strings, than all," was

Ed Sullivan's summary in the *New York Daily News*. This was November 1, and Sullivan was already warning his readers that the "Hollywood big shots" would shortly be caving in before the anxieties of their financiers.[15]

On November 24, fifty members of the Motion Picture Association met at the Waldorf-Astoria hotel in New York. Two days later, they issued a statement saying that although Hollywood believed passionately in free speech, it was also determined to rid itself of all subversives. The Association, it said, deplored the "action of the ten Hollywood men who have been cited for contempt . . . we do not desire to pre-judge their legal rights, but their actions have been a disservice to their employers and have impaired their usefulness to the industry":

> we will forthwith discharge or suspend without compensation those in our employ and we will not re-employ any of the ten until such time as he is acquitted or has purged himself of contempt and declares under oath that he is not a Communist.

From now on, the statement continued, Hollywood would be vigilant and would never "knowingly . . . employ a Communist or a member of any party or group which advocates the overthrow of the Government by force or by any illegal or unconstitutional means." This resolve, it was recognized, could create "an atmosphere of fear," and there was a risk of "innocent people" being hurt: "We will guard against this danger, this risk, this fear."

The Hollywood blacklist was now official. Loyalty oaths would be compulsory. The Ten, thoroughly sold down the river, were now unemployed—"numbed," as Ring Lardner, Jr., put it, by the treachery of their bosses. The *Los Angeles Times* commented:

> A few weeks ago Mr. Johnston was chiding the Committee on UnAmerican Activities with smearing Hollywood. . . . Now, less than a month later, Mr. Johnston issues a statement in New York which will surprise the members of the Thomas Committee and quite a few Americans who are not in Congress. Of the ten witnesses who refused to avow or disavow communism, he says, "Their refusal to stand up and be counted resulted in confusion of the issues before the Committee." But it will seem to those who read Mr. Johnston's full-page newspaper advertisements and his

statement to the committee that his own contribution to the confusion has been substantial. First the committee was wrong in questioning; then the witnesses were wrong in not answering the question.[16]

The story of Ring Lardner, Jr.'s, dismissal by 20th Century–Fox well typifies the several small outbreaks of shame and confusion that afflicted some part of almost every studio in the days following Eric Johnston's Waldorf declaration. Lardner, after the hearings, had good reason to believe that all would be well. He had actually been put to work on a new picture since getting back from Washington. He was admired by Zanuck, who would surely protect him all the way. Other Fox writers, like Philip Dunne, had seemed to loathe HUAC just as much as he did. On the day after the Waldorf statement, Zanuck announced that "he wasn't going to fire anybody unless he was specifically urged to do so by his board of directors." Lardner recalls:

> The Twentieth Century–Fox board got together and obliged him. . . . When I went to Zanuck's office, I was shunted off and did not get to see Zanuck himself but his assistant, Lou Schreiber, who told me that my contract was terminated and I was supposed to leave the premises.[17]

And this was 20th Century–Fox, the writers' studio. Philip Dunne has recalled: "Conscience is the only reliable guide to behavior. I disobeyed mine only once: when I failed to resign the day Ring Lardner was fired . . . my own inglorious Day of the Chicken."[18] As to Zanuck, his biographer Mel Gussow treats 1947 as a missing year.

The Ten were abandoned not only by the producers but also by the Committee for the First Amendment, now defunct, and by the Screen Writers Guild, which—although professing opposition to the Waldorf declaration—was also busy purging its own executive of left-wing elements. Eventually, the Guild would collaborate with HUAC to the extent of agreeing to hand over all its records—files and minutes dating back to the mid-1930s: a feast indeed for the committee's investigators. For the next two years, the Ten were engaged in a series of expensive legal battles—appealing against the contempt citations and filing suits against the studios for breach of contract. They raised funds by giving lectures and, in one or two instances, by black market scriptwriting, but several of them had to sell their houses and take out crippling loans. Any help they got from their Hollywood former colleagues was of course clandestine.

In the end, the Ten took their appeal to the Supreme Court; this, they had believed from the outset, would be their trump card. However, the deaths of two liberal justices altered the balance of the court in HUAC's favor, and the appeal did not get a hearing. In 1950, the Ten were each sentenced to one year's imprisonment. In Danbury Prison, Ring Lardner, Jr., and Lester Cole were amused one day to observe the arrival of a new coprisoner: none other than J. Parnell Thomas, arrived to serve eighteen months for payroll padding. Thomas was put to work tending the jail's chicken coop. "I see that you are still shoveling chicken shit," said Cole.

The Ten served their time, and only one of them, Edward Dmytryk, recanted. But by then it was 1951, and the Hollywood witch-hunt had intensified, in accord with the mood of the whole nation. Korea, Alger Hiss, China, the Russian atom bomb, the Rosenbergs: when HUAC reconvened in 1951, there was a rush of friendly witnesses, all desperate for a "clearance" that would keep them off the industry's lengthening blacklist. A Motion Picture Industry Council was set up by Roy Brewer, Hollywood's arch anti-Communist "labor organizer." The Council (which had Ronald Reagan on its board) offered "rehabilitation" to anyone who felt himself threatened by the new HUAC hearings. The Council's prescription was straightforward: confess, name names, apologize, and take the pledge. And this was roughly the advice offered by a "clearance" lawyer named Martin Gang, an ex-liberal who now told his nervous clients that "war was coming on and to oppose the committee and these lists could only lead to the concentration camp." Thus, if a Hollywood figure wished to stay in work, his shrewdest move would be to get in touch with Brewer or with Gang: they would ease his way with the committee and afterward see to it that his name was expunged from any black or gray list that his potential employers might consult. Needless to say, it was Brewer or Gang whom the studios consulted when they did their checking. Said Joseph Losey: "The most terrifying thing about the atmosphere was seeing people succumb, and seeing all protest disappear. Because if you did protest, you'd had it."[19]

There was resistance, but not much. Some unfriendly witnesses subpoenaed by the committee elected to plead the Fifth Amendment, as Dashiell Hammett had when, in the summer of 1951, he had been asked to name names in a federal court. Hammett was a trustee of a bail fund set up for the eleven leaders of the Civil Rights Congress when they were convicted of subversion under the 1940 Smith Act. Four of the leaders jumped bail, and Hammett was summoned really to help track them down. He refused to do so and refused also to answer any questions on the grounds that an "answer might tend to incriminate me." This was hardly true, but Hammett was not prepared to "let cops or judges tell me what democracy is." He was judged to be in contempt and got five months in jail.

To potential HUAC witnesses, then, it was clear from this Hammett trial that taking the Fifth would be to risk citation for contempt of Congress. It would also without much doubt mean an asterisked billing on the blacklist. Lillian Hellman, who badly did not want to go to jail but was not too alarmed about the blacklist, had been with Hammett the night before he took the Fifth and had asked him why he didn't plead ignorance instead. "I don't know why," he said. "I guess it has something to do with keeping my word, but I don't want to talk about that." When her HUAC subpoena arrived, Hellman wrote a now famous letter to the committee saying that although she would answer any questions put to her about her own politics, she would not inform on others:

> to hurt innocent people whom I knew many years ago in order to save myself is, to me, inhuman and indecent and dishonorable. I cannot and will not cut my conscience to fit this year's fashions, even though I long ago came to the conclusion that I was not a political person and could have no comfortable place in any political group.[20]

Of course, by testifying about her own politics, Hellman would automatically surrender her right to plead the Fifth and thus stand in contempt if she refused to speak of others. Her lawyer has amusingly recalled:

> She came into my office and said, "I will not go to jail. I am not the kind of person who can go to jail. I do not want to plead the Fifth. It would make me look bad in the press. And I will not name names." So those were the givens I had to work with: no jail, no Fifth and no names. It was like an algebra problem. But then I began to see it as primarily a public relations problem. I know that

if the headlines in the *New York Times* the next day read "HELL-
MAN REFUSES TO NAME NAMES," I had won; if it said "HELLMAN
PLEADS THE FIFTH," I had lost. . . . To me the truly courageous
position was the one Arthur Miller took when I represented him
in the same situation. He said to me, "I don't give a shit if they send
me to jail, I am not co-operating."[21]

The *New York Times* headline read: LILLIAN HELLMAN BALKS
HOUSE UNIT. The committee also found her strategy something of
an algebra problem. The Fifth she finally invoked was a "diminished
Fifth." She answered some questions and not others and did indeed
"balk" the committee. In her own account of the proceedings, she
tells of a man yelling from the public gallery: "Thank God somebody
finally had the guts to do it!" Nobody else can recall such an interrup-
tion; nor is anybody at all clear about what gutsy thing it was that
Hellman did. Public relations being what it is, though, she is still idly
remembered as a heroine of HUAC. That reputation depends, really, on her having supplied two splendid lines of screenplay: "I
cannot and will not cut my conscience to fit this year's fashions" and
"Thank God somebody finally had the guts to do it." If Mr. Smith
had come to Washington in 1951 (well, 1951 to 1954), such would have
been the rhetoric. (Ironically, Sidney Buchman, the writer of *Mr.
Smith Goes to Washington,* had been called before HUAC shortly
before Hellman: he had admitted his own communism but refused
to name others. Because of a procedural technicality that Mr. Smith
would have savored, Buchman got off with a year's probation and
a fine.)

The original Ten were still in jail when the 1951 hearings began,
and Richard Collins, one of the Nineteen, was among the first witnesses to be called. He gave the committee twenty-six names. "The
first snitch, stoolie, squealer," Lester Cole called him. And after
Collins, the deluge: Budd Schulberg, Clifford Odets, Elia Kazan,
Robert Rossen, Larry Parks, Lee J. Cobb, Edward G. Robinson,
Sterling Hayden, and so on. "I was a real daddy longlegs of a worm
when it came to crawling," said Hayden. It was, Kazan said recently,
"a degradation ceremony, in which the acts of informing were more
important than the information conveyed. I didn't doubt they knew
all the names they were asking for."[22]

At the time, Albert Maltz wrote to Herbert Biberman: "Oh the
moral horror of this parade of stool pigeons, what a sickness it

spreads over the entire land. That which we predicted is here—the complete triumph of the Motion Picture Alliance for American Ideals. My God."[23] And at Danbury jail, one of the regular convicts listened with Lester Cole to the HUAC broadcasts on the radio. After a bit, he said: "Lester, if you *are* a Communist you'd better get the hell out. Any movement with that many finks in it is no damn good."

3

"I didn't have the strength to resist corruption but I was strong enough to fight for a piece of it"; "it's all addition and subtraction, the rest is conversation." In Abraham Polonsky's *Force of Evil*, moral decency is reduced to whatever dregs of self-esteem can be salvaged from a world in which wrong conduct is now inescapable, the way it has to be. Nobody is any good, but maybe some villains have the faintest moral edge on others. "That's where the moral authority is," said Polonsky, "in the undestroyed element left in human nature."

Polonsky would soon be blacklisted and driven out of Hollywood, but in this intensely written movie he turns to underworld melodrama for a metaphor that might do justice to the industry's sense of itself, post-1947. In Polonsky's earlier film *Body and Soul*, the boxer who in the end refuses to throw a fight faces up to the hood who has been running him. "What makes you think you can get away with this?" the hood asks. "What are you going to do?" replies the boxer. "Kill me? Everybody dies."

Polonsky's films (the first directed by Robert Rossen, the second by Polonsky himself) were consciously political in their intent, and unusually literate, but their malevolent worldview was echoed in a score of movies released in the two or three postwar years before the studio blacklists and loyalty oaths began to bite. We all know the images so well: the early-hours backstreet, the lone streetlamp, the drizzle, the flashing neon sign, and then the hiding or hurrying submilitary raincoat, the stairwells, the cramped elevators, the rain-flecked windshields, the single-lane train corridors (your papers, please), the interrogation rooms, and the faces, half-visibly distraught, barred and slatted by shadows, shadows put there by cinematographers newly educated in making an expressionist-

documentary virtue out of wretchedly poor light. And then there
are the errant wartime women, fueling the psychoses of war-
damaged, nervous-from-the-service vets *(Deception, The Unfaithful)*, the psychopathic family men *(Monsieur Verdoux)*, the stran-
gers without pasts, the smoothie bigamists or widowers, romancing
young girls into nightmare trials of wedlock *(Gaslight, The Two
Mrs. Carrolls)*. Disloyalty, revenge, neurotic instability, mental
cruelty, obsession: were these themes chosen by the market, or did
they signify some aberration in the merchant? It was hard for anyone to tell, since by 1948 the market itself seemed to be going
crazy.

The Snake Pit in 1948 was Hollywood's first knowing effort to
fathom the mysteries of mental breakdown. Although the inquiry
now seems anesthetized, it was thought to be intrepid at the time—
and timely too. The maddened heroine is transfigured by the love
of a good doctor and thus rescued from the perils of an underfunded
hospital system. Hollywood's attachment to a vaguely Freudian
"buried key" approach to mental illness is to be expected: as Hitchcock would soon demonstrate, too often, the "buried key" or
"sunken link" method has a rich plot potential, and it affords much
scope for cinematic trickery. Also, the one-to-one relationship between patient and analyst can excite romantic expectations. Drugs,
hypnosis, incarceration, and so on are usually the province of evil,
often foreign medics, themselves mad much of the time, or of
scheming relatives intent on bagging all the family loot. In postwar
Hollywood, wrong accusations of insanity update the old gangland
frame-up, the false witness: how terrible to be "put away" because
they say that you are mad.

By 1948, though, Hollywood itself had fallen victim to an outbreak
of unreason, a sense of impending collapse that was not exclusively
generated by the witch-hunts and the blacklists. And by 1951, when
the second wave of HUAC hearings started up, the industry was well
advanced in panic. Audiences were still falling and would shortly
level out at around fifty million a week—what they used to be back
in the silent days. The British and other foreigners were imposing
crippling taxes on American film company earnings (and showed
signs anyway of preferring their own movies). Also, in 1948, a Supreme Court decision had declared Hollywood's theater ownerships
and block booking methods to be in breach of antitrust legislation.

For twenty-five years, the industry had been under investigation by the Federal Trade Commission but had somehow managed to keep its monopoly afloat. The 1948 decision was in response to a Justice Department plea that breaking the monopoly was not just in the interests of free trade. It was also to do with the "free" distribution of ideas:

> The content of films, regardless of who produces and exhibits them, must necessarily be conditioned by the prejudices and moral attitudes of those who control the channels of distribution.

In 1948, it was pretty clear which "prejudices and moral attitudes" were being targeted. The Supreme Court ruling effectively destroyed the basis of the Hollywood studio system and more than any other single factor caused the end of the industry's so-called Golden Age. The "independents" would no longer have to suck up to the big boys.

As if this were not enough to have to stomach, 1948 was also the year in which the number of television sets in the United States for the first time reached one million. By 1950, that figure had risen to eleven million. "This is one medium that I don't believe Hollywood can give the old run-around," said Hedda Hopper. The moguls, after a first wave of bluster, began to think she might be right: they began issuing visionary statements about the amazing properties of new techniques like Magnascope ("a device that, with the press of a button, enlarges the screen and the images on it to the full width of the stage"), the Third Dimension ("the engineers . . . are promising movie executives concrete results within the next few years, probably by the time television reaches manhood, if not before"), drive-ins ("so you don't even have to leave your car while looking at a movie"), and high fidelity. "All in all, the film industry is looking ahead to meet squarely any emergency or competition, be it television or some other form of entertainment that may come along."

Well, we know what happened. But to anyone who lived through the thirties and forties in Hollywood, the mood in 1951 was becoming seriously elegiac: things would never be like *that* again—it had been too good, too bad, to last. In Billy Wilder's *Sunset Boulevard*, released in 1950, a silent-movie queen is tended in her rotting mansion by her former husband and director, now her butler and general factotum. The movie star is played by Gloria Swanson; the butler by Erich von Stroheim. The pair of them live in the past, insanely. The

tennis court is overgrown, rats scuttle in the grounds. The pathos of
it all is described for us, voice over, by a screenwriter whose predicament is also in its way pathetic. He is a hack out of the Midwest, a
former newsman with two B pictures to his credit, and now he has
set up as a gigolo ghost writer for Miss Swanson, who ludicrously
plans a comeback: he hates himself, doesn't much like her, and finds
the work demeaning and absurd. In the end, she destroys him as he
and his kind had once destroyed the silent pictures: "You made a
rope of words and strangled this business." This was Brackett and
Wilder's last picture together, and the image that lingers is of a dead
writer face downward in the swimming pool of a demented movie
star. "I always wanted a swimming pool," he tells us.

NOTES

Chapter One

1. Terry Ramsaye, *A Million and One Nights* (1926; New York: Simon & Schuster/ Touchstone, 1986), p. 268.

2. Lillian Gish, *The Movies, Mr. Griffith and Me* (London: Columbus Books, 1988), p. 55.

3. Ramsaye, p. 514.

4. Epes Winthrop Sargent, "The Literary Side of Pictures," *Motion Picture World*, July 11, 1914, p. 199.

5. Ramsaye, p. 514.

6. William de Mille, *Hollywood Saga* (New York: E. P. Dutton, 1939), pp. 14–16.

7. Lillian Gish, p. 159.

8. Sargent, p. 199.

9. Ibid.

10. Anita Loos, *Kiss Hollywood Goodbye* (London: W. H. Allen, 1974), p. 7.

11. Gary Carey, *Anita Loos: A Biography* (London: Bloomsbury, 1988), p. 44.

12. C. Gardner Sullivan scripts quoted by Tom Stempel, *Framework* (New York: Continuum, 1988), p. 44.

13. Frank Capra, *The Name Above the Title* (New York: Vintage Books, 1985), pp. 50–1.

14. Ibid.

15. Ibid.

16. H. L. Mencken, "Appendix from Moronia," in *Prejudices* (New York: Knopf, 1937), reprinted in Harry M. Geduld (ed.), *Rumors on Film* (Indiana University Press, 1972) pp. 92–103.

17. David Bordwell, "The Classical Hollywood Style 1917–60," in *The Classical Hollywood Cinema* (London: Routledge, 1985), p. 3.

18. David Robinson, *Hollywood in the Twenties* (London: Zwemmers, 1968), p. 30.

Chapter Two

1. Jesse L. Lasky, "The Screen Needs a Shakespeare," *The Motion Picture Director* (n.d.), p. 26.

2. Elmer Rice, *Minority Report* (New York: Simon & Schuster, 1963), p. 179.

3. Samuel Goldwyn, *Behind the Screen* (New York: George H. Doran, 1923), p. 343.

4. A. Scott Berg, *Goldwyn: A Biography* (New York: Knopf, 1989), p. 96.

5. Ibid.

6. W. Somerset Maugham, "On Writing for the Films," *North American Review* 213 (May 1921), pp. 670–75.

7. Ted Morgan, *Somerset Maugham* (London: Cape, 1980), p. 248.

8. Anthony Glyn, *Elinor Glyn* (London: Hutchinson, 1955), p. 278.

9. Ramsaye, *A Million and One Nights,* pp. 797–98.

10. Ibid., p. 802.

11. Joel W. Finler, ed., *Greed: a film by Erich von Stroheim* (New York: Simon & Schuster, 1972), pp. 7–8.

12. Ibid., p. 26.

13. Ibid., p. 24.

14. Ibid., pp. 39–40.

15. Erich von Stroheim, in Lewis Jacobs, *The Rise of the American Film* (New York: Harcourt Brace, 1939), p. 351.

16. William Lord Wright, *Photoplay Writing* (New York: Falk Publishing Co., 1922), pp. 78–81.

17. Richard Meryman, *Mank* (New York: William Morrow, 1978), p. 133.

18. Ben Hecht, *A Child of the Century* (New York: Signet, 1955), p. 447.

19. Josef von Sternberg, *Fun in a Chinese Laundry* (London: Columbus Books, 1987), p. 215.

20. Ibid., p. 351.

21. Leslie Halliwell, *The Filmgoer's Companion* (London: Paladin, 1985), p. 498.

22. Doug Fetherling, *The Five Lives of Ben Hecht* (Toronto: Lester and Orpen, 1977), p. 62.

23. Margaret Reid, "Has the Flapper Changed," interview with F. Scott Fitzgerald, *Motion Picture,* July 1927, p. 104.

24. James Montgomery Flagg, *Roses and Buckshot* (New York: Putnam's, 1948), pp. 210–11.

25. Tom Dardis, *Some Time in the Sun* (London: Deutsch, 1976), p. 48.

26. H. L. Mencken to F. Scott Fitzgerald, March 15, 1927, in James R. Mellon, *Invented Lives* (London: Souvenir Press, 1984), p. 288.

Chapter Three

1. Samson Raphaelson, Columbia Oral History Transcription, in introduction to *The Jazz Singer,* ed. Robert L. Carringer (Madison: University of Wisconsin Press, 1979), p. 20.

2. Ibid., p. 21.

3. James G. Stewart, in "The Evolution of Cinematic Sound," *Sound and the Cinema,* ed. Evan William Cameron (New York: Redgrave Publishing Co., 1980), p. 43. Stewart was postproduction sound chief at RKO, 1933–45; his credits include *Citizen Kane* and *The Magnificent Ambersons.*

4. Hal Mohr, in *Sound and the Cinema,* pp. 71–2.

5. Richard Griffith, in Paul Rotha, *The Film Till Now* (London: Spring Books, 1967), p. 417.

6. V. I. Pudovkin, *Film Technique* (London: Gollancz, 1929), pp. 30–1.

7. Rudolf Arnheim, in Roger Manvell, *Film* (London: Penguin, 1944), p. 53.

8. Aldous Huxley, "Silence Is Golden," *Do What You Will* (New York: Harper, 1929); reprinted in *Authors on Film,* ed. Harry M. Geduld (Bloomington: Indiana University Press, 1972), p. 73.

9. George Jean Nathan, *Art of the Night* (New York: Knopf, 1928), p. 139.

10. Budd Schulberg, "The Writer in Hollywood," *Harper's,* October 1959.

11. John Lee Mahin, interview in *Backstory,* ed. Pat McGilligan (Berkeley: University of California Press, 1986), p. 251.

12. S. J. Perelman, quoted in William Wolf, *Landmark Films* (New York and London: Paddington Press, 1979), p. 59.

13. Wells Root, interview in *Screenwriter,* ed. Lee Server (Pittstown, N.J.. Main Street Press, 1987), p. 174.

14. Ethan Mordden, *The American Theatre* (New York: Oxford University Press, 1981), p. 89.

15. Alexander Walker, *The Shattered Silents* (London: Harrap, 1986), epigraph.

16. Lewis Milestone, in *Film Makers Speak,* ed. Jay Leyda (New York: Da Capo Press, 1977), p. 312.

17. Arthur Knight, *The Liveliest Art* (New York: Mentor/NAL, 1957), p. 169.

18. *Variety,* October 31, 1929.

19. Alan L. Gansberg, *Little Caesar: A Biography of Edward G. Robinson* (London: New English Library, 1983), p. 62.

20. W. R. Burnett, interview in *Backstory,* pp. 57–8.

21. Ibid., pp. 58–9.

22. Frances Donaldson, *P. G. Wodehouse: The Authorized Biography* (London: Weidenfeld & Nicolson, 1982), p. 139.

23. Ibid., pp. 142–43.

24. Ibid., p. 143.

25. Jay Martin, *Nathanael West: The Art of His life* (London: Secker & Warburg, 1970), p. 205.

26. Ibid., p. 203.

27. W. A. Swanberg, *Dreiser* (New York: Bantam, 1967), p. 447.

28. Ibid., p. 454.

29. Theodore Dreiser, "The Real Sins of Hollywood," *Liberty,* June 11, 1932, pp. 6–11.

30. Josef von Sternberg, *Fun in a Chinese Laundry* (London: Columbus Books, 1987), p. 259.

31. Swanberg, p. 448.

Chapter Four

1. Raymond Chandler, "Oscar Night in Hollywood," in *Sight and Sound* anthology (London: Faber, 1982), p. 58.

2. Murray Schumach, *The Face on the Cutting Room Floor* (New York: Da Capo, 1975), p. 18.

3. Raymond Moley, *The Hays Office* (Bobbs-Merrill, 1945), in Gerald Mast, ed., *The Movies in Our Midst* (University of Chicago Press, 1982), pp. 320–21.

4. Lamar Trotti to Will Hays, April 30, 1932 (Margaret Herrick Library of the Academy of Motion Picture Arts and Sciences).

5. Ibid., April 22, 1932.

6. Jason S. Joy to John Hammell, September 16, 1932 (Margaret Herrick Library).

7. Fergus Cashin, *Mae West* (London: W. H. Allen, 1981), p. 106.

8. Martin Quigley, *Decency in Motion Pictures* (New York: Macmillan, 1937), in Mast, pp. 340–44.

9. Olga J. Martin, *Hollywood's Movie Commandments* (H. W. Wilson, 1937), in Mast, pp. 333–39.

10. Cashin, p. 125.

11. "An Interview with Mae West," *Take One* (Quebec), January 22, 1974, p. 19.

12. Philip Dunne, *Take Two—A Life in Movies and Politics* (New York: McGraw-Hill, 1980), p. 184.

13. Paul F. Boller, Jr., and Ronald L. Davis, *Hollywood Anecdotes* (New York: Ballantine Books, 1987), p. 191.

Chapter Five

1. Hecht, *Child of the Century*, p. 474.

2. Ibid., p. 449.

3. Rudy Behlmer, ed., *Memo from David O. Selznick* (New York: Avon, 1973), p. 104.

4. Opening for *Trilby*, in Fetherling, *Five Lives of Ben Hecht*, p. 141.

5. Hecht, *Child of the Century*, pp. 455–56.

6. Howard Hawks, interview with Joseph McBride for the Directors Guild of America, October 21–23, 1977.

7. W. R. Burnett, interview in *Backstory*, p. 69.

8. John Lee Mahin, ibid., p. 247.

9. Gerald Mast, *Howard Hawks, Storyteller* (New York: Oxford University Press, 1982), p. 84.

10. Dunne, *Take Two*, p. 45.

11. Casey Robinson, interview in *Backstory*, pp. 296–97.

12. Allen Scott, ibid., p. 315.

13. Capra, *The Name Above the Title*, p. 233.

14. Ibid., p. 234.

15. Behlmer, *Memo from David O. Selznick*, pp. 55–56.

16. Leo C. Rosten, *Hollywood: The Movie Colony, The Movie Makers* (New York: Harcourt, Brace, 1941), p. 37.

17. Orson Welles, in Richard Corliss, *Talking Pictures* (Woodstock, N.Y.: Overlook Press, 1985), p. xxii.

18. Hecht, *Child of the Century,* p. 442.

19. Kenneth Tynan, "The Girl in the Black Helmet," *The New Yorker,* June 11, 1979, p. 47.

20. Fetherling, p. 149.

21. Ben Hecht, *Charlie* (New York: Harper, 1957), p. 185.

22. Geoff Brown, "Better Than Metro Isn't Good Enough," *Sight and Sound,* Summer 1975, p. 153.

23. Fetherling, p. 149.

24. Hecht, *Charlie,* p. 191.

25. Frances Hackett, quoted in Schwartz, p. 37.

26. Greg Mitchell, "How Hollywood Fixed an Election," *American Film,* November 1988, p. 30.

27. Ibid., p. 31.

28. Ibid., p. 27.

Chapter Six

1. Samuel Marx, *Mayer and Thalberg: The Make Believe Saints* (New York: Warner Books, 1980), pp. 258–59.

2. Larry Ceplair and Steven Englund, *The Inquisition in Hollywood* (Berkeley: University of California Press, 1983), p. 20.

3. Donald Ogden Stewart, interview in *Backstory,* pp. 341–42.

4. Curt Siodmak, interview in *Screenwriter,* p. 217.

5. Mary C. McCall, Jr., "A Brief History of the Guild," *The Screen Writer,* April 1948, pp. 25–31.

6. Nancy Lynn Schwartz, *The Hollywood Writers' Wars* (New York: Knopf, 1982), p. 60.

7. Ibid.

8. Frances Marion, *Off With Their Heads* (New York: Macmillan, 1971), p. 240.

9. Ceplair and Englund, p. 38.

10. Meryman, *Mank,* p. 171.

11. John Lee Mahin, interview in *Backstory,* pp. 258–59.

12. Schwartz, p. 67.

13. Ibid.

14. Ibid., p. 68.

15. Ibid., pp. 69–70.

16. Ceplair and Englund, p. 43.

17. Schwartz, p. 76.

18. Ibid.

19. S. J. Perelman, quoted in Neil Gabler, *An Empire of Their Own* (New York: Crown, 1988), p. 223.

20. Ceplair and Englund, p. 46.

21. John Bright, quoted in Schwartz, p. 18.

22. Gary Carr, *The Left Side of Paradise: The Screenwriting of John Howard Lawson* (Ann Arbor, Mich.: UMI Research Press, 1984), p. 7.

23. Ibid., p. 13.

24. Ibid., p. 45.

25. Ibid., p. 50.

26. Ring Lardner, Jr., *The Lardners: My Family Remembered* (New York: Harper Colophon, 1976), p. 245.

27. Donald Ogden Stewart, *By a Stroke of Luck* (London: Paddington Press, 1975), p. 216.

28. John Keats, *You Might as Well Live: The Life and Times of Dorothy Parker* (London: Penguin, 1970), p. 188.

29. Ibid., p. 204.

30. Ceplair and Englund, p. 117.

31. Gabler, *An Empire of Their Own,* p. 328.

32. Ibid., p. 327.

33. Schwartz, p. 47.

Chapter Seven

1. Schwartz, *The Hollywood Writers' Wars,* p. 101.

2. Ibid.

3. Gabler, *An Empire of Their Own,* p. 194.

4. Ibid., p. 195.

5. Otto Friedrich, *City of Nets* (New York: Harper & Row, 1986), p. 76.

6. Rudy Behlmer, *Inside Warner Bros. (1935–1951)* (New York: Simon & Schuster/Fireside Books, 1985), pp. 9–10.

7. Casey Robinson, interview in *Backstory,* p. 294.

8. John Bright, interview in *Screenwriter,* p. 70.

9. Ibid., p. 84.

10. *I Am a Fugitive from a Chain Gang,* ed. John E. O'Connor (Madison: University of Wisconsin Press, 1981), pp. 9–10.

11. Ibid., pp. 186–87.

12. Nick Roddick, *A New Deal in Entertainment: Warner Brothers in the 1930s* (London: BFI Books, 1983), p. 126.

13. Mervyn LeRoy, *Take One* (London: W. H. Allen, 1974), pp. 110–11.

14. Ibid., p. 110.

15. *New York Times,* July 5, 1941.

16. Ezra Goodman, *The Fifty Year Decline and Fall of Hollywood* (New York: Simon & Schuster, 1961), p. 182.

17. Jason S. Joy to Irving Thalberg, February 26, 1932 (Academy Library).

18. Joseph I. Breen to Will H. Hays, December 18, 1935 (Academy Library).

19. *New York Times,* Feb. 16, 1936.

20. Gabler, p. 338.

21. Ibid., p. 340.

22. Ibid p. 344.

23. John Davis, "Notes on Warner Brothers' Foreign Policy, 1918–1948," *The Velvet Light Trap* 4, pp. 23–33.

24. *The Sea Hawk,* ed. Rudy Behlmer (Madison: University of Wisconsin Press, 1982) p. 207.

25. Howard Koch, *As Time Goes By: Memoirs of a Writer* (New York: Harcourt Brace Jovanovich, 1979), p. 46.

26. William Hughes, "Howard Koch," *Dictionary of Literary Biography* 26 (Detroit: Gale Research Co., 1984) pp. 178–85.

27. Koch, *As Time Goes By,* p. 7.

28. Ibid., p. 42.

29. Joseph Breen to John Hammell, March 11, 1937 (Margaret Herrick Library).

30. Frederick L. Herron to Geoffrey Shurlock, March 25, 1937.

31. Dave Davis and Neal Goldberg, "Interview with John Howard Lawson," *Cineaste* 8, p. 10, in Ceplair and Englund, p. 307.

32. Ceplair and Englund, p. 308.

33. John Howard Lawson, *Film: The Creative Process* (New York: Hill & Wang, 1964), p. 127.

Chapter Eight

1. Virginia M. Clark, *Aldous Huxley and Film* (Metuchen, N.J.: Scarecrow Press, 1987), p. 17.

2. Ibid., quoting George Woodcock.

3. David King Dunaway, *Huxley in Hollywood* (New York: Harper & Row, 1989), p. 83.

4. Ibid., p. 103.

5. Aldous Huxley, *Letters of Aldous Huxley,* ed. Grover Smith, Letter to Julian Huxley, Jan. 14, 1940 (London: Chatto & Windus, 1969), p. 450.

6. Ibid., Letter to Eugene F. Saxton, Nov. 2, 1939, p. 447.

7. Dunaway, *Huxley in Hollywood,* p. 154.

8. Ibid.

9. Ibid., p. 175.

10. *The Letters of F. Scott Fitzgerald,* ed. Andrew Turnbull, Letter to Frances Scott Fitzgerald, July 1937 (London: Penguin, 1968), p. 31.

11. F. Scott Fitzgerald, "Crazy Sunday," *The Stories of F. Scott Fitzgerald,* ed. Malcolm Cowley (New York: Scribner, 1951), p. 407.

12. Ibid., p. 416.

13. Fitzgerald to Beatrice Dance, September 15, 1936, in *Letters,* p. 561.

14. Fitzgerald to Harold Ober, January 10, 1935, in *As Ever, Scott Fitz,* ed. Matthew J. Bruccoli (London: Woburn Press, 1973), p. 216.

15. Harold Ober to Fitzgerald, December 13, 1935, in ibid., p. 234.

16. Fitzgerald to Harold Ober, December 31, 1935, in ibid., p. 241.

17. F. Scott Fitzgerald, *"The Crack-Up,"* ed. Edmund Wilson (Norfolk, Conn., and New York: New Directions, 1945), p. 78.

18. Gore Vidal, *Pink Triangle and Yellow Star* (London: Heinemann, 1982), p. 15.

19. Harold Ober to Fitzgerald, June 5, 1936, in *As Ever,* p. 273.

20. Fitzgerald to Harold Ober, received March 22, 1937, in ibid., p. 300.

21. Fitzgerald to Frances Scott Fitzgerald, July 1937, in *Letters*, pp. 30–31.

22. Fitzgerald to Anne Ober, July 26, 1937, in *As Ever*, p. 330.

23. *Three Comrades* (Carbondale: Southern Illinois University Press, 1978), p. 44.

24. Ibid., p. 5.

25. Jacques Bontemps and Richard Overstreet, " 'Measure for Measure': Interviews with Joseph Mankiewicz," *Cahiers du Cinema in English* 18 (February 1967), p. 31.

26. *Three Comrades*, p. 30.

27. Ibid., pp. 287–88.

28. Ibid., pp. 124–25.

29. Ibid., p. 264 (Afterword by Matthew J. Bruccoli).

30. Ibid., p. 265.

31. Ibid., p. 251.

32. Ibid., p. 266–67.

33. Sheilah Graham, *Beloved Infidel* (London: Cassell, 1959), p. 197.

34. Nunnally Johnson to Tom Dardis, December 1974, in *Some Time in the Sun* (London: Deutsch, 1976), p. 57.

35. Fitzgerald to Beatrice Dance, March 4, 1938, in *Correspondence of Scott Fitzgerald*, ed. Matthew J. Bruccoli and Margaret M. Duggan (New York: Random House, 1980), p. 489.

36. Aaron Latham, *Crazy Sundays* (London: Secker & Warburg, 1972), p. 26.

37. Ibid., p. 291.

38. Ibid., p. 204.

39. Fitzgerald to Harold Ober, December 29, 1938, in *As Ever*, p. 360.

40. Nunnally Johnson to Tom Dardis, in *Some Time in the Sun*, p. 58.

41. Fitzgerald to Budd Schulberg, February 28, 1939, quoted in Latham, *Crazy Sundays*, p. 229.

42. Fitzgerald to Zelda Fitzgerald, October 11, 1940, in *Letters*, p. 145.

43. Latham, *Crazy Sundays*, p. 263.

44. Martin, *Nathanael West*, p. 9.

45. Milton Sperling, in Martin, *Nathanael West*, p. 288.

46. Nathanael West, *The Day of the Locust and His Other Novels* (London: Heinemann, 1983), p. 261.

47. Arthur Strawn, in Jay Martin, *Nathanael West*, p. 274.

48. Nathanael West to S. J. Perelman, in ibid., pp. 266–67.

49. Ibid., p. 268.

50. Ibid.

51. S. J. Perelman in ibid., p. 345.

52. Nathanael West to S. J. Perelman, in ibid., p. 365.

53. Ibid., p. 366.

54. Ibid. p. 340.

55. Nathanael West to Edmund Wilson in ibid., p. 341.

Chapter Nine

1. Quoted in Paul Jensen, "The Career of Dudley Nichols," *Film Comment,* Winter 1970–71, p. 56.

2. *This Land Is Mine,* RKO Classic Screenplays (New York: Ungar, 1970), p. 109.

3. *Stagecoach,* Classic Film Scripts (London: Lorrimer, 1971), pp. 90–1.

4. Dudley Nichols, "The Writer and the Film," *Theatre Arts,* October 1943, pp. 591–602.

5. Dudley Nichols, "Film Writing," *Theatre Arts,* December 1942, pp. 770–74.

6. Lindsay Anderson, "On the Films of John Ford," *Cinema* 3 (Spring 1971), vol. 6, no. 3, pp. 21–36.

7. Peter Bogdanovich, *John Ford,* rev. ed. (Berkeley: University of California Press, 1978), p. 52.

8. Dan Ford, *The Unquiet Man: The Life of John Ford* (London: William Kimber, 1982), p. 51.

9. Ibid., p. 113.

10. Bogdanovich, pp. 63–64.

11. Ford, p. 84.

12. Andrew Sinclair, *John Ford* (London: Allen & Unwin, 1979), p. 57.

13. Ford, p. 155.

14. Nichols, "Film Writing," p. 772.

15. *This Land Is Mine,* pp. 39–40.

16. Ibid., p. 32.

17. Richard Corliss, *Talking Pictures* (Woodstock, New York: Overlook Press, 1985), p. 233.

18. James Agee, *Agee on Film* (London: Peter Owen, 1963), p. 46.

19. Ibid., p. 49.

20. Jackson L. Benson, *The True Adventures of John Steinbeck, Writer* (London: Heinemann, 1984), pp. 410–11.

21. Ibid., p. 409.

22. *Letters of Nunnally Johnson,* ed. Dorris Johnson and Ellen Leventhal (New York: Knopf, 1981), pp. 34–5.

23. Tom Stempel, *Screenwriter: The Life and Times of Nunnally Johnson* (New York: A. S. Barnes, 1980), p. 37.

24. Mel Gussow, *Don't Say Yes Until I Finish Talking* (New York: Pocket Books, 1972), p. 60.

25. Johnson, *Letters,* p. 9.

26. Stempel, p. 92.

27. Ibid., p. 147.

28. Johnson, *Letters,* p. 80.

Chapter Ten

1. Dardis, *Some Time in the Sun,* p. 103.

2. *Paris Review,* Spring 1956; reprinted in *Writers at Work,* ed. Malcolm Cowley (London: Secker & Warburg, 1958), pp. 115–16.

3. Joseph Blotner, *Faulkner: A Biography* (New York: Random House, 1974), p. 802.

4. *Writers at Work*, pp. 115–116.

5. Gussow, *Don't Say Yes*, pp. 69–70.

6. Stephen B. Oates, *Faulkner: The Man and the Artist* (New York: Perennial Library, 1988), pp. 145–46.

7. Jack Warner, *My First Hundred Years in Hollywood* (New York: Random House, 1965), p. 309–10.

8. Samuel Marx, *A Gaudy Spree* (New York: Franklin Watts, 1987), pp. 79–81.

9. Blotner, p. 773.

10. *Faulkner's MGM Screenplays*, ed. Bruce F. Kawin (Knoxville: University of Tennessee Press, 1982), p. xxviii.

11. A. I. Bezzerides, interview in *Screenwriter*, p. 39.

12. Dardis, p. 99.

13. Oates, p. 158.

14. Blotner, p. 1107.

15. Oates, p. 188.

16. *Screenwriter*, p. 38.

17. Ibid.

18. Dardis, p. 123.

19. Fay Wray, *On the Other Hand* (New York: St. Martin's Press, 1989), pp. 227–28.

20. *Air Force*, ed. Lawrence Howard Suid (Madison: University of Wisconsin Press, 1983), pp. 168–69.

21. Bruce F. Kawin, *Faulkner and Film* (New York: Ungar, 1977), p. 108.

22. *To Have and Have Not*, ed. Bruce F. Kawin (Madison: University of Wisconsin Press, 1980), p. 33.

23. Leigh Brackett, "From *The Big Sleep* to *The Long Goodbye* and More or Less How We Got There," *Take One* 4, no. 1 (1974), pp. 26–28.

24. Oates, p. 203.

25. Ibid., pp. 205–6.

26. Behlmer, *Inside Warner Bros.*, pp. 250–51.

Chapter Eleven

1. In Peter Roffman and Jim Purdy, *The Hollywood Social Problem Film* (Bloomington: Indiana University Press, 1981), p. 215.

2. Hays Office files (Margaret Herrick Library).

3. *Hollywood Reporter*, April 28, 1939.

4. Behlmer, *Inside Warner Bros.*, pp. 188–89.

5. Ceplair and Englund, *The Inquisition in Hollywood*, p. 310.

6. *Air Force*, p. 117.

7. Ibid., p. 121.

8. "Government Information Manual for the Motion Picture Industry," Summer 1942, in Clayton R. Koppes and Gregory D. Black, *Hollywood Goes to War* (London: I. B. Tauris, 1987), p. 142.

9. Koppes and Black, p. 140.

10. Schwartz, *The Hollywood Writers' Wars*, p. 182.

11. Ibid.

12. Ibid., p. 188.

13. Ibid., p. 189.

14. *Mission to Moscow*, ed. David Culbert (Madison: University of Wisconsin Press, 1980), pp. 169–70.

15. Koppes and Black, p. 205.

16. Berg, *Goldwyn*, pp. 374–79.

17. Ibid., p. 263.

18. David Talbot and Barbara Zheutlin, *Creative Differences, Profiles of Hollywood Dissidents* (Boston: South End Press, 1978), p. 17.

19. Dalton Trumbo, *Johnny Got His Gun* (New York: Bantam, 1967), p. 241.

20. *Writers' Congress:* The Proceedings of the Conference Held in October 1943 under the sponsorship of the Hollywood Writers' Mobilization and the University of California (Berkeley: University of California Press, 1944), p. 31.

21. Schwartz, p. 202.

22. Ibid., p. 203.

23. Martin Dies, in Schwartz, p. 211.

Chapter Twelve

1. Meryman, *Mank*, p. 255.

2. Ibid., p. 234.

3. Ibid., p. 248.

4. Ibid., p. 258.

5. Barbara Leaming, *Orson Welles* (London: Penguin, 1987), p. 202.

6. Meryman, p. 270.

7. Ibid., p. 272.

8. Julius J. Epstein, interview in *Backstory*, p. 185.

9. Ingrid Bergman and Alan Burgess, *Ingrid Bergman, My Story* (London: Sphere Books, 1980), pp. 121–22.

10. Casey Robinson, interview in *Backstory*, p. 303.

11. Ibid., p. 308.

12. Ibid.

13. *Casablanca*, Hays Office file (Margaret Herrick Library).

14. *Sound and the Cinema*, pp. 105–6.

15. *Backstory*, p. 185.

16. John Houseman, "Brecht in Hollywood," *Brecht Annual* (Berkeley: Pacifica Foundation, 1965), p. 9.

17. Bruce Cook, *Brecht in Exile* (New York: Holt, Rinehart & Winston, 1982), p. 85.

18. Ibid., p. 88.

19. James K. Lyon, *Bertolt Brecht in America* (London: Methuen, 1982), p. 64.

20. Ibid., p. 66.

21. Cook, p. 89.

22. Lyon, pp. 69–70.

23. Ibid., p. 68.

Chapter Thirteen

1. Maurice Zolotow, *Billy Wilder in Hollywood* (London: Pavilion, 1988), p. 129.

2. Diane Johnson, *The Life of Dashiell Hammett* (London: Chatto & Windus, 1984), p. 151.

3. Richard Layman, *Shadow Man: The Life of Dashiell Hammett* (London: Junction Books, 1981), p. 162.

4. Al Clark, *Raymond Chandler in Hollywood* (New York: Proteus Books, 1982), p. 62.

5. Ibid., p. 63.

6. *The World of Raymond Chandler,* ed. Miriam Gross (London: Weidenfeld & Nicolson, 1977), p. 50.

7. Ibid.

8. Zolotow, pp. 113–14.

9. *Selected Letters of Raymond Chandler,* ed. Frank MacShane (London: Cape, 1981), p. 237.

10. Zolotow, pp. 65–6.

11. Ibid., p. 90.

12. Ibid., p. 106.

13. Preston Sturges to Carol Lorraine Noble, July 3, 1934 (Sturges Collection, Theatre Arts Library, UCLA).

14. Ibid.

15. James Curtis, *Between Flops: A Life of Preston Sturges* (New York: Limelight Editions, 1984), p. 128.

16. Manny Farber, *Negative Space* (London: Studio Vista, 1971), p. 98.

17. *Five Screenplays by Preston Sturges,* ed. Brian Henderson. pp. 670–71.

18. Preston Sturges to Bosley Crowther, July 22, 1947 (Sturges Collection).

19. Koppes and Black, p. 93.

20. Dudley Nichols to Preston Sturges, September 29, 1944 (Sturges Collection).

21. Gussow, *Don't Say Yes,* pp. 132–33.

22. Earl Felton, in Halliwell, *Filmgoer's Companion,* p. 975.

Chapter Fourteen

1. *Writers' Congress,* p. 31.

2. Friedrich, *City of Nets,* p. 179.

3. Robert Rossen, "An Approach to Character, 1943," *Writers' Congress,* pp. 61–7.

4. In Thomas J. Knock, "History with Lightning: The Forgotten Film *Wilson,*" in *Hollywood as Historian,* ed. Peter C. Rollins (Lexington: University Press of Kentucky, 1983), p. 99.

5. Gussow, *Don't Say Yes,* p. 110.

6. Ibid., p. 111.

7. Bosley Crowther, *New York Times,* Jan. 13, 1944.

8. Axel Madsen, *William Wyler* (London: W. H. Allen, 1974), p. 264.

9. John Cogley, *Report on Blacklisting* (The Fund for the Republic, 1956), vol. I, p. 11.

10. Schwartz, *The Hollywood Writers' Wars,* pp. 266–67.

11. Cook, *Brecht in Exile,* p. 197.

12. Ibid., p. 198.

13. Friedrich, p. 326.

14. Philip Dunne, interviewed in BBC-TV's "Writers on Trial," transmitted from London, November 4, 1973.

15. Cogley, p. 23.

16. Ibid.

17. Ring Lardner, Jr., interview by Barry Strugatz, *Film Comment,* October 1988, p. 67.

18. Philip Dunne, *Take Two* (New York: McGraw-Hill, 1980), p. 220.

19. Ceplair and Englund, *The Inquisition in Hollywood,* p. 364.

20. Cogley, pp. 100–1.

21. William Wright, *Lillian Hellman: The Image, The Woman* (London: Sidgwick & Jackson, 1987), p. 249.

22. Elia Kazan, *A Life* (New York: Knopf, 1988), p. 220.

23. Ceplair and Englund, p. 377.

INDEX